TAPESTRY

A · MULTICULTURAL · ANTHOLOGY

Alan C. Purves
General Editor

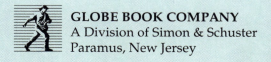
GLOBE BOOK COMPANY
A Division of Simon & Schuster
Paramus, New Jersey

Executive Editor: Virginia Seeley
Project Editor: Bernice Golden
Editors: Karen Hill, William Winfield
Editorial Support: Lynn W. Kloss
Copy Chief: June Bodansky
Art Director: Nancy Sharkey
Production Manager: Winston Sukhnanand
Production Coordinator: Lisa Cowart
Marketing Managers: Elmer Ildefonso, Sandra Hutchison

Interior Electronic Design: Function Thru Form Inc.
Art Insert: Carole Anson
Photo Research: Omni-Photo Communications, Inc.

Cover: B B + K Design Inc.
Cover Illustration: John Jinks

Printed in the United States of America. 2 3 4 5 6 7 8 9 10 96 95 94 93

ISBN: 0-835-90510-1(softcover)
        0-835-90728-7(hardcover)

 GLOBE BOOK COMPANY
A Division of Simon & Schuster
Paramus, New Jersey

ABOUT THE GENERAL EDITOR

ALAN C. PURVES, Professor of Education and Humanities at The University of Albany, State University of New York, is also the Director of Multicultural Studies at the National Center for Research on Literature Teaching and Learning and the Director of the Center for Writing and Literacy, both at SUNY Albany. He has edited a journal of translations of world literature as well as multicultural literature anthologies, and has done cross-cultural studies of literature learning, literary criticism, composition, and reading. He is currently researching the teaching of multicultural literature in the United States.

CONSULTANTS

Miriam Bat-Ami
Assistant Professor of English
Western Michigan University
Kalamazoo, Michigan

Beverly Chin
Professor of English
University of Montana
Missoula, Montana

Rodolfo J. Cortina
Professor of Modern Languages
Florida International University
Miami, Florida

Barbara Cruz
Assistant Professor of Social Science
    Education
University of South Florida
Tampa, Florida

Florence Hongo
Instructor of Asian American Studies
College of San Mateo
San Mateo, California

Mary Catherine Rainwater
Assistant Professor of English
St. Edward's University
Austin, Texas

Joseph T. Skerrett, Junior
Professor of English
University of Massachusetts
Amherst, Massachusetts

Gabrielle Tayac
Ph.D. candidate, Sociology
Graduate School of Arts and Sciences
Harvard University
Cambridge, Massachusetts

Joyce Carol Thomas
Professor of English
University of Tennessee
Knoxville, Tennessee

REVIEWERS

Lula L. Baker
Savannah High School
Savannah, Georgia

Rebecca Ball
Savannah-Chatham County
    Board of Education
Savannah, Georgia

Dr. Noreen Benton
Guilderland Central High School
Guilderland Center, New York

Dr. Lynn F. Carhart
Neptune High School
Neptune, New Jersey

Gwyneth DeGraf
Jamaica High School
Jamaica, New York

Joe Ann Dunbar
Department Chair
Johnson High School
Savannah, Georgia

Kenneth Fallender
Middletown Township Schools
Middletown, New Jersey

Dr. George I. Ferris, Jr.
Moorestown High School
Moorestown, New Jersey

Deborah A. Fitch
Linton High School
Schenectady, New York

Geri L. Flanary
Jenkins High School
Savannah, Georgia

Mary Glover
Office of Education
San Diego, California

Jackie Henry
George Washington Preparatory
    High School
Los Angeles, California

Gladys Kosty
Lewis and Clark High School
Spokane, Washington

Judy LaVigne
Neptune High School
Neptune, New Jersey

Nancy Michelson
Ravena-Coeymans-Selkirk
    High School
Ravena, New York

Chiquetta O. Mitchell
Academic Facilitator
Hubert Middle School
Chatham County, Georgia

Sally P. Pfeifer
English Department Chair
Lewis and Clark High School
Spokane, Washington

Joseph Quattrini
English Department Chair
Canajoharie High School
Canajoharie, New York

Judith K. Rothstein
English Supervisor
Guilderland Central Schools
Guilderland Center, New York

Huxsie D. Scott
Chatham-Savannah Schools
Savannah, Georgia

Martha W. Serensits
Reading Specialist
Robert Goddard Combined School
Prince George's County Public Schools
Seabrook, Maryland

Michael L. Stacey
Principal
Bartlett Middle School
Savannah, Georgia

Essie Stewart Johnson
Savannah-Chatham Public Schools
Savannah, Georgia

Bernice Thompkins
Freemont High School
Oakland, California

Janie R. Tolbert
Middle School Reading Coordinator
Kettering Middle School
Prince George's County Public Schools
Upper Marlboro, Maryland

Dr. Anne Ware
G. Holmes Braddock Senior High School
Miami, Florida

Philip Weinberg
High School of Telecommunication Arts
    and Technology
Brooklyn, New York

Dr. Rita J. Womack
Coordinating Supervisor of Reading
Prince George's County Public Schools
Landover, Maryland

TABLE OF CONTENTS

Unit 2: Arrival and Settlement

Unit 3: Struggle and Recognition   220

DEAR STUDENT,

In the not-so-distant past, it was very difficult for students and teachers to find and use literature that reflected the extraordinary mix of people and cultures in the United States. This was the case, in part, because many people believed that the experiences of some people were not worthy of being discussed in your classroom. Times have changed. In this book, you will meet people whose stories, plays, poems, folktales, and essays are glorious reflections of our country's magnificent people.

You will experience the similarities and differences of many people. Every culture has a rich literary tradition. The joy and pain in each of the selections you are about to read will introduce you to a part of a tradition that has shaped our history. In this literature, there are ideas about life, values, love, peace, and struggle.

This Tapestry of Multicultural Literature has been organized to place at your fingertips a slice of the American tradition that most adults have not read.

Some of the literature is funny, some sad. These selections are full of rich ideas and memorable characters. Some of the ideas and people you will perhaps instantly like. Others will grow on you over time.

What matters greatly to my colleagues and me is that your experience in school be one that includes the literature that we did not receive. This is important to us because our country has the most amazing mix of people and cultures in the world, and each of us, especially you, should know something about those neighbors who are a part of us.

It is also important to us that you learn the skills of good writing, critical and creative thinking, and the elements and structure of literature. These skills are essential to effective communication in your community and in your future work.

This book is about you. I encourage you to allow the voices and experiences of your fellow Americans to expand your world. Enjoy.

Irving Hamer, Jr.
President, Globe Book Company

North Mountain. *Museum of Northern Arizona.* Painting of a planting ceremony by Navajo artist Haskay Yah Ne Yah (Harrison Begay).

The Tree of Life. *Museum of International Folk Art, Santa Fe, New Mexico.* Painted earthenware by Heron Martinez, an artist from Puebla, Mexico.

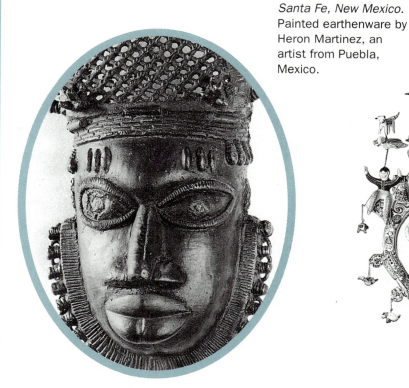

Bronze mask from the Kingdom of Benin (1350–1680) in Nigeria, West Africa.

ORIGINS AND CEREMONIES

Unit 1

THEMES

▼ A Heritage
   of Traditional
   Stories

▼ Exploring
   Ancestral
   Roots

▼ Celebrating
   Growth and
   Change

PEOPLE TALK about a "multicultural" society in the United States. What does that mean? *Multi* means "many," and *culture* means "something grown." *Cultured* pearls and *agriculture* are words that clearly suggest growing. But what does culture mean when it refers to a society?

Generally, the term *culture* is used to describe the way of life of a group of people who share some common characteristics. You may think of culture simply as art, music, and literature. In this book, *culture* refers to all the ideas and beliefs created by a group as well as their customs, language, traditions, and values.

A cultural group is larger than a family. It is a group that shares certain beliefs. These beliefs are often expressed and shared through the telling of traditional stories. The group also shares in ceremonies and rites, those activities that surround the important events in people's lives, such as birth, growing into the adult world, courtship and marriage, and death. Every culture has developed customs, stories, songs, and dramas to celebrate these events.

A culture can often be understood most clearly through its creative expressions, and that is what this unit explores. The literature in this unit follows the personal journeys several writers have made to find their origins and roots—their own past and the history of their people as they find out who they are.

A cultural group defines itself through its various ceremonies and beliefs, by the way it goes about doing things. It used to be said that a culture can be identified through the ways it views the supernatural, through the ways in which it handles marriage, and through the ways it deals with death. In most cultures these are considered the most important areas of human life, and people develop ceremonies around them. Different groups have different marriage ceremonies, for example, or different ways of dealing with death and funerals. Some societies have whole sets of ceremonies that determine when a person has stopped being a child and has become a member of the adult world.

Very often a group will pass on its beliefs about these matters through stories and songs. Some of these we call *folktales* or *folk songs*. This term suggests that these stories and songs come from ordinary people. They are handed down from older to younger. Some of these traditional stories are intended to amuse. Others are meant to teach something about the culture's history. Some tales explain how aspects of nature began. Folktales are not always far away in time or place. We are surrounded by them in our daily lives. There are stories about individuals who have

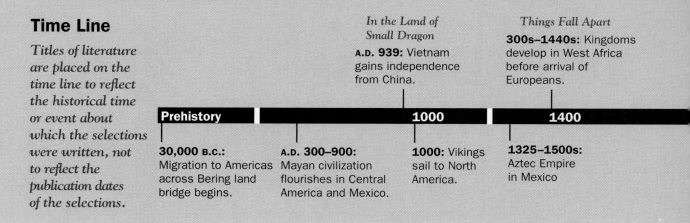

Time Line

Titles of literature are placed on the time line to reflect the historical time or event about which the selections were written, not to reflect the publication dates of the selections.

In the Land of Small Dragon
A.D. 939: Vietnam gains independence from China.

Things Fall Apart
300s–1440s: Kingdoms develop in West Africa before arrival of Europeans.

Prehistory | **1000** | **1400**

30,000 B.C.: Migration to Americas across Bering land bridge begins.

A.D. 300–900: Mayan civilization flourishes in Central America and Mexico.

1000: Vikings sail to North America.

1325–1500s: Aztec Empire in Mexico

---

extraordinary mental or physical powers and tales about visitors from other worlds.

Each person in the world is a member of a group and has a culture, but how does a person come to terms with that sense of belonging? Do people need to give up their individuality? Do people find their identities by becoming part of a group? What about you? What are some of the folktales of your community? Your school? The sport or hobby you participate in? What are the important ceremonies in your life and in the lives of your friends? The driver's license? The first date? The school dance? Joining a neighborhood group or club?

Are there any stories that you, your friends, or your family tell over and over? How do these tales hold the group together? How do you find out what sort of person you are and whether you belong to a particular group? Can you be yourself and a member of a culture, too? The literature in this unit raises these questions.

Historical Background and Thematic Organization

All the cultures that make up the United States have deep roots in history. The ancestors of these groups held a variety of beliefs about where they came from and how their world was made. In many of these earlier societies, the stories revolved around a central figure—a person or animal that came to stand for much of what the people believed, admired, or feared. For the First Nations of the North American continent, the central figure was an animal. In the eastern woodlands it was often the rabbit; in the West it was Coyote. In West Africa it was Anansi the spider or the tortoise; in Asia it was the dragon. These animal figures often had human characteristics. Through stories that feature figures like these, people explained how the world was made, how the first humans came to populate the earth, or how various important practices such as agriculture or hunting originated.

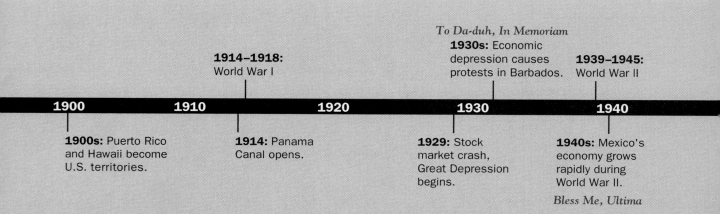

To Da-duh, In Memoriam
1930s: Economic depression causes protests in Barbados.

1914–1918: World War I

1939–1945: World War II

1900 | **1910** | **1920** | **1930** | **1940**

1900s: Puerto Rico and Hawaii become U.S. territories.

1914: Panama Canal opens.

1929: Stock market crash, Great Depression begins.

1940s: Mexico's economy grows rapidly during World War II.

Bless Me, Ultima

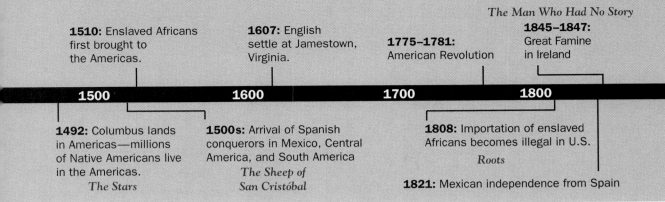

1510: Enslaved Africans first brought to the Americas.

1607: English settle at Jamestown, Virginia.

1775–1781: American Revolution

The Man Who Had No Story
1845–1847: Great Famine in Ireland

1500 **1600** **1700** **1800**

1492: Columbus lands in Americas—millions of Native Americans live in the Americas.
The Stars

1500s: Arrival of Spanish conquerors in Mexico, Central America, and South America
The Sheep of San Cristóbal

1808: Importation of enslaved Africans becomes illegal in U.S.
Roots

1821: Mexican independence from Spain

The first thematic section of this unit, "A Heritage of Traditional Stories," contains several of these kinds of tales and stories, which come from Mexico, Nigeria, Vietnam, Ireland, and the Tewa of the Southwest United States. Many of the tales were passed on from parent to child. Others were told in villages by special storytellers who were believed to possess magical powers. These traditional stories were forms of entertainment, history, religious instruction, and the main means by which a culture maintained its heritage. These kinds of stories form the basis on which many modern writers tie their work back to their cultural roots.

In the selections in Theme 2, "Exploring Ancestral Roots," contemporary writers seek to find their personal roots in their culture. The cultures represented here are African American, Filipino, Mexican American, and Native American. Many people today feel cut off from their past as they look around a modern world. Writers and artists often ex-

press the desire that many of us have, to find out who we are by looking at where we came from. As we look back to our ancestors, we often discover aspects of our own beliefs, attitudes, customs, and values. Can we find our roots? If we find them, do we find ourselves?

One way in which people connect themselves to their cultural roots is through rituals and ceremonies. If you have been to a wedding or a funeral, you have probably noticed that some of the customs performed are connected to the specific ethnic group to which the members belong. Theme 3, "Celebrating Growth and Change," explores how several writers have depicted the ways that people within a culture deal with the major stages and processes of life. These include coming of age or entering the adult world, courtship and marriage, and spiritual instruction. These are the rituals and celebrations that people cherish, and sometimes need to change, as you will see in the literature of this unit.

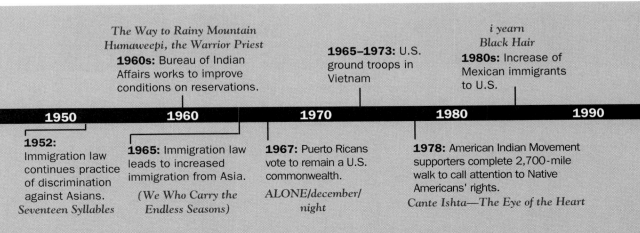

The Way to Rainy Mountain
Humaweepi, the Warrior Priest
1960s: Bureau of Indian Affairs works to improve conditions on reservations.

1965–1973: U.S. ground troops in Vietnam

i yearn
Black Hair
1980s: Increase of Mexican immigrants to U.S.

1950 **1960** **1970** **1980** **1990**

1952: Immigration law continues practice of discrimination against Asians.
Seventeen Syllables

1965: Immigration law leads to increased immigration from Asia.
(We Who Carry the Endless Seasons)

1967: Puerto Ricans vote to remain a U.S. commonwealth.
ALONE/december/ night

1978: American Indian Movement supporters complete 2,700-mile walk to call attention to Native Americans' rights.
Cante Ishta—The Eye of the Heart

A Heritage of Traditional Stories

THE BEGINNING OF ALL LITERATURE is traditional stories, which are told by grandparents and parents and are handed down by word of mouth by children to their children. Through the oral and written traditions of storytelling, a culture not only creates a form of entertainment but also gives expression to its collective ideals, values, and goals.

In this theme you will read stories from several cultures. The forms of these stories are as different as a quest or search tale, a moral tale, a fantasy, and a poem. The stories come from a Native American people, the Tewa, as well as from Mexico, Nigeria, Ireland, and Vietnam. Some of them are very old and some were written down recently. Through these tales, storytellers explore the customs, values, and beliefs of their cultures and explain their ideas about how things came to be. Above all, the stories entertain listeners and readers with the adventures of colorful characters.

Tatei Urianaka, Goddess of the Earth Ready for Planting by Cresencio Peréz Robles. *The Fine Arts Museum of San Francisco.* Yarn on plywood, a traditional art form of the Huichol people of Mexico. How do you think this yarn art might tell a story about the beliefs of the Huichol people?

The Stars

Reading the Story in a Cultural Context

For hundreds of years, Native American peoples have relied on storytelling to pass on their traditions. In the Native American storytelling tradition, words are alive. Imagine yourself sitting by a campfire, and someone is telling you a story. The words swirl around you, and you become a part of them, a part of the story. Storytelling serves two purposes. It instructs and it delights. The Native American children listening to traditional stories are entertained, and they are also taught about their heritage. At the same time, they are reliving the story and making it happen again. The beliefs and customs of the culture are celebrated through storytelling.

Native American stories have been called circular because of their quality of timelessness. Many of the stories have a never-ending nature that flows from the intensely personal relationship that many Native Americans have traditionally had with the earth. Animals are humankind's brothers and sisters, and it is not clear where our animalness ends and our humanness begins. The boundaries between nature and people are crossed in Native American stories and beliefs. As you read the following creation story, think about how it achieves a quality of timelessness.

"The Stars" is a story from the Tewa (TEE-wah), a group of Native Americans of the Southwest. The early Spanish settlers in this region tried first to convert the Tewa to Christianity and then to rule them. When these efforts failed, the Spanish tried to eliminate them because they would not give up their spiritual traditions and accept Catholicism. The Hopi offered protection to the Tewa, and the two groups formed a complementary relationship, sharing protection and mingling beliefs.

Like all creation stories, "The Stars" describes the making of a world. As you read, notice what elements of the Southwest appear in this tale.

Focusing on the Selection

As you follow the adventures of Long Sash and his people, think about the values, customs, and beliefs that the story communicates. What lessons does Long Sash learn and teach about how to live together with all groups of people?

The Stars

PABLITA VELARDE

MANY STARS made bright holes in the clear, cold autumn sky. In the village plaza a fire danced and children danced around it. They were happy and excited because Old Father was in the village and would begin tonight to tell them the winter's stories.

"Tell us a story, tell us a story." They loved Old Father, and he loved them and understood them. His kindness made a warmth like the fire. He laughed and asked, "What kind of a story?", and a tiny voice came tumbling, "Why are some stars brighter than all the others? And why don't they ever fall where we can find them?"

The children settled around the fire as Old Father gazed up at the stars with a faraway smile. Pointing first toward Orion[1] in the east, he said:

* * * *

That is "Long Sash,"[2] the guide of our ancestors; he led our people to this beautiful land where we now live. Our people followed him without question, for he was a great warrior who had won many battles. He had grown tired of seeing misery all around him, his own people suffering because of the cruel ruler they had lived under for so many years. During his battles he had been in distant lands, and when he told his people about these places they asked him to take them there. They were determined to end their suffering by going away to a new land.

---

1. **Orion** (oh-REYE-uhn) *n.* the name of a constellation, or star pattern, in the Roman and Western European tradition; Orion was a great hunter
2. **Long Sash** the name of this guide, also the name for Orion

He tried to discourage them, telling them they had nothing to take along. He warned them of the hardships, the sickness, and the deaths they would face, but they were determined people, and in the end he could not refuse them.

They traveled with empty stomachs and scant clothing. Many died from hunger and disease, but they continued on and on. Long Sash taught them to hunt for their food, to make clothing from animal skins and bird feathers. After a time he led them into a land where no man, not even he, had been. It was daylight all the time, and they rested only when they were too weary to travel any more. Many children were born, and some died, but the brave spirit of these people kept them going.

Old Father paused to look around him. He saw all the children were gazing upward as if the stars, gleaming like mica, had hypnotized them. Waving his hand across the sky, Old Father raised the pitch of his voice, bringing the children out of their trance. They followed him, wide-eyed and open-mouthed.

"See that milky white belt across the middle of the sky?"

"Yes," they all answered at once.

"Well," continued Old Father, "that is the Endless Trail they were traveling on." In time, some of the people became doubtful and hard to reason with, and violence began to show itself here and there. Thereupon Long Sash decided that force was to be used on no one, that those who wished to follow him could come, and those who wanted to turn back could do so. In order to give everyone an opportunity to rest and make his own decision, he had them camp on the spot. It was time for many of the women to bear their babies.

"See those two big bright stars (Gemini)[3] to the north of Long Sash?" Old Father waited for an answer, but when none came he smiled and continued:

They are stars of decision. We must all make choices between forward or backward, good or bad. They mark the trail where Long Sash told his people, "If we choose to go forward, it will be a good choice, for the lives of the young stretch long before them. Choose the road back and you know what torture you will live. We have our signs ahead of us; let us not close our eyes, to see only the darkness!"

It did not take long for the people to decide to follow their leader. They all went on with lighter hearts and greater hopes. Long Sash sang loudly as he led his people on what seemed an endless journey. He hoped they would reach their destination soon, but he had prepared his

---

3. Gemini (JEM-ihn-eye) *n.* another star pattern; the Roman idea is that it represents twins who sit across the Milky Way from Orion (Long Sash); Native Americans called them stars of decision

people well, he had taught them patience, tolerance,[4] and love for one another. Yet for some reason there was an emptiness in his own soul, and he could not understand the reason why.

He himself was growing tired of the long wandering, and when he was by himself he wept in despair. He began to feel strange beings around him and to hear unfamiliar voices. Not understanding these things, his first thought was that he must be losing his mind, but he was determined that he would lead his people to safety before anything happened to him. While he was resting he began talking aloud, and his people thought he was talking to them, and they gathered around him.

His voice was strange: "My fathers and my mothers, wherever you are, hear me, give me your guidance and give me strength to find our home. My people are tired now, and I am not young as I once was. Give me wisdom and strength to decide for them, and give me an omen,[5] give me an omen!"

The people looked at each other fearfully, feeling the need for someone stronger than Long Sash to depend upon. They looked at him, who was now asleep. They discussed what he had said and wondered about the unseen beings with whom he had spoken. They became afraid of him, and when he awoke he sensed that something was troubling his people, so he gathered them about him and told them he had had a dream with many omens in it. He told them the most difficult part of their journey was over; traveling would be easier for the rest of the trip. He told them of the unseen beings and the voices he had sensed, and commanded that they be addressed as "Fathers and Mothers," and that the people ask for their aid whenever the need for help was felt. "Always have faith in them, for they will answer you with their blessings. I am not sick of mind. Now my mind is clearer than it has ever been. I will leave my headdress here as a symbol to all the others who may need a reminder of the greater spirits."

Old Father again pointed to the heavens toward the cluster of seven bright stars in the shape of a bonnet[6] (Cancer),[7] saying, "That represents the war bonnet of Long Sash." The children shifted a little and closed their mouths, dry by this time. He continued:

As they traveled they learned many new ways to carry loads. At first they bore their belongings on their backs, but now, with more babies to be carried, the younger men teamed up in pairs to drag the loads on poles. See the three stars (Leo)[8] north of the headdress? They represent

---

4. **tolerance** (TAHL-er-uhnz) *n.* allowing and accepting differences
5. **omen** (OH-men) *n.* sign, something that tells about the future
6. **bonnet** (BAHN-iht) *n.* a war bonnet, or Native American headdress with feathers
7. **Cancer** (KAN-ser) *n.* a star pattern and sign of the zodiac
8. **Leo** (LEE-oh) *n.* a star pattern and sign of the zodiac

love, tolerance, and understanding, and were personified by two young men dragging their load and saving their people from worse hardship.

After a long time they came into darkness and everyone was afraid again, but their leader kept on, following a bright light coming through a very small opening (*sipapu* in Hopi; *sipo-pede*[9] in Tewa). From somewhere they heard something digging and scratching. Still following the bright light they came closer to the noise, and when they reached the opening they found a little mole digging away. Long Sash thanked the small creature for helping them to find the opening, but the mole only replied, "Go, and when you again find my sign, you will have found your home." They found a cord hanging and climbed toward the opening.

Through the opening Long Sash saw Old Spider Woman, busy weaving, and he asked permission to enter. Replied Old Spider Woman, "You are welcome to pass through my house. Do not destroy anything and I will help you find your way out and show you the direction to take. When you see my sign again, you will have found your home." Long Sash thanked her, but he could not understand at the time what she meant.

Continuing on their way they came to a very cold, beautiful land to the north where they rested for many years. Some stayed to make their homes, for they were tired of moving. Long Sash told his people, "This is the land of ice and snow, and your helper is the bear, for he is big and powerful, as one must be in order to live here. Those who wish to continue I will lead, for we have not yet found any signs of the mole and spider."

The people asked Long Sash why he did not follow the sun to the west, and they went in the direction of the setting sun and came to a place where the land was hot and dry. They rested here for many years, some of them staying to make it their home.

Long Sash was restless, so he prepared to leave, saying, "This is the land of the coyote, the sun is hot and the air is dry, the wind echoes the wails of the creatures who live in the surrounding hills. It has its own beauty, but you who remain here will follow the ways of the coyote and wander about aimlessly preying on whatever you find on your way. Those who wish to follow me will go with me to the land of the sunrise where we will seek the sign of the spider and the mole."

Once more they traveled, this time until they reached the land to the east. There they found tall trees, plenty of water, and earth covered with green wherever they looked. Here indeed, they thought, was the land promised by the two prophetic[10] creatures. Here life was easier, and

---

9. **sipapu** and **sipo-pede** (see-PAH-poo), (see-POH-pay-day) *n.* the hole in the floor of a council meeting room from which the people's ancestors were thought to have first emerged

10. **prophetic** (proh-FET-ihk) *adj.* telling the future

many of the people were happy to make this their home, despite the ever present danger of wild beasts who often pounced upon them. The seasons were short.

Still they had not found the signs of the mole and spider, so Long Sash said to his people, "This is indeed a beautiful land where game is plentiful, but the seasons of warmth are short and the changes are too swift. This is the land of the cougar. He is dangerous and unpredictable as the seasons, so we will go to the south in search of the signs."

So, sad because brothers and sisters had parted, but with hope in their hearts and faith in their leader, they again set out until they came to a land in the south where the seasons were long, food was easier to find, and there was not the danger from lurking beasts. Still they were not sure this was their home, for they had not found the signs they were seeking, even though they searched all over the land of the south, to the borders of the lands of the bear, the coyote, and the cougar.

Long Sash called again for help from his spiritual ancestors, praying that they would again show him a sign. He felt low in spirit, but he taught his followers how to talk from their hearts, how to find happiness in their misery, and how to read signs. From him they learned a new way of life, guided by a new belief. Many of our ancient ceremonials born of that belief are still with us, but many others have passed with time.

After Long Sash's communication with the spirits of his forefathers, a great bird flew overhead and circled the people four times before dropping two feathers from its tail. Falling to the ground, one feather pointed in the direction of the coyote, while the other pointed to the people. Long Sash then declared, "Here is our sign from our powerful messenger, the eagle. He tells us to follow in this direction!"

When they came to the new land, they found it to have seasons wet and dry, hot and cold, with good soil and bad. There was game, but it was hard to get. Here and there they found little scratches or tracks, but they had not found the mole as they had expected to do. However, close to the banks of a muddy river they found an ugly little creature with a very rough skin and on his back a stone-like shell. He made the tracks of a mole, yet he was not a mole. Long Sash studied him for a long time before he exclaimed, "Look, he carries his home with him and is protected by it at all times because when he is drawn up inside it he looks and rolls like a rock. He travels slowly, as we have done. On his back we can see plainly that he carries the sign of the spider; and when he moves, his feet make tracks like those of the mole."

This made the people very happy, for now they were certain they had found their homeland here where we are today. We move about a little now and then, but we will never leave this land, for this is where we belong.

The signs in the sky will always be there to guide us. Long Sash (Orion) is still up there leading many lost tribes over the Endless Trail (Milky Way).[11] The Twins (Gemini), the two stars of decision, are choices we always have. There is the headdress (Cancer) of Long Sash, reminding us of his spiritual guidance; there is the team of young men dragging their load (Leo) to remind us of love, tolerance, and understanding. The big star (North Star)[12] which guided our ancestors through the darkness is still there.

See those seven bright stars (Big Dipper)[13] that form an animal with its tail hanging downward? That is Long Tail. Each star in this group represents a sign given us by one of the creatures I told you of, the mole, the spider, the bear, the coyote, the cougar, the eagle, and the turtle.

Look at the four high mountain peaks around you: to the north, Bear Mountain (Taos Mountains); to the west (Mt. Taylor), the Coyote; to the east (Sangre de Cristo Mountains), the Cougar; and to the south, the Turtle (Sandia) Mountains. Within these boundaries our people found their home.

Why don't you find stars after they fall? Well, Long Sash is playing a game, and he catches them before they reach you!

* * * *

The children sat and gazed upward, still hearing the voices of the past, as Old Father rose and stretched, saying, "I will pass here again, with other stories. Go home to your parents and sleep well. *Songe-de-ho*,[14] goodbye!"

Male storyteller with 17 children. Ceramic figure created in 1971 by Helen Cordero of the Cochiti Pueblo in New Mexico.

---

11. **Milky Way** the Western European name for a wide band of milky light across the night sky; it is caused by the light of thousands of faint stars
12. **North Star** traditional Western European name for a star used to find direction
13. **Big Dipper** a star pattern
14. *Songe-de-ho* (sahn-gah-DAY-hoh) the Hopi word for "goodbye"

Critical Thinking

1. What values and beliefs of Tewa culture does the story tell you about?
2. Why do you think storytelling has been an important tradition in the heritage of Native Americans?
3. What similarities do you see between the journey described in "The Stars" and the goals and values of the community or the group to which you belong?

Writing Your Response to "The Stars"

What event, character, or idea in this story speaks most directly to you? What part of the story seems to have a connection to your life? In your journal, write about what you identify with most.

Going Back Into the Text: Author's Craft

"The Stars" is the story of a **quest**. In quest tales, the characters undertake adventurous journeys in search of something that is very important to them or to the society of which they are a member. For example, "The Stars" tells about a quest for a new homeland. Leading the quest is often a hero, a character of great strength and ability. Sometimes the hero is a spiritual leader or has special, super-human powers.

The quest is often filled with hardships and obstacles. Sometimes the hero and other characters are given help or guidance by higher powers. The goal of a quest and the way in which the characters reach that goal tell about the beliefs and values of the culture in which the quest tale is told.

With a partner, use these questions to review how "The Stars" is an example of a quest story.

1. What is the goal of the quest in "The Stars"? Why is the goal important?
2. What obstacles and adventures do the people meet in their quest? How do they overcome them?
3. Describe the quests in other stories or movies you have enjoyed.

The Sheep of San Cristóbal

Reading the Story in a Cultural Context

The Spanish heritage behind the following Mexican folktale has a long history. The first European settlement in what is today the United States was established by Spain in 1526 in present-day Georgia. By the end of the 17th century, the Spanish had settled throughout the Southwest. Among the important things that the Spanish brought with them from Europe were Catholicism and sheep, as you will see in the story.

Because the region that includes what is now Texas, New Mexico, Arizona, Nevada, Utah, and California was first Spanish and then Mexican territory, the Spanish influences continue to be felt in the region. Many people living in this part of the United States have retained the Spanish language, Catholicism is still an important religion, and sheep remain important.

"The Sheep of San Cristóbal" is set in this region of the southwestern United States, which was once part of Mexico. The theme of the story is very old. Many different religious leaders, from Buddha to Jesus, have suggested that the way to peace and fulfillment is by giving away one's money and possessions. Like so many folktales, this story was passed on by word of mouth, changing a little as times and circumstances changed. Still, the main themes of the story have remained the same. Storytellers help preserve the values and beliefs of communities. Even after the stories are finally written down, they continue to be handed down from generation to generation by word of mouth.

Folktales often contain a hero who must do something to receive a reward. In the process, the character learns something important about life, which is the lesson, or moral, of the tale. There is usually a villain or trickster who plays practical jokes, a little bit of magic, and some guiding force that will help the hero win. "The Sheep of San Cristóbal" contains all of these elements. Look for them as you read the folktale.

Focusing on the Selection

As you read "The Sheep of San Cristóbal," think about the values of right and wrong illustrated in the story. What is the moral lesson of the tale? How does the tale portray the Spanish-speaking people of Mexico? Write your responses in your journal.

The Sheep of San Cristóbal[1]

TOLD BY TERRI BUENO

In the time when New Mexico belonged to Spain, a woman named Felipa[2] farms a small plot of land near the village of Las Colonias. There is hostility between the Spanish settlers and the Ute[3] Indians, who believe that the settlers have taken their land. One day Felipa returns home from the fields to find that her seven-year-old son Manuel is missing, taken away by Utes. Felipa believes there is no hope of getting the child back. Despite her terrible misfortune, she prays for strength to go on living.

. . . IN THE DAYS that followed, deep sorrow never left Felipa. . . . But little by little, she learned to do what she had to do. She had always been very religious, and now she spent at least an hour a day on her knees at the shrine. The rest of the time she worked in her field—digging, planting, hoeing, picking. Sometimes she carried a basket of vegetables to the center of Las Colonias[4] to sell. The people of the little town had always liked Felipa, and now they felt sorry for her. They would buy from her first. Men who cut firewood often dropped off

---

1. **San Cristóbal** (SAHN krees-TOH-bahl) *n.* Saint Christopher
2. **Felipa** (fay-LEE-pah) *n.* a woman's name, Philippa
3. **Ute** (YOOT) *n.* a Native American people
4. **Las Colonias** (LAHS koh-LOH-nee-ahs) *n.* name of a town

a few pieces as they went by her doorstep. Other people did her other little favors, and Felipa always remembered to thank them.

There was one man, however, whose favors Felipa did not want. This was Don José Vigil.[5] From his father, Don José had inherited a huge flock of sheep. People said he was the richest man in town, but people also knew that he never gave anything to the poor. It was not Don José's habit to help anyone but himself. Felipa soon learned the reason for his favors to her: He was a young man without a wife, and she was a young woman without a husband.

The Mexican Museum of San Francisco. Shepherd and sheep, a crèche grouping. Traditional hand-painted clay figures from San Pedro Tlaquepaque, Mexico.

At night Don José kept his sheep in a corral beside his house in town. In the daytime he took them to the top of a huge mesa[6] to eat grass. This meant that twice a day, morning and evening, Don José had to pass Felipa's house with his sheep. Felipa would groan when she saw them coming up the dirt road. Leading the way would be Sancho,[7] Don José's big dog; then would come the sheep, and finally Don José himself. Always he would smile and stop to talk.

Felipa did nothing to lead Don José on—but he would not be stopped. If she would not talk to him, he would talk for both of them. If she refused a present, he would leave it on the ground. If she hid in the house, he would simply open the door and walk in. Only if she locked the door would Don José leave, angry and silent. Felipa didn't like making anyone mad, but locking the door was better than listening to all his fatuous[8] talk of marriage.

Soon Felipa found herself locking the door twice a day. And to her surprise, she sometimes found herself thinking evil thoughts about Don José. "If only Don José would fall off the mesa and break his neck!" she would think. Then, realizing how mean her thoughts had been, she would sigh and pray to Our Lady for forgiveness.

Before long, however, Don José found a way to get Felipa out of her house. He changed places with Sancho, the big brown dog. Instead of having Sancho lead the sheep, he led them himself. When he got to Felipa's house, he stopped. For a few minutes the sheep would stand still on the road. But soon, left to themselves, they would wander into Felipa's field. They would begin to eat her half-grown bean plants. Felipa had no choice. She would come tearing out of the house, shouting and waving her arms at the sheep, as Don José stood in the road and laughed.

---

5. **Don José Vigil** (DOHN hoh-SAY VEE-hil) *n. don* is a title of respect in Spanish; José Vigil is the man's name
6. **mesa** (MAY-suh) *n.* large, flat-topped hill
7. **Sancho** (SAHN-choh) *n.* a name
8. **fatuous** (FACH-oo-us) *adj.* silly, foolish

The same thing happened every morning for a week. Felipa was puzzled. What was Don José trying to do? Was he trying to punish her for not liking him? Was he trying to force her to marry him? Without the beans to sell, Felipa would soon have no money. Then what would she do? What could she do?

One morning Don José's sheep arrived very early. Waking up to hear them already in her field, Felipa quickly looked out the window. They were eating the last of the beans.

Wild with anger, Felipa bolted out of the house. First she screamed at the sheep. But what was the use? Her beans had already disappeared. Then she screamed at Don José:

"You are a bad man, Don José Vigil! A bad man! May San Cristóbal throw you off the mesa today! May he break your neck! May you—"

Bursting into tears, Felipa ran back into the house. The door slammed behind her. She didn't watch as Don José shook his head, laughed once, and followed the last of his sheep toward the mesa. The peaceful dog Sancho was already way ahead.

Four hours later, the body of Don José Vigil was carried past Felipa's house. His foot had landed on the wrong small round stone on the narrow path up the side of the mesa. He had slipped, fallen to the plain far below, and broken his neck.

The news made Felipa feel dead herself. Her anger turned inward, toward herself. She was sure that her curse had caused Don José's death. All day long she prayed to Nuestra Señora de los Dolores,[9] Our Lady of Sorrows. She could eat nothing, and that night she could not sleep. She kept seeing the reproachful[10] eyes of Don José as he fell to his death. They seemed to look right at her, and they made her feel very guilty.

Early the next morning, Felipa hurried to the church. There was only one thing to do. She would have to ask for penance, for some kind of punishment that would make up for her evil words.

"Padre,"[11] Felipa whispered to the priest. "I am guilty of the death of Don José Vigil." Then she sobbingly told the whole story.

"No," the priest finally said, "you did not cause Don José to die. San Cristóbal would not listen to such a plea. He would not do such a thing. He would never listen to a wicked prayer made by an angry woman."

The old priest looked into Felipa's big brown eyes and went on: "But yes, you are guilty. You are guilty of a very wicked prayer. And for that evil act, you must do penance."

---

9. Nuestra Señora de los Dolores (noo-AYS-trah say-NYOR-ah DAY LOHS doh-LOH-rays) *n.* Our Lady of Sorrows, a name for Mary, the mother of Jesus Christ
10. reproachful (rih-PROHCH-fuhl) *adj.* blaming, disappointed
11. Padre (PAH-dray) *n.* Father; priest's title in Spanish

"Yes," murmured Felipa, "I know. Without the penance, the rest of my life would be empty."

"Here is what you must do," the priest told her. "You must do penance for your own evil wishes. But more important, you must do penance for Don José, too. You see, he was in some ways an evil man. He had much money, yet he never gave to the poor. But no man is all evil. Right now, could he join us again on earth, Don José would want to do good. That is why your penance must be for him also."

Felipa listened as the priest went on. First she was to go to the mesa and gather Don José's sheep together. Then she was to drive them all over New Mexico, to every village. Everywhere she went, she was to search for indigent[12] people in real need. To each of these people she was to give a single sheep. Felipa was to give the sheep away in the name of Don José, with the blessing of San Cristóbal. She was to beg for bread, and eat nothing else. She was to carry only a cup, and use it only for sheep milk.

"If anyone asks you," the priest finished, "say that the sheep are the sheep of San Cristóbal. Have faith, my daughter. San Cristóbal will guide you. Pray often. And at the end, he will give you a sign. You will know that your penance is over, and that you are free of your sin."

Felipa did as she'd been told. First she went to her house to get a cup. Should she change her clothes? No, she decided. She'd keep on what she'd worn to the church, a simple black robe with a hood. Then she headed for the mesa. Her whole body shook as she walked up the dangerous path where Don José had fallen.

On the mesa's flat top, she found the sheep in a group. The faithful dog Sancho had kept them together during the night.

Sancho barked with joy when he saw Felipa coming. He ran up and nuzzled his short brown nose against her leg. Then he led her into some bushes not far away. There on the ground, Felipa saw the bones of three lambs. She knew that coyotes must have taken them during the night.

"You are a good, good dog, Sancho," Felipa scratched the big brown head by her knee. "But some lambs have been lost, am I right? You could not do the whole job, could you? Now you have me to help you. And I have you to help me."

Felipa milked one of the sheep. She held the cup of milk out to Sancho, and he lapped it up quickly. Then they drove the sheep toward the path leading off the mesa. Once safely down, and with Sancho leading, they headed for town. Felipa passed her own house, wondering when she'd ever see it again. A few minutes later they came to the house of Don José. Sancho started to drive the sheep into the corral, as he had always done. Felipa ran forward and headed the sheep back onto the

---

12. **indigent** (IN-duh-juhnt) *adj.* poor

road. She pulled the corral gate shut and urged the sheep on by. Sancho stood next to the corral, his head tipped to one side.

Now the sheep were past Don José's house, and almost to the center of Las Colonias. Felipa looked back at Don José's corral. Sancho was still standing there, watching her.

"Come, Sancho!" Felipa called. "Come! Come!" She clapped her hands together.

For a moment Sancho didn't move. Then all at once he seemed to make up his mind. He rushed toward Felipa, passed her, and took his place far up, in front of the sheep.

The sheep moved through Las Colonias and headed out of town. Felipa tried to count them. Because they were moving and close together, it wasn't an easy job. The first time she counted 172. The second time she got 167. Then she noticed that a large black ewe had dropped back to walk at her side. An hour later, the ewe[13] was still there. Felipa looked at the animal carefully. "I think this sheep wants to be milked," she told herself. "She must be one of the ewes who lost their lambs to the coyotes."

Coming to a grassy spot, Felipa decided that it was time for the whole procession to rest. As the other sheep browsed,[14] Felipa milked the large black ewe. She drank the first cup of warm milk herself. The second she gave to Sancho. That was all, and the ewe then wandered off to graze on the thin grass. But as soon as they started down the dusty road again, the ewe came back to Felipa's side.

"You are a good friend, black ewe," Felipa said aloud. "Do you know that I too have lost a child? Can you tell that I share your sadness? Is that why you stay here next to me?"

Before the sun set that day, Felipa had given the black ewe a name: Negrita.[15] In the evening Felipa milked her again, and again the ewe moved away to eat. But as it got dark, and the rest of the sheep settled down for the night, Negrita came back to Felipa and lay down. Felipa lay down, too, using Negrita's soft side as a pillow. She knew that Sancho would stay half awake and watch the sheep.

Soon Felipa was sound asleep. Later she dreamed of Don José's face—smiling at her.

Early the next morning the journey continued, with Negrita still at Felipa's side. About noon they got to the first town, San José. Felipa was surprised to find that everyone was waiting for her. The news of her penance and her journey had traveled on ahead. Many people offered her bread, more than she could have eaten in a week. She asked and asked, but she could find no one poor enough to be given a sheep.

---

13. ewe (YOO) *n.* female sheep
14. browsed (BROWZD) *v.* nibbled plants or grass
15. Negrita (nay-GREE-tah) *n.* little black one; the name she gives the sheep

The same reception greeted Felipa in the next village, except that there she gave away her first sheep. And in the town after that she had the same experience. Continuing on, everywhere she went, she found that people had heard of her. On the third day her shoes wore out, and at first the dry desert sand hurt her feet. But she kept going. She traveled down the Rio Grande valley, where she found many poor people. Once she discovered a wrinkled old Indian woman who was starving in a mud hut. "In the name of Don José, and with the blessing of San Cristóbal, I give you this large sheep," Felipa told her. She knew without asking that the woman was a Ute.

The days turned into weeks, and the weeks turned into months. Felipa walked through Santa Cruz, headed north to Chimayo, and then south toward Pogoáqua. Nearly every day, she gave away a sheep. The number of sheep grew smaller and smaller. She went past Tesúque,[16] then over the hills to Santa Fe. Finally there were only a few sheep left. There was no need for Sancho to lead them. He now walked on one side of Felipa, with the good sheep Negrita on the other.

In Albuquerque, Felipa gave away her next-to-last sheep. Now only Negrita was left. The next town, Felipa knew, was Bajada, and for the first time she didn't want to go on. She prayed that there would be no one in La Bajada[17] poor enough to deserve a sheep. But she also knew that if she found the right person, even Negrita would have to go.

Negrita did have to go. Felipa offered her to an emaciated[18] old man who lay on a mat in the shade of a tree. He was almost too weak to stand up.

"Good-bye, Negrita," Felipa said. "You have been a good friend. Good-bye. Good-bye. Good-bye."

As the old man took hold of Negrita, Felipa got down on her knees. She buried her face in Negrita's soft neck. Suddenly feeling tears come to her eyes, she stood up quickly and turned to leave. But all at once, there was Negrita at her side again. The old man had not been strong enough to hold her.

"No, Negrita!" Felipa said. Now the tears were on her cheeks. "You must stay here!" She found a piece of rope and tied Negrita to the tree next to the old man. But when she again started to leave, a strange thing happened. Sancho stayed behind. He growled at the old man; then he growled at Negrita. Suddenly he started to bark. He ran at Negrita, sinking his sharp teeth into one of her back legs. The rope broke, and in an instant both animals were back at Felipa's side.

What should she do? Take Negrita back to the man again? No, Felipa decided. Perplexed, she walked on in silence. She could not force

16. **Tesúque** (tay-SOO-kay) n. name of a town
17. **La Bajada** (LAH bah-HAH-dah) n. name of a town
18. **emaciated** (ih-MAY-shee-ay-tihd) adj. very thin

herself to return Negrita to the old man once more. But how long, really, could she keep Negrita? The next village was Socorro[19] (which at the time was the last town in lower New Mexico). Surely, someone there would be poor enough to deserve the last of San Cristóbal's sheep.

Felipa entered Socorro with a heavy heart. As usual, the people already knew she was on her way. They offered her bread and answered her questions. No, they said, there was really no one poor enough to get a sheep. But Felipa didn't feel quite sure that everyone was telling the truth. She then looked into every house. She held her breath at every doorway, but she found no one poor enough to deserve Negrita.

Beyond the town, on the edge of the desert, was one old house. It was a hut, really, adobe,[20] poles, and animal skins. Felipa, with Negrita and Sancho by her side, approached it slowly. A tall man stepped out and stood at the doorway. His face mirrored the hue of the sun-baked desert sand. His wide-brimmed hat was filled with holes, and his clothes were rags.

"Certainly," Felipa told herself, "this is the person."

"In the name of Don José, and with the blessing of San Cristóbal—" Felipa began.

"Ah!" said the man. "So you are Felipa Sandoval!"[21]

Felipa nodded. She watched the man as he smiled at her suddenly.

"No," he said, shaking his head slowly. "You will not give your last sheep to me. I am getting old, but I can still work. I am not as poor as I look."

Felipa's heart rose—then began to plummet again as the man went on:

"You should give your sheep to the child in my hut. He seems to be really in need. I got him from some Navajo[22] Indians yesterday, for just a piece of cheap turquoise. The Navajos told me they got him from the Utes."

Felipa went into the hut. There in the shadows, dressed in Indian clothing, stood her son Manuel.[23]

Feeling her head swimming, Felipa fell to her knees. Was it true? . . .

The boy ran toward her arms, and Felipa knew it was true.

This was her son. Her only son. Her son Manuel. She had not held him close to her in a little more than a year.

Bark, bark—it was the dog Sancho, from outside the hut. Felipa pulled the boy toward the door, and stepped outside. Negrita came up and nuzzled Felipa's leg as she stood blinking in the bright sunlight. Where was the man? She walked around the hut. Had he simply vanished?

Felipa hurried back to the center of Socorro. She asked about the tall stranger. Even though she described him clearly, the people in town said they

---

19. **Socorro** (soh-KO-roh) *n.* name of a town
20. **adobe** (uh-DOH-bee) *n.* sun-dried bricks
21. **Sandoval** (SAHN-doh-vahl) *n.* Felipa's family name
22. **Navajo** (NAH-vah-hoh) *n.* name of a Native American people
23. **Manuel** (mahn-WEL) *n.* a man's name

had never seen such a man. The hut, they said, had been built years before for goats. No one had ever lived in it. Now even the goats had given it up.

Suddenly Felipa stopped listening. She knew intuitively who the man had been. She knew that San Cristóbal himself had delivered her little boy to her. And she knew, too, as the cloud of her guilt left her, that her penance was over.

For many years, people in New Mexico talked about Felipa Sandoval. They remembered her long walk with the sheep to Socorro. And they remembered even better her journey back home. No one ever forgot the young woman with the kind and joyful face, the little boy, the brown dog, and the black ewe.

Back in Las Colonias, Felipa found only happiness. Her neighbors had cared for her field, and beans were ready to be picked. She and Manuel picked them in peace, happy to be home, and not really caring that their story spread throughout the whole Southwest and then to the rest of the country.

POSTREADING

Critical Thinking

1. What does the story tell you about the beliefs and values of the Spanish-speaking people of Mexico? What moral lesson does the tale teach?
2. How do different historical traditions and forces come together in the tale?
3. What similarities do you see between the moral values illustrated in this tale and the values held by your own cultural group?

Writing Your Response to "The Sheep of San Cristóbal"

In your journal, write about a feeling, a question, an issue, or a character that impressed you while reading "The Sheep of San Cristóbal."

Going Back Into the Text: Author's Craft

"The Sheep of San Cristóbal" is a **moral tale.** Moral tales focus on right and wrong behavior. In these stories, a wrongful action occurs, the person who commits it takes action to make up for the misdeed, and a reward usually follows. The purpose of a moral tale is to teach a lesson or a moral about right actions.

Because the plot, characters, and setting in this type of story are chosen to highlight the lesson, moral tales often present a simplified view of life. The emphasis is on the moral and spiritual nature of the characters in the story, rather than on details about the appearance of the characters or the setting of the story.

With a partner, use the following questions to review how "The Sheep of San Cristóbal" is a moral tale.

1. What wrongful action is committed? Why is it committed?
2. What penance is performed? Is the penance effective? How do you know?
3. What other moral tales do you know? What are the lessons they teach?

from Things Fall Apart

Reading the Story in a Cultural Context

Writing was not yet commonly used as a form of communication in parts of Africa in the 18th century. For centuries, peoples passed down their histories, traditions, and beliefs through oral storytelling and song. The stories and songs were an important means of sharing culture for Africans. Of course, stories and songs were valued for entertainment, as well. Professional storytellers called *griots* were highly respected. However, stories were also told by other villagers as they gathered together in the compound at night.

Most of these stories had no known authors, and so the tellers usually told their own versions of tales. Favorite subjects included the deeds of heroes and the mysteries of the supernatural. The best loved were humorous tales about animal characters. Hare, Tortoise, Monkey, and Spider were the most popular characters of these beast fables. As you read the folktale that follows, think about the qualities of its main character, Tortoise.

In some African folktales, the central animal character is a trickster. This is a figure whose ridiculous antics and deceptive or outrageous behavior entertained audiences. The trickster also might have magical powers of transformation or wild and destructive aspects.

In the fables, animals had human characteristics, and events befalling them were often the result of weaknesses in their characters. The object of such morality tales was to teach a lesson about behavior to listeners.

Another object for many of the stories was to provide an explanation—usually humorous—of the beginning of some phenomenon observed in nature. Throughout history, people worldwide have been curious about the world around them. Before science developed experimental ways to explain natural events, it was common in most cultures to create stories as explanations for what people saw. Think about what the following folktale explains.

Chinua Achebe was born in 1930 in Nigeria. In the folktale that follows, from Achebe's novel *Things Fall Apart*, he describes some of the customs of Nigerian village life in the days before Europeans came to Africa. Family members lived in clusters of huts. Besides yams, a main crop was kola nuts, which were offered to guests. During holidays and other special occasions, speeches were popular. As you read the following tale, notice how the author weaves these realistic details into the fantastic story.

Focusing on the Selection

As you read the tale from *Things Fall Apart*, think about the purpose of the story. What understanding of human nature and community values does the storyteller share? Which parts of the story are fantasy? Which details are realistic? Write your responses in your journal.

from *Things Fall Apart*

CHINUA ACHEBE

... L OW VOICES, broken now and again by singing, reached Okonkwo from his wives'[1] huts as each woman and her children told folk stories. Ekwefi[2] and her daughter, Ezinma,[3] sat on a mat on the floor. It was Ekwefi's turn to tell a story.

"Once upon a time," she began, "all the birds were invited to a feast in the sky. They were very happy and began to prepare themselves for the great day. They painted their bodies with red cam wood and drew beautiful patterns on them with uli.[4]

"Tortoise saw all these preparations and soon discovered what it all meant. Nothing that happened in the world of the animals ever escaped his notice; he was full of cunning. As soon as he heard of the great feast in the sky his throat began to itch at the very thought. There was a famine in those days and Tortoise had not eaten a good meal for two moons. His body rattled like a piece of dry stick in his empty shell. So he began to plan how he would go to the sky."

---

1. **wives'** Having more than one wife is an ancient, although uncommon, practice in Africa.
2. **Ekwefi** (ek-WEE-fee) *n.* a woman's name
3. **Ezinma** (e-ZIHN-mah) *n.* a girl's name
4. **uli** (OO-lee) *n.* dye

"But he had no wings," said Ezinma.

"Be patient," replied her mother. "That is the story. Tortoise had no wings, but he went to the birds and asked to be allowed to go with them.

" 'We know you too well,' said the birds when they had heard him. 'You are full of cunning and you are ungrateful. If we allow you to come with us you will soon begin your mischief.'

" 'You do not know me,' said Tortoise. 'I am a changed man. I have learned that a man who makes trouble for others is also making it for himself.'

"Tortoise had a sweet tongue, and within a short time all the birds agreed that he was a changed man, and they each gave him a feather, with which he made two wings.

"At last the great day came and Tortoise was the first to arrive at the meeting place. When all the birds had gathered together, they set off in a body.[5] Tortoise was very happy and voluble[6] as he flew among the birds, and he was soon chosen as the man to speak for the party because he was a great orator.

" 'There is one important thing which we must not forget,' he said as they flew on their way. 'When people are invited to a great feast like this, they take new names for the occasion. Our hosts in the sky will expect us to honor this age-old custom.'

"None of the birds had heard of this custom but they knew that Tortoise, in spite of his failings in other directions, was a widely traveled man who knew the customs of different peoples. And so they each took a new name. When they had all taken, Tortoise also took one. He was to be called *All of you.*

Staatliche Museum, Berlin. Gaming chips or counters from the Beti culture of Cameroon, West Africa. Carved from fruit stones, or pits. How do these gaming chips emphasize the importance of animals in Beti culture?

5. **in a body** (IHN UH BAHD-ee) *prep. phrase* all together
6. **voluble** (VAHL-yoo-buhl) *adj.* talkative

"At last the party arrived in the sky and their hosts were very happy to see them. Tortoise stood up in his many-colored plumage and thanked them for their invitation. His speech was so eloquent that all the birds were glad they had brought him, and nodded their heads in approval of all he said. Their hosts took him as the king of the birds, especially as he looked somewhat different from the others.

"After kola nuts had been presented and eaten, the people of the sky set before their guests the most delectable dishes Tortoise had ever seen or dreamed of. The soup was brought out hot from the fire and in the very pot in which it had been cooked. It was full of meat and fish. Tortoise began to sniff aloud. There was pounded yam and also yam pottage cooked with palm-oil and fresh fish. There were also pots of palm-wine. When everything had been set before the guests, one of the people of the sky came forward and tasted a little from each pot. He then invited the birds to eat. But Tortoise jumped to his feet and asked: 'For whom have you prepared this feast?'

" 'For all of you,' replied the man.

"Tortoise turned to the birds and said: 'You remember that my name is *All of you*. The custom here is to serve the spokesman first and others later. They will serve you when I have eaten.'

"He began to eat and the birds grumbled angrily. The people of the sky thought it must be their custom to leave all the food for their king. And so Tortoise ate the best part of the food and then drank two pots of palm-wine, so that he was full of food and drink and his body grew fat enough to fill out in his shell.

"The birds gathered round to eat what was left and to peck at the bones he had thrown all about the floor. Some of them were too angry to eat. They chose to fly home on an empty stomach. But before they left each took back the feather he had lent to Tortoise. And there he stood in his hard shell full of food and wine but without any wings to fly home. He asked the birds to take a message for his wife, but they all refused. In the end Parrot, who had felt more angry than the others, suddenly changed his mind and agreed to take the message.

" 'Tell my wife,' said Tortoise, 'to bring out all the soft things in my house and cover the compound[7] with them so that I can jump down from the sky without very great danger.'

"Parrot promised to deliver the message, and then flew away. But when he reached Tortoise's house he told his wife to bring out all the hard things in the house. And so she brought out her husband's hoes, machetes,[8] spears, guns, and even his cannon. Tortoise looked down

---

7. **compound** (KAHM-pownd) *n.* yard, walled-in area around a house and other buildings
8. **machetes** (muh-SHET-eez) *n. pl.* heavy knives used for cutting sugar cane and underbrush, or as weapons

from the sky and saw his wife bringing things out, but it was too far to see what they were. When all seemed ready he let himself go. He fell and fell and fell until he began to fear that he would never stop falling. And then like the sound of his cannon he crashed on the compound."

"Did he die?" asked Ezinma.

"No," replied Ekwefi. "His shell broke into pieces. But there was a great medicine man[9] in the neighborhood. Tortoise's wife sent for him and he gathered all the bits of shell and stuck them together. That is why Tortoise's shell is not smooth." . . .

---

9. medicine man (MED-uh-sihn MAN) *n.* priestly healer

POSTREADING

Critical Thinking

1. Why do you think this story might have been told among the villages of Nigeria? What is the storyteller's purpose?
2. What human qualities are illustrated in the story? What do you think is the narrator's attitude about those traits?
3. How does the message of the story apply to life in your community? Give examples from your own experience.

Writing Your Response to *Things Fall Apart*

What interests you most about the characters, setting, or dialogue in the folktale? What parts struck you as especially funny or colorful? In your journal, write about what stands out most vividly for you in this story. What, if anything, in the story relates to your own life?

Going Back Into the Text: Author's Craft

Like many traditional tales, the story from *Things Fall Apart* combines **fantasy** and **realism.** The plot is fanciful. The characters are animals, but they speak and act like people. However, the tale also contains realistic details about life in Nigeria.

The fantastic plot of the story holds the attention of readers. It assures them that the story will be entertaining. The details of village life help the audience imagine events and identify with characters. Together these elements help create a story that mixes the familiar with the startling.

Use the questions below to review the elements of fantasy and realism in the tale.

1. What parts of the story are pure fantasy?
2. What parts have realistic details?
3. How are realism and fantasy combined in the last scene of the story?

In the Land of Small Dragon:
A Vietnamese Folktale

Reading the Story in a Cultural Context

In Vietnam, generations of parents have enjoyed their roles as storytellers for their children. The stories they have told reflect 4,000 years of Vietnamese history and culture. Many of the stories stress the value of good behavior. Some tell about emperors who struggled for the freedom of their people. Mostly, the stories are told for fun.

Storytelling has always provided escape for the hard-working Vietnamese. Through stories they could enjoy a magical world of dragons, beautiful princesses, and wealthy emperors.

The stories provide insight into the Vietnamese people, too. The tales often reflect beliefs in ancestor worship and in a spirit world within nature. Characters exhibit duty and honor to family, especially to elders. In the tales, the spirits of animals and landforms resemble human personalities, but with greater power. The explanations of natural events found in these stories provide fascinating glimpses into an ancient culture.

In the folktale that follows, elements of the Cinderella story are blended with the traditions of the Vietnamese culture. The Cinderella story is one of the most retold of world folktales and may have begun in China. This version contains proverbs. Proverbs are short sayings enjoyed for their wisdom. As you read, notice how a familiar story takes on new qualities when it appears in a different culture.

Focusing on the Selection

As you read this Vietnamese folktale, consider the ideas about beauty that are illustrated in the story. How are the traditions and customs of Vietnam blended with elements of the ancient tale known in English as the Cinderella story? What do the sayings within this Vietnamese tale tell you about the values of the culture? In what ways is the poem like a story? Record your responses in your journal.

In the Land of Small Dragon: A Vietnamese Folktale

TOLD BY DANG MANH KHA

One

Man cannot know the whole world,
But can know his own small part.
In the Land of Small Dragon,
In the Year of the Chicken,
In a Village of No-Name,
In the bend of the river,
There were many small houses
Tied together by walkways.
Mulberry and apricot,
Pear tree and flowering vine
Dropped their delicate blossoms
On a carpet of new grass.
In a Village of No-Name
Lived a man and two daughters.
T'âm[1] was the elder daughter;
Her mother died at her birth.
A jewel box of gold and jade
Holds only jewels of great price.
T'âm's face was a golden moon,
Her eyes dark as a storm cloud,
Her feet delicate flowers
Stepping lightly on the wind.
No envy lived in her heart,
Nor bitterness in her tears.
Cám was the younger daughter,
Child of Number Two Wife.
Cám's[2] face was long and ugly,
Scowling and discontented,
Frowning in deep displeasure.
Indolent, slow and idle,
Her heart was filled with hatred

For her beautiful sister.
An evil heart keeps records
On the face of its owner.
The father loved both daughters,
One not more than the other.
He did not permit his heart
To call one name more dearly.
He lived his days in justice,
Standing strong against the wind.
Father had a little land,
A house made of mats and clay,
A grove of mulberry trees
Enclosed by growing bamboo,
A garden and rice paddy,[3]
Two great water buffalo,
A well for drinking water,
And twin fish ponds for the fish.
Cám's mother, Number Two Wife,
Cared only for her own child.
Her mind had only one thought:
What would give pleasure to Cám.
Her heart had only one door
And only Cám could enter.
Number Two Wife was jealous
Of T'âm, the elder daughter,
Who was beautiful and good,
So the mother planned revenge
On the good, beautiful child.
To Cám she gave everything,
But nothing but work to T'âm.
T'âm carried water buckets,
Hanging from her bamboo pole.
T'âm carried forest fagots[4]

---

1. **T'âm** (TAHM) a girl's name
2. **Cám** (CAM) a girl's name
3. **rice paddy** n. wet land on which rice is grown
4. **fagots** (FAG-uhtz) n. pl. bundles of sticks

To burn in the kitchen fire.
T'âm transplanted young rice plants
From seed bed to rice paddy.
T'âm flailed the rice on a rock,
Then she winnowed and gleaned it.
T'âm's body ached with tiredness,
Her heart was heavy and sad.
She said, "Wise Father, listen!
I am your elder daughter;
Therefore why may I not be
Number One Daughter, also?
"A Number One Daughter works,
But she works with dignity.
If I were your Number One
The honor would ease my pain.
As it is, I am a slave,
Without honor or dignity."
Waiting for wisdom to come,
Father was slow to give answer.
"Both my daughters share my heart.
I cannot choose between them.
One of you must earn the right
To be my Number One child."
A man's worth is what he does,
Not what he says he can do.
"Go, Daughters, to the fish pond;
Take your fish baskets with you.
Fish until night moon-mist comes.
Bring your fish catch back to me.
She who brings a full basket
Is my Number One Daughter.
Your work, not my heart, decides
Your place in your father's house."
T'âm listened to her father
And was quick to obey him.
With her basket, she waded
In the mud of the fish pond.
With quick-moving, graceful hands
She caught the quick-darting fish.

Slowly the long hours went by.
Slowly her fish basket filled.
Cám sat on the high, dry bank
Trying to think of some plan,
Her basket empty of fish,
But her mind full of cunning.
"I, wade in that mud?" she thought.
"There must be some better way."
At last she knew what to do
To be Number One Daughter.
"T'âm," she called, "elder sister,
Our father needs a bright flower,
A flower to gladden his heart.
Get it for him, dear sister."
T'âm, the good, gentle sister,
Set her fish basket aside
And ran into the forest
To pick the night-blooming flowers.
Cám crept to T'âm's fish basket,
Emptied it into her own.
Now her fish basket was full.
T'âm's held only one small fish.
Quickly Cám ran to Father,
Calling, "See my full basket!"
T'âm ran back to the fish pond
With an armload of bright flowers.
"Cám," she called, "what has happened?
What has happened to my fish?"
Slowly T'âm went to Father
Bringing him the flowers and fish.
Father looked at both baskets.
Speaking slowly, he told them,
"The test was a full basket,
Not flowers and one small fish.
Take your fish, Elder Daughter.
It is much too small to eat.
Cám has earned the right to be
Honorable Number One."

Two

T'âm looked at the little fish.
Her heart was filled with pity
At its loneliness and fright.
"Little fish, dear little fish,
I will put you in the well."
At night T'âm brought her rice bowl,
Sharing her food with the fish—
Talked to the thin fish, saying,
"Little fish, come eat with me"—
Stayed at the well at nighttime
With the stars for company.
The fish grew big and trustful.
It grew fat and not afraid.
It knew T'âm's voice and answered,
Swimming to her outstretched hand.
Cám sat in the dark shadows,
Her heart full of jealousy,
Her mind full of wicked thoughts.
Sweetly she called, "T'âm, sister.
Our father is overtired.
Come sing him a pretty song
That will bring sweet dreams to him."
Quickly T'âm ran to her father,
Singing him a nightbird song.
Cám was hiding near the well,
Watching, waiting and watching.
When she heard T'âm's pretty song
She crept closer to the fish,
Whispering, "Dear little fish,
Come to me! Come eat with me."
The fish came, and greedy Cám
Touched it, caught it and ate it!
T'âm returned. Her fish was gone.
"Little fish, dear little fish,
Come to me! Come eat with me!"
Bitterly she cried for it.
The stars looked down in pity;
The clouds shed teardrops of rain.

Three

T'âm's tears falling in the well
Made the water rise higher.
And from it rose Nâng Tien,[5]
A lovely cloud-dressed fairy.
Her voice was a silver bell
Ringing clear in the moonlight.
"My child, why are you crying?"
"My dear little fish is gone!
He does not come when I call."
"Ask Red Rooster to help you.
His hens will find Little Fish."
Soon the hens came in a line
Sadly bringing the fish bones.
T'âm cried, holding the fish bones.
"Your dear fish will not forget.
Place his bones in a clay pot
Safe beneath your sleeping mat.
Those we love never leave us.
Cherished bones keep love alive."
In her treasured clay pot, T'âm
Made a bed of flower petals
For the bones of Little Fish
And put him away with love.
But she did not forget him;
When the moon was full again,
T'âm, so lonely for her fish,
Dug up the buried clay pot.
T'âm found, instead of fish bones,
A silken dress and two jeweled *hai*.[6]
Her Nâng Tien spoke again.
"Your dear little fish loves you.
Clothe yourself in the garments
His love has given you."
T'âm put on the small jeweled *hai*.
They fit like a velvet skin
Made of moonlight and stardust
And the love of Little Fish.
T'âm heard music in her heart
That sent her small feet dancing,
Flitting like two butterflies,

---

5. **Nâng Tien** (NAHNG TIHN)
6. *hai* (HEYE) *n. pl.* shoes

Skimming like two flying birds,
Dancing by the twin fish ponds,
Dancing in the rice paddy.
But the mud in the rice paddy
Kept one jeweled *hai* for its own.
Night Wind brought the *hai* to T'âm.
"What is yours I bring to you."
Water in the well bubbled,
"I will wash your *hai* for you."
Water buffalo came by.
"Dry your *hai* on my sharp horn."
A blackbird flew by singing,
"I know where this *hai* belongs.
In a garden far away
I will take this *hai* for you."

Four

What is to be must happen
As day follows after night.
In the Emperor's garden,
Sweet with perfume of roses,
The Emperor's son, the Prince,
Walked alone in the moonlight.
A bird, black against the moon,
Flew along the garden path,
Dropping a star in its flight.
"Look! A star!" exclaimed the Prince.
Carefully he picked it up
And found it was the small jeweled *hai.*
"Only a beautiful maid
Can wear this beautiful *hai.*"
The Prince whispered to his heart,
And his heart answered, "Find her."
In truth, beauty seeks goodness:
What is beautiful is good.
The Prince went to his father:
"A bird dropped this at my feet.
Surely it must come as truth,
Good and fair the maid it fits.
Sire, if it is your pleasure
I would take this maid for wife."

The Great Emperor was pleased
With the wishes of his son.
He called his servants to him,
His drummers and his crier,
Proclaiming a Festival
To find one who owned the *hai.*
In the Village of No-Name
The Emperor's subjects heard—
They heard the Royal Command.
There was praise and rejoicing.
They were pleased the Royal Son
Would wed one of their daughters.

Five

Father's house was filled with clothes,
Embroidered *áo-dài*[7] and *hai*
Of heavy silks and rich colors.
Father went outside to sit.
Cám and her mother whispered
Their hopes, their dreams and their plans.
Cám, Number One Daughter, asked,
"Mother, will the Prince choose me?"
Mother said, "Of course he will.
You will be the fairest there!
When you curtsy to the Prince
His heart will go out to you."
T'âm, Daughter Number Two, said,
"May I go with you and Cám?"
Cám's mother answered curtly,
"Yes, if you have done this task:
Separating rice and husks
From one basket into two."
T'âm knew Cám's mother had mixed
The cleaned rice with rice unhusked.
She looked at the big basket
Full to brim with rice and husks.
Separating the cleaned rice
From that of rice unhusked
Would take all harvest moon time,
When the Festival would end.
A cloud passed over the moon.

---

7. *áo-dài* (ow-DEYE) *n. pl.* long robes

T'âm arrives at the Emperor's palace. Pen and ink drawing by Tony Chen. From the book *In the Land of Small Dragon: A Vietnamese Folktale* by Dang Manh Kha.

Whirring wings outsung the wind.
A flock of blackbirds lighted
On the pile of leaves and grain.
Picking the grain from the leaves,
They dropped clean rice at T'âm's feet.
T'âm could almost not believe
That the endless task was done.
T'âm, the elder daughter, said,
"May I go? May I go, too,
Now that all my work is done?"
Cám taunted, "How could you go?
You have nothing fit to wear."
"If I had a dress to wear
Could I go to the Palace?"
"If wishes were dresses, yes,

But wishes are not dresses."
When Mother left she said,
"Our dear Cám is ravishing.
Stay at home, you Number Two!
Cám will be the one to wed."
T'âm dug up the big clay pot
The dress and one *hai* were there—
As soft as misty moon clouds,
Delicate as rose perfume.
T'âm washed her face in the well,
Combed her hair by the fish pond.
She smoothed down the silken dress,
Tied one *hai* unto her belt
And, though her feet were bare,
Hurried, scurried, ran and ran.
She ran to the Festival
In the King's Royal Garden.
At the Palace gates the Guards
Bowed before her, very low.
Pretty girls stood in a line
With their mothers standing near;
One by one they tried to fit
A foot into a small, jeweled *hai*.
Cám stood beside her mother,
By the gilded throne-room door.
Her face was dark and angry
Like a brooding monsoon wind.
Cám, wiping her tears away,
Sobbed and whimpered and complained,
"My small foot fits his old shoe—
Everything but my big toe."
T'âm stood shyly by the door
Looking in great wonderment
While trumpeters and drummers
Made music for her entrance.
People looked at gentle T'âm.
Everyone was whispering,
"Oh! She is so beautiful!
She must be a Princess fair
From some distant foreign land."
Then the Prince looked up and saw
A lady walking toward him.

Stepping from his Royal Throne,
He quickly went to meet her,
And taking her hand led her
To His Majesty the King.
What is to be must happen
As day happens after night.
Real beauty mirrors goodness.
What is one is the other.
Kneeling, the Prince placed the *hai*
On T'âm's dainty little foot.
T'âm untied the *hai* she wore
And slid her bare foot in it.

Beauty is not painted on.
It is the spirit showing.
The Prince spoke to his father.
"I would take this maid for wife."
His Royal Highness nodded.
"We will have a Wedding Feast."
All the birds in all the trees
Sang a song of happiness:
"T'âm, the Number Two Daughter,
Is to be Wife Number One."
That is written in the stars
Cannot be changed or altered.

POSTREADING

Critical Thinking

1. What are the views of beauty expressed in this Vietnamese folktale? Give examples from the story.
2. What do the proverbs, or sayings, suggest about the values and beliefs of the Vietnamese culture?
3. How has reading this folktale affected your thoughts about beauty and ugliness? Compare and contrast your ideas with the attitudes expressed in the story.

Writing Your Response to "In the Land of Small Dragon"

What image, saying, or event in this story especially appealed to your imagination? In your journal, write your thoughts and feelings about it. Why is it special? How does it relate to your experience?

Going Back Into the Text: Author's Craft

A **narrative poem** tells a story in verse form. Like short stories, narrative poems often tell about characters involved in a plot, which usually revolves around a central conflict, or problem. Narrative poetry also frequently contains dialogue, or conversations between characters. Narrative poems such as ballads are divided into four- and six-line stanzas, and often contain a repeating stanza called a *refrain.*

With a partner, review "In the Land of Small Dragon" to identify its narrative elements. Use the following questions as guidelines.

1. What elements of narrative poetry can you find in the selection?
2. Which of these elements do you think are most effective in the poem?
3. What other poems or songs that you know are examples of narrative poetry?

MAKING CONNECTIONS

Vietnamese Culture

The Vietnamese trace their culture to a people who lived in the Ma River valley southwest of Hanoi more than 4,000 years ago. That heritage is evident not only in legends and folktales but also in the Vietnamese language. Despite 1,000 years of Chinese rule (from 111 B.C. to A.D. 939), the Vietnamese people have preserved their rich and ancient culture.

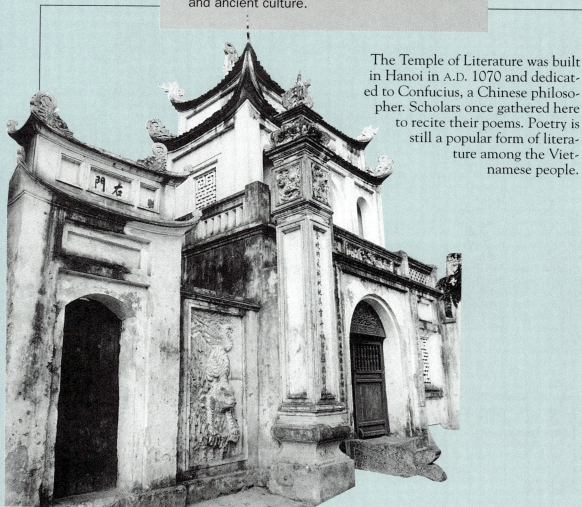

The Temple of Literature was built in Hanoi in A.D. 1070 and dedicated to Confucius, a Chinese philosopher. Scholars once gathered here to recite their poems. Poetry is still a popular form of literature among the Vietnamese people.

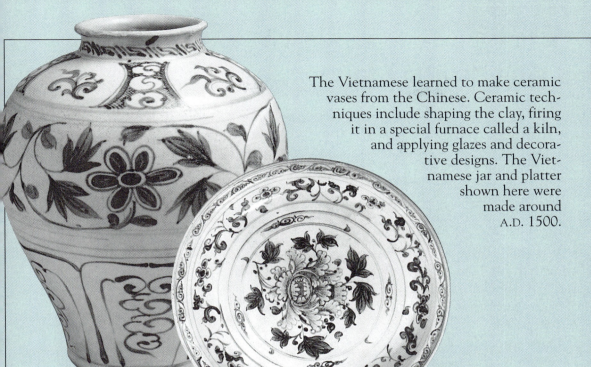

The Vietnamese learned to make ceramic vases from the Chinese. Ceramic techniques include shaping the clay, firing it in a special furnace called a kiln, and applying glazes and decorative designs. The Vietnamese jar and platter shown here were made around A.D. 1500.

Vietnamese scholars, even in the United States, still teach children calligraphy, the ancient art of beautiful handwriting. Each set of brush strokes is a character or symbol that has a special meaning. The characters that this calligrapher is writing stand for prosperity, wealth, and long life.

LINKING
Literature, Culture, and Theme

Compare the aspects of Vietnamese culture represented on these pages with those expressed in "In the Land of Small Dragon: A Vietnamese Folktale."

▼ Art is sometimes called a window to the soul of a nation. What do the pictures shown here suggest about the values of the Vietnamese people?

▼ How are these cultural values expressed in the Vietnamese folktale?

▼ In what ways do art and literature pass cultural values from one generation to another?

The Man Who Had No Story

Reading the Story in a Cultural Context

As in many other cultures, the story-telling tradition in Ireland has helped to express the Irish people's beliefs, values, social customs, and views of nature and life.

During the Middle Ages, between A.D. 1200 and 1600, Irish historians and storytellers were known throughout the western world as masters. People came from all over the world to train with them. The Irish bards, or poets, had to know about 200 tales, word for word. These stories have been handed down so accurately that 20th-century retellings of tales match exactly the words in the ancient manuscripts.

Irish poets studied the art of storytelling for several years. During this period they would also study philosophy, astronomy, and magic, to name only a few subjects. Then they memorized important stories and traveled about. People would give them food and shelter in exchange for their stories.

One part of the Irish heritage of stories was tales of the "good folk," the "little people," or fairies. These magic beings inhabited another world. The fairies were thought to be earth spirits or fallen angels. One legend suggests that fairies were descended from early Irish non-Christian gods. As more and more Irish people became Christian, these beings became smaller and smaller until they were tiny. Fairies were lively and loved feasting, fighting, and making beautiful music.

They could do mischief, such as stealing things, causing cows to have no milk, and striking people or cattle with paralysis. People could win the fairies' good will and kindness by leaving a saucer of milk on a windowsill for them.

Every county and village in Ireland has its own local fairy tales and special places that were believed to be doorways into the fairy kingdom. Stories abound of humans taken away by the fairies and returned many years later. Fairies were not always tiny, and a person could have magical adventures without knowing until afterward that he or she was dealing with fairies. Look for these elements as you read "The Man Who Had No Story."

The ancient hero sagas, or long adventure stories, were told in a sad-sounding musical chant. This method reflected the rhythmic, musical quality in the Irish language and in Irish tale telling. Notice these qualities as you read the tale.

Focusing on the Selection

What do the details of this story suggest to you about life in Ireland in earlier times? What does the story suggest about Irish beliefs and traditions? As you read, notice how certain story elements and lines of dialogue repeat. Think about the effect these patterns have. What do they suggest about the traditional Irish storytelling? Write your response in your journal.

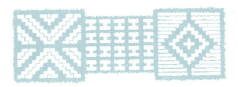

The Man Who Had No Story

MICHAEL JAMES TIMONEY
SÉAMUS Ó CATHÁIN

WELL, THERE WAS A MAN down here in Barr an Ghaoith[1] a long time ago and his name was Brian Ó Braonacháin.[2] The trade that he had was cutting rods,[3] making baskets of them, and selling them in Glenties and in Dunloe[4] and in Fintown and everywhere he could get them sold.

But one year he was down here and there wasn't a single rod in the whole of Bar an Ghaoith that he hadn't cut, made baskets of, sold, and then spent the money.

Those were bad times—the English were in power and they wouldn't let the Irish earn a single penny in any way. And Brian didn't know what to do.

But in those days there was a little glen outside of Barr an Ghaoith that they called Alt an Torr[5] and there were remarkably fine rods grow-

---

1. **Barr an Ghaoith** (BAWR ahn GWEE-hah)
2. **Brian Ó Braonacháin** (BREEN oh BRAYN-uh-kahn)
3. **rods** (RAHDZ) *n.* straight, slender sticks growing on trees or bushes
4. **Glenties** (GLEN-teez) . . . **Dunloe** (duhn-LOH)
5. **Alt an Torr** (AHLT ahn TOWR)

ing there. But nobody dared cut any rods there, for everyone made out that it was a fairy glen.

But one morning Brian said to his wife that if she made him up a little lunch he would go out and cut the makings of a couple of baskets and perhaps no harm would come to him.

The wife got up and made up a lunch for him. He put it in his pocket and he took a hook and a rope under his arm.

He went out to the glen and he wasn't long in the glen until he had cut two fine bundles of rods.

When he was tying them together so that he could carry them with the rope on his back, a terrible fog started to gather around him. He decided that he would sit down and eat his lunch and perhaps that the fog would clear. He sat down and he ate the lunch he had with him and when he had finished eating it was so dark that he could not see his finger in front of him.

He stood up and he got terribly scared. He looked to the east and he looked to the west and he saw a light. Where there is light there must be people, he thought, and he headed for the light. And he tripped and fell the whole time, but in the end he came up to the light. There was a big long house there. The door was open and there was a fine light coming out of the window and the door.

He put his head in the door and an old woman was sitting in the corner and an old man on the other side of the fire. Both of them saluted Brian Ó Braonacháin from Barr an Ghaoith and wished him welcome, and they asked him to come up and sit in at the fire.

Brian came up and he sat in at the fire between the pair of them. They talked for a while. But he had not been sitting there long when the old man asked him to tell a fairy tale.[6]

"That is something that I never did in all my life," said Brian, "tell a story of any kind. I can't tell Fenian[7] tales or fairy tales of any kind."

"Well," said the old woman, said she, "take that bucket and go down to the well below the house and fetch a bucket of water and do something for your keep."

"I'll do anything," said Brian, "except tell a story."

He took the bucket, went down to the well and filled it with water from the well. He left it standing on the flagstone beside the well, so that the water would run off it, before he brought it in. But a big blast of wind came and he was swept off up into the sky. He was blown east and he was blown west and when he fell to the ground he could see neither the bucket nor the well nor anything at all.

---

6. fairy tale *n.* a story about a human's adventures with the "Little people," or fairies. A magical world inhabited by fairies and other beings is part of Irish folklore.

7. Fenian (FEE-nee-uhn) *adj.* pertaining to the struggle for Irish independence and its supporters

He looked around and he saw a light and he made out that where there was light there must be people and he headed for the light. He tripped and fell the whole time, it was so dark. But at last he came to the light. There was a big long house there, far bigger than the first house, two lights in it and a fine light out of the door.

He put his head in the door, and what was it but a wake-house.[8] There was a row of men sitting by the back wall of the house and a row of men sitting by the front wall of the house and up at the fire there was a girl with curly black hair sitting on a chair. She saluted and welcomed Brian Ó Braonacháin from Barr an Ghaoith and she asked him to come up and sit beside her on the chair.

Brian came up and he sat beside her on the chair and very shy he was, too. But he had not been sitting long when a big man who was in the company stood up.

"It is a very lonely wake we are having here tonight," said he, "a couple of us must go to get a fiddler, so that we can start dancing."

"Oh," said the girl with the curly black hair, "you don't need to go for any fiddler tonight," said she, "you have the best fiddler in Ireland among you here tonight," said she, "Brian Ó Braonacháin from Barr an Ghaoith."

"Oh, that is something I never did in my life," said Brian, "play a tune on a fiddle, and there is no music or singing or fiddling of any kind in my head."

"Oh," said she, "don't make me a liar, you are the very man who can fiddle."

Before Brian knew he had the bow and the fiddle in his hand and he played away and they danced away, and they all said that they had never heard any fiddler playing a tune on a fiddle better than Brian Ó Braonacháin from Barr an Ghaoith. . . .

Then the corpse was placed in a coffin outside the door and four men put the coffin on their shoulders. They were three fairly short men and one big tall man and the coffin was terribly shaky.

"One or two of us," said the big man who was in the company, said he, "must go for a doctor so that we can cut a piece off the legs of that big man to make him level with the other three."

"Oh," said the girl with the curly black hair, "you don't need to go for any doctor tonight, the best doctor in Ireland is here among you tonight, Brian Ó Braonacháin from Barr an Ghaoith."

"Oh, that is something I never did in my life," said Brian, "doctoring of any sort. I never got any doctor's schooling at all."

---

8. **wake-house** n. a house in which a wake, or watch over a dead person, is taking place

"You'll do that just as well as you did the rest," said she.

The lances were given to Brian and he cut a piece off the big man's legs, under his knees, and he stuck the legs back on, and he made him level with the other three men.

Then they put the coffin on their shoulders and they walked gently and carefully west, until they came to the graveyard. There was a big stone wall around the graveyard, ten feet high, or maybe twelve. And they had to lift one man up on the wall first and they were going up one by one and going down into the graveyard on the other side. And the last man on top of the wall ready to go down into the graveyard was Brian Ó Braonacháin.

But a big blast of wind came and he was swept off up into the sky. He was blown to the east and he was blown to the west. When he fell down to the ground, he could see neither the graveyard nor the coffin nor the funeral. But where did he fall? He fell down on the flagstone beside the well where he had been at the beginning of the night. He looked at the bucket and the water was hardly dry on the outside of it.

He took the bucket and up he went into the house. And the old man and the old woman were sitting where he had left them at nightfall. He left the bucket by the dresser and he came up and sat in between the pair of them again.

"Now, Brian," said the old man, "can you tell a fairy tale?"

"I can," said he, "I am the man who has got a story to tell."

He began to tell the old woman and the old man what he had gone through since nightfall.

"Well, Brian," said the old man, "wherever you are from now on," said he, "and whenever anybody asks you to tell a story, tell them that story, and you are the man who will have a story to tell."

The old woman got up and made Brian a good supper. And when he had had his supper she made up a feather bed for him and he went to bed. And he wasn't in bed long before he fell asleep, for he was tired after all he had gone through since nightfall.

But when he woke in the morning, where was he? He was lying in Alt an Torr outside Barr an Ghaoith with his head on the two bundles of rods. He got up and went home and he never cut a rod from that day to this.

The Fiddler of Glenbirnie.
19th-century Irish engraving by I. Kay. What does the appearance of a fiddler in this tale tell you about the cultural traditions of the Irish people?

Critical Thinking

1. What Irish traditions and beliefs does the story suggest? What cultural value does the story title indicate?
2. Why do you think storytelling has been an important Irish tradition? Give evidence from the story to support your answer.
3. What value does the culture you come from place on the tradition of storytelling? How is this value similar to that illustrated in the Irish story?

Writing Your Response to "The Man Who Had No Story"

What situation, event, or character in this story do you find most striking or intriguing? In your journal, write about the aspects of the story that create strong pictures in your imagination. What parts relate to your own life?

Going Back Into the Text: Author's Craft

Speakers and storytellers use **repetition** for emphasis and to provide a pleasurable feeling of recognition when familiar words chime in. In stories, whole sections of the plot may repeat, with variations. The repetition makes readers believe they know what comes next, but it also creates suspense, because they also know that something will be different. The listener can almost anticipate the storyteller in the repeat sections of the story, yet the details that vary with each repetition create a sense of surprise.

Repetitive language in a poem or tale adds a rhythmic feeling and can act as an informal, irregular refrain. The first few words of a repeated line catch the reader's attention and then satisfy the audience's expectation by completing the familiar line.

Use the following questions to help you analyze the use of repetition in "The Man Who Had No Story." Work with a partner, rereading parts of the story aloud to hear the rhythmic effect of the repetition.

1. What plot sections in this story are repeated? What elements change in the repeated sections? What elements stay the same?
2. What phrases are repeated? What is the effect of this repetition? Give examples of repetition in other stories you know.
3. Give examples of repetition in other stories you enjoy.

Reviewing the Theme

1. Compare the morals, or lessons about life, illustrated by two or more stories in this theme. What similarities can you find? Do the values and beliefs reinforce or contradict one another? Could they all exist in one culture? Why or why not?

2. Analyze the forms of two stories in this theme. How are the forms similar? How are they different? How does the form of each story convey the values the storyteller wants to express?

3. Which story or stories confirmed your own values and beliefs? Which made you think differently about your understanding of life? Explain your answer.

Theme 2:
Exploring Ancestral Roots

Horn Player. Bronze figure from the Kingdom of Benin (1350–1680) in Nigeria, West Africa.

THE AUTHORS of the following selections write from the belief that their ancestors and their cultural backgrounds are an essential part of their lives. Together, the writings in this section explore many different backgrounds. However, the writers describe the kinds of conflicts that may occur as young and old, past and present, traditional and modern come together. You will read about Mexican Americans who are dealing with conflicts within their own society. You will also learn about African Americans whose ancestral roots were lost during generations of slavery. Other selections tell about Native Americans whose heritage is close to the land and West Indians who visit their Caribbean homeland.

The writers of these selections explore relationships with the past and with older relatives as a way of finding out about themselves. In the process of exploring their family histories, they gain a new sense of self-understanding.

MODEL LESSON

from Bless Me, Ultima

Responding to Literature

Notice the sidenotes in the margins of this selection. These notes reflect one student's reading of *Bless Me, Ultima*. The student sees how Anaya's background is reflected in the story. The student also notices how the author uses some common story elements like foreshadowing and dialogue to construct his story and to describe his characters. The student also has some personal responses to the story. Compare these observations with your own critical reading of this fictional piece.

Reading the Author in a Cultural Context

The search for one's roots is not a new journey. For centuries, people have visited ancestral sites, whether this meant a trip to an ancient castle or to a parent's house. Sometimes the journey is an exploration of traditions, of values, of culture. Such is the case with Rudolfo Anaya (roo-DOHL-foh ah-NEYE-ah), a Mexican American writer from New Mexico. Anaya's novel, *Bless Me, Ultima*, from which the following selection has been taken, is a journey into the language and traditions of his ancestry.

Anaya's work blends the hard reality of the Southwest and the spiritual qualities of his Catholic and Indian heritages. His work is different from that of many other Mexican American writers in that it is not political. Instead, Anaya uses the social customs and values of his family, the language of his people, and the magic of his childhood to create a poetic account of his boyhood.

Anaya began writing to try to create some type of faith for himself. The religion that he questioned was the Catholicism brought to the Americas by the Spanish. This religion blended over time with Aztec and other traditional beliefs. Tension is created in this selection by the influence of Christian ideas and the presence of the *curandera*, or healer. Within Antonio's family, there is conflict between the settled farmers, called *rancheros* (rahn-CHAY-rohs), of his mother's family and the free-roaming *vaqueros* (bah-KAY-rohs), or cowboys, of his father's.

More important than life's contradictions, however, is its continuity. Anaya belongs to a culture that stresses the importance of *cuentos* (KWEN-tohs), or stories, in tying together the past and the present.

Focusing on the Selection

As you read, think about how Anaya depicts the cultural roots of Antonio's family. Why is la Grande so important to Antonio? What does the selection tell you about the conflicts in Antonio's family? What descriptive details most help Antonio's world come to life for you?

from *Bless Me, Ultima*

RUDOLFO A. ANAYA

ULTIMA CAME TO STAY with us the summer I was almost seven. When she came the beauty of the llano[1] unfolded before my eyes, and the gurgling waters of the river sang to the hum of the turning earth. The magical time of childhood stood still, and the pulse of the living earth pressed its mystery into my living blood. She took my hand, and the silent, magic powers she possessed made beauty from the raw, sun-baked llano, the green river valley, and the blue bowl which was the white sun's home. My bare feet felt the throbbing earth and my body trembled with excitement. Time stood still, and it shared with me all that had been, and all that was to come. . . .

That night I lay very quietly in my bed, and I heard my father and mother speak of Ultima.

"Está sola," my father said, "ya no queda gente en el pueblito de Las Pasturas—"[2]

He spoke in Spanish, and the village he mentioned was his home. My father had been a vaquero all his life, a calling as ancient as the coming of the Spaniard to Nuevo Méjico. Even after the big rancheros and the tejanos came and fenced the beautiful llano, he and those like him continued to work there, I guess because only in that wide expanse of land and sky could they feel the freedom their spirits needed.

"¡Qué lástima,"[3] my mother answered, and I knew her nimble fingers worked the pattern on the doily she crocheted for the big chair in the sala.

I heard her sigh, and she must have shuddered too when she thought of Ultima living alone in the loneliness of the wide llano. My mother was not a woman of the llano, she was the daughter of a farmer. She could not see beauty in the llano and she could not understand the coarse men who lived half their lifetimes on horseback. After I was born in Las Pasturas she persuaded my father to leave the llano and bring her family to the town of Guadalupe where she said there would be opportunity and school for us. The move lowered my father in the esteem of his compadres, the other vaqueros of the llano who clung tenaciously to their way of life and freedom. There was no room to keep animals in

---

1. **llano** (YAHN-oh) *n.* a flat area, like a prairie
2. **Está sola, ya no queda gente en el pueblito de Las Pasturas** (ay-STAH SO-lah, YAH NO KAY-dah HEN-tay AYN EL POOAY-bleeto DAY LAHS pahs-TOO-rahs) She is alone, there is no one left in the little town of Las Pasturas.
3. **¡Qué lástima!** (kay LAHS-tee-mah) What a pity!

Market scene. *Museum of International Folk Art, Santa Fe, New Mexico.* Contemporary ceramic folk art from San Pedro Tlaquepaque, Mexico. What does this art tell you about how the *vaqueros* felt about leaving the *llano*?

town so my father had to sell his small herd, but he would not sell his horse so he gave it to a good friend, Benito Campos. But Campos could not keep the animal penned up because somehow the horse was very close to the spirit of the man, and so the horse was allowed to roam free and no vaquero on that llano would throw a lazo on that horse. It was as if someone had died, and they turned their gaze from the spirit that walked the earth.

It hurt my father's pride. He saw less and less of his old compadres. . . . but he was never close to the men of the town. Some weekends the llaneros would come into town for supplies and old amigos[4] like Bonney or Campos or the Gonzales brothers would come by to visit. Then my father's eyes lit up as they . . . talked of the old days and told the old stories. But when the western sun touched the clouds with orange and gold the vaqueros got in their trucks and headed home, and my father was left . . . alone in the long night. Sunday morning he would get up very crudo[5] and complain about having to go to early mass.

The character of the father is connected with the earth, the animals, and the past. His old way of life is vanishing.

---

4. llaneros (yahn-AY-rohs) . . . **amigos** (ah-MEE-gohs) *n. pl.* plainsmen . . . friends
5. crudo (KROO-doh) *adj.* feeling ill

Maybe the mother is a strong Catholic. She makes the sign of the cross in conversation.

"—She served the people all her life, and now the people are scattered, driven like tumbleweeds by the winds of war. The war sucks everything dry," my father said solemnly, "it takes the young boys overseas, and their families move to California where there is work—"

"Ave María Purísima,"[6] my mother made the sign of the cross for my three brothers who were away at war. "Gabriel," she said to my father, "it is not right that la Grande be alone in her old age—"

"No," my father agreed.

"When I married you and went to the llano to live with you and raise your family, I could not have survived without la Grande's help. Oh, those were hard years—"

"Those were good years," my father countered. But my mother would not argue.

"There isn't a family she did not help," she continued, "no road was too long for her to walk to its end to snatch somebody from the jaws of death, and not even the blizzards of the llano could keep her from the appointed place where a baby was to be delivered—"

"Es verdad,"[7] my father nodded.

The mother and father have a lot of respect for la Grande. I think this respect means that it is the custom of their people to take care of old people.

"She tended me at the birth of my sons—" And then I knew her eyes glanced briefly at my father. "Gabriel, we cannot let her live her last days in loneliness—"

"No," my father agreed, "it is not the way of our people."

"It would be a great honor to provide a home for la Grande," my mother murmured. My mother called Ultima la Grande out of respect. It meant the woman was old and wise.

"I have already sent word with Campos that Ultima is to come and live with us," my father said with some satisfaction. He knew it would please my mother.

"I am grateful," my mother said tenderly, "perhaps we can repay a little of the kindness la Grande has given to so many."

Maybe la Grande just knows good natural medicine.

"And the children?" my father asked. I knew why he expressed concern for me and my sisters. It was because Ultima was a curandera,[8] a woman who knew the herbs and remedies of the ancients, a miracle-worker who could heal the sick. And I had heard that Ultima could lift the curses laid by brujas,[9] that she could exorcise the evil the witches planted in people to make them sick. And because a curandera had this power she was misunderstood and often suspected of practicing witchcraft herself.

---

6. **Ave María Purísima** (AH-vay mah-REE-ah poor-EES-ee-mah) Hail Mary, most pure; a reference to the Immaculate Conception
7. **Es verdad** (AYS bair-DAHD) it is true
8. **curandera** (koor-ahn-DAI-rah) *n.* healer
9. **brujas** (BROO-hahs) *n. pl.* witches

I shuddered and my heart turned cold at the thought. The cuentos of the people were full of the tales of evil done by brujas.

"She helped bring them into the world, she cannot be but good for the children," my mother answered.

"Está bien,"[10] my father yawned, "I will go for her in the morning."

So it was decided that Ultima should come and live with us. I knew that my father and mother did good by providing a home for Ultima. It was the custom to provide for the old and the sick. There was always room in the safety and warmth of la familia[11] for one more person, be that person stranger or friend.

It was warm in the attic, and as I lay quietly listening to the sounds of the house falling asleep and repeating a Hail Mary over and over in my thoughts, I drifted into the time of dreams. Once I had told my mother about my dreams and she said they were visions from God and she was happy, because her own dream was that I should grow up and become a priest. After that I did not tell her about my dreams, and they remained in me forever and ever . . .

In my dream I flew over the rolling hills of the llano. My soul wandered over the dark plain until it came to a cluster of adobe[12] huts. I recognized the village of Las Pasturas and my heart grew happy. One mud hut had a lighted window, and the vision of my dream swept me towards it to be witness at the birth of a baby. . . .

Now the people who had waited patiently in the dark were allowed to come in and speak to the mother and deliver their gifts to the baby. I recognized my mother's brothers, my uncles from El Puerto de los Lunas. They entered ceremoniously. A patient hope stirred in their dark, brooding eyes.

This one will be a Luna,[13] the old man said, he will be a farmer and keep our customs and traditions. Perhaps God will bless our family and make the baby a priest.

And to show their hope they rubbed the dark earth of the river valley on the baby's forehead, and they surrounded the bed with the fruits of their harvest so the small room smelled of fresh green chile and corn, ripe apples and peaches, pumpkins and green beans.

Then the silence was shattered with the thunder of hoofbeats; vaqueros surrounded the small house with shouts and gunshots, and when they entered the room they were laughing and singing and drinking.

Gabriel, they shouted, you have a fine son! He will make a fine vaquero! And they smashed the fruits and vegetables that surrounded the bed and

The boy is the narrator of the novel. We see everything from his point of view. He may have stopped telling his mother his dreams because he wanted to keep them to himself.

This is an amazing dream. It's also an important part of the plot of the story. My dreams aren't complete stories like this one.

---

10. **Está bien** (ay-STAH BEE-yen) it's all right
11. **la familia** (lah fah-MEE-lee-ah) *n.* the family
12. **adobe** (uh-DOH-bee) *n.* a house built from sundried mud bricks
13. **Luna** (LOO-nah) *n.* the mother's family name

replaced them with a saddle, horse blankets, bottles of whiskey, a new rope, bridles,[14] chapas,[15] and an old guitar. And they rubbed the stain of earth from the baby's forehead because man was not to be tied to the earth but free upon it.

These were the people of my father, the vaqueros of the llano. They were an exuberant, restless people, wandering across the ocean of the plain. . . .

Curses and threats filled the air, pistols were drawn, and the opposing sides made ready for battle. But the clash was stopped by the old woman who delivered the baby. . . .

The dream began to dissolve. When I opened my eyes I heard my father cranking the truck outside. I wanted to go with him, I wanted to see Las Pasturas, I wanted to see Ultima. I dressed hurriedly, but I was too late. The truck was bouncing down the goat path that led to the bridge and the highway.

I turned, as I always did, and looked down the slope of our hill to the green of the river, and I raised my eyes and saw the town of Guadalupe. Towering above the housetops and the trees of the town was the church tower. I made the sign of the cross on my lips. The only other building that rose above the housetops to compete with the church tower was the yellow top of the schoolhouse. This fall I would be going to school.

My heart sank. When I thought of leaving my mother and going to school a warm, sick feeling came to my stomach. To get rid of it I ran to the pens we kept by the molino[16] to feed the animals. I had fed the rabbits that night and they all had alfalfa and so I only changed their water. I scattered some grain for the hungry chickens and watched their mad scramble as the rooster called them to peck. I milked the cow and turned her loose. During the day she would forage[17] along the highway where the grass was thick and green, then she would return at nightfall. She was a good cow and there were very few times when I had to run and bring her back in the evening. Then I dreaded it, because she might wander into the hills where the bats flew at dusk and there was only the sound of my heart beating as I ran and it made me sad and frightened to be alone.

I collected three eggs in the chicken house and returned for breakfast.

"Antonio," my mother smiled and took the eggs and milk, "come and eat your breakfast."

I sat across the table from Deborah and Theresa and ate my atole and the hot tortilla[18] with butter. I said very little. I usually spoke very

The quiet farmers are very different from the rowdy vaqueros. It's as if they have stereotyped ideas of each other.

I've had that scared feeling of knowing something was going to change. The boy goes to see the animals for comfort and to take away the fear.

---

14. **bridles** (BREYE-duhls) *n. pl.* leather gear used to lead or guide horses
15. **chapas** (CHAH-pahs) *n. pl.* chaps, leather leg protectors worn by cowboys
16. **molino** (moh-LEE-noh) *n.* a mill
17. **forage** (FOHR-ihj) *v.* look for food
18. **atole** (ah-TOH-lay) . . . **tortilla** (tawr-TEE-yah) cornmeal breakfast foods: porridge and a pancake

little to my two sisters. They were older than I and they were very close. They usually spent the entire day in the attic, playing dolls and giggling. I did not concern myself with those things.

"Your father has gone to Las Pasturas," my mother chattered, "he has gone to bring la Grande." Her hands were white with the flour of the dough. I watched carefully. "—And when he returns, I want you children to show your manners. You must not shame your father or your mother—"

"Isn't her real name Ultima?" Deborah asked. She was like that, always asking grown-up questions.

"You will address her as la Grande," my mother said flatly. I looked at her and wondered if this woman with the black hair and laughing eyes was the woman who gave birth in my dream.

"Grande," Theresa repeated.

"Is it true she is a witch?" Deborah asked. Oh, she was in for it. I saw my mother whirl then pause and control herself.

"No!" she scolded. "You must not speak of such things. Oh, I don't know where you learn such ways—" Her eyes flooded with tears. She always cried when she thought we were learning the ways of my father, the ways of the Márez.[19] "She is a woman of learning," she went on and I knew she didn't have time to stop and cry, "she has worked hard for all the people of the village. Oh, I would never have survived those hard years if it had not been for her—so show her respect. We are honored that she comes to live with us, understand?"

"Sí, mamá,"[20] Deborah said half willingly.

"Sí, mamá," Theresa repeated. . . .

"Was Ultima at my birth?" I asked.

"¡Ay Dios mío!"[21] my mother cried. She came to where I sat and ran her hand through my hair. She smelled warm, like bread. "Where do you get such questions, my son. Yes," she smiled, "la Grande was there to help me. She was there to help at the birth of all of my children—"

"And my uncles from El Puerto were there?"

"Of course," she answered, "my brothers have always been at my side when I needed them. They have always prayed that I would bless them with a—"

I did not hear what she said because I was hearing the sounds of the dream, and I was seeing the dream again. The warm cereal in my stomach made me feel sick.

"And my father's brother was there, the Márez' and their friends, the vaqueros—"

---

19. **Márez** (MAH-rays) *n.* Márez is their family name; the father's relatives
20. **Sí, mamá** (SEE mah-MAH) yes, mother
21. **¡Ay Dios Mío!** (AI DEE-ohs MEE-oh) Oh, my God!

I think the boy feels that it is very important to his mother that the children understand and treat la Grande respectfully. This culture really respects old people.

Antonio must think that if the people he dreamed were really there, then the part about the old woman knowing his future is true also.

Maybe Antonio doesn't want to be a priest. That's why he is so interested in la Grande, because she will know his future.

Antonio is making the garden to please his mother. The novelist has included a lot of vivid details in his descriptions here.

It seems that manners matter a lot in this family. The mother warned her daughters to be polite.

"Ay!" she cried out, "Don't speak to me of those worthless Márez and their friends!"

"There was a fight?" I asked.

"No," she said, "a silly argument. They wanted to start a fight with my brothers—that is all they are good for. Vaqueros, they call themselves, they are worthless drunks! Thieves! Always on the move, like gypsies, always dragging their families around the country like vagabonds—"

As long as I could remember she always raged about the Márez family and their friends. She called the village of Las Pasturas beautiful; she had gotten used to the loneliness, but she had never accepted its people. She was the daughter of farmers.

But the dream was true. It was as I had seen it. Ultima knew.

"But you will not be like them." She caught her breath and stopped. She kissed my forehead. "You will be like my brothers. You will be a Luna, Antonio. You will be a man of the people, and perhaps a priest." She smiled.

. . . I felt a cool sweat on my forehead and I knew I had to run, I had to clear my mind of the dream. . . .

While I waited for my father to return with Ultima I worked in the garden. Every day I had to work in the garden. Every day I reclaimed from the rocky soil of the hill a few more feet of earth to cultivate. The land of the llano was not good for farming, the good land was along the river. But my mother wanted a garden and I worked to make her happy. Already we had a few chile and tomato plants growing. It was hard work. My fingers bled from scraping out the rocks and it seemed that a square yard of ground produced a wheelbarrow full of rocks which I had to push down to the retaining wall.

The sun was white in the bright blue sky. The shade of the clouds would not come until the afternoon. The sweat was sticky on my brown body. I heard the truck and turned to see it chugging up the dusty goat path. My father was returning with Ultima.

"¡Mamá!" I called. My mother came running out, Deborah and Theresa trailed after her.

"I'm afraid," I heard Theresa whimper.

"There's nothing to be afraid of," Deborah said confidently. My mother said there was too much Márez blood in Deborah. Her eyes and hair were very dark, and she was always running. She had been to school two years and she spoke only English. She was teaching Theresa and half the time I didn't understand what they were saying.

"Madre de Dios,[22] but mind your manners!" my mother scolded. The truck stopped and she ran to greet Ultima. "Buenos días le de Dios,

22. **Madre de Dios** (MAHD-ray day DEE-ohs) Mother of God; Mary, the mother of Jesus Christ

Grande,"[23] my mother cried. She smiled and hugged and kissed the old woman.

"Ay, María Luna," Ultima smiled, "Buenos días te de Dios, a ti y a tu familia."[24] She wrapped the black shawl around her hair and shoulders. Her face was brown and very wrinkled. When she smiled her teeth were brown. I remembered the dream.

"Come, come!" my mother urged us forward. It was the custom to greet the old. "Deborah!" my mother urged. Deborah stepped forward and took Ultima's withered hand.

"Buenos días, Grande," she smiled. She even bowed slightly. Then she pulled Theresa forward and told her to greet la Grande. My mother beamed. Deborah's good manners surprised her, but they made her happy, because a family was judged by its manners.

"What beautiful daughters you have raised," Ultima nodded to my mother. Nothing could have pleased my mother more. She looked proudly at my father who stood leaning against the truck, watching and judging the introductions.

"Antonio," he said simply. I stepped forward and took Ultima's hand. I looked up into her clear brown eyes and shivered. Her face was old and wrinkled, but her eyes were clear and sparkling, like the eyes of a young child.

"Antonio," she smiled. She took my hand and I felt the power of a whirlwind sweep around me. Her eyes swept the surrounding hills and through them I saw for the first time the wild beauty of our hills and the magic of the green river. My nostrils quivered as I felt the song of the mockingbirds and the drone of the grasshoppers mingle with the pulse of the earth. The four directions of the llano met in me, and the white sun shone on my soul. The granules of sand at my feet and the sun and sky above me seemed to dissolve into one strange, complete being.

A cry came to my throat, and I wanted to shout it and run in the beauty I had found.

"Antonio." I felt my mother prod me. Deborah giggled because she had made the right greeting, and I who was to be my mother's hope and joy stood voiceless.

"Buenos días le de Dios, Ultima," I muttered. I saw in her eyes my dream. I saw the old woman who had delivered me from my mother's womb. I knew she held the secret of my destiny.

"¡Antonio!" My mother was shocked I had used her name instead of calling her Grande. But Ultima held up her hand.

It seems as if la Grande has some magic that makes the world change for Antonio. Maybe it's because she is a link with his roots.

I can see that Antonio does something very rude; he calls Ultima by her first name. But she says it's all right because they have a special relationship.

---

23. **Buenos días le de Dios, Grande** (BWAY-nohs DEE-ahs lay day DEE-ohs, GRAHN-day) God grant you a good day, Grande
24. **a ti y a tu familia** (ah TEE ee ah TOO fah-MEE-lee-ah) to you and your family

November in New Mexico. *Albert M. Bender Collection.* Oil painting
on canvas by Andrew Michael Dasburg, created in 1926.
What was life like for the *rancheros* and *vaqueros* living on the
llanos, or wide, grassy plains, of the Southwest?

"Let it be," she smiled. "This was the last child I pulled from your
womb, María. I knew there would be something between us."

My mother who had started to mumble apologies was quiet. "As you
wish, Grande," she nodded.

"I have come to spend the last days of my life here, Antonio," Ultima said to me.

"You will never die, Ultima," I answered. "I will take care of you—"
She let go of my hand and laughed. Then my father said, "pase, Grande,
pase. Nuestra casa es su casa.[25] It is too hot to stand and visit in the sun—"

"Sí, sí," my mother urged. I watched them go in. My father carried
on his shoulders the large blue-tin trunk which later I learned contained
all of Ultima's earthly possessions, the black dresses and shawls she wore,
and the magic of her sweet smelling herbs.

As Ultima walked past me I smelled for the first time a trace of the
sweet fragrance of herbs that always lingered in her wake. Many years
later, long after Ultima was gone and I had grown to be a man, I would
awaken sometimes at night and think I caught a scent of her fragrance
in the cool-night breeze.

The scent of
herbs becomes a
reminder of la
Grande for
Antonio. The
herbs she uses
as a healer are
part of the old
Native American
customs.

---

25. **pase, Grande, pase. Nuestra casa es su casa** (PAH-say GRAHN-day, PAH-say.
    noo-AYS-trah CAH-sah ays soo CAH-sah) Come in Grande, come in. Our
    home is your home.

And with Ultima came the owl. I heard it that night for the first time in the juniper tree outside of Ultima's window. I knew it was her owl because the other owls of the llano did not come that near the house. At first it disturbed me, and Deborah and Theresa too. I heard them whispering through the partition. I heard Deborah reassuring Theresa that she would take care of her, and then she took Theresa in her arms and rocked her until they were both asleep.

I waited. I was sure my father would get up and shoot the owl with the old rifle he kept on the kitchen wall. But he didn't, and I accepted his understanding. In many cuentos I had heard the owl was one of the disguises a bruja took, and so it struck a chord of fear in the heart to hear them hooting at night. But not Ultima's owl. Its soft hooting was like a song, and as it grew rhythmic it calmed the moonlit hills and lulled us to sleep. Its song seemed to say that it had come to watch over us. . . .

At first, the owl disturbs the children, but Antonio comes to find it soothing. It's a symbol for him.

One of Anaya's themes in the novel seems to be that who you are is strongly influenced by your cultural roots.

POSTREADING

Critical Thinking

1. What does Rudolfo Anaya tell you about the attitudes Antonio has about his ancestral roots?
2. How do you think Anaya's life and family history influenced him to write a novel about a young boy and an old woman who is a healer?
3. How did this story influence your own attitudes about exploring your ancestry? How are Antonio's feelings about his ancestors similar to your own?

Writing Your Response to *Bless Me, Ultima*

In your journal, tell about one event, character, or description from the selection that had special meaning for you. Why was it special? Did Anaya's language affect you in any way? How? How does the excerpt that you chose relate to experiences in your own life?

Going Back Into the Text: Author's Craft

Writers often use **sensory details** to help create a mood or tone and bring their descriptions to life for the reader. Sensory details may describe how something looks, sounds, feels, tastes, or smells.

With a partner, review the selection from *Bless Me, Ultima* to see how Anaya uses sensory details in his descriptions. Use these questions as guidelines.

1. What sensory details does Anaya use to describe the landscape?
2. What sensory details does he use to describe people?
3. Which descriptions do you think are most effective? Why?

from Roots

Reading the Author in a Cultural Context

In 1976, *Roots* took its place in a long and rich tradition of storytelling in African American literature. Many African tales and characters came to the Americas with enslaved Africans. For example, an animal trickster in stories from the Ashanti (uh-SHAN-tuh) people of what is now Ghana appears in African American tales as Brer Rabbit. In the 20th century, the African American tradition of storytelling became known in the United States with the publication of African folktales. These tales featured stories and characters that had been passed down through generations.

Alex Haley used the name of his ancestor Kunta Kinte (KOON-tuh kihn-TAY) and some African words from stories handed down in his family as clues to find the African village from which Kunta was stolen and sold into slavery. Haley truly found his roots—the culture and people that his family came from. *Roots* is Haley's imagined reconstruction of Kunta Kinte's life in what is now The Gambia in West Africa, his enslavement in North America, and the growth of his family over time in slavery and in freedom.

Haley's original source of information was the stories that he heard his grandmother and her sisters sharing. Haley wrote that his own mother did not like the talk, and "would abruptly snap something like, 'Oh, Maw, I wish you'd stop all that old-time slavery stuff, it's entirely embarrassing!' Grandma would snap right back, 'If you don't care who and where you come from, I does!' "

The term *faction* has been used to describe the storytelling technique Haley used to write *Roots*. This method combines fact and fiction, using historical events but invented characters and dialogue. In his research, Haley learned of very old men called griots (GREE-ohz), who memorize the histories of villages, families, and clans over hundreds of years. He found a griot of his ancestral village who was able to tell him about his relatives and his homeland from as long ago as the 1700s. Haley used information that the griot shared with him and his own imagination to construct the world in which Kunta lived.

In reconstructing his past, Haley created a personal and familial history to share with millions of African Americans who had long been denied such a history. *Roots* was an enormous success with U.S. television viewers. Haley believed that this was due to his intention neither to blame nor to stir up anger, but to find out who he was. Finding one's roots is a great human equalizer.

Focusing on the Selection

As you read, think about the customs that Haley explores in his search for his ancestral roots. What is the function of the Council of Elders in this village? What might happen if this tradition were lost or forgotten? Think about which parts of the selection may be facts Haley learned from the griot. Which parts may be fiction, things he made up or changed to make a good story?

from *Roots*

ALEX HALEY

A S NEW MEN[1] were permitted to do whenever there was no conflict with their duties, Kunta and the others of his kafo[2] would sit at the outermost edges of the formal sessions of the Council of Elders, which were held once each moon under Juffure's[3] ancient baobab.[4] Sitting beneath it on cured hides very close together, the six senior elders seemed almost as old as the tree, Kunta thought, and to have been carved from the same wood, except that they were as black as ebony against the white of their long robes and round skullcaps. Seated facing them were those with troubles or disputes to be resolved. Behind the petitioners,[5] in rows, according to their ages, sat junior elders such as Omoro, and behind them sat the new men of Kunta's kafo. And behind them the village women could sit, though they rarely attended except when someone in their immediate family was involved in a matter to be heard. . . .

No women at all attended when the Council met to discuss purely administrative affairs, such as Juffure's relationship with other villages.

---

1. **new men** *n. pl.* young men formally accepted into the adult male community
2. **kafo** (KAH-foh) *n.* young men who have come to manhood at the same time
3. **Juffure's** (joo-FOO-rahz) *n.* belonging to the village of Juffure
4. **baobab** (BAH-oh-bab) *n.* kind of tree with a broad trunk
5. **petitioners** (puh-TIHSH-uhn-erz) *n. pl.* people asking for help

High Museum, Atlanta, Georgia. 19th-century bronze staff of office from the Abeokuta culture in Nigeria, West Africa.

On the day for matters of the people, however, the audience was large and noisy—but all settled quickly into silence when the most senior of the elders raised his stick, sewn with bright-colored beads, to strike out on the talking drum before him the name of the first person to be heard. This was done according to their ages, to serve the needs of the oldest first. Whoever it was would stand, stating his case, the senior elders all staring at the ground, listening until he finished and sat down. At this point, any of the elders might ask him questions.

If the matter involved a dispute, the second person now presented his side, followed by more questions, whereupon the elders turned around to present their backs as they huddled to discuss the matter, which could take a long time. One or more might turn with further questions. But all finally turned back around toward the front, one motioning the person or persons being heard to stand again, and the senior elder then spoke their decision, after which the next name was drumtalked.[6]

Even for new men like Kunta, most of these hearings were routine matters. People with babies recently born asked for a bigger farm plot for the husband and an additional rice plot for the wife—requests that were almost always quickly granted, as were the first farming-land requests of unmarried men like Kunta and his mates. During man-training,[7] the kintango[8] had directed them never to miss any Council of Elders sessions unless they had to, as the witnessing of its decisions would broaden a man's knowledge as his own rains[9] increased until he too would be a senior elder. Attending his first session, Kunta had looked at Omoro seated ahead of him, wondering how many hundreds of decisions his father must have in his head, though he wasn't even a senior elder yet.

At his first session, Kunta witnessed a land matter involving a dispute. Two men both claimed the fruit of some trees originally planted

---

6. **drumtalked** (DRUM-tawkd) *v.* communicated using drums
7. **man-training** (MAN-trayn-ihng) *n.* formal preparation for becoming a man
8. **kintango** (kin-TANG-goh) *n.* leader who supervises the man-training
9. **rains** (RAYNZ) *n. pl.* years. Since there is one rainy season a year, counting rainy seasons is the same as counting years.

by the first man on land to which the second man now had the farming rights, since the first man's family had decreased. The Council of Elders awarded the fruit to the first man, saying, "If he hadn't planted the trees, that fruit wouldn't be there."

At later sessions, Kunta saw people frequently charged with breaking or losing something borrowed from an irate lender who claimed that the articles had been both valuable and brand-new. Unless the borrower had witnesses to disprove that, he was usually ordered to pay for or replace the article at the value of a new one. Kunta also saw furious people accusing others of inflicting bad fortune on them through evil magic. One man testified that another had touched him with a cock's spur, making him violently ill. A young wife declared that her new mother-in-law had hidden some bourein shrub in the wife's kitchen, causing whatever was cooked there to turn out badly. And a widow claimed that an old man whose advances[10] she had spurned[11] had sprinkled powdered eggshells in her path, making her walk into a long succession of troubles, which she proceeded to describe. If presented with enough impressive evidence of evil magic's motives and results, the Council would command immediate corrective[12] magic to be done by the nearest traveling magic man, whom a drumtalk message would summon to Juffure at the expense of the evildoer.

Kunta saw debtors ordered to pay up, even if they had to sell their possessions; or with nothing to sell, to work off the amount as the lender's slave.[13] He saw slaves charging their masters with cruelty, or with providing unsuitable food or lodgings, or with taking more than their half share of what the slaves' work had produced. Masters, in turn, accused slaves of cheating by hiding some of their produce, or of insufficient work, or of deliberately breaking farm tools. Kunta saw the Council weigh carefully the evidence in these cases, along with each person's past record in the village, and it was not uncommon for some slaves' reputations to be better than their masters'!

But sometimes there was no dispute between a master and his slave. Indeed, Kunta saw them coming together asking permission for the slave to marry into the master's family. But any couple intending to marry, first had to obtain the Council's permission. Couples judged by the

---

10. **advances** (ad-VAN-sez) *n. pl.* efforts to court or win the love of

11. **spurned** (SPERND) *v.* rejected

12. **corrective** (kuh-REK-tihv) *adj.* intended to fix

13. **lender's slave** *n.* Debtor who had to work off the debt to the lender

Council to be too close of kinship were refused out of hand,[14] but for those not thus disqualified, there was a waiting period of one moon between the request and the reply, during which the villagers were expected to pay quiet visits to any senior elder and reveal any private information, either good or bad, about the couple in question. Since childhood, had each of them always demonstrated a good home training? Had either of them ever caused undue trouble to anyone, including their own families? Had either of them ever displayed any undesirable tendencies of any kind, such as cheating or telling less than the full truth? Was the girl known for being irritable and argumentative? Was the man known for beating goats unmercifully? If so, the marriage was refused, for it was believed that such a person might pass these traits along to his or her children. But as Kunta knew even before he began attending the Council sessions, most couples won approval for marriage, because both sets of parents involved had already learned the answers to these questions, and found them satisfactory, before granting their own permission.

At the Council sessions, however, Kunta learned that sometimes parents hadn't been told things that people did tell the senior elders. Kunta saw one marriage permission flatly refused when a witness came forth to testify that the young man of the planned marriage, as a young goatherd, had once stolen a basket from him, thinking he hadn't been seen. The crime hadn't been reported then, out of compassion for the fact that he was still a boy; if it had been reported, the law would have dictated that his right hand be cut off. Kunta sat riveted as the young thief, exposed at last, burst into tears, blurting out his guilt before his horrified parents and the girl he was asking to marry, who began screaming. Soon afterward, he disappeared from Juffure and was never seen or heard of again . . . .

---

14. out of hand *prep. phrase* at once

Critical Thinking

1. What does Alex Haley tell you in this selection about his ancestral roots?
2. What events in Haley's life do you think prompted him to write the story of Kunta?
3. Do you think the Council's way of resolving problems is effective? What might your community learn from the Council's methods?

Writing Your Response to *Roots*

In your journal, write about one scene or idea that was memorable to you. What made it stand out for you? Did the passage remind you of something in your own life? How?

Going Back Into the Text: Author's Craft

Roots is a **historical novel** based on a real place, real people, and real customs. As in many historical stories, the author mixes facts, such as the kinds of cases the Council of Elders decided, with elements that may be fiction, such as details of specific cases. Together these elements help give the reader a clear picture of an unfamiliar culture or historical period.

In a historical novel, you can often tell what is fiction by thinking about what the author could or could not know. For example, an author would probably need to make up the private thoughts of a long-dead historical figure. With a partner, review the selection and decide which parts are most likely historically true statements about the Council and the villagers and which parts were probably imagined by the author. Use the following questions as guidelines in your discussion.

1. What factual information about village government does the selection give?
2. What parts of the selection were probably the author's invention? Where do you think the author got his ideas for the fictional parts of the novel?
3. What other stories do you know that mix fiction with historical facts?

To Da-duh, In Memoriam

Reading the Author in a Cultural Context

Paule Marshall is a first-generation American. She was born in Brooklyn in 1929, the daughter of parents who had been born in Barbados in the Caribbean. When she was a child, she visited Barbados, where she stayed for a year before returning to New York City. "To Da-duh, In Memoriam" grew out of that visit to her mother's home.

In the 1930s, during the time that Paule Marshall visited Barbados and when the story is set, New York offered a refuge to African Americans in the arts. Many of these actors, musicians, artists, and writers found their work accepted in the dominant white society. But the 1930s were a troubled time. At the time of the story, the United States and the world were deep in the Great Depression, and poverty was widespread. The era was marked by "separate-but-equal" laws for African Americans, laws that were later judged to be unconstitutional. By 1920, women had won the right to vote, but that was only one step toward social and political equality. These events are the background to the story of the child's encounter with her grandmother Da-duh. The little girl is growing up in a world that is anything but stable. As you read, consider how these events influence the story.

The story contains several conflicts. There is tension between Da-duh and her daughter Adry. There is a hint of conflict between Adry and her husband, who calls her trip back to Barbados "foolishness." He fears that returning to the island might undermine all that Adry has gained by leaving home.

Other points of conflict are feelings about race and the forces of history. Da-duh has spent her life among people with the same history. The little girl is an African American in New York City. She shares a history of slavery with other African Americans but with a twist—she has a West Indian heritage. She is different from children whose parents grew up in the United States, and she does not have an extended family to help her forge her own identity. She and her sister are the first of their family to be born into U.S. citizenship, with all its privileges and problems.

Focusing on the Selection

As you read, think about the relationship between the nine-year-old city child and her grandmother, who has lived her whole life in an island village. What does each character admire and value? What are the strengths and weaknesses of each? What does each character do to gain an advantage over the other? What is Marshall saying about the two cultures represented by these two characters?

To Da-duh, In Memoriam

PAULE MARSHALL

I DID NOT SEE HER at first I remember. For not only was it dark in-side the crowded disembarkation shed[1] in spite of the daylight flooding in from outside, but standing there waiting for her with my mother and sister I was still somewhat blinded from the sheen of tropi-cal sunlight on the water of the bay which we had just crossed in the landing boat, leaving behind us the ship that had brought us from New York lying in the offing. Besides, being only nine years of age at the time and knowing nothing of islands I was busy attending to the alien sights and sounds of Barbados, the unfamiliar smells.

I did not see her, but I was alerted to her approach by my mother's hand which suddenly tightened around mine, and looking up I traced her gaze through the gloom in the shed until I finally made out the small, purposeful, painfully erect figure of the old woman headed our way.

Her face was drowned in the shadow of an ugly rolled-brim brown felt hat, but the details of her slight body and of the struggle taking place within it were clear enough—an intense, unrelenting[2] struggle between her back which was beginning to bend ever so slightly under the weight of her eighty-odd years and the rest of her which sought to

---

1. **disembarkation shed** (dihs-em-bahr-KAY-shuhn SHED) *n.* building through which passengers arriving by ship go ashore
2. **unrelenting** (un-rih-LEN-tihng) *adj.* not letting up, never ending

deny those years and hold that back straight, keep it in line. Moving swiftly toward us (so swiftly it seemed she did not intend stopping when she reached us but would sweep past us out the doorway which opened onto the sea and like Christ walk upon the water!), she was caught between the sunlight at her end of the building and the darkness inside—and for a moment she appeared to contain them both: the light in the long severe old-fashioned white dress she wore which brought the sense of a past that was still alive into our bustling present and in the snatch of white at her eye; the darkness in her black high-top shoes and in her face which was visible now that she was closer.

It was as stark and fleshless as a death mask, that face. The maggots might have already done their work, leaving only the framework of bone beneath the ruined skin and deep wells at the temple and jaw. But her eyes were alive, unnervingly[3] so for one so old, with a sharp light that flicked out of the dim clouded depths like a lizard's tongue to snap up all in her view. Those eyes betrayed a child's curiosity about the world, and I wondered vaguely seeing them, and seeing the way the bodice[4] of her ancient dress had collapsed in on her flat chest (what had happened to her breasts?), whether she might not be some kind of child at the same time that she was a woman, with fourteen children, my mother included, to prove it. Perhaps she was both, both child and woman, darkness and light, past and present, life and death—all the opposites contained and reconciled in her.

"My Da-duh," my mother said formally and stepped forward. The name sounded like thunder fading softly in the distance.

"Child," Da-duh said, and her tone, her quick scrutiny of my mother, the brief embrace in which they appeared to shy from each other rather than touch, wiped out the fifteen years my mother had been away and restored the old relationship. My mother, who was such a formidable[5] figure in my eyes, had suddenly with a word been reduced to my status.

"Yes, God is good," Da-duh said with a nod that was like a tic. "He has spared me to see my child again."

We were led forward then, apologetically because not only did Da-duh prefer boys but she also liked her grandchildren to be "white," that is, fair-skinned; and we had, I was to discover, a number of cousins, the outside children of white estate managers and the like, who qualified. We, though, were as black as she.

My sister being the oldest was presented first. "This one takes after the father," my mother said and waited to be reproved.

---

3. **unnervingly** (un-NERV-ihng-lee) *adv.* disturbingly
4. **bodice** (BAHD-ihs) *n.* top part of a dress
5. **formidable** (FAWR-mihd-uh-buhl) *adj.* frightening, powerful

Frowning, Da-duh tilted my sister's face toward the light. But her frown soon gave way to a grudging smile, for my sister with her large mild eyes and little broad winged nose, with our father's high-cheeked Barbadian cast[6] to her face, was pretty.

"She's goin' be lucky," Da-duh said and patted her once on the cheek. "Any girl child that takes after the father does be lucky."

She turned then to me. But oddly enough she did not touch me. Instead leaning close, she peered hard at me, and then quickly drew back. I thought I saw her hand start up as though to shield her eyes. It was almost as if she saw not only me, a thin truculent[7] child who it was said took after no one but myself, but something in me which for some reason she found disturbing, even threatening. We looked silently at each other for a long time there in the noisy shed, our gaze locked. She was the first to look away.

"But Adry," she said to my mother and her laugh was cracked, thin, apprehensive. "Where did you get this one here with this fierce look?"

"We don't know where she came out of, my Da-duh," my mother said, laughing also. Even I smiled to myself. After all I had won the encounter. Da-duh had recognized my small strength—and this was all I ever asked of the adults in my life then.

"Come, soul,"[8] Da-duh said and took my hand. "You must be one of those New York terrors you hear so much about."

She led us, me at her side and my sister and mother behind, out of the shed into the sunlight that was like a bright driving summer rain and over to a group of people clustered beside a decrepit lorry.[9] They were our relatives, most of them from St. Andrews although Da-duh herself lived in St. Thomas, the women wearing bright print dresses, the colors vivid against their darkness, the men rusty black suits that encased them like straitjackets. Da-duh, holding fast to my hand, became my anchor as they circled round us like a nervous sea, exclaiming, touching us with their calloused hands, embracing us shyly. They laughed in awed bursts: "But look Adry got big-big children!"/"And see the nice things they wearing, wrist watch and all!"/"I tell you, Adry has done all right for sheself in New York. . . ."

Da-duh, ashamed at their wonder, embarrassed for them, admonished[10] them the while. "But oh Christ," she said, "why you all got to get on like you never saw people from 'Away' before? You would think New York is the only place in the world to hear

6. **Barbadian cast** (bar-BAY-dee-uhn KAST) looking like someone from Barbados
7. **truculent** (TRUK-yoo-luhnt) *adj.* fierce
8. **soul** (SOHL) *n.* a way of addressing a person, similar to "child" or "girl"
9. **lorry** (LAWR-ee) *n.* a British word for *truck*
10. **admonished** (ad-MAHN-ihshd) *v.* warned

Photograph of woman of Barbados.

wunna.[11] That's why I don't like to go anyplace with you St. Andrews people, you know. You all ain't been colonized."[12]

We were in the back of the lorry finally, packed in among the barrels of ham, flour, cornmeal and rice and the trunks of clothes that my mother had brought as gifts. We made our way slowly through Bridgetown's clogged streets, part of a funereal procession of cars and open-sided buses, bicycles and donkey carts. The dim little limestone shops and offices along the way marched with us, at the same mournful pace, toward the same grave ceremony—as did the people, the women balancing huge baskets on top their heads as if they were no more than hats they wore to shade them from the sun. Looking over the edge of the lorry I watched as their feet slurred the dust. I listened, and their voices, raw and loud and dissonant in the heat, seemed to be grappling with each other high overhead.

Da-duh sat on a trunk in our midst, a monarch amid her court. She still held my hand, but it was different now. I had suddenly become her anchor, for I felt her fear of the lorry with its asthmatic motor (a fear and distrust, I later learned, she held of all machines) beating like a pulse in her rough palm.

As soon as we left Bridgetown behind though, she relaxed, and while the others around us talked she gazed at the canes standing tall on

11. **wunna** (WUN-nah) *pron.* everybody; all of you
12. **colonized** (KAHL-uh-neyezd) *v.* Da-duh means *civilized*

either side of the winding marl[13] road. "C'dear,"[14] she said softly to herself after a time. "The canes this side are pretty enough."

They were too much for me. I thought of them as giant weeds that had overrun the island, leaving scarcely any room for the small tottering houses of sunbleached pine we passed or the people, dark streaks as our lorry hurtled by. I suddenly feared that we were journeying, unaware that we were, toward some dangerous place where the canes, grown as high and thick as a forest, would close in on us and run us through with their stiletto blades. I longed then for the familiar: for the street in Brooklyn where I lived, for my father who had refused to accompany us ("Blowing out good money on foolishness," he had said of the trip), for a game of tag with my friends under the chestnut tree outside our aging brownstone house.

"Yes, but wait till you see St. Thomas canes," Da-duh was saying to me. "They's canes father, bo,"[15] she gave a proud arrogant nod. "Tomorrow, God willing, I goin' take you out in the ground and show them to you."

True to her word Da-duh took me with her the following day out into the ground. It was a fairly large plot adjoining her weathered board and shingle house and consisting of a small orchard, a good-sized cane-piece and behind the canes, where the land sloped abruptly down, a gully. She had purchased it with Panama money[16] sent her by her eldest son, my uncle Joseph, who had died working on the canal. We entered the ground along a trail no wider than her body and as devious and complex as her reasons for showing me her land. Da-duh strode briskly ahead, her slight form filled out this morning by the layers of sacking petticoats she wore under her working dress to protect her against the damp. A fresh white cloth, elaborately arranged around her head, added to her height, and lent her a vain, almost roguish air.

Her pace slowed once we reached the orchard, and glancing back at me occasionally over her shoulder, she pointed out the various trees.

"This here is a breadfruit," she said. "That one yonder is a papaw. Here's a guava. This is a mango. I know you don't have anything like these in New York. Here's a sugar apple."[17] (The fruit looked more like artichokes than apples to me.) "This one bears limes. . . ." She went on

---

13. **marl** (MAHRL) *n.* mixture of dirt and shell fragments
14. **C'dear** (kuh-DEER) a fond expression, "Come, dear" or "Good Dear"
15. **bo** (BOH) *interj.* you see; you understand
16. **Panama money** (PAN-uh-mah MUN-ee) money earned from working on the Panama Canal
17. **breadfruit** (bred-FROOT) . . . **papaw** (PAW-paw) also called *papaya* . . . **guava** (GWAH-vuh) . . . **mango** (MANG-goh) . . . **sugar apple** (SHUG-er AP-puhl) fruit trees common to Barbados

for some time, intoning the names of the trees as though they were those of her gods. Finally, turning to me, she said, "I know you don't have anything this nice where you come from." Then, as I hesitated, "I said I know you don't have anything this nice where you come from. . . ."

"No," I said and my world did seem lacking.

Da-duh nodded and passed on. The orchard ended and we were on the narrow cart road that led through the canepiece, the canes clashing like swords above my cowering head. Again she turned and her thin muscular arms spread wide, her dim gaze embracing the small field of canes, she said—and her voice almost broke under the weight of her pride, "Tell me, have you got anything like these in that place where you were born?"

"No."

"I din't think so. I bet you don't even know that these canes here and the sugar you eat is one and the same thing. That they does throw the canes into some damn machine at the factory and squeeze out all the little life in them to make sugar for you all so in New York to eat. I bet you don't know that."

"I've got two cavities and I'm not allowed to eat a lot of sugar."

But Da-duh didn't hear me. She had turned with an inexplicably angry motion and was making her way rapidly out of the canes and down the slope at the edge of the field which led to the gully below. Following her apprehensively down the incline amid a stand of banana plants whose leaves flapped like elephants' ears in the wind, I found myself in the middle of a small tropical wood—a place dense and damp and gloomy and tremulous with the fitful play of light and shadow as the leaves high above moved against the sun that was almost hidden from view. It was a violent place, the tangled foliage fighting each other for a chance at the sunlight, the branches of the trees locked in what seemed an immemorial struggle, one both necessary and inevitable. But despite the violence, it was pleasant, almost peaceful in the gully, and beneath the thick undergrowth the earth smelled like spring.

This time Da-duh didn't even bother to ask her usual question, but simply turned and waited for me to speak.

"No," I said, my head bowed. "We don't have anything like this in New York."

"Ah," she cried, her triumph complete. "I din' think so. Why, I've heard that's a place where you can walk till you near drop and never see a tree."

"We've got a chestnut tree in front of our house," I said.

"Does it bear?" She waited. "I ask you, does it bear?"

"Not anymore," I muttered. "It used to, but not anymore."

Photograph of deserted beach with palm trees on the Atlantic coast of Barbados, an island in the Caribbean Sea. How does the beach in this photograph suggest a contrast between Da-duh's home and the narrator's home?

She gave the nod that was like a nervous twitch. "You see," she said, "Nothing can bear there." Then, secure behind her scorn, she added, "But tell me, what's this snow like that you hear so much about?"

Looking up, I studied her closely, sensing my chance, and then I told her, describing at length and with as much drama as I could summon not only what snow in the city was like, but what it would be like here, in her perennial[18] summer kingdom.

". . . And you see all these trees you got here," I said. "Well, they'd be bare. No leaves, no fruit, nothing. They'd be covered in snow. You see your canes. They'd be buried under tons of snow. The snow would be higher than your head, higher than your house, and you wouldn't be able to come down into this here gully because it would be snowed under. . . ."

She searched my face for the lie, still scornful but intrigued. "What a thing, huh?" she said finally, whispering it softly to herself.

"And when it snows you couldn't dress like you are now," I said. "Oh no, you'd freeze to death. You'd have to wear a hat and gloves and galoshes and ear muffs so your ears wouldn't freeze and drop off, and a heavy coat. I've got a Shirley Temple coat with fur on the collar. I can dance. You wanna see?"

Before she could answer I began, with a dance called the Truck which was popular back then in the 1930's. My right forefinger waving, I trucked around the nearby trees and around Da-duh's awed and rigid form. After the Truck I did the Suzy-Q, my lean hips swishing, my sneakers sidling zigzag over the ground. "I can sing," I said and did so, starting with "I'm Gonna Sit Right Down and Write Myself a Letter," then without pausing, "Tea For Two," and ending with "I Found a Million Dollar Baby in a Five and Ten Cent Store."

For long moments afterwards Da-duh stared at me as if I were a creature from Mars, an emissary[19] from some world she did not know but which intrigued her and whose power she both felt and feared. Yet something about my performance must have pleased her, because bending down she slowly lifted her long skirt and then, one by one, the layers of petticoats until she came to a drawstring purse dangling at the end of a long strip of cloth tied round her waist. Opening the purse she handed me a penny. "Here," she said half-smiling against her will. "Take this to buy yourself a sweet at the shop up the road. There's nothing to be done with you, soul."

From then on, whenever I wasn't taken to visit relatives, I accompanied Da-duh out into the ground, and alone with her amid the canes or

---

18. **perennial** (puh-REN-ee-uhl) *adj.* every year, everlasting
19. **emissary** (EM-uh-ser-ee) *n.* messenger

down in the gully I told her about New York. It always began with some slighting remark on her part: "I know they don't have anything this nice where you come from," or "Tell me, I hear those foolish people in New York does do such and such. . . ." But as I answered, recreating my towering world of steel and concrete and machines for her, building the city out of words, I would feel her give way. I came to know the signs of her surrender: the total stillness that would come over her little hard dry form, the probing gaze that like a surgeon's knife sought to cut through my skull to get at the images there, to see if I were lying; above all, her fear, a fear nameless and profound, the same one I had felt beating in the palm of her hand that day in the lorry.

Over the weeks I told her about refrigerators, radios, gas stoves, elevators, trolley cars, wringer washing machines, movies, airplanes, the cyclone at Coney Island, subways, toasters, electric lights: "At night, see, all you have to do is flip this little switch on the wall and all the lights in the house go on. Just like that. Like magic. It's like turning on the sun at night."

"But tell me," she said to me once with a faint mocking smile, "do the white people have all these things too or it's only the people looking like us?"

I laughed. "What d'ya mean," I said. "The white people have even better." Then: "I beat up a white girl in my class last term."

"Beating up white people!" Her tone was incredulous.[20]

"How you mean!" I said, using an expression of hers. "She called me a name."

For some reason Da-duh could not quite get over this and repeated in the same hushed, shocked voice, "Beating up white people now! Oh, the lord, the world's changing up so I can scarce recognize it anymore."

One morning toward the end of our stay, Da-duh led me into a part of the gully that we had never visited before, an area darker and more thickly overgrown than the rest, almost impenetrable. There in a small clearing amid the dense bush, she stopped before an incredibly tall royal palm which rose cleanly out of the ground, and drawing the eye up with it, soared high above the trees around it into the sky. It appeared to be touching the blue dome of sky, to be flaunting[21] its dark crown of fronds[22] right in the blinding white face of the late morning sun.

Da-duh watched me a long time before she spoke, and then she said, very quietly, "All right, now, tell me if you've got anything this tall in that place you're from."

---

20. **incredulous** (ihn-KREJ-oo-luhs) *adj.* unbelieving
21. **flaunting** (FLAWNT-ihng) *v.* showing off
22. **fronds** (FRAHNDZ) *n. pl.* leaves of palm trees

I almost wished, seeing her face, that I could have said no. "Yes," I said. "We've got buildings hundreds of times this tall in New York. There's one called the Empire State Building that's the tallest in the world. My class visited it last year and I went all the way to the top. It's got over a hundred floors. I can't describe how tall it is. Wait a minute. What's the name of that hill I went to visit the other day, where they have the police station?"

"You mean Bissex?"

"Yes, Bissex. Well, the Empire State Building is way taller than that."

"You're lying now!" she shouted, trembling with rage. Her hand lifted to strike me.

"No, I'm not," I said. "It really is, if you don't believe me I'll send you a picture postcard of it soon as I get back home so you can see for yourself. But it's way taller than Bissex."

All the fight went out of her at that. The hand poised to strike me fell limp to her side, and as she stared at me, seeing not me but the building that was taller than the highest hill she knew, the small stubborn light in her eyes (it was the same amber as the flame in the kerosene lamp she lit at dusk) began to fail. Finally, with a vague gesture that even in the midst of her defeat still tried to dismiss me and my world, she turned and started back through the gully, walking slowly, her steps groping and uncertain, as if she were suddenly no longer sure of the way, while I followed triumphant yet strangely saddened behind.

The next morning I found her dressed for our morning walk but stretched out on the Berbice chair[23] in the tiny drawing room where she sometimes napped during the afternoon heat, her face turned to the window beside her. She appeared thinner and suddenly indescribably old.

"My Da-duh," I said.

"Yes, nuh," she said. Her voice was listless and the face she slowly turned my way was, now that I think back on it, like a Benin mask,[24] the features drawn and almost distorted by an ancient abstract sorrow.

"Don't you feel well?" I asked.

"Girl, I don't know."

"My Da-duh, I goin' boil you some bush tea?," my aunt, Da-duh's youngest child, who lived with her, called from the shed roof kitchen.

"Who tell you I need bush tea?" she cried, her voice assuming for a moment its old authority. "You can't even rest nowadays without some malicious person looking for you to be dead. Come girl," she motioned me to a place beside her on the old-fashioned lounge chair, "give us a tune."

---

23. **Berbice chair** (BER-bihs CHAIR) kind of lounge chair
24. **Benin mask** (be-NEEN MASK) mask from a former kingdom in West Africa

I sang for her until breakfast at eleven, all my brash irreverent Tin Pan Alley songs, and then just before noon we went out into the ground. But it was a short, dispirited walk. Da-duh didn't even notice that the mangoes were beginning to ripen and would have to be picked before the village boys got to them. And when she paused occasionally and looked out across the canes or up at her trees it wasn't as if she were seeing them but something else. Some huge, monolithic shape had imposed itself, it seemed, between her and the land, obstructing her vision. Returning to the house she slept the entire afternoon on the Berbice chair.

She remained like this until we left, languishing[25] away the mornings on the chair at the window gazing out at the land as if it were already doomed; then, at noon, taking the brief stroll with me through the ground during which she seldom spoke and afterwards returning home to sleep till almost dusk sometimes.

On the day of our departure she put on the austere, ankle length white dress, the black shoes and brown felt hat (her town clothes she called them), but she did not go with us to town. She saw us off on the road outside her house and in the midst of my mother's tearful protracted[26] farewell, she leaned down and whispered in my ear, "Girl, you're not to forget now to send me the picture of that building, you hear."

By the time I mailed her the large colored picture postcard of the Empire State Building she was dead. She died during the famous '37 strike[27] which began shortly after we left. On the day of her death England sent planes flying low over the island in a show of force—so low, according to my aunt's letter, that the downdraft from them shook the ripened mangoes from the trees in Da-duh's orchard. Frightened, everyone in the village fled into the canes. Except Da-duh. She remained in the house at the window so my aunt said, watching as the planes came swooping and screaming like monstrous birds down over the village, over her house, rattling her trees and flattening the young canes in her field. It must have seemed to her lying there that they did not intend pulling out of their dive, but like the hardback beetles which hurled themselves with suicidal force against the walls of the house at night, those menacing silver shapes would hurl themselves in an ecstasy of self-immolation onto the land, destroying it utterly.

When the planes finally left and the villagers returned they found her dead on the Berbice chair at the window.

---

25. **languishing** (LANG-gwihsh-ihng) *adj.* lying weakly
26. **protracted** (proh-TRAKT-ed) *adj.* long and drawn out
27. **'37 strike** In 1937, economic conditions in Barbados were so severe that riots broke out.

She died and I lived, but always, to this day even, within the shadow of her death. For a brief period after I was grown I went to live alone, like one doing penance, in a loft above a noisy factory in downtown New York and there painted seas of sugar-cane and huge swirling Van Gogh[28] suns and palm trees striding like brightly-plumed Tutsi[29] warriors across a tropical landscape, while the thunderous tread of the machines downstairs jarred the floor beneath my easel, mocking my efforts.

---

28. **Van Gogh** (van GOH) *n.* a Dutch painter known for using vivid colors
29. **Tutsi** (TUHT-see) *adj.* referring to a specific African people

POSTREADING

Critical Thinking

1. In this story about visiting her ancestral home, what attitudes does Paule Marshall express through the character of the little girl?
2. Which experiences in Marshall's life do you think most influenced these attitudes?
3. Did reading this story affect your thoughts and feelings about your own cultural roots? How are your attitudes similar to Marshall's?

Writing Your Response to "To Da-duh, In Memoriam"

In your journal, tell about a part of the story that was especially meaningful to you. How does this passage relate to an experience in your own life or the life of someone you know?

Going Back Into the Text: Author's Craft

A **conflict** is a struggle between opposing forces. The struggle may be internal, or inside a character, or it may be external, involving another character. "To Da-duh, In Memoriam" contains both types of conflict.

As you review the conflicts in the story, use these questions as guidelines.

1. What internal conflicts does the girl experience?
2. What external conflicts does she face?
3. How does the author connect these two types of conflict in the story?

from The Way to Rainy Mountain

Reading the Author in a Cultural Context

For hundreds of years, Native Americans have relied on storytelling to pass on the traditions of their ways of life. Exact repetition of words is essential, for words are believed to have a life of their own. Once uttered, they live on, always ready to be recalled. Therefore, one should not use words carelessly. The power of words is perceived to be so strong, in fact, that Native Americans believe that language can actually shape the world. N. Scott Momaday says, "A word has power in and of itself. It comes from nothing into sound and meaning; it gives origin to all things. By means of words can a man deal with the world in equal terms."

Momaday's written words are his attempt to deal with his world, a world in which the identity of his people has changed. Through his writing, he tries to keep their valuable beliefs and traditions alive. Momaday is of the Kiowa (KEYE-oh-wah) nation, a Native American group whose way of life changed drastically in the mid-1800s, when settlers killed the buffalo in great numbers. Buffalo provided the meat and hides that were the Kiowa's livelihood, as well as part of their religion. The loss of this sacred animal along with the attacks by the settlers, aided by government policies, forced the Kiowa from the freedom of the southern plains onto a reservation.

In this excerpt, you hear the voice of Momaday, a young man traveling from Yellowstone in Wyoming to the reservation in Oklahoma where his grandmother has died. He expresses personal sadness over the loss of a beloved family member. There is also the voice of the proud Kiowa, who retells some of his nation's stories. Together, these voices are part of a collective history. Collective history includes not only the facts but also the memories that people share with one another. An older person who knows your parents and your aunts and uncles and maybe even your grandparents knows a great deal about you just by knowing about your family and culture. Such a person offers you parts of your history that you may not learn from any other source. As you read, think about the voices and stories that make up your family's collective history.

Focusing on the Selection

As you read, notice how Momaday links the life of his grandmother with the story of his people. What does his grandmother stand for in his mind? What methods does Momaday use to describe the character of his ancestor? What does he feel he has lost with her death?

from *The Way to Rainy Mountain*

N. Scott Momaday

A SINGLE KNOLL[1] rises out of the plain in Oklahoma, north and west of the Wichita Range. For my people, the Kiowas, it is an old landmark, and they gave it the name Rainy Mountain. The hardest weather in the world is there. Winter brings blizzards, hot tornadic winds arise in the spring, and in summer the prairie is an anvil's edge.[2] The grass turns brittle and brown, and it cracks beneath your feet. There are green belts along the rivers and creeks, linear groves of hickory and pecan, willow and witch hazel. At a distance in July or August the steaming foliage seems almost to writhe in fire. Great green and yellow grasshoppers are everywhere in the tall grass, popping up like corn to sting the flesh, and tortoises crawl about on the red earth, going nowhere in the plenty of time. Loneliness is an aspect of the land. All things in the plain are isolate; there is no confusion of objects in the eye, but one hill or one tree or one man. To look upon that landscape in the early morning, with the sun at your back, is to lose the sense of proportion. Your imagination comes to life, and this, you think, is where Creation was begun.

---

1. **knoll** (NOHL) *n.* small hill
2. **anvil's edge** edge of the iron block on which a blacksmith hammers metal

I returned to Rainy Mountain in July. My grandmother had died in the spring, and I wanted to be at her grave. She had lived to be very old and at last infirm. Her only living daughter was with her when she died, and I was told that in death her face was that of a child.

I like to think of her as a child. When she was born, the Kiowas were living the last great moment of their history. For more than a hundred years they had controlled the open range from the Smoky Hill River to the Red, from the headwaters of the Canadian to the fork of the Arkansas and Cimarron. In alliance with the Comanches, they had ruled the whole of the southern Plains. War was their sacred business, and they were among the finest horsemen the world has ever known. But warfare for the Kiowas was preeminently a matter of disposition rather than of survival, and they never understood the grim, unrelenting[3] advance of the U.S. Cavalry. When at last, divided and ill-provisioned,[4] they were driven onto the Staked Plains in the cold rains of autumn, they fell into panic. In Palo Duro Canyon they abandoned their crucial stores to pillage[5] and had nothing then but their lives. In order to save themselves, they surrendered to the soldiers at Fort Sill and were imprisoned in the old stone corral that now stands as a military museum. My grandmother was spared the humiliation of those high gray walls by eight or ten years, but she must have known from birth the affliction of defeat, the dark brooding of old warriors.

Her name was Aho, and she belonged to the last culture to evolve in North America. Her forebears came down from the high country in western Montana nearly three centuries ago. They were a mountain people, a mysterious tribe of hunters whose language has never been positively classified in any major group. In the late seventeenth century they began a long migration to the south and east. It was a journey toward the dawn, and it led to a golden age. Along the way the Kiowas were befriended by the Crows, who gave them the culture and religion of the Plains. They acquired horses, and their ancient nomadic[6] spirit was suddenly free of the ground. They acquired Tai-me,[7] the sacred Sun Dance doll, from that moment the object and symbol of their worship, and so shared in the divinity of the sun. Not least, they acquired the sense of destiny, therefore courage and pride. When they entered upon the southern Plains they had been transformed. No longer were they slaves to the simple necessity of survival; they were a lordly and dangerous society of fighters and thieves, hunters and priests of the sun.

---

3. **unrelenting** (uhn-rih-LEN-tihng) *adj.* not letting up
4. **ill-provisioned** (ihl-pruh-VIHZH-uhnd) *adj.* poorly supplied
5. **pillage** (PIHL-ihj) *n.* theft
6. **nomadic** (noh-MAD-ihk) *adj.* wandering
7. **Tai-me** (teye-MEE)

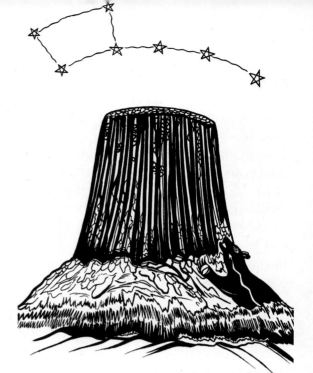

Devil's Tower. Drawing by Al Momaday, the father of N. Scott Momaday. From the book *The Way to Rainy Mountain*. How does this illustration portray the Kiowa legend that Momaday's grandmother told?

According to their origin myth, they entered the world through a hollow log. From one point of view, their migration was the fruit of an old prophecy, for indeed they emerged from a sunless world.

Although my grandmother lived out her long life in the shadow of Rainy Mountain, the immense landscape of the continental interior lay like memory in her blood. She could tell of the Crows, whom she had never seen, and of the Black Hills, where she had never been. I wanted to see in reality what she had seen more perfectly in the mind's eye, and traveled fifteen hundred miles to begin my pilgrimage. . . .

A dark mist lay over the Black Hills, and the land was like iron. At the top of a ridge I caught sight of Devil's Tower upthrust against the gray sky as if in the birth of time the core of the earth had broken through its crust and the motion of the world was begun. There are things in nature that engender[8] an awful[9] quiet in the heart of man; Devil's Tower is one of them. Two centuries ago, because they could not do otherwise, the Kiowas made a legend at the base of the rock. My grandmother said:

Eight children were there at play, seven sisters and their brother. Suddenly the boy was struck dumb; he trembled and began to run upon his hands and feet. His fingers became claws, and his body was covered with fur. Directly there was a bear where the boy had been. The sisters were terrified; they ran, and the bear after them. They came to the stump of a great tree, and the tree

---

8. engender (ihn-JEN-der) *v.* cause to grow
9. awful (AW-fuhl) *adj.* full of deep respect

*spoke to them. It bade them climb upon it, and as they did so it began to rise
into the air. The bear came to kill them, but they were just beyond its reach. It
reared against the tree and scored the bark all around with its claws. The seven
sisters were borne into the sky, and they became the stars of the Big Dipper.*
From that moment, and so long as the legend lives, the Kiowas have
kinsmen in the night sky. Whatever they were in the mountains, they
could be no more. However tenuous[10] their well-being, however much
they had suffered and would suffer again, they had found a way out of
the wilderness.

My grandmother had a reverence for the sun, a holy regard that now
is all but gone out of mankind. There was a wariness[11] in her, and an
ancient awe. She was a Christian in her later years, but she had come a
long way about, and she never forgot her birthright.[12] As a child she
had been to the Sun Dances; she had taken part in those annual rites,
and by them she had learned the restoration of her people in the presence
of Tai-me. She was about seven when the last Kiowa Sun Dance
was held in 1887 on the Washita River above Rainy Mountain Creek.
The buffalo were gone. In order to consummate[13] the ancient sacrifice—to
impale the head of a buffalo bull upon the medicine tree—a
delegation of old men journeyed into Texas, there to beg and barter for
an animal from the Goodnight herd. She was ten when the Kiowas
came together for the last time as a living Sun Dance culture. They
could find no buffalo; they had to hang an old hide from the sacred tree.
Before the dance could begin, a company of soldiers rode out from Fort
Sill under orders to disperse the tribe. Forbidden without cause the essential
act of their faith, having seen the wild herds slaughtered and left
to rot upon the ground, the Kiowas backed away forever from the
medicine tree. That was July 20, 1890, at the great bend of the Washita.
My grandmother was there. Without bitterness, and for as long as she
lived, she bore a vision of deicide.[14]

Now that I can have her only in memory, I see my grandmother in
the several postures that were peculiar to her: standing at the wood
stove on a winter morning and turning meat in a great iron skillet; sitting
at the south window, bent above her beadwork, and afterwards,
when her vision failed, looking down for a long time into the fold of her
hands; going out upon a cane, very slowly as she did when the weight of
age came upon her; praying. I remember her most often at prayer. She
made long, rambling prayers out of suffering and hope, having seen

---

10. **tenuous** (TEN-yoo-uhs) *adj.* shaky
11. **wariness** (WER-ee-nihs) *n.* watchfulness
12. **birthright** (BERTH-reyet) *n.* what was hers from birth
13. **consummate** (KAHN-suh-mayt) *adj.* complete
14. **deicide** (DEE-ih-seyed) *n.* killing of a god

many things. I was never sure that I had the right to hear, so exclusive were they of all mere custom and company. The last time I saw her she prayed standing by the side of her bed at night. . . . I do not speak Kiowa, and I never understood her prayers, but there was something inherently sad in the sound, some merest hesitation upon the syllables of sorrow. She began in a high and descending pitch, exhausting her breath to silence; then again and again—and always the same intensity of effort, of something that is, and is not, like urgency in the human voice. Transported so in the dancing light among the shadows of her room, she seemed beyond the reach of time. But that was illusion; I think I knew then that I should not see her again.

Houses are like sentinels[15] in the plain, old keepers of the weather watch. There, in a very little while, wood takes on the appearance of great age. All colors wear soon away in the wind and rain, and then the wood is burned gray and the grain appears and the nails turn red with rust. The windowpanes are black and opaque;[16] you imagine there is nothing within, and indeed there are many ghosts, bones given up to the land. They stand here and there against the sky, and you approach them for a longer time than you expect. They belong in the distance; it is their domain.

Once there was a lot of sound in my grandmother's house, a lot of coming and going, feasting and talk. The summers there were full of excitement and reunion. The Kiowas are a summer people; they abide the cold and keep to themselves, but when the season turns and the land becomes warm and vital they cannot hold still; an old love of going returns upon them. The aged visitors who came to my grandmother's house when I was a child were made of lean and leather, and they bore themselves upright. They wore great black hats and bright ample shirts that shook in the wind. They rubbed fat upon their hair and wound their braids with strips of colored cloth. Some of them painted their faces and carried the scars of old and cherished enmities.[17] They were an old council of warlords, come to remind and be reminded of who they were. Their wives and daughters served them well. The women might indulge themselves; gossip was at once the mark and compensation of their servitude. They made loud and elaborate talk among themselves, full of jest and gesture, fright and false alarm. They went abroad in fringed and flowered shawls, bright beadwork and German silver. They were at home in the kitchen, and they prepared meals that were banquets.

There were frequent prayer meetings, and great nocturnal[18] feasts. When I was a child I played with my cousins outside, where the lamp-

---

15. **sentinels** (SEN-tih-nuhlz) *n.* watchers or guards
16. **opaque** (oh-PAYK) *adj.* not clear; not letting light go through
17. **enmities** (EN-me-teez) *n.* hatreds
18. **nocturnal** (nahk-TER-nuhl) *adj.* night-time

light fell upon the ground and the singing of the old people rose up around us and carried away into the darkness. There were a lot of good things to eat, a lot of laughter and surprise. And afterwards, when the quiet returned, I lay down with my grandmother and could hear the frogs away by the river and feel the motion of the air.

Now there is a funeral silence in the rooms, the endless wake of some final word. The walls have closed in upon my grandmother's house. When I returned to it in mourning, I saw for the first time in my life how small it was. It was late at night, and there was a white moon, nearly full. I sat for a long time on the stone steps by the kitchen door. From there I could see out across the land; I could see the long row of trees by the creek, the low light upon the rolling plains, and the stars of the Big Dipper. Once I looked at the moon and caught sight of a strange thing. A cricket had perched upon the handrail, only a few inches away from me. My line of vision was such that the creature filled the moon like a fossil. It had gone there, I thought, to live and die, for there, of all places, was its small definition made whole and eternal. A warm wind rose up and purled[19] like the longing within me.

The next morning I awoke at dawn and went out on the dirt road to Rainy Mountain. It was already hot, and the grasshoppers began to fill the air. Still, it was early in the morning, and the birds sang out of the shadows. The long yellow grass on the mountain shone in the bright light, and a scissortail[20] hied[21] above the land. There, where it ought to be, at the end of a long and legendary way, was my grandmother's grave. Here and there on the dark stones were ancestral names. Looking back once, I saw the mountain and came away.

XXIV

East of my grandmother's house, south of the pecan grove, there is buried a woman in a beautiful dress. Mammedaty used to know where she is buried, but now no one knows. If you stand on the front porch of the house and look eastward towards Carnegie, you know that the woman is buried somewhere within the range of your vision. But her grave is unmarked. She was buried in a cabinet, and she wore a beautiful dress. How beautiful it was! It was one of those fine buckskin dresses, and it was decorated with elk's teeth and beadwork. That dress is still there, under the ground.

Aho's high moccasins are made of softest, cream-colored skins. On each instep there is a bright disc of beadwork—an eight-pointed star, red and pale

---

19. **purled** (PERLD) *v.* rippled, moved gently
20. **scissortail** (SIHZ-er-tayl) *n.* a bird with a deeply forked tail
21. **hied** (HEYED) *v.* hurried

blue on a white field—and there are bands of beadwork at the soles and ankles. The flaps of the leggings are wide and richly ornamented with blue and red and green and white and lavender beads.

East of my grandmother's house the sun rises out of the plain. Once in his life a man ought to concentrate his mind upon the remembered earth, I believe. He ought to give himself up to a particular landscape in his experience, to look at it from as many angles as he can, to wonder about it, to dwell upon it. He ought to imagine that he touches it with his hands at every season and listens to the sounds that are made upon it. He ought to imagine the creatures there and all the faintest motions of the wind. He ought to recollect the glare of noon and all the colors of the dawn and dusk.

POSTREADING

Critical Thinking

1. What feelings and attitudes does the selection express about Momaday's search for his ancestral roots?
2. How does Momaday connect his grandmother with his people's history?
3. How might you react if the cultural group you belonged to experienced a history like that of the Kiowa? How are your reactions similar to Momaday's?

Writing Your Response to *The Way to Rainy Mountain*

In your journal, write about an idea, a feeling, or a question you had while reading the selection. What did the passage make you think of? Can you relate the selection to something in your own life?

Going Back Into the Text: Author's Craft

Characters in stories are called round or flat, depending on how they are developed by the author. **Round characters** are complex and have several qualities. This mixture of traits makes them seem like real people. **Flat characters** have only one or two basic characteristics.

With a partner, review the selection to see how Momaday develops the character of the grandmother. Use the following questions.

1. Does Momaday write about his grandmother as a round or a flat character?
2. What mixture of qualities does the grandmother have?
3. What other round and flat characters can you find in the selections in this theme?

i yearn
[We Who Carry the Endless Seasons]

Reading the Authors in a Cultural Context

Many people who have moved to the United States have felt the isolation that comes from confronting a culture different from their own. These people often hold on to their past as a way of coping with the new and often difficult times they must face. Practicing the customs, speaking the language, and eating the foods of their ancestors are ways of preserving their heritage. These practices are also ways of preserving their own personal identity that has grown from their past.

In the two poems that follow, both writers explore their cultural heritages. The first poem, by Ricardo Sánchez, a Mexican American poet, captures his longing for home. Sánchez was raised in the Mexican American barrio, or neighborhood, in El Paso, Texas. The barrio provided support to Mexicans who arrived in this country. It also was considered home to the following generations that were born there. Sánchez left the barrio to attend college. As a writer, Sánchez preserves his cultural identity, which he considers a mixture of Mexican American and U.S. mainstream cultures. The combination of Spanish and English within the poem enhances Sánchez's sense of himself. At the same time, it captures the values and life-style of the barrio in which he was raised. Sánchez distinguishes even further between Spanish and caló, the dialect spoken in the barrio.

Virginia Cerenio is a Filipino American from San Francisco, California. She also reflects on her ancestral past in "We Who Carry the Endless Seasons." Cerenio was born and raised in the United States yet feels naturally linked to her ancestral roots in the Philippines. The Philippines, a large group of islands off the southeast coast of Asia, was under Spanish rule for more than 300 years. It was then under U.S. control for another 48 years. Because of this history, the country has many political and religious ties to the West. However, its people consider themselves Asian in their values and aspirations. In the following poem, Cerenio conveys this unique blend of cultures through references to Catholicism and through the use of her ancestors' language. Notice how the poem expresses the connection between Cerenio's American-born generation and the previous generations of Filipino women.

Focusing on the Selections

As you read the poems, think about the attitudes they express about the past and about cultural roots. What hopes and desires do the poems convey? How does language reflect each poet's sense of cultural identity? Think about the effect that is created by the use of different line lengths. Record your responses in your journal.

i yearn

RICARDO SÁNCHEZ

i yearn this morning
what i've yearned
since i left

    almost a year ago . . .

it is hollow
this
being away
from everyday life
in the barrios
of my homeland . . .
all those cities
like el paso, los angeles,
albuquerque,
denver, san antonio
    (off into chicano
      infinitum!);

i yearn
to hear spanish
spoken in caló—
that special way

chicanos roll their
    tongues
to form
words
which dart or glide;

i yearn
for foods
that have character
and strength—the kind
that assail yet caress
you with the zest of life;

more than anything,
i yearn, my people,
for the warmth of you
greeting me with "¿qué tal,
hermano?"[1]
and the knowing that you
    mean it
when you tell me that you love
the fact that we exist . . .

---

1. **"¿qué tal, hermano?"** (KAY TAHL uhr-MAH-noh) Spanish for "how goes it, brother?"

[We Who Carry the Endless Seasons]

VIRGINIA CERENIO

we who carry the endless seasons
    of tropical rain in our blood
still weep our mother's tears
feel the pain of their birth
              their growing
              as women in america

we wear guilt for their minor sins
                      singing lullabies
                      in foreign tongue
                            "... o ilaw sa gabing madilim
                            wangis mo'y bituin sa langit ..."[1]
           their desires
                      wanting us
                      their daughters
                      to marry only
                            "... a boy from the islands ...
                            ang guapo lalake[2] ... and
                            from a good family too...."

    like shadows
    attached to our feet
    we cannot walk away

though we are oceans and dreams apart
waves carry the constant clicking of their rosary beads
                      like heartbeats
                      in our every breathing

---

1. **o ilaw sa gabing madilim wangis mo'y bituin sa langit** (Oh EE-low SAH GAHB-ihng mah-dih-LEEM WAHNG-ees MOI bih-TWEEN SAH LAHNG-iht)
   Light in the middle of the night/your face like stars in the sky.
2. **ang guapo lalake** (AHNG GWAHP-oh lah-LAHK-ay) a handsome man

POSTREADING

Critical Thinking

1. What aspects of the poet's ancestral and personal history are most important in each poem?
2. What relationship with his or her heritage does each poet express? What are the poet's feelings in the moment captured in each poem?
3. How might you react if you were separated from the people of your culture? Think about how your ideas and feelings are similar to those expressed in the poems.

Writing Your Response to "i yearn" and ["We Who Carry the Endless Seasons"]

What phrases or images from the poems made the strongest impression on you? Why? In your journal, write about how the poems relate to experiences in your life or the life of someone you know.

Going Back Into the Text: Author's Craft

Both "i yearn" and "We Who Carry the Endless Seasons" are written in **free verse**. Free verse is poetry that does not have a fixed metrical pattern. In metrical poetry, there is a regular pattern of stresses and line lengths, a predictable rhythm. In free verse, the poet uses rhythms of everyday speech and makes his or her own rules about line length. This may include not using conventional punctuation or capital letters.

The length of the line in free verse may be determined by natural speech rhythms or by the thoughts the poet wants to express. Line length may even be chosen according to how the poem will look on the page. The line length and word placement tell the reader where to pause and how to read the poem. The form may suggest reading in long, thoughtful phrases or in short, choppy bursts of action. Free verse may emphasize certain ideas by unusual breaks or word placement.

With a partner, reread the poems aloud and use the following questions to review the use of free verse in each poem.

1. In what ways are the poems examples of free verse?
2. How do the length and placement of lines in each poem help to convey the poet's meaning?
3. Find another example of free verse in this book. How do free verse techniques help to make the poem effective?

Reviewing the Theme

1. Choose two of the ancestral figures described in the selections for this theme. Compare the relationships the authors or narrators have with each character. What did each one gain from the ancestor? Describe the similarities and differences between the attitudes they have toward their roots.

2. Choose two selections and describe the relationship with the natural world that is part of each author's heritage. Give examples to support your answer.

3. Which selection relates most closely to your personal experience? Support your answer with details from the selection and from your own life.

Theme 3:
Celebrating Growth and Change

THE FICTIONAL CHARACTERS and real-life people who are depicted in "Celebrating Growth and Change" experience personal change in very different, sometimes surprising, ways. Through traditions and ceremonies, the young people portrayed in the selections move from childhood into adulthood. In some cases, the customs they explore are hundreds of years old. Through them, individuals and families are connected to a spiritual life that lies beyond the everyday physical world. They feel changed as they recognize new values and new perspectives on themselves and the world.

This section explores the theme of growth and change through three different cultures—Native American, Asian, and Hispanic. Two of the selections follow the per-

This photograph shows a Japanese bride dressed in traditional wedding garments, each of which has symbolic meaning. The white hood, for example, represents the bride's promise to hide any jealous feelings.

sonal development of young Native Americans—one a Laguna, and the other a Lakota. A story focusing on a Japanese American girl and her mother highlights the differences between a traditional Japanese upbringing and growing up in the United States. Two poems by Hispanic writers reflect feelings that are at once personal and universal. These authors share their celebration of—and questions about—the role of ancient heritages and ceremonies in a contemporary world.

Seventeen Syllables

Reading the Author in a Cultural Context

Communication between generations is often difficult. This may be especially true if your parents are Issei (Japanese immigrants to the United States) and you are Nisei (the first generation born in the United States). This is the case for Rosie, the 15-year-old main character of Hisaye Yamamoto's "Seventeen Syllables."

Rosie's parents came to the United States as adults. They were raised according to traditional Japanese customs and values. In Japan, marriages were often arranged by a matchmaker. Duty toward one's spouse and children was more important than romantic love.

The matchmaking tradition continued among the Japanese men who came alone to settle in the United States. Japanese Americans were forced to live in separate areas. They had little opportunity to associate with people of other cultural backgrounds. Marriages continued to be arranged with women in Japan. These women then traveled by ship to the West Coast of the United States, with only a picture to identify their future husbands among the crowd on shore.

Such a bride had to adjust not only to a new husband but also to a new land. Instead of golden opportunity, the couple faced hardship. The Issei's agricultural background in Japan prepared them to be excellent farmers. But land laws in California and then World War II prevented many from owning their own land until the early 1950s. Until that time, Japanese immigrants rented land or were farm laborers.

There were also educational and social class differences in Japan that the younger generation of Nisei did not always appreciate. Many educated people kept a tradition of writing elegant verse—the haiku of 17 syllables—and collecting fine-brush paintings. They spoke a formal literary language that was different from everyday speech. This might have seemed dry and old-fashioned to the young people.

Hisaye Yamamoto, a Nisei born in 1921 in California, says that "Seventeen Syllables" is her mother's story. The short story is set during the 1950s. During that time, Nisei children began to attend English-speaking schools. They became more comfortable with American ways or customs than with the traditions of their parents. As a result, Issei mothers faced further disappointment. They had made sacrifices for their children's sakes, but the Nisei did not have the customary sense of duty to their parents. They began developing new life-styles and values as you will see in the story.

Focusing on the Selection

As you read, notice the differences in values between the generations of this Japanese family. What causes the changes they experience? How do the characters respond to the changes? What conflicts lead to a high point of action in the story? Use your journal to record your responses.

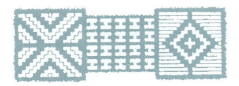

Seventeen Syllables

HISAYE YAMAMOTO

THE FIRST ROSIE KNEW that her mother had taken to writing poems was one evening when she finished one and read it aloud for her daughter's approval. It was about cats, and Rosie pretended to understand it thoroughly and appreciate it no end, partly because she hesitated to disillusion her mother about the quantity and quality of Japanese she had learned in all the years now that she had been going to Japanese school every Saturday (and Wednesday, too, in the summer). Even so, her mother must have been skeptical about the depth of Rosie's understanding, because she explained afterwards about the kind of poem she was trying to write.

See, Rosie, she said, it was a *haiku*,[1] a poem in which she must pack all her meaning into seventeen syllables only, which were divided into three lines of five, seven, and five syllables. In the one she had just read, she had tried to capture the charm of a kitten, as well as comment on the superstition that owning a cat of three colors meant good luck.

"Yes, yes, I understand. How utterly lovely," Rosie said, and her mother, either satisfied or seeing through the deception and resigned, went back to composing.

The truth was that Rosie was lazy; English lay ready on the tongue but Japanese had to be searched for and examined, and even then put

---

1. *haiku* (HEYE-koo) *n.* a traditional Japanese poetic form

The Poetess Ono-No-Komaki. *Museo Chiossone, Genoa, Italy.*
Traditional Japanese painting by a student of Mitsu Shighe Tosa.

forth tentatively (probably to meet with laughter). It was so much easier to say yes, yes, even when one meant no, no. Besides, this was what was in her mind to say: I was looking through one of your magazines from Japan last night, Mother, and towards the back I found some *haiku* in English that delighted me. There was one that made me giggle off and on until I fell asleep—

> *It is morning, and lo!*
> *I lie awake, comme il faut,[2]*
> *sighing for some dough.*

Now, how to reach her mother, how to communicate the melancholy song? Rosie knew formal Japanese by fits and starts, her mother had even less English, no French. It was much more possible to say yes, yes.

It developed that her mother was writing the *haiku* for a daily newspaper, the *Mainichi Shimbun*, that was published in San Francisco. Los Angeles, to be sure, was closer to the farming community in which the Hayashi[3] family lived and several Japanese vernaculars were printed

---

2. *comme il faut* (KUM EEL FOH) French phrase meaning "as I must"
3. *Mainichi Shimbun* (MEYE-een-nee-chee SHEEM-boon) . . . **Hayashi** (HEYE-yah-shee)

there, but Rosie's parents said they preferred the tone of the northern paper. Once a week, the *Mainichi* would have a section devoted to *haiku*, and her mother became an extravagant contributor, taking for herself the blossoming pen name, Ume Hanazono.[4]

So Rosie and her father lived for awhile with two women, her mother and Ume Hanazono. Her mother (Tome Hayashi[5] by name) kept house, cooked, washed, and, along with her husband and the Carrascos, the Mexican family hired for the harvest, did her ample share of picking tomatoes out in the sweltering fields and boxing them in tidy strata in the cool packing shed. Ume Hanazono, who came to life after the dinner dishes were done, was an earnest, muttering stranger who often neglected speaking when spoken to and stayed busy at the parlor table as late as midnight scribbling with pencil on scratch paper or carefully copying characters on good paper with her fat, pale green Parker.

The new interest had some repercussions on the household routine. Before, Rosie had been accustomed to her parents and herself taking their hot baths early and going to bed almost immediately afterwards, unless her parents challenged each other to a game of flower cards or unless company dropped in. Now if her father wanted to play cards, he had to resort to solitaire (at which he always cheated fearlessly), and if a group of friends came over, it was bound to contain someone who was also writing *haiku*, and the small assemblage would be split in two, her father entertaining the non-literary members and her mother comparing ecstatic notes with the visiting poet.

If they went out, it was more of the same thing. But Ume Hanazono's life span, even for a poet's, was very brief—perhaps three months at most.

One night they went over to see the Hayano[6] family in the neighboring town to the west. . . . On this visit, Mrs. Hayano sat all evening in the rocker, as motionless and unobtrusive as it was possible for her to be, and Rosie found the greater part of the evening practically anaesthetic. . . . Rosie noticed that her mother and Mr. Hayano were talking together at the little table—they were discussing a *haiku* that Mr. Hayano was planning to send to the *Mainichi*, while her father was sitting at one end of the sofa looking through a copy of *Life*, the new picture magazine. . . . "Come on, Rosie, we're going home now."

"Already?" asked Rosie.

"Work tomorrow," he said.

He sounded irritated, and Rosie, puzzled, . . . stood up to go, while the sisters began protesting, as was their wont.[7] . . .

---

4. **Ume Hanazono** (OO-may HAH-nah-zoh-noh)
5. **Tome Hayashi** (TOH-may HEYE-yah-shee)
6. **Hayano** (HEYE-yah-noh)
7. **wont** (WAWNT) *n.* custom, usual way of behaving

Rosie, following, saw that her mother and Mr. Hayano were sipping tea and still talking together, ... Her father, saying nothing, went out the door, onto the bright porch, and down the steps. Her mother looked up and asked, "Where is he going?"

"Where is he going?" Rosie said. "He said we were going home now."

"Going home?" Her mother looked with embarrassment at Mr. Hayano and his absorbed wife and then forced a smile. "He must be tired," she said. . . .

Rosie's father looked ahead into the windshield as the two joined him. "I'm sorry," her mother said. "You must be tired." Her father, stepping on the starter, said nothing. "You know how I get when it's *haiku*," she continued, "I forget what time it is." He only grunted.

As they rode homeward silently, Rosie, sitting between, felt a rush of hate for both—for her mother for begging, for her father for denying her mother. . . .

Rosie ran between two patches of tomatoes, her heart working more rambunctiously[8] than she had ever known it to. How lucky it was that Aunt Taka and Uncle Gimpachi[9] had come tonight, though, how very lucky. Otherwise she might not have really kept her half-promise to meet Jesus Carrasco.[10] Jesus was going to be a senior in September at the same school she went to, and his parents were the ones helping with the tomatoes this year. She and Jesus, who hardly remembered seeing each other at Cleveland High where there were so many other people and two whole grades between them, had become great friends this summer. . . .

What she enjoyed most was racing him to see which could finish picking a double row first. He, who could work faster, would tease her by slowing down until she thought she would surely pass him this time, then speeding up furiously to leave her several sprawling vines behind. Once he had made her screech hideously by crossing over, while her back was turned, to place atop the tomatoes in her green-stained bucket a truly monstrous, pale green worm (it had looked more like an infant snake). And it was when they had finished a contest this morning, after she had pantingly pointed a green finger at the immature tomatoes evident in the lugs at the end of his row and he had returned the accusation (with justice), that he had startlingly brought up the matter of their possibly meeting outside the range of both their parents' dubious[11] eyes.

---

8. **rambunctiously** (ram-BUNK-shuhs-lee) *adv.* uncontrollably
9. **Taka** (TAH-kah) . . . **Gimpachi** (geem-PAH-chee)
10. **Jesus Carrasco** (HAY-soos kah-RAHS-koh)
11. **dubious** (DOO-bee-uhs) *adj.* doubtful or suspicious

"What for?" she had asked.

"I've got a secret I want to tell you," he said.

"Tell me now," she demanded.

"It won't be ready till tonight," he said.

She laughed. "Tell me tomorrow then."

"It'll be gone tomorrow," he threatened.

"Well, for seven hakes,[12] what is it?" she had asked, more than twice, and when he had suggested that the packing shed would be an appropriate place to find out, she had cautiously answered maybe. She had not been certain she was going to keep the appointment until the arrival of mother's sister and her husband. Their coming seemed a sort of signal of permission, of grace, and she had definitely made up her mind to lie and leave as she was bowing them welcome.

So as soon as everyone appeared settled back for the evening, she announced loudly that she was going to the privy[13] outside, "I'm going to the *benjo*!" and slipped out the door. And now that she was actually on her way, her heart pumped in such an undisciplined way that she could hear it with her ears. It's because I'm running, she told herself, slowing to a walk. The shed was up ahead, one more patch away, in the middle of the fields. Its bulk, looming in the dimness, took on a sinisterness[14] that was funny when Rosie reminded herself that it was only a wooden frame with a canvas roof and three canvas walls that made a slapping noise on breezy days.

Jesus was sitting on the narrow plank that was the sorting platform and she went around to the other side and jumped backwards to seat herself on the rim of a packing stand. "Well, tell me," she said without greeting, thinking her voice sounded reassuringly familiar.

"I saw you coming out the door," Jesus said. "I heard you running part of the way, too."

"Uh-huh," Rosie said. "Now tell me the secret."

"I was afraid you wouldn't come," he said.

Rosie delved around on the chicken-wire bottom of the stall for number two tomatoes, ripe, which she was sitting beside, and came up with a left-over that felt edible. She bit into it and began sucking out the pulp and seeds. "I'm here," she pointed out.

"Rosie, are you sorry you came?"

"Sorry? What for?" she said. "You said you were going to tell me something."

---

12. **for seven hakes** turned-around version of the common expression "for heaven's sakes"

13. **privy** (PRIHV-ee) *n.* outdoor toilet in a small shed

14. **sinisterness** (SIHN-ihs-tuhr-nes) *n.* hint of evil or danger

"I will, I will," Jesus said, but his voice contained disappointment, and Rosie fleetingly felt the older of the two, realizing a brand-new power which vanished without category under her recognition.

"I have to go back in a minute," she said. "My aunt and uncle are here from Wintersburg. I told them I was going to the privy."

Jesus laughed. "You funny thing," he said. "You slay me!"

"Just because you have a bathroom *inside*," Rosie said. "Come on, tell me."

Chuckling, Jesus came around to lean on the stand facing her. They still could not see each other very clearly, but Rosie noticed that Jesus became very sober again as he took the hollow tomato from her hand and dropped it back into the stall. When he took hold of her empty hand, she could find no words to protest; her vocabulary had become distressingly constricted and she thought desperately that all that remained intact now was yes and no and oh, and even these few sounds would not easily out. Thus, kissed by Jesus, Rosie fell for the first time entirely victim to a helplessness delectable[15] beyond speech. . . .

Rosie stopped running as she approached the lights from the windows of home. How long since she had left? She could not guess, but gasping yet, she went to the privy in back and locked herself in. Her own breathing deafened her in the dark, close space, and she sat and waited until she could hear at last the nightly calling of the frogs and crickets. Even then, all she could think to say was oh, my, and the pressure of Jesus' face against her face would not leave. . . .

At Japanese school the next day (Wednesday, it was), Rosie was grave and giddy by turns. . . . Her father came after her at noon, bringing her sandwiches of minced ham and two nectarines to eat while she rode, so that she could pitch right into the sorting when they got home. . . .

It *was* hot, probably the hottest day of the year, and Rosie's blouse stuck damply to her back even under the protection of the canvas. But she worked as efficiently as a flawless machine and kept the stalls heaped, with one part of her mind listening in to the parental murmuring about the heat and the tomatoes and with another part planning the exact words she would say to Jesus when he drove up with the first load of the afternoon. But when at last she saw that the pick-up was coming, her hands went berserk and the tomatoes started falling in the wrong stalls, and her father said, "Hey, hey! Rosie, watch what you're doing!"

"Well, I have to go to the *benjo*," she said, hiding panic.

"Go in the weeds over there," he said, only half-joking.

"Oh, Father!" she protested.

"Oh, go on home," her mother said. "We'll make out for awhile."

---

15. **delectable** (dih-LEK-tuh-buhl) *adj.* delightful

In the privy Rosie peered through a knothole toward the fields, watching as much as she could of Jesus. Happily she thought she saw him look in the direction of the house from time to time before he finished unloading and went back toward the patch where his mother and father worked. As she was heading for the shed, a very presentable black car purred up the dirt driveway to the house and its driver motioned to her. Was this the Hayashi home, he wanted to know. She nodded. Was she a Hayashi? Yes, she said, thinking that he was a good-looking man. He got out of the car with a huge, flat package and she saw that he warmly wore a business suit. "I have something here for your mother then," he said, in a more elegant Japanese than she was used to.

She told him where her mother was and he came along with her, patting his face with an immaculate white handkerchief and saying something about the coolness of San Francisco. To her surprised mother and father, he bowed and introduced himself as, among other things, the *haiku* editor of the *Mainichi Shimbun*, saying that since he had been coming as far as Los Angeles anyway, he had decided to bring her the first prize she had won in the recent contest.

"First prize?" her mother echoed, believing and not believing, pleased and overwhelmed. Handed the package with a bow, she bobbed her head up and down numerous times to express her utter gratitude.

"It is nothing much," he added, "but I hope it will serve as a token of our great appreciation for your contributions and our great admiration of your considerable talent."

"I am not worthy," she said, falling easily into his style. "It is I who should make some sign of my humble thanks for being permitted to contribute."

"No, no, to the contrary," he said, bowing again.

But Rosie's mother insisted, and then saying that she knew she was being unorthodox,[16] she asked if she might open the package because her curiosity was so great. Certainly she might. In fact, he would like her reaction to it, for personally, it was one of his favorite *Hiroshiges*.[17]

Rosie thought it was a pleasant picture, which looked to have been sketched with delicate quickness. There were pink clouds, containing some graceful calligraphy,[18] and a sea that was a pale blue except at the edges, containing four sampans[19] with indications of people in them. Pines edged the water and on the far-off beach there was a cluster of thatched huts towered over by pine-dotted mountains of grey and blue. The frame was scalloped and gilt.

---

16. unorthodox (uhn-AWR-thuh-dahks) *adj.* unconventional, out of the ordinary

17. Hiroshiges (HEE-roh-shee-gayz) *n. pl.* beautiful block prints by the famous Japanese artist Hiroshige

18. calligraphy (kuh-LIHG-ruh-fee) *n.* beautiful, ornamental writing or script

19. sampans (SAM-panz) *n. pl.* small boats used in China and Japan

After Rosie's mother pronounced it without peer and somewhat prodded her father into nodding agreement, she said Mr. Kuroda must at least have a cup of tea after coming all this way, and although Mr. Kuroda did not want to impose, he soon agreed that a cup of tea would be refreshing and went along with her to the house, carrying the picture for her.

"Ha, your mother's crazy!" Rosie's father said, and Rosie laughed uneasily as she resumed judgment on the tomatoes. She had emptied six lugs when he broke into an imaginary conversation with Jesus to tell her to go and remind her mother of the tomatoes, and she went slowly. . . .

"Tell him I shall only be a minute," her mother said, speaking the language of Mr. Kuroda.

When Rosie carried the reply to her father, he did not seem to hear and she said again, "Mother says she'll be back in a minute."

"All right, all right," he nodded, and they worked again in silence. But suddenly, her father uttered an incredible noise, exactly like the cork of a bottle popping, and the next Rosie knew, he was stalking angrily toward the house, almost running in fact, and she chased after him crying, "Father! Father! What are you going to do?"

He stopped long enough to order her back to the shed. "Never mind!" he shouted. "Get on with the sorting."

And from the place in the fields where she stood, frightened and vacillating, Rosie saw her father enter the house. Soon Mr. Kuroda came out alone, putting on his coat. Mr. Kuroda got into his car and backed out down the driveway onto the highway. Next her father emerged, also alone, something in his arms (it was the picture, she realized), and, going over to the bathhouse woodpile, he threw the picture on the ground and picked up the axe. Smashing the picture, glass and all (she heard the explosion faintly), he reached over for the kerosene that was used to encourage the bath fire and poured it over the wreckage. I am dreaming, Rosie said to herself, I am dreaming, but her father, having made sure that his act of cremation was irrevocable,[20] was even then returning to the fields.

Rosie ran past him and toward the house. What had become of her mother? She burst into the parlor and found her mother at the back window watching the dying fire. They watched together until there remained only a feeble smoke under the blazing sun. Her mother was very calm.

"Do you know why I married your father?" she said without turning.

"No," said Rosie. It was the most frightening question she had ever been called upon to answer. Don't tell me now, she wanted to say, tell me tomorrow, tell me next week, don't tell me today. But she knew she would be told now, that the telling would combine with the other

---

20. irrevocable (ih-REV-uh-kuh-buhl) *adj.* not able to be called back or changed

violence of the hot afternoon to level her life, her world to the very ground. . . .

At eighteen she had been in love with the first son of one of the well-to-do families in her village. The two had met whenever and wherever they could, secretly, because it would not have done for his family to see him favor her—her father had no money; he was a drunkard and a gambler besides. She had learned she was with child; an excellent match[21] had already been arranged for her lover. Despised by her family, she had given premature birth to a stillborn son, who would be seventeen now. Her family did not turn her out, but she could no longer project herself in any direction without refreshing in them the memory of her indiscretion.[22] She wrote to Aunt Taka, her favorite sister in America, threatening to kill herself if Aunt Taka would not send for her. Aunt Taka hastily arranged a marriage with a young man of whom she knew, but lately arrived from Japan, a young man of simple mind, it was said, but of kindly heart. The young man was never told why his unseen betrothed[23] was so eager to hasten the day of meeting.

The story was told perfectly, with neither groping for words nor untoward passion. It was as though her mother had memorized it by heart, reciting it to herself so many times over that its nagging vileness[24] had long since gone. . . .

Suddenly, her mother knelt on the floor and took her by the wrists. "Rosie," she said urgently, "Promise me you will never marry!" Shocked more by the request than the revelation,[25] Rosie stared at her mother's face. Jesus, Jesus, she called silently, not certain whether she was invoking the help of the son of the Carrascos or of God, until there returned sweetly the memory of Jesus' hand, how it had touched her and where. Still her mother waited for an answer, holding her wrists so tightly that her hands were going numb. She tried to pull free. Promise, her mother whispered fiercely, promise. Yes, yes, I promise, Rosie said. But for an instant she turned away, and her mother, hearing the familiar glib agreement, released her. Oh, you, you, you, her eyes and twisted mouth said, you fool. Rosie, covering her face, began at last to cry, and the embrace and consoling hand came much later than she expected.

---

21. **match** (MACH) *n.* arranged marriage
22. **indiscretion** (ihn-dihs-KRESH-uhn) *n.* unwise act; in this case, the love affair and pregnancy
23. **betrothed** (bih-TROTHD) *n.* person one is engaged to marry
24. **vileness** (VEYEL-nes) *n.* ugliness, horror
25. **revelation** (rev-uh-LAY-shuhn) *n.* telling of previously unknown information

Critical Thinking

1. What does Hisaye Yamamoto say about the changes that are happening in the lives of Rosie and her mother?
2. What aspects of Yamamoto's cultural background may have led her to write about the changing traditions described in the story?
3. How did reading the story affect your thinking about the ways a person's cultural heritage affects his or her development? Give other examples of how a person's traditional culture may affect his or her growth.

Writing Your Response to "Seventeen Syllables"

What scene or character in this story affected your feelings or thoughts most deeply? What surprised or troubled you most? How does the story relate to experiences in your life or in the life of someone you know? Write your responses in your journal.

Going Back Into the Text: Author's Craft

The **climax** is the high point of a story, the moment of greatest emotional intensity. The conflicts and action in the plot lead up to this moment of crisis. Often the climax happens near the end of a story.

With a partner, use the questions below to review how Yamamoto leads the action in "Seventeen Syllables" to a climax.

1. What is the climax of the story? What conflicts and events in the story lead to the climax?
2. What emotional tension and pain in the mother's life lead her to speak as she does? How does this fit with what is happening in Rosie's life?
3. What is the climax in other stories in this unit?

from Humaweepi, the Warrior Priest

Reading the Author in a Cultural Context

Recognized as a Native American writer, Leslie Marmon Silko is of Laguna, Mexican, and European descent. Her great-grandfather was a trader who became a governor of the Laguna Pueblo (lah-GOO-nuh PWEB-loh) where the family lived. Being a descendant of these cultures endows Silko with many themes and voices. But it also suggests that perhaps she feels that she does not belong anywhere. Silko thought that the fact that her family's house was on the edge of the village was significant. It seemed to show that her family was not really part of the community.

Silko's stories combine elements of her diverse background. She has long been aware of how stories can bring a community together. ("Stories" can be anything that people tell others, from gossip to tribal beliefs told through ceremonies.) The fact that she is recognized as a Native American writer means that through her own storytelling, she has found a way to show that she does belong to a community.

In her stories, Silko includes beliefs and thoughts of people who share her Laguna background. But her stories are told as modern fiction, and not as old legends. For example, Humaweepi (hoo-mah-WEE-pee), the Native American character in the following novel excerpt, wears cowboy boots. This lets you know that the story is somewhat modern. However, Humaweepi also sings to the Bear, an ancient Native American symbol of power and life.

Humaweepi has been singled out as a future leader. He lives apart from the pueblo, with his uncle, because he is being trained to be a warrior priest. However, he does not realize this. What he does know is that he does not really feel like part of the village.

Many people feel at times as if they do not really belong anywhere, that they live on the outskirts of a society. But in growing older, individuals can begin to share a culture with others, and the feeling of isolation often disappears. In the following selection, think about how Humaweepi grows into his own history, how he discovers his destiny.

Focusing on the Selection

As you read, notice how Humaweepi responds to the events in his life. How does the old man assist in Humaweepi's personal growth? What general ideas about growth and change do you think the author wants to convey in the selection? Record your answers in your journal.

from *Humaweepi,*
the Warrior Priest

LESLIE MARMON SILKO

THE OLD MAN DIDN'T REALLY TEACH HIM MUCH; mostly they just lived. Occasionally Humaweepi would meet friends his own age who still lived with their families in the pueblo,[1] and they would ask him what he was doing; they seemed disappointed when he told them.

"That's nothing," they would say.

Once this had made Humaweepi sad and his uncle noticed. "Oh," he said when Humaweepi told him, "that shows you how little they know."

They returned to the pueblo for the ceremonials and special days. His uncle stayed in the kiva[2] with the other priests, and Humaweepi usually stayed with clan members because his mother and father had been very old when he was born and now they were gone. Sometimes during these stays, when the pueblo was full of the activity and excitement of the dances or the fiesta when the Christians paraded out of the pueblo church carrying the saint, Humaweepi would wonder why he was living out in the hills with the old man. When he was twelve he thought he had it all figured out: the old man just wanted someone to

---

1. **pueblo** (PWEB-loh) *n.* type of village built by some Native American peoples
2. **kiva** (KEE-vuh) *n.* structure used for religious and other purposes

live with him and help him with the goat and to chop wood and carry water. But it was peaceful in this place, and Humaweepi discovered that after all these years of sitting beside his uncle in the evenings, he knew the songs and chants for all the seasons, and he was beginning to learn the prayers for the trees and plants and animals. "Oh," Humaweepi said to himself, "I have been learning all this time and I didn't even know it."

Once the old man told Humaweepi to prepare for a long trip.

"Overnight?"

The old man nodded.

So Humaweepi got out a white cotton sack and started filling it with jerked venison,[3] piki bread,[4] and dried apples. But the old man shook his head sternly. It was late June then, so Humaweepi didn't bother to bring the blankets; he had learned to sleep on the ground like the old man did.

"Human beings are special," his uncle had told him once, "which means they can do anything. They can sleep on the ground like the doe and fawn."

And so Humaweepi had learned how to find the places in the scrub-oak thickets where the deer had slept, where the dry oak leaves were arranged into nests. This is where he and his uncle slept, even in the autumn when the nights were cold and Humaweepi could hear the leaves snap in the middle of the night and drift to the ground.

Sometimes they carried food from home, but often they went without food or blankets. When Humaweepi asked him what they would eat, the old man had waved his hand at the sky and earth around them. "I am a human being, Humaweepi," he said; "I eat anything." On these trips they had gathered grass roots and washed them in little sandstone basins made by the wind to catch rain water. The roots had a rich, mealy taste. Then they left the desert below and climbed into the mesa[5] country, and the old man had led Humaweepi to green leafy vines hanging from crevasses in the face of the sandstone cliffs. "Wild grapes," he said as he dropped some tiny dark-purple berries into Humaweepi's open palms. And in the high mountains there were wild iris roots and the bulbs from wild tulips which grew among the lacy ferns and green grass beside the mountain streams. They had gone out like this in each season. Summer and fall, and finally, spring and winter. "Winter isn't easy," the old man had said. "All the animals are hungry—not just you."

So this time, when his uncle shook his head at the food, Humaweepi left it behind as he had many times before. His uncle took the special leather pouch off the nail on the wall, and Humaweepi pulled his own

---

3. **jerked venison** dried deer meat
4. **piki bread** (PEE-kee BRED) crisp flat bread made from cornmeal
5. **mesa** (MAY-suh) *n.* land formation that looks like a hill or mountain with a flat top

buckskin bundle out from under his mattress. Inside he had a few objects of his own. A dried blossom. Fragile and yellow. A smooth pink quartz crystal in the shape of a star. Tiny turquoise beads the color of a summer sky. And a black obsidian[6] arrowhead, shiny and sharp. They each had special meaning to him, and the old man had instructed him to assemble these things with special meaning. "Someday maybe you will derive strength from these things." That's what the old man had said.

They walked west toward the distant blue images of the mountain peaks. The water in the Rio Grande was still cold. Humaweepi was aware of the dampness on his feet: when he got back from his journey he decided he would make sandals for himself because it took hours for his boots to dry out again. His uncle wore old sandals woven from twisted yucca fiber[7] and they dried out almost immediately. The old man didn't approve of boots and shoes—bad for you, he said. In the winter he wore buckskin moccasins and in the warm months, these yucca sandals.

They walked all day, steadily, stopping occasionally when the old man found a flower or herb or stone that he wanted Humaweepi to see. And it seemed to Humaweepi that he had learned the names of everything, and he said so to his uncle.

The old man frowned and poked at a small blue flower with his walking stick. "That's what a priest must know," he said and walked rapidly then, pointing at stones and shrubs. "How old are you?" he demanded.

"Nineteen," Humaweepi answered.

"All your life," he said, "every day, I have been teaching you."

After that they walked along in silence, and Humaweepi began to feel anxious; all of a sudden he knew that something was going to happen on this journey. That night they reached the white sandstone cliffs at the foot of the mountain foothills. At the base of these cliffs were shallow overhangs with sandy floors. They slept in the sand under the rock overhang; in the night Humaweepi woke up to the call of a young owl; the sky was bright with stars and a half-moon. The smell of the night air made him shiver and he buried himself more deeply in the cliff sand.

In the morning they gathered tumbleweed sprouts that were succulent[8] and tender. As they climbed the cliffs there were wild grapevines, and under the fallen leaves around the vine roots, the old man uncovered dried grapes shrunken into tiny sweet raisins. By noon they had reached the first of the mountain streams. There they washed and drank water and rested.

The old man frowned and pointed at Humaweepi's boots. "Take them off," he told Humaweepi; "leave them here until we come back."

---

6. **obsidian** (ahb-SIHD-ee-uhn) n. a hard volcanic glass
7. **yucca fiber** (YUK-kuh FEYE-ber) threadlike parts of the yucca plant
8. **succulent** (SUK-yoo-luhnt) adj. juicy

So Humaweepi pulled off his cowboy boots and put them under a lichen-covered[9] boulder near a big oak tree where he could find them. Then Humaweepi relaxed, feeling the coolness of air on his bare feet. He watched his uncle, dozing in the sun with his back against a big pine. The old man's hair had been white and long ever since Humaweepi could remember; but the old face was changing, and Humaweepi could see the weariness there—a weariness not from their little journey but from a much longer time in this world. Someday he will die, Humaweepi was thinking. He will be gone and I will be by myself. I will have to do the things he did. I will have to take care of things.

Humaweepi had never seen the lake before. It appeared suddenly as they reached the top of a hill covered with aspen trees. Humaweepi looked at his uncle and was going to ask him about the lake, but the old man was singing and feeding corn pollen from his leather pouch to the mountain winds. Humaweepi stared at the lake and listened to the songs. The songs were snowstorms with sounds as soft and cold as snowflakes; the songs were spring rain and wild ducks returning. Humaweepi could hear this; he could hear his uncle's voice become the night wind—high-pitched and whining in the trees. Time was lost and there was only the space, the depth, the distance of the lake surrounded by the mountain peaks.

When Humaweepi looked up from the lake he noticed that the sun had moved down into the western part of the sky. He looked around to find his uncle. The old man was below him, kneeling on the edge of the lake, touching a big gray boulder and singing softly. Humaweepi made his way down the narrow rocky trail to the edge of the lake. The water was crystal and clear like air; Humaweepi could see the golden rainbow colors of the trout that lived there. Finally the old man motioned for Humaweepi to come to him. He pointed at the gray boulder that lay half in the lake and half on the shore. It was then that Humaweepi saw what it was. The bear. Magic creature of the mountains, powerful ally to men. Humaweepi unrolled his buckskin bundle and picked up the tiny beads—sky-blue turquoise and coral[10] that was dark red. He sang the bear song and stepped into the icy, clear water to lay the beads on bear's head, gray granite rock, resting above the lake, facing west.

Native American standing on a cliff. Photograph by Edward Curtis. Seattle, 1907. Curtis (1868–1952) was the author and photographer for a 20-volume history of Native Americans.

---

9. **lichen-covered** (LEYE-kuhn KUV-erd) covered with gray or greenish plant growth
10. **coral** (KAWR-uhl) *n.* shell-like substance formed from the skeletons of tiny sea animals, used in jewelry

> *"Bear*
>   *resting in the mountains*
>   *sleeping by the lake*
> *Bear*
>   *I come to you, a man,*
>   *to ask you:*
> *Stand beside us in our battles*
>   *walk with us in peace.*
> *Bear*
>   *I ask you for your power*
>   *I am the warrior priest.*
>   *I ask you for your power*
>   *I am the warrior priest."*

It wasn't until he had finished singing the song that Humaweepi realized what the words said. He turned his head toward the old man. He smiled at Humaweepi and nodded his head. Humaweepi nodded back.

Humaweepi and his friend were silent for a long time. Finally Humaweepi said, "I'll tell you what my uncle told me, one winter, before he left. We took a trip to the mountain. It was early January, but the sun was warm and down here the snow was gone. We left early in the morning when the sky in the east was dark gray and the brightest star was still shining low in the western sky. I remember he didn't wear his ceremonial moccasins; he wore his old yucca sandals. I asked him about that.

"He said, 'Oh, you know the badger and the squirrel. Same shoes summer and winter,' but I think he was making that up, because when we got to the sandstone cliffs he buried the sandals in the sandy bottom of the cave where we slept and after that he walked on bare feet—up the cliff and along the mountain trail.

"There was snow on the shady side of the trees and big rocks, but the path we followed was in the sun and it was dry. I could hear melting snow—the icy water trickling down into the little streams and the little streams flowing into the big stream in the canyon where yellow bee flowers grow all summer. The sun felt warm on my body, touching me, but my breath still made steam in the cold mountain air.

" 'Aren't your feet cold?' I asked him.

"He stopped and looked at me for a long time, then shook his head. 'Look at these old feet,' he said. 'Do you see any corns[11] or bunions?'[12]

"I shook my head.

" 'That's right,' he said, 'my feet are beautiful. No one has feet like

---

11. corns (KAWRNZ) *n.* thick, hard, sometimes painful growths on the toes
12. bunions (BUN-yuhnz) *n.* inflamed swellings on the big toes

these. Especially you people who wear shoes and boots.' He walked on ahead before he said anything else. 'You have seen babies, haven't you?' he asked.

"I nodded, but I was wondering what this had to do with the old man's feet.

" 'Well, then you've noticed their grandmothers and their mothers, always worried about keeping the feet warm. But have you watched the babies? Do they care? No!' the old man said triumphantly, 'they do not care. They play outside on a cold winter day, no shoes, no jacket, because they aren't cold.' He hiked on, moving rapidly, excited by his own words; then he stopped at the stream. 'But human beings are what they are. It's not long before they are taught to be cold and they cry for their shoes.'

"The old man started digging around the edge of a stream, using a crooked, dry branch to poke through the melting snow. 'Here,' he said as he gave me a fat, round root, 'try this.'

"I squatted at the edge of the rushing, swirling water, full of mountain dirt, churning, swelling, and rolling—rich and brown and muddy with ice pieces flashing in the sun. I held the root motionless under the force of the stream water; the ice coldness of the water felt pure and clear as the ice that clung to the rocks in midstream. When I pulled my hand back it was stiff. I shook it and the root and lifted them high toward the sky.

"The old man laughed, and his mouth was full of the milky fibers of the root. He walked up the hill, away from the sound of the muddy stream surging through the snowbanks. At the top of the hill there was a grove of big aspens;[13] it was colder, and the snow hadn't melted much.

" 'Your feet,' I said to him. 'They'll freeze.'

" 'The snow was up to my ankles now. He was sitting on a fallen aspen, with his feet stretched out in front of him and his eyes half closed, facing into the sun.

" 'Does the wolf freeze his feet?' the old man asked me.

" I shook my head.

" 'Well then,' he said.

" 'But you aren't a wolf,' I started to say.

"The old man's eyes opened wide and then looked at me narrowly, sharply, squinting and shining. He gave a long, wailing, wolf cry with his head raised toward the winter sky.

"It was all white—pale white—the sky, the aspens bare white, smooth and white as the snow frozen on the ground. The wolf cry echoed off the rocky mountain slopes around us; in the distance I thought I heard a wailing answer."

---

13. **aspens** (AS-penz) *n.* slender-trunked trees

POSTREADING

Critical Thinking

1. What do you think Leslie Marmon Silko is saying about how growth and change came to Humaweepi?
2. What is there in Silko's life experience that might have led her to write about these ideas?
3. How do Humaweepi's experiences of change in his life compare with the events that have been most important in shaping your own life? Explain the similarities and differences.

Writing Your Response to *Humaweepi, the Warrior Priest*

In your journal, write about one conversation, scene, or idea in the selection that has special meaning for you. What is it about the scene that made it meaningful? How does it relate to your own life?

Going Back Into the Text: Author's Craft

The central message about life that a writer conveys is called the **theme** of the writing. The theme involves some insight about human values or beliefs. A long, complex work like a novel may express several broad ideas about human life and have several themes.

In some pieces of writing, the author states the theme directly. In a fable, for example, the theme is often summarized as a moral. More often, however, the author reveals the theme indirectly—that is, through the title, the setting, the characters and their words and actions, and the working out of the plot. The writer expects the reader to figure out the theme from these clues.

With a partner, review the selection from *Humaweepi, the Warrior Priest* to explore your understanding of Silko's theme. Use these questions to help you.

1. What theme does Silko develop in this novel excerpt?
2. What scenes or events most clearly reveal the theme?
3. How does the author's theme compare with your own attitudes and beliefs about change, learning, and human growth?

Cante Ishta–The Eye of the Heart

Reading the Author in a Cultural Context

Mary Crow Dog, of Lakota heritage, grew up not speaking her people's language or knowing very much about Native American ways. One reason for this was that Mary's family had become Christians and rejected the traditional Lakota religion. Another reason was the U.S. government's policy of sending Native American children away from home to missionary boarding schools. This practice was supposed to give them the same school experience as other American children. What it did, actually, was to isolate Native Americans from their heritage, since in school they could not speak their language or practice their religion.

Mary Crow Dog became a rebel. She left school because of disagreements with teachers, and she began a period of drifting. Joining the American Indian Movement (AIM) gave Mary's life new purpose. AIM is a political group trying to change the government's policies toward Native Americans. Mary Crow Dog was an active member. For example, in 1972 she marched with AIM into Washington, D.C., where the group staged a sit-in (a peaceful protest) at the Bureau of Indian Affairs.

The selection that follows is from a book Mary Crow Dog wrote called *Lakota Woman*. This book is her story about the Native American protests of the late 1960s and the 1970s. It is also a personal exploration of what it means to be a Native American—for Mary Crow Dog, a search for dignity and pride in spite of being made to feel ashamed.

You can read this excerpt from *Lakota Woman* in different ways. You can read it as an outsider, interested in learning what the author is going to teach you about Lakota ways and ceremonies. Or you can read from the point of view of the narrator, discovering what it means to be Lakota, what it means to see "with the eye in your heart."

Focusing on the Selection

As you read, think about the ceremonial ritual that Mary Crow Dog participates in to learn how to open "the eye of the heart." Why is this important to her? How does this change her? What comparisons does the author make in her descriptions? Record your responses in your journal.

Cante Ishta[1]– The Eye of the Heart

from *Lakota Woman*

MARY CROW DOG

> You got to look at things
> with the eye in your heart,
> not with the eye in your head.
> —*Lame Deer*[2]

SOME OF OUR MEDICINE MEN always say that one must view the world through the eye in one's heart rather than just trust the eyes in one's head. "Look at the real reality beneath the sham[3] realities of things and gadgets," Leonard always tells me. "Look through the eye in your heart. That's the meaning of Indian religion."

The eye of my heart was still blind when I joined Leonard to become his wife. I knew little of traditional ways. I had been to a few peyote[4] meetings without really understanding them. I had watched one Sun Dance, and later the Ghost Dance held at Wounded Knee, like a

---

1. **Cante Ishta** (KAHN-tay IHSH-tah)
2. **Lame Deer** medicine man of the Oglala people
3. **sham** (SHAM) *adj.* false
4. **peyote** (pay-OHT-ee) *n.* drug that comes from cactus buttons

spectator—an emotional spectator, maybe, but not different from white friends watching these dances. They, too, felt emotion. Like myself they did not penetrate through symbolism to the real meaning. I had not yet participated in many ancient rituals of our tribe—the sweat bath, the vision quest, yuwipi,[5] the making of relatives, the soul keeping. I did not even know that these ceremonies were still being performed. There were some rituals I did not even know existed.

I was now the wife of a medicine man who had been a finder and seer since boyhood, because the elders of the tribe had noticed his spiritual gifts when he was still very young, about eight years old. They had said, "Watch this boy. He's the one," and had taught and prepared him for his future life as a medicine man. Because going to a white school would spoil him for the role the elders had chosen for him, Old Henry had driven the truant officers away with his shotgun, telling them, "I will rather go to jail before I let this boy go to your school!" Now Leonard would teach me to be a medicine man's wife, and I was eager to learn.

I think it was not easy for him to teach his wife. She knows him during the day and during the night, too. Knowing his strengths, she cannot fail to see his weaknesses also. And he knows the good and the bad in her likewise. We were under stress from the outside all the time, and so we had our ups and downs. Also, with the kind of life I had before, I did not respect him just because he was a man, as some Sioux[6] women do. Some of those old macho Sioux proverbs like "Woman should not walk before man" I did not think were meant for me. We loved each other, and sometimes we fought each other. Under the conditions under which we had to live, how could it have been otherwise? But always, always I felt, and was enraptured[7] by, his tremendous power—raw power, spiritual Indian power coming from deep within him. It was raw because, never having been at school and being unable to read or write, there is no white-man intellectualism[8] in him. At the same time, his thinking and ideas are often extremely sophisticated—unique, original, even frightening.

I was at first very unsure about the role of a medicine man's wife, about the part women played, or were allowed to play, in Indian religion. . . . Leonard helped me overcome these feelings of insecurity. He told me about Ptesan Win,[9] the White Buffalo Woman, who brought the sacred pipe to our tribes. He told me about medicine women. He

---

5. **yuwipi** (yoo-WEE-pee) *n.* a healing ceremony done by Lakota and other Plains medicine men
6. **Sioux** (SOO) *n.* a Native American nation that lives on the plains
7. **enraptured** (en-RAP-cherd) *v.* filled with delight
8. **intellectualism** (ihn-tuhl-ek-choo-wuhl-ihzum) *n.* focus on logical thought
9. **Ptesan Win** (TAY-sah WEE)

said that in 1964 he went to Allen, South Dakota, to take part in a number of ceremonies. While there he met a medicine woman. She said good things to the people at this ceremony. Her name was Bessie Good Road. She used a buffalo skull in her rituals, and always a buffalo came into her meetings. She had the spiritual buffalo power. Every time the buffalo spirit moved his legs, his hoofs struck sparks of lightning. Every time the buffalo grunted, flashes of light shot from his nostrils. Every time the buffalo swung his tail, one could see a flaming circle. "I took my drum and sang for her," he told me. "I had never seen a medicine woman before and I was awed by her power." She told him: "Someday I won't be here anymore. I want to leave these things, this power for my people to stand on. We are losing many sacred things, losing sacred knowledge, but to this place the buffalo spirit still comes."

The medicine woman did not talk much. She had to wait a long time until she could use her medicine. . . . He was not ashamed to have this holy woman teach him. Hearing this made me feel good.

In this way Crow Dog talked to me. It did not matter where. Riding in a car, at the table eating fry bread and hamburger, around the stove with other people listening, or at night lying by his side. He taught me how to listen. Sound is important. Our sound is the sound of nature and animals, not the notes of a white man's scale.[10] Our language comes from the water, the flowers, the wild creatures, the winds. Crow Dog believes that the newborn child can understand this universal language, but later he forgets it. He teaches about harmony between humans and the earth, between man and man and between man and woman. He always says: "What's the saddle good for without a horse? Get the horse, and a saddle blanket, and the saddle together. That's what the sacred hoop means."

Tunkashila,[11] the Grandfather Spirit, has filled this universe with powers, powers to use—for good, not for bad. We only have to suffer this power to enter into us, to fill us, not to resist it. Medicine men, Leonard told me, have a sort of secret language. Sioux, Crow, Blackfeet medicine men, before they start talking, they already know what they'll be saying to each other. I guess that goes for medicine women, too.

I had to learn about the sweat bath, because it precedes all sacred ceremonies, and is at the same time a ceremony all by itself. It is probably the oldest of all our rituals because it is connected with the glowing stones, evoking thoughts of Tunka, the rock, our oldest god. Our family's sweat lodge, our oinikaga tipi, is near the river which flows through Crow Dog's land. That is good. Pure, flowing water plays a great part

---

10. **notes of a white man's scale** specific musical notes of European musical tradition
11. **Tunkashila** (toon-KAH-shee-lah)

American Museum of Natural History, New York City.
Dakota Sun Dance painted by Short Bull, Chief of the Oglala Dakota.

National Museum of the American Indian, Smithsonian Institution, Washington, D.C. Painted buffalo skull used in the Sun Dance ceremony by the Arapaho people. Photographed in Wyoming in the early 20th century. What do this painted skull and the painting of the Sun Dance above tell you about the role of animals in Native American cultures?

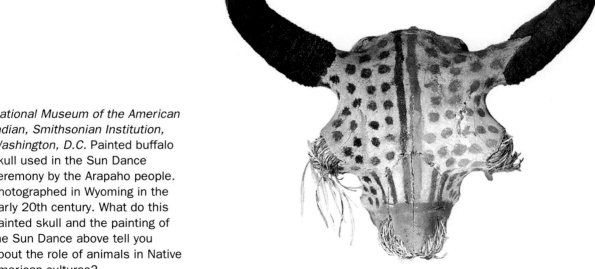

during a sweat. Always at the lodge we can hear the river's voice, the murmur of its waters. Along its banks grows washte wikcemna,[12] a sweet-smelling aromatic herb—Indian perfume.

The lodge is made of sixteen willow sticks, tough but resilient and easy to bend. They are formed into a beehive-shaped dome. The sweat lodges vary in size. They can accommodate anywhere from eight to twenty-four people. The bent willow sticks are fastened together with strips of red trade cloth.[13] Sometimes offerings of Bull Durham tobacco are tied to the frame, which is then covered with blankets or a tarp. In the old days buffalo skins were used for the covering, but these are hard to come by now. The floor of the little lodge is covered with sage. In the center is a circular pit to receive the heated rocks. In building a lodge, people should forget old quarrels and have only good thoughts.

Outside the lodge, wood is piled up in a certain manner to make the fire in which the rocks will be heated—peta owihankeshni[14]—the "fire without end" which is passed on from generation to generation. After it has blazed for a while, white limestone rocks are placed in its center. These rocks do not crack apart in the heat. They come from the hills. Some of them are covered with a spidery network of green moss. This is supposed by some to represent secret spirit writing.

The scooped-out earth from the firepit inside the lodge is formed up into a little path leading from the lodge entrance and ending in a small mound. It represents Unci—Grandmother Earth. A prayer is said when this mound is made. A man is then chosen to take care of the fire, to bring the hot rocks to the lodge, often on a pitchfork, and to handle the entrance flap.

In some places men and women sweat together. We do not do this. Among us, men and women do their sweat separately. Those taking part in a sweat strip, and wrapped in their towels, crawl into the little lodge, entering clockwise. In the darkness inside they take their towels off and hunker down naked. I was astounded to see how many people could be swallowed up by this small, waist-high, igloo-shaped hut. The rocks are then placed into the lodge, one by one. Each stone is touched with the pipe bowl as, resting in the fork of a deer antler, it is put into the center pit. The leader goes in first, sitting down near the entrance on the right side. Opposite him, at the other side of the entrance sits his helper. The leader has near him a pail full of cold, pure water and a ladle. Green cedar is sprinkled over the hot rocks, filling the air with its aromatic

---

12. **Tunka** (toon-KAH) . . . **oinikaga tipi** (oi-NEE-kah-gah TEE-pee) . . . **washte wikcemna** (wah-SHTAI week-CHEM-nah)

13. **trade cloth** (TRAYD KLAWTH) *n.* cheap cloth offered by European traders to Native Americans, whose clothing was made from animal skins

14. **peta owihankeshni** (pay-TAH oh-wee-HAHNK-shnee)

odor. Outside the entrance flap is a buffalo-skull altar. Tobacco ties are fastened to its horns. There is also a rack for the pipe to rest on.

Anywhere from twelve to sixty rocks can be used in this ceremony. The more rocks, the hotter it will be. Once the rocks have been passed into the lodge, the flap is closed. Inside it is dark except for the red glow of the rocks in the pit. Now the purification[15] begins. As sage or cedar is sprinkled on the rocks, the men or women participating catch the sacred smoke with their hands, inhaling it, rubbing it all over their face and body. Then cold water is poured on the rocks. The rising cloud of white steam, "grandfather's breath," fills the lodge. A sweat has four "doors," meaning that the flap is opened four times during the purification to let some cool outside air in, bringing relief to the participants.

Everybody has the privilege to pray or speak of sacred things during the ceremony. It is important that all take part in the ritual with their hearts, souls, and minds. When women have their sweats, a medicine man runs them—which is all right because it is so dark inside that he cannot see you.

The first time I was inside the oinikaga tipi, the sweat lodge, when water was poured over the rocks and the hot steam got to me, I thought that I could not endure it. The heat was beyond anything I had imagined. I thought I would not be able to breathe because it was like inhaling liquid fire. With my cupped hands I created a slightly cooler space over my eyes and mouth. After a while I noticed that the heat which had hurt me at first became soothing, penetrating to the center of my body, going into my bones, giving me a wonderful feeling. If the heat is more than a person can stand, he or she can call out "Mitakuye oyasin!"[16]—All my relatives!—and the flap will be opened to let the inside cool off a bit. I was proud not to have cried out. After the sweat I really felt newly born. My pores were opened and so was my mind. My body tingled. I felt as if I had never experienced pain. I was deliciously light-headed, elated, drunk with the spirit. Soon I began looking forward to a good sweat.

Once we were in California testifying for an Indian brother on trial in Los Angeles. Some of the local Indians invited us to a sweat somewhere in the desert eighty miles from L.A. As I was hunkering down inside the lodge, they started passing in the rocks. When about twenty were in the pit, the usual number for a woman's sweat, I expected them to close the flap and start the ceremony. Instead more and more rocks, a big heap, were coming in. I stared at the huge pile of glowing, hissing rocks rising higher and higher. I tried to back away from the rocks, but

---

15. **purification** (pyoor-ih-fih-KAY-shuhn) *n.* making pure, clearing of guilt or imperfections
16. **Mitakuye oyasin** (mee-tah-kee AH-SAY)

there was no room. My knees started to blister. Already the heat was terrific and they had not even poured the water yet. I cringed at the thought of what cold water on this big mound of fiery rocks would do. Then it came, the water. I thought I would die. Never, never thereafter would I eat lobsters, knowing what these poor creatures have to go through. I felt I could not cry out to have the flap opened. After all, I represented the Sioux women on this occasion. . . . There were some anguished cries: "All my relatives!" The door was opened, but it was so hot outside in the desert that it brought me no relief. The flap was closed again and more water poured. The prayers started. I was praying too, silently: "Please make the prayers short," but they were long. When it was all over we could not get out quickly enough. Some women were in such a hurry they did not even wrap their towels around themselves and came out stark naked. The relief of being out of that particular sweat lodge was indescribable. Leonard told me that they had used more stones in the men's sweat than in ours. I could not see how that was possible. . . .

POSTREADING

Critical Thinking

1. What does Mary Crow Dog tell you about how being a medicine man's wife has changed her life?
2. What experiences in Mary Crow Dog's life do you think led her to write about Sioux traditions?
3. How has reading this selection influenced your ideas about Native American culture? How can you apply the idea of looking "with the eye in your heart" to your own life?

Writing Your Response to "Cante Ishta–The Eye of the Heart"

What idea, scene, or image in this selection stands out the most for you? What thoughts or feelings did it bring to mind? Write about it in your journal.

Going Back Into the Text: Author's Craft

Personification is a type of figurative language in which a nonhuman subject is given human qualities—for example, "The waves marched along the shore." Writers use personification to add freshness, vividness, and surprise to their writing. Personification can also give the reader new insight into a subject.

With a partner, discuss "Cante Ishta—The Eye of the Heart." Use the following questions to help you.

1. How is the title of the selection an example of personification?
2. How does the use of personification help you understand the ideas in the selection?
3. What other uses of personification can you find in this theme?

Black Hair
ALONE/december/night

Responding to Literature

Notice the sidenotes in the margins of the two selections. These notes reflect one student's reading of "Black Hair" and "ALONE/december/night." The student notices that although the poems are very different in style, both Soto and Hernandez Cruz describe their connection to their own cultural heritage and their feelings of isolation from mainstream U.S. society. The student also has some personal responses to the poems. Compare these observations with your own reading of these poems.

Reading the Authors in a Cultural Context

Writers very often draw from their own life experiences to develop certain themes, characters, and situations in their work. Gary Soto and Victor Hernandez Cruz base much of their poetry on their own lives.

Born in 1952 in the San Joaquin Valley of California, Gary Soto is a Mexican American who spent much of his childhood moving from farm to farm as a migrant worker. In his first book of poetry, *The Elements of San Joaquin*, Soto vividly describes the harsh realities of life for migrant workers, as well as reflecting on his own memories and dreams.

The following poem, "Black Hair," is about a young boy's fascination with baseball and specifically with one Mexican American baseball player, Hector Moreno. As you read the poem, notice how Hector's talent and success offer hope to Mexican Americans.

Similarly, in the poem "ALONE/december/night," Victor Hernandez Cruz conveys a sense of alienation and isolation in the United States. Although this poem is very abstract and therefore very different from Soto's concrete imagery and simple style, both Hernandez Cruz and Soto reveal their pride in and attachment to their cultural heritage.

Victor Hernandez Cruz was born in a small village in Puerto Rico in 1949. When he was four, he moved with his family to New York City. Hernandez Cruz recalls that his childhood in New York was always filled with the music of his heritage. As you read the poem, think about the words and images Hernandez Cruz uses to convey his message.

Focusing on the Selections

As you read the poems, think about the feelings each poet expresses about changes in his life. What conflicts do the poems illustrate? What solutions to these problems are suggested? What words and images do the poets use to express feelings and thoughts? Record your responses in your journal.

Black Hair

GARY SOTO

At eight I was brilliant with my body.
In July, that ring of heat
We all jumped through, I sat in the bleachers
Of Romain Playground, in the lengthening
Shade that rose from our dirty feet.
The game before us was more than baseball.
It was a figure—Hector Moreno
Quick and hard with turned muscles,
His crouch the one I assumed before an altar
Of worn baseball cards, in my room.
I came here because I was Mexican, a stick
Of brown light in love with those
Who could do it—the triple and hard slide,
The gloves eating balls into double plays.
What could I do with 50 pounds, my shyness,
My black torch of hair, about to go out?
Father was dead, his face no longer
Hanging over the table or our sleep,
And mother was the terror of mouths
Twisting hurt by butter knives.
In the bleachers I was brilliant with my body,
Waving players in and stomping my feet,
Growing sweaty in the presence of white shirts.
I chewed sunflower seeds. I drank water
And bit my arm through the late innings.
When Hector lined balls into deep
Center, in my mind I rounded the bases
With him, my face flared, my hair lifting
Beautifully, because we were coming home
to the arms of brown people.

ALONE/*december/night*

VICTOR HERNANDEZ CRUZ

it's been so long
speaking to people
who think it all
too complex
stupidity in their eyes
&
it's been so long
so far from the truth
so far from a roof
to talk to
or a hand to touch
or anything to really
love

it's been so long
talking to myself
alone
in the night
listening to a music
that is me.

I think the title suggests loneliness. All the words in the title suggest a sense of isolation.

The speaker is talking to people he can't relate to. Maybe the speaker is from a different cultural group.

The similar sounds in "roof" and "truth" and the repetition of "so far" add rhythm.

I wonder why the poet puts "love" on a separate line. Maybe he is emphasizing the importance or the absence of love in his life.

The music could refer to the poetry that the poet writes to overcome his sense of isolation. I never thought that writing might be able to do that.

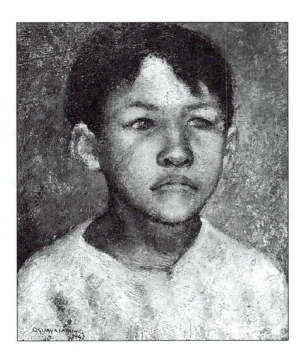

My Brother. *Museum of Modern Art, New York City.* Oil painting on wood by Oswaldo Guayasamin. Ecuador, 1942.

Critical Thinking

1. Compare the attitudes that each poet expresses about his life. How does each speaker seem to have dealt with change?
2. What events may have led each poet to the situations and attitudes conveyed in the poems?
3. How does your community provide young people with ceremonies and rituals of growth and change?

Writing Your Response to "Black Hair" and "ALONE/december/night"

In your journal, write about the image, a character, or a feeling in one of these poems that you find most meaningful. What makes it so striking? How can you relate it to a situation, a person, or a feeling you have known?

Going Back Into the Text: Author's Craft

Using words to describe sensory experiences is called **imagery**. A writer's imagery may make you aware of sights, sounds, tastes, textures, and smells that are new to you. The writer may use the imagery associated with an event, like a baseball game, to help express emotions and ideas.

The imagery in a poem can create a tone or a feeling about its subject. Images may be strong and hard-hitting, full of sensations. A poem can also be striking for the delicacy, simplicity, and sparseness of its imagery.

With a partner, use the following questions to review the imagery in "Black Hair" and "ALONE/december/night."

1. What imagery is used in each poem?
2. How does the imagery in each poem help to express the feelings, attitudes, and thoughts of the speaker?
3. Describe the imagery in other poems or songs you know.

Reviewing the Theme

1. Select two of the authors represented in this chapter. Compare their perspectives on the theme of personal growth and change through cultural rites, customs, and values. What similarities and differences do you see?
2. What is the role of the family in personal growth and change? Choose one or two selections in this chapter and discuss this question as it applies to them.
3. Have you participated in any ceremonies of change? What were they? In what ways have these ceremonies resulted in your growth?

FOCUSING THE UNIT THEME

COOPERATIVE/COLLABORATIVE LEARNING

With three of your classmates, discuss the works presented in this unit as they relate to the theme and to your own lives. Below is a sample dialogue that one group of students used to start their discussion. You may wish to use it as a starting point for your discussion. At the end of the allotted time, summarize the main ideas expressed by your group and share them with the class.

STUDENT 1: Long Sash taught the people to be tolerant. Quite a few of the selections teach some lesson about what's important in life or how to live.

STUDENT 2: There's a political aspect, too. Mary Crow Dog suggests that getting in touch with the old ways can help us change our lives and our society. But in "To Da-duh" and "Seventeen Syllables," old ways sometimes conflict with what's happening today. I think sometimes the old has to give way to the new.

STUDENT 3: I'm impressed by how strongly the authors feel about their cultural origins. Momaday made a long trip just to visit his grandmother's grave. Anaya's character, Antonio, believed that his future was in the hands of an older family friend. I think that learning about each other's cultural roots helps me see how alike we all are.

STUDENT 4: I'm struck by the proverbs in the Vietnamese tale, like "Beauty is not painted on. It is the spirit showing." In "The Way to Rainy Mountain," too, Momaday is saying, "My people live in me; my grandmother lives in me."

Writing Process

Review all the journal notes you have made for the literature in this unit. Rethink your responses in terms of the unit theme. Choose two or more selections that were the most helpful and meaningful to you in developing an understanding of this theme.

Write an expository essay that explains how the literature you have selected contributes to the unit theme. In your essay, draw conclusions about the importance of origins and ceremonies to all cultures. Use examples from the literature to support your ideas. Use the writing process described on pages 393-402 of the Handbook to help you write your essay. If necessary, use the model essays provided.

Problem Solving

One of the challenges of living in a multicultural society is staying in touch with one's cultural roots. Choose one or more of the cultural groups portrayed in the unit and identify the values, beliefs, and customs they have that may be a source of strength. Which values or beliefs are the same from culture to culture, and how are they the same? Which are different, and how are they different? How does understanding another person's cultural roots help you understand that person better? Does it help you understand yourself better? In a skit, a debate, a dance, a musical arrangement, a news show, or an art composition, express your thoughts about how similarities and differences among cultures can help to bring people together.

Photograph of a Chinatown street in San Francisco about 1900.

Photograph of an immigrant family looking at the Statue of Liberty from Ellis Island in 1930.

Photograph of Cuban Americans at Miami Airport welcoming newcomers from Havana in May 1961.

ARRIVAL AND SETTLEMENT

THEMES

▼ Voices of the First Nations

▼ The Long Road from Slavery

▼ Stories of Newcomers

IN UNIT 2, you will read about several groups of people who helped create what is now the United States. The experiences of these people provide distinct perspectives on arrival and settlement in the United States. They also provide an understanding of the nation's cultural diversity.

As you read the stories, poems, and primary sources in this unit, you will learn about the conflicts each group has encountered. How did the Native American peoples of the First Nations view the early explorers and settlers who took over their lands? What was the Middle Passage like for enslaved Africans? What were the hopes of the early immigrants from Europe and Asia who flooded the gates at Ellis and Angel islands? What problems have recent Hispanic immigrants faced after arriving in their new home?

As each group settled, a new group arrived. This process of arriving and settling has repeated itself throughout U.S. history. Think about the challenges each group has confronted. How were new groups accepted? In what ways did cultures change as groups of people built communities?

While reading the selections in this unit, look for the diverse perspectives of the groups of people who are represented. Consider the unique problems each group faced as well as the similar goals they shared. Also think about how you respond to newcomers. Are you curious? Resentful? Accepting? Have you ever been a newcomer? How have you felt in a new or unfamiliar group? How did you resolve any problems of adjustment? How does any outsider finally become part of a group?

Historical Background and Thematic Organization

The United States has been described as a nation of immigrants. The only true Native Americans are the people Christopher Columbus mistakenly referred to as "Indians." Native Americans have never been a single people. In 1492, the year Columbus arrived in the Americas, there were about 2,000 separate Native American nations, each with its own language, land, and culture. Although these groups traded with one another, they had little contact with people on other continents. The same was true of nations in Europe, Asia, and Africa.

About the year A.D. 1000, among the first outsiders to arrive in the Western Hemisphere were sailors from Scandinavia. They did not stay. For the next 500 years, the only other Europeans to visit the Americas were fishers, who cast their nets in the rich fishing grounds off the coast of Labrador.

Then in 1492, the first Spanish ships reached the Caribbean Sea. In the years that followed, hundreds of other vessels arrived in harbors throughout the Americas. The Spaniards did not come to explore or to fish.

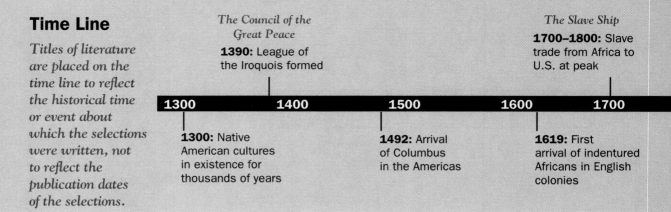

Time Line

Titles of literature are placed on the time line to reflect the historical time or event about which the selections were written, not to reflect the publication dates of the selections.

The Council of the Great Peace
1390: League of the Iroquois formed

The Slave Ship
1700–1800: Slave trade from Africa to U.S. at peak

| 1300 | 1400 | 1500 | 1600 | 1700 |

1300: Native American cultures in existence for thousands of years

1492: Arrival of Columbus in the Americas

1619: First arrival of indentured Africans in English colonies

They came to stay. They built colonies on islands in the Caribbean and then took control of Mexico, on the mainland of North America. From there, they sailed south and then north.

By the late 1500s, groups from other parts of Europe were also arriving in the Americas. Among them were people from Portugal, England, France, the Netherlands, and Sweden. As each group built communities on the two continents, the newcomers adapted their ways of life to a new set of living conditions. In the process, each group helped create a nation.

The literature in Theme 4 focuses on the way the Native Americans responded to the newcomers. Some of these perspectives were introduced in Unit 1. In Unit 2, you will explore the thoughts and feelings of the peoples of the First Nations as they became outsiders in the land they had lived on for thousands of years.

Theme 5 highlights the experiences of the millions of Africans who were forced into slavery and then shipped to the Western

Hemisphere. More than one million died during the Middle Passage—the journey from West Africa to the Americas. Those who survived were forced to work on farms and plantations. They also cleared forests, drained swamps, and built countless cities and towns throughout the Americas.

Africans, like Europeans and Native Americans, were not a single people. Although most of those who were brought to the Americas came from West Africa, the region was not a united one. Then, as now, West Africans had many different ways of life and spoke many different languages. Slave owners in the Americas tried to destroy those cultures. Yet, somehow, Africans managed to preserve much of their heritage for their children and their children's children.

Other newcomers came to the United States voluntarily. Some were seeking religious freedom. Others hoped to find economic opportunity in a new land. Still others came for political freedom. In all, more than

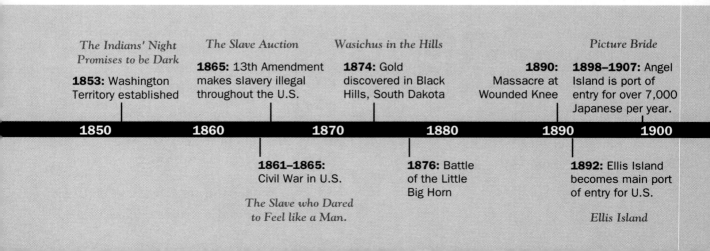

The Indians' Night Promises to be Dark
1853: Washington Territory established

The Slave Auction
1865: 13th Amendment makes slavery illegal throughout the U.S.

Wasichus in the Hills
1874: Gold discovered in Black Hills, South Dakota

1890: Massacre at Wounded Knee

Picture Bride
1898–1907: Angel Island is port of entry for over 7,000 Japanese per year.

| 1850 | 1860 | 1870 | 1880 | 1890 | 1900 |

1861–1865: Civil War in U.S.

The Slave who Dared to Feel like a Man.

1876: Battle of the Little Big Horn

1892: Ellis Island becomes main port of entry for U.S.

Ellis Island

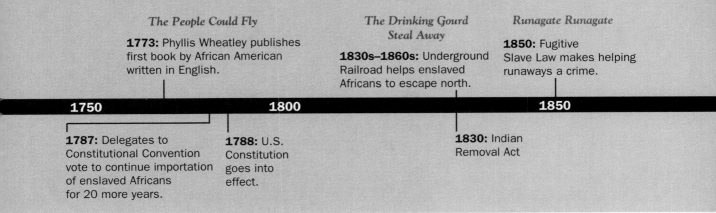

The People Could Fly

1773: Phyllis Wheatley publishes first book by African American written in English.

*The Drinking Gourd
Steal Away*

1830s–1860s: Underground Railroad helps enslaved Africans to escape north.

Runagate Runagate

1850: Fugitive Slave Law makes helping runaways a crime.

1750

1800

1850

1787: Delegates to Constitutional Convention vote to continue importation of enslaved Africans for 20 more years.

1788: U.S. Constitution goes into effect.

1830: Indian Removal Act

45 million immigrants have settled in the United States since 1776.

The newcomers did not arrive all at once. They tended to come in large numbers whenever conditions in their native lands became unbearable. Those who arrived in the years before the Civil War were mainly from countries in northern Europe. In the mid-1800s, these newcomers were joined by immigrants from China. By the late 1800s, most immigrants were from southern and eastern Europe, Asia, and the Middle East.

As the immigrant population grew, many Americans became fearful of the new arrivals. They claimed that the newcomers were "too different" to become Americans. Therefore, in 1882, Congress passed the first in a series of laws that restricted immigration.

By 1924, only 165,000 newcomers could enter the United States in a single year. Just a dozen years earlier, nearly a million immigrants were arriving every year. The new laws also set quotas. The number of people who could come from any one country was based on immigration patterns before the Civil War. Thus, the quotas favored immigrants from Great Britain, Germany, and Sweden.

After World War II, Congress changed the law somewhat to help refugees from war-torn countries. In 1965, it ended the quota system. As a result, Asians, Africans, and people from other countries of the Americas could enter the country more freely.

In Theme 6 you will read about the experiences of newcomers from Puerto Rico, recent immigrants from South Africa and Mexico, as well as the stories of earlier arrivals. Although each viewpoint is individual, these stories have elements in common. Look for similarities and differences as you read. Think also about your own cultural heritage. What does your family have in common with the people portrayed in Theme 6? How do newcomers find a place in your community today? How do they develop a sense of being a part of the nation?

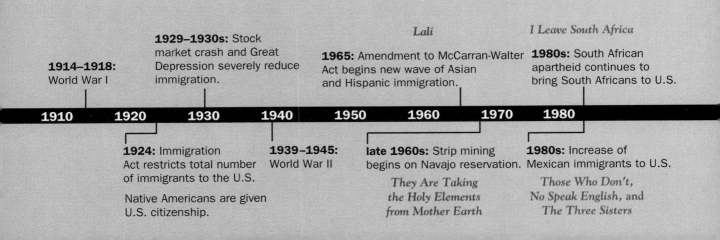

Lali

1965: Amendment to McCarran-Walter Act begins new wave of Asian and Hispanic immigration.

I Leave South Africa

1980s: South African apartheid continues to bring South Africans to U.S.

1914–1918: World War I

1929–1930s: Stock market crash and Great Depression severely reduce immigration.

1910 **1920** **1930** **1940** **1950** **1960** **1970** **1980**

1924: Immigration Act restricts total number of immigrants to the U.S.

Native Americans are given U.S. citizenship.

1939–1945: World War II

late 1960s: Strip mining begins on Navajo reservation.

*They Are Taking
the Holy Elements
from Mother Earth*

1980s: Increase of Mexican immigrants to U.S.

*Those Who Don't,
No Speak English, and
The Three Sisters*

Theme 4:
Voices of the First Nations

ALTHOUGH the Native Americans whose works are presented in the following section are no longer alive, their attitudes, values, and traditions continue to be heard today. Their ancestors belonged to the first nations to settle in North America, thousands of years before Europeans arrived. The voices in this section span six centuries and come from four regions of what is now the continental United States—Northeast, Midwest, Southwest, and Northwest. Yet each speaker's words reflect a strong love and respect for the land and for heritage.

Most of the voices in this section tell of experiences with white

Navajo wall painting depicting a Spanish cavalry expedition against the Navajo in 1804–1805. Painted on a ledge at Canyon de Chelly National Monument, Arizona.

people—newcomers—who moved onto the land, ignored the rights of Native Americans, and changed these people's ways of life forever. The voices in three of the selections you will read come from individuals: a holy man of the Lakota (lah-KOH-tuh), a Navajo (NAH-vu-hoh) woman, and a Suquamish (soo-KWAHM-ihsh) Chief. The voice in the other selection speaks for a group of many people—five nations who gathered together to build a body of laws to live by. Together, the voices represented in these selections show Native American dignity and eloquence despite the tragedies suffered.

Wasichus in the Hills

Reading the Author in a Cultural Context

Black Elk was a holy man of the Oglala (oh-GLAH-lah) Lakota, who lived on the Great Plains. In his lifetime, he saw the Lakota nation—along with the Cheyenne (sheye-AN), Arapaho (ah-RAP-ah-hoh), and many other peoples who had flourished in North America for centuries before European settlers arrived—suffer total devastation. The destruction of these first nations began before Black Elk was born. The newcomers had little regard for the Native American belief that the land (Mother Earth) belonged to no individual, but rather was to be shared and used and replenished by all.

Much about the development of the United States has been written from the white point of view. However, some great Native American voices of the time can be heard through translations of speeches and interviews into English. *Black Elk Speaks*, published in 1932, is the result of long narrative sessions with John G. Neihardt, an author of books and poems about Native American nations and the U.S. West. Black Elk's son translated his father's words into English for Neihardt. Black Elk's telling of his life and his people's beliefs and traditions was perhaps a way of fulfilling his vision from childhood that he would help preserve the culture of his people.

Visions are an important part of Native American life. When a man or woman has a recurring dream—waking or sleeping—he or she is thought to be receiving a message from the spirit world. The person then discusses the vision with the community's spiritual leaders, and goes on a *vision quest*, which includes retreating to an isolated spot, fasting, and praying for guidance. The person is sometimes visited by a bear, buffalo, eagle, wolf, or hawk that turns into human form and explains the responsibilities of the vision, what the person should do to perform it, and why he or she was chosen.

In the excerpt you will read, Black Elk tells of some events that happened during the years 1874 and 1875 when he was 11 and 12 years old. His people had long been living in the Black Hills of South Dakota, although they had already been forced to fight battles to keep their homes and sacred grounds. He tells of simple boyhood pranks, of rituals, visions, and of the experiences of fleeing from camp to camp after gold was discovered in the Black Hills in 1874.

Focusing on the Selection

As you read "Wasichus in the Hills," notice what Black Elk tells about his culture and about how it is affected by the soldiers and others moving onto Lakota lands. What values do Black Elk and his band reveal through their actions? Also look for comparisons that Black Elk uses to help you imagine the events and feelings more clearly. Record your responses in your journal as you read.

Wasichus[1] in the Hills

from *Black Elk Speaks*

AS TOLD TO JOHN G. NEIHARDT

IT WAS THE NEXT SUMMER, when I was 11 years old (1874), that the first sign of a new trouble came to us. Our band[2] had been camping on Split-Toe Creek in the Black Hills, and from there we moved to Spring Creek, then to Rapid Creek where it comes out into the prairie. That evening just before sunset, a big thunder cloud came up from the west, and just before the wind struck, there were clouds of split-tail swallows flying all around above us. It was like a part of my vision, and it made me feel queer. The boys tried to hit the swallows with stones and it hurt me to see them doing this, but I could not tell them. I got a stone and acted as though I were going to throw, but I did not. The swallows seemed holy. Nobody hit one, and when I thought about this I knew that of course they could not.

The next day some of the people were building a sweat tepee for a medicine man by the name of Chips, who was going to perform a ceremony and had to be purified first. They say he was the first man who

---

1. **Wasichus** (wah-SEE-choos) literally "stealers of the fat" in Lakota (Sioux); the name Lakota and Dakota people call white people
2. **band** (BAND) *n.* a group made up of several families who lived and traveled together; similar to clans; often identified by its leader, as in Crazy Horse's band

made a sacred ornament for our great chief, Crazy Horse. While they were heating the stones for the sweat tepee, some boys asked me to go with them to shoot squirrels. We went out, and when I was about to shoot at one, I felt very uneasy all at once. So I sat down, feeling queer, and wondered about it. While I sat there I heard a voice that said: "Go at once! Go home!" I told the boys we must go home at once, and we all hurried. When we got back, everybody was excited, breaking camp, catching the ponies and loading the drags; and I heard that while Chips was in the sweat tepee a voice had told him that the band must flee at once because something was going to happen there.

It was nearly sundown when we started, and we fled all that night on the back trail toward Spring Creek, then down that creek to the south fork of the Good River. I rode most of the night in a pony drag because I got too sleepy to stay on a horse. We camped at Good River in the morning, but we stayed only long enough to eat. Then we fled again, upstream, all day long until we reached the mouth of Horse Creek. We were going to stay there, but scouts came to us and said that many soldiers had come into the Black Hills; and that was what Chips saw while he was in the sweat tepee. So we hurried on in the night towards Smoky Earth River (the White), and when we got there, I woke up and it was daybreak. We camped a while to eat, and then went up the Smoky Earth, two camps, to Robinson, for we were afraid of the soldiers up there.

Afterward I learned that it was Pahuska[3] who had led his soldiers into the Black Hills that summer to see what he could find. He had no right to go in there, because all that country was ours. Also the Wasichus had made a treaty with Red Cloud[4] (1868) that said it would be ours as long as grass should grow and water flow. Later I learned too that Pahuska had found there much of the yellow metal that makes the Wasichus crazy; and that is what made the bad trouble, just as it did before, when the hundred were rubbed out.

Our people knew there was yellow metal in little chunks up there; but they did not bother with it, because it was not good for anything.

We stayed all winter at the Soldiers' Town, and all the while the bad trouble was coming fast; for in the fall we heard that some Wasichus had come from the Missouri River to dig in the Black Hills for the yellow metal, because Pahuska had told about it with a voice that went everywhere. Later he got rubbed out for doing that.[5]

---

3. **Pahuska** (pa-HUS-kah) "Long Hair," a name for U.S. General George Custer
4. **Red Cloud** (RED KLOWD) Oglala chief
5. **Later he got rubbed out for doing that** a reference to the Battle of the Little Bighorn (June 25, 1876), in which the Lakota, under the leadership of Chief Crazy Horse and Chief Sitting Bull, killed Custer and his men

South Dakota Historical Society. Black Elk of the Oglala Lakota nation.
Photograph by Joseph Epes.

The people talked about this all winter. Crazy Horse was in the Powder River country and Sitting Bull was somewhere north of the Hills.
Our people at the Soldiers' Town thought we ought to get together and
do something. Red Cloud's people said that the soldiers had gone in
there to keep the diggers out, but we, who were only visiting, did not believe it. We called Red Cloud's people "Hangs-Around-The-Fort," and

our people said they were standing up for the Wasichus, and if we did not do something we should lose the Black Hills. . . .

In the Moon When the Calves Grow Hair (September) there was a big council with the Wasichus on the Smoky Earth River at the mouth of White Clay Creek. I can remember the council, but I did not understand much of it then. Many of the Lakotas were there, also Shyelas and Blue Clouds;[6] but Crazy Horse and Sitting Bull stayed away. In the middle of the circle there was a shade made of canvas. Under this the councilors sat and talked, and all around them there was a crowd of people on foot and horseback. They talked and talked for days, but it was just like wind blowing in the end. I asked my father what they were talking about in there, and he told me that the Grandfather at Washington wanted to lease the Black Hills so that the Wasichus could dig yellow metal, and that the chief of the soldiers had said if we did not do this, the Black Hills would be just like melting snow held in our hands, because the Wasichus would take that country anyway.

It made me sad to hear this. It was such a good place to play and the people were always happy in that country. Also I thought of my vision, and of how the spirits took me there to the center of the world.

After the council we heard that creeks of Wasichus were flowing into the Hills and becoming rivers, and that they were already making towns up there. It looked like bad trouble coming, so our band broke camp and started out to join Crazy Horse on Powder River. We camped on Horsehead Creek, then on the War Bonnet after we crossed the old Wasichu's road[7] that made the trouble that time when the hundred were rubbed out. Grass was growing on it. Then we camped at Sage Creek, then on the Beaver, then on Driftwood Creek, and came again to the Plain of Pine Trees at the edge of the Hills.

The nights were sharp now, but the days were clear and still; and while we were camping there I went up into the Hills alone and sat a long while under a tree. I thought maybe my vision would come back and tell me how I could save that country for my people, but I could not see anything clear. . . .

6. **Shyelas and Blue Clouds** (SHEYE-las) Cheyenne and Arapaho
7. **the old Wasichu's road** the Bozeman Trail, which ran from Fort Laramie, Colorado, to the mining town of Virginia City, Montana: Native Americans objected to settlers' use of this road by gold prospectors because it crossed their main hunting grounds.

POSTREADING

Critical Thinking

1. What did you discover about the values of Black Elk and his people? Which parts of the narrative helped you make this discovery?
2. What do you think would have happened if Black Elk's band had not moved from camp to camp?
3. Which events that Black Elk describes are new to you? How does this knowledge change your understandings of the time and people involved?

Writing Your Response to "Wasichus in the Hills"

In your journal, write your reactions to an event, a scene, or an issue in the excerpt that stands out in your mind. What is it about the situation that makes it memorable? In what way can you relate it to an experience or feeling or issue in the world of today?

Going Back Into the Text: Author's Craft

Speakers and writers often use **comparisons** to help listeners and readers better understand the events, ideas, or feelings being described. In a comparison, something unfamiliar or difficult to explain is compared to something familiar and recognizable to most people. In one kind of comparison, called a **simile**, the word *like* or *as* is used to signal that a comparison is being made.

Black Elk uses a simile when he describes the big council between the Lakota, Shyelas, and Blue Clouds, and the white men: *They talked and talked for days, but it was just like wind blowing in the end.* He compares the talk to wind blowing to help us understand his feelings about the meeting.

With a partner, review the comparisons in the selection, using the following questions as a guide.

1. What do you think Black Elk meant about the council meeting when he compared it to the wind?
2. What other comparison can you find in the excerpt? What two things are being compared? What meaning is made clear to you through the use of this comparison?
3. Would you agree that comparisons are an effective way to make a point clear? Why or why not?

The Council of the Great Peace

Reading the Document in a Cultural Context

The Five Nations of the Iroquois (IHR-uh-kwoi) lived in what is now the northeastern United States. They were independent groups with similar dialects and customs. These individual nations—the Mohawk (MOH-hawk), the Oneida (oh-NEYE-duh), the Onondaga (ahn-uhn-DAW-guh), the Cayuga (kay-YOO-guh), and the Seneca (SEN-ih-kuh)—were often at war with one another. They also faced invasions by other nations who were hostile to them. These situations made the Iroquois' lives very insecure and dangerous. The invasions by other nations made them recognize the need to organize to protect themselves and their land.

According to respected historians and historical papers, the League of the Iroquois, or Confederation of the Five Nations, was formed around 1390. The year was determined according to traditions that were passed on orally from generation to generation. The date was recorded in a document prepared in 1900 by a committee of Iroquois chiefs. The chiefs, who were appointed by the Six Nations Council of Grand River, Canada, met to chronicle the cultural heritage of the Iroquois. (A sixth nation, the Tuscarora (tus-kuh-RAWR-uh), joined the League in 1724.) The written record they prepared became part of a book of historical papers by and about the Iroquois.

In the written account of 1900 created by the chiefs, Dekanawidah (deh-gahn-ah-WEE-dah) is credited with bringing together the nations. According to Iroquois stories that were passed down, he was a great hero. He established the Great Peace between the Five Nations by calling them to sit in council beneath the Tree of the Great Peace. He then presented to the lords (representatives) of the Five Nations the laws and principles by which they would all live. This Code of Dekanawidah became the Constitution of the Five Nations, or the Iroquois constitution. Because the Iroquois did not have a written language, the representatives of each nation memorized the laws and regulations and passed them on orally for generations. Many of these laws were also represented by different symbols on wampum (WAHM-puhm) belts and strings. Each belt or string recalled each law and regulation. Although many of the wampums were lost or destroyed long ago, some survived. They are in the New York State Museum in Albany.

Focusing on the Selection

As you read the excerpts from "The Council of the Great Peace," look for what they reveal about the values and ideals of the Five Nations. What do the codes of behavior and the guides for council procedure tell you about the Iroquois traditions? How does the selection help you understand how powerful the Five Nations of the Iroquois were?

The Council of the Great Peace

from *The Constitution of the Five Nations*

LEAGUE OF THE IROQUOIS

The Great Binding Law, Gayanashagowa[1]

1 I AM DEKANAWIDAH and with the Five Nations' Confederate[2] Lords I plant the Tree of the Great Peace. I plant it in your territory, Adodarhoh,[3] and the Onondaga Nation, in the territory of you who are Firekeepers.

I name the tree the Tree of the Great Long Leaves. Under the shade of this Tree of the Great Peace we spread the soft white feathery down of the globe thistle as seats for you, Adodarhoh, and your cousin Lords.

We place you upon those seats, spread soft with the feathery down of the globe thistle, there beneath the shade of the spreading branches of the Tree of Peace. There shall you sit and watch the Council Fire of

---

1. **Gayanashagowa** (geye-ahn-ah-shah-GOW-uh)
2. **Confederate** (kuhn-FED-er-et) *adj.* a person or group united with others for a common purpose
3. **Adodarhoh** (ah-doh-DAR-hoh) *n.* Chief of Chiefs

the Confederacy of the Five Nations, and all the affairs of the Five Nations shall be transacted at this place before you, Adodarhoh, and your cousin Lords, by the Confederate Lords of the Five Nations.

2 Roots have spread out from the Tree of the Great Peace, one to the north, one to the east, one to the south and one to the west. The name of these roots is The Great White Roots and their nature is Peace and Strength.

If any man or any nation outside the Five Nations shall obey the laws of the Great Peace and make known their disposition[4] to the Lords of the Confederacy, they may trace the Roots to the Tree and if their minds are clean and they are obedient and promise to obey the wishes of the Confederate Council, they shall be welcomed to take shelter beneath the Tree of the Long Leaves.

We place at the top of the Tree of the Long Leaves an Eagle who is able to see afar. If he sees in the distance any evil approaching or any danger threatening he will at once warn the people of the Confederacy.

3 To you Adodarhoh, the Onondaga cousin Lords, I and the other Confederate Lords have entrusted the caretaking and the watching of the Five Nations Council Fire. . . .

When the Lords are assembled the Council Fire shall be kindled, but not with chestnut wood,[5] and Adodarhoh shall formally open the Council.

Then shall Adodarhoh and his cousin Lords, the Fire Keepers, announce the subject for discussion.

The Smoke of the Confederate Council Fire shall ever ascend and pierce the sky so that other nations who may be allies may see the Council Fire of the Great Peace. . . .

7 Whenever the Confederate Lords shall assemble for the purpose of holding a council, the Onondaga Lords shall open it by expressing their gratitude to their cousin Lords and greeting them, and they shall make an address and offer thanks to the earth where men dwell, to the streams of water, the pools, the springs and the lakes, to the maize and the fruits, to the medicinal herbs and trees, to the forest trees for their usefulness, to the animals that serve as food and give their pelts for clothing, to the great winds and the lesser winds, to the Thunderers, to the Sun, the mighty warrior, to the moon, to the messengers of the Creator who reveal his wishes and to the Great Creator who dwells in the heavens above, who gives all the things useful to men, and who is the source and the ruler of health and life.

Then shall the Onondaga Lords declare the council open.

The council shall not sit after darkness has set in.

---

4. **disposition** (dihs-poh-ZISH-uhn) *n.* intention
5. **chestnut wood** Chestnut wood in burning throws out sparks, which would disturb the council.

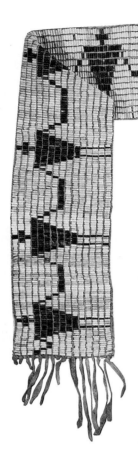

The Washington Covenant Belt. *New York State Museum.* This belt, made of strung beads, or wampum, commemorated the peace agreement between the 13 original colonies and the Iroquois League. What does the belt suggest about the values and ideals of the Iroquois League?

8 The Firekeepers shall formally open and close all councils of the Confederate Lords, they shall pass upon all matters deliberated upon by the two sides and render their decision.

Every Onondaga Lord (or his deputy) must be present at every Confederate Council and must agree with the majority without unwarrantable dissent, so that a unanimous decision may be rendered.

If Adodarhoh or any of his cousin Lords are absent from a Confederate Council, any other Firekeeper may open and close the Council, but the Firekeepers present may not give any decisions, unless the matter is of small importance.

9 All the business of the Five Nations Confederate Council shall be conducted by the two combined bodies of Confederate Lords. First the question shall be passed upon by the Mohawk and Seneca Lords, then it shall be discussed and passed by the Oneida and Cayuga Lords. Their decisions shall then be referred to the Onondaga Lords, (Fire Keepers) for final judgment.

The same process shall obtain when a question is brought before the council by an individual or a War Chief. . . .

17 A bunch of a certain number of shell (wampum) strings each two spans in length shall be given to each of the female families in which the Lordship titles are vested. The right of bestowing the title shall be hereditary in the family of females legally possessing the bunch of shell strings and the strings shall be the token that the females of the family have the proprietary right[6] to the Lordship title for all time to come, subject to certain restrictions hereinafter mentioned.

18 If any Confederate Lord neglects or refuses to attend the Confederate Council, the other Lords of the Nation of which he is a member shall require their War Chief to request the female sponsors of the Lord so guilty of defection to demand his attendance of the Council. If he refuses, the women holding the title shall immediately select another candidate for the title.

---

6. proprietary right (pruh-PREYE-uh-ter-ee REYET) right of ownership

No Lord shall be asked more than once to attend the Confederate Council.

19 If at any time it shall be manifest that a Confederate Lord has not in mind the welfare of the people or disobeys the rules of this Great Law, the men or the women of the Confederacy, or both jointly, shall come to the Council and upbraid the erring Lord through his War Chief. If the complaint of the people through the War Chief is not heeded the first time it shall be uttered again and then if no attention is given a third complaint and warning shall be given. If the Lord is still contumacious[7] the matter shall go to the council of War Chiefs. The War Chiefs shall then divest the erring Lord of his title by order of the women in whom the titleship is vested. When the Lord is deposed the women shall notify the Confederate Lords through their War Chief, and the Confederate Lords shall sanction the act. The women will then select another of their sons as a candidate and the Lords shall elect him. Then shall the chosen one be installed by the Installation Ceremony. . . .

23 Any Lord of the Five Nations Confederacy may construct shell strings (or wampum belts) of any size or length as pledges or records of matters of national or international importance.

When it is necessary to dispatch a shell string by a War Chief or other messenger as the token of a summons, the messenger shall recite the contents of the string to the party to whom it is sent. That party shall repeat the message and return the shell string and if there has been a summons he shall make ready for the journey.

Any of the people of the Five Nations may use shells (or wampum) as the record of a pledge, contract or an agreement entered into and the same shall be binding as soon as shell strings shall have been exchanged by both parties.

24 The Lords of the Confederacy of the Five Nations shall be mentors of the people for all time. The thickness of their skin shall be seven spans—which is to say that they shall be proof against anger, offensive actions and criticism. Their hearts shall be full of peace and good will and their minds filled with a yearning for the welfare of the people of the Confederacy. With endless patience they shall carry out their duty and their firmness shall be tempered with a tenderness for their people. Neither anger nor fury shall find lodgement in their minds and all their words and actions shall be marked by calm deliberation.

25 If a Lord of the Confederacy should seek to establish any authority independent of the jurisdiction of the Confederacy of the Great Peace, which is the Five Nations, he shall be warned three times in open council, first by the women relatives, second by the men relatives and finally by the Lords of the Confederacy of the Nation to which he

---

7. contumacious (kahn-too-MAY-shuhs) *adj.* disobedient

belongs. If the offending Lord is still obdurate[8] he shall be dismissed by the War Chief of his nation for refusing to conform to the laws of the Great Peace. His nation shall then install the candidate nominated by the female name holders of his family. . . .

27 All Lords of the Five Nations Confederacy must be honest in all things. They must not idle or gossip, but be men possessing those honorable qualities that make true royaneh.[9] It shall be a serious wrong for anyone to lead a Lord into trivial affairs, for the people must ever hold their Lords high in estimation out of respect to their honorable positions.

28 When a candidate Lord is to be installed he shall furnish four strings of shells (or wampum) one span in length bound together at one end. Such will constitute the evidence of his pledge to the Confederate Lords that he will live according to the constitution of the Great Peace and exercise justice in all affairs.

When the pledge is furnished the Speaker of the Council must hold the shell strings in his hand and address the opposite side of the Council Fire and he shall commence his address saying: "Now behold him. He has now become a Confederate Lord. See how splendid he looks." An address may then follow. At the end of it he shall send the bunch of shell strings to the opposite side and they shall be received as evidence of the pledge. Then shall the opposite side say:

"We now do crown you with the sacred emblem of the deer's antlers, the emblem of your Lordship. You shall now become a mentor of the people of the Five Nations. The thickness of your skin shall be seven spans—which is to say that you shall be proof against anger, offensive actions and criticism. Your heart shall be filled with peace and good will and your mind filled with a yearning for the welfare of the people of the Confederacy. With endless patience you shall carry out your duty and your firmness shall be tempered with tenderness for your people. Neither anger nor fury shall find lodgement in your mind and all your words and actions shall be marked with calm deliberation. In all of your deliberations in the Confederate Council, in your efforts at law making, in all your official acts, self interest shall be cast into oblivion. Cast not over your shoulder behind you the warnings of the nephews and nieces should they chide[10] you for any error or wrong you may do, but return to the way of the Great Law which is just and right. Look and listen for the welfare of the whole people and have always in view not only the present but also the coming generations, even those whose faces are yet beneath the surface of the ground—the unborn of the future Nation."...

---

8. **obdurate** (AHB-duhr-uht) *adj.* stubbornly persistent in behaving improperly or wrongly

9. **royaneh** (LOY-ah-nee) *n.* lords

10. **chide** (CHEYED) *v.* scold

Critical Thinking

1. What did you learn about the values and ideals of the Five Nations of the Iroquois from their constitution?
2. What does the Tree of Peace stand for? Do you think it is a good symbol for the Five Nations? Why or why not?
3. In what ways is the Iroquois constitution similar to the U.S. constitution? In what ways is it different?

Writing Your Response to "The Council of the Great Peace"

In the Iroquois constitution, Dekanawidah identifies several qualities he expects the confederation lords to have. In your journal, choose one quality from this list that you feel is, or is not, important for a lawmaker to possess. Do you think this quality is as important today as it was at the time of the Iroquois League?

Going Back Into the Text: Author's Craft

In learning about history, readers have a variety of sources available to them. Some of these are called **primary sources**. A primary source is a firsthand account that is produced or recorded by a person or persons who see or participate in an event. Examples of some primary sources include diaries, letters, newspapers, laws, and treaties. Primary sources are also written versions of oral sources. Stories, songs, speeches, and interviews are examples of oral sources. Though some written versions are created long after events have taken place, and are based on the memories and traditions of a group of people, these versions are no less valuable than are firsthand accounts. A reader does have to be aware, however, that these accounts may not be completely accurate. There also may be more than one version of the same event. This is due to differences in people's memories and to translators' various interpretations of words. In addition, as explanations are passed down through generations, people contribute their own individual touches. Thus, a reader must try to separate fact from fiction by carefully evaluating historical explanations. The written record of the Iroquois constitution is considered to be a primary source. It is based on Iroquois oral traditions.

With a partner, use the following questions to help you evaluate what you have read.

1. Who produced the information?
2. Why was the account written?
3. When was it written?
4. What relationship does the writer or writers have to the event or situations described?
5. What information does the writer or writers give about the event, the time, and the people involved?
6. What other sources of information might be checked to provide another view?

The Indians' Night Promises to be Dark

Responding to Literature

Notice the sidenotes in the margins of this selection. These notes reflect one student's reading of Chief Seattle's speech, "The Indians' Night Promises to be Dark." The student sees how Seattle's values and traditions influenced his attitude toward white people. Compare this student's observations with your own.

Reading the Author in a Cultural Context

Seattle (1786-1866), whose real name according to some sources was See-ahth (SEE-ahth), was chief of the Suquamish (soo-KWAHM-ish) and Duwamish (doo-WAHM-ish) nations in the Pacific Northwest region of what is now the United States. Around the time Seattle was born, the United States was a young nation.

By the time Seattle became chief of his people, U.S. settlers had moved west, pushing the Native Americans out of their homelands and onto reservations. Despite what had happened in other areas, Seattle and his people remained at peace with the whites who had moved into the Northwest. Seattle's bands kept the peace even after their lands were included in the Washington Territory, organized by the U.S. government in 1853.

In 1855, Isaac Stevens, the first Governor of the Washington Territory, held councils with Seattle's bands. He told of the plans for placing them, and other Northwest bands, on reservations. The speech that follows is Chief Seattle's response to the Governor's address.

It is important to note that speeches made by Native Americans were usually written down by white people who were familiar with the language of the speaker or who recorded the words of an interpreter. But translations were not always exact, and interpreters did not always give the meaning the Native Americans intended. In addition, years of retellings and rewritings often led to versions with made-up details. The text of Chief Seattle's speech that follows, however, is considered by historians to be the most accurate in translation and meaning.

Focusing on the Selection

As you read "The Indians' Night Promises to be Dark," look for the special way Seattle reveals how he feels about the governor's plans and why. What does he convey about the differences between the values and traditions of his people and those of white people? Also keep in mind that Seattle spoke to an audience made up of his people and some white settlers. Why do you think he chose the words he did?

The Indians' Night Promises to be Dark

CHIEF SEATTLE

YONDER SKY THAT HAS WEPT TEARS of compassion upon my people for centuries untold, and which to us appears changeless and eternal, may change. Today is fair. Tomorrow it may be overcast with clouds. My words are like the stars that never change. Whatever Seattle says the great chief at Washington can rely upon with as much certainty as he can upon the return of the sun or the seasons. The White Chief[1] says that Big Chief at Washington[2] sends us greetings of friendship and goodwill. This is kind of him for we know he has little need of our friendship in return. His people are many. They are like the grass that covers vast prairies. My people are few. They resemble the scattering trees of a storm-swept plain. The great—and I presume—good White Chief sends us word that he wishes to buy our lands but is willing to allow us enough to live comfortably. This indeed appears just, even generous, for the Red Man no longer has rights that he need respect, and the offer may be wise also, as we are no longer in need of an extensive country.

There was a time when our people covered the land as the waves of a wind-ruffled sea cover its shell paved floor, but that time long since passed away with the greatness of tribes that are now but a mournful memory. I will not dwell on, nor mourn over, our untimely decay, nor reproach my paleface brothers with hastening it as we too may have been somewhat to blame.

Youth is impulsive. When our young men grow angry at some real or imaginary wrong, and disfigure their faces with black paint, it denotes that their hearts are black, and that they are often cruel and relentless, and our old men and old women are unable to restrain them. Thus it has ever been. Thus it was when the white man first began to push our forefathers westward. But let us hope that the hostilities between us may never return. We would have everything to lose and nothing to gain. Revenge by young men is considered gain, even at the cost of their own lives, but old men who stay at home in times of war, and mothers who have sons to lose, know better.

I know from studying U.S. history that the government broke agreements with Native Americans. I think that's why Seattle said he wouldn't change his mind.

Seattle shows a willingness to give in to a situation that he can't change. His words here seem to contain a mixture of sadness and sarcasm. I wonder how he sounded when he said those words.

Seattle said those words almost 150 years ago, yet what he says applies even today to people everywhere.

---

1. **White Chief** refers to Governor Isaac Stevens
2. **Big Chief at Washington** refers to President Franklin Pierce, the 14th President of the United States

Photograph of Chief Seattle of the Suquamish and Duwamish nations of the present-day northwestern United States.

Did Seattle speak these words in anger? Perhaps not, but he certainly must have raised his voice and commanded attention from his audience.

Our good father at Washington—for I presume he is now our father as well as yours, since King George has moved his boundaries further north—our great and good father, I say, sends us words that if we do as he desires he will protect us. His brave warriors will be to us a bristling wall of strength, and his wonderful ships of war will fill our harbors so that our ancient enemies far to the northward—the Hydas and Tsimpsians[3]—will cease to frighten our women, children and old men. Then in reality will he be our father and we his children. But can that ever be? Your God is not our God! Your God loves your people and hates mine. He folds his strong protecting arms lovingly about the pale face and leads him by the hand as a father leads his infant son—but He has forsaken His red children—if they really are His. Our God, the Great Spirit, seems also to have forsaken us. Your God makes your people wax[4] strong every day. Soon they will fill all the land. Our people are ebbing away like a rapidly receding tide that will never return. The white man's God cannot love our people or He would protect them. They seem to be orphans who can look nowhere for help. How then can we be brothers?

3. **Hydas** (HEYE-dahz) *n.* literally means "people"; and **Tsimpsians** (TSIMP-see-unz) *n.* literally means "people of the Skeena River"
4. **wax** (WAKS) *v.* grow in strength or number

How can your God become our God and renew our prosperity and awaken in us dreams of returning greatness. If we have a common heavenly father He must be partial—for He came to His paleface children. We never saw Him. He gave you laws but had no word for his red children whose teeming multitudes once filled this vast continent as stars fill the firmament. No; we are two distinct races with separate origins and separate destinies. There is little in common between us.

To us the ashes of our ancestors are sacred and their resting place is hallowed ground. You wander far from the graves of your ancestors and seemingly without regret. Your religion was written upon tables of stone[5] by the iron finger of your God so that you could not forget. The Red Man could never comprehend nor remember it. Our religion is the traditions of our ancestors—the dreams of our old men, given them in the solemn hours of night by the Great Spirit; and the visions of our sachems,[6] and is written in the hearts of our people.

Your dead cease to love you and the land of their nativity as soon as they pass the portals of the tomb and wander way beyond the stars. They are soon forgotten and never return. Our dead never forget the beautiful world that gave them being. They still love its verdant valleys, its murmuring rivers, its magnificent mountains, sequestered vales and verdant lined lakes and bays, and ever yearn in tender, fond affection over the lonely hearted living, and often return from the Happy Hunting Ground to visit, guide, console and comfort them.

Day and night cannot dwell together. The Red Man has ever fled the approach of the White Man, as the morning mist flees before the morning sun.

However, your proposition seems fair and I think that my people will accept it and will retire to the reservation you offer them. Then we will dwell in peace, for the words of the Great White Chief seem to be the words of nature speaking to my people out of dense darkness.

It matters little where we pass the remnant of our days. They will not be many. The Indians' night promises to be dark. Not a single star of hope hovers above his horizon. Sad-voiced winds moan in the distance. Grim fate seems to be on the Red Man's trail, and wherever he goes he will hear the approaching footsteps of his fell[7] destroyer and prepare stolidly[8] to meet his doom, as does the wounded doe that hears the approaching footsteps of the hunter.

I know that the Native Americans honored their ancestors. Here Seattle is saying that they believe their ancestors are still all around them. They do not separate their past and present because both are bound together in the way they live every day of their lives.

Seattle uses a comparison to make his point about the Native Americans and whites not being able to live together.

Now I understand the title, "The Indians' Night Promises to be Dark." Seattle seems to see no hope for his people. How sad that must have been for him to say those words.

---

5. tables of stone the Ten Commandments
6. sachems (SAY-chemz) *n.* leaders or chiefs of the people
7. fell (FEL) *adj.* fierce, terrible
8. stolidly (STAH-lihd-lee) *adv.* showing no emotion

A few more moons.[9] A few more winters—and not one of the descendants of the mighty hosts that once moved over this broad land or lived in happy homes, protected by the Great Spirit, will remain to mourn over the graves of a people—once more powerful and hopeful than yours. But why should I mourn at the untimely fate of my people? Tribe follows tribe, and nation follows nation, like the waves of the sea. It is the order of nature, and regret is useless. Your time of decay may be distant, but it will surely come, for even the White Man whose God walked and talked with him as friend with friend, cannot be exempt from the common destiny. We may be brothers after all. We will see.

We will ponder your proposition and when we decide will let you know. But should we accept it, I here and now make this condition that we will not be denied the privilege without molestation[10] of visiting at any time the tombs of our ancestors, friends and children. Every part of this soil is sacred in the estimation of my people. Every hillside, every valley, every plain and grove, has been hallowed by some sad or happy event in days long vanished. Even the rocks, which seem to be dumb and dead as they swelter in the sun along the silent shore, thrill with memories of stirring events connected with the lives of my people, and the very dust upon which you now stand responds more lovingly to their footsteps than to yours, because it is rich with the blood of our ancestors and our bare feet are conscious of the sympathetic touch. Our departed braves, fond mothers, glad, happy-hearted maidens, and even our little children who lived here and rejoiced here for a brief season, will love these somber solitudes and at eventide they greet shadowy returning spirits. And when the last Red Man shall be perished, and the memory of my tribe shall have become a myth among the White Men, these shores will swarm with the invisible dead of my tribe, and when your children's children think themselves alone in the field, the store, the shop, upon the highway, or in the silence of the pathless woods, they will not be alone. In all the earth there is no place dedicated to solitude. At night when the streets of your cities and villages are silent and you think them deserted, they will throng with the returning hosts that once filled them and still love this beautiful land. The White Man will never be alone.

Let him be just and deal kindly with my people, for the dead are not powerless. Dead, did I say? There is no death, only a change of worlds.

---

9. **moons** (MOONZ) *n.* months
10. **molestation** (moh-les-TAY-shun) *n.* interference

POSTREADING

Critical Thinking

1. What were Chief Seattle's feelings about the U.S. government's plans for the Washington Territory?
2. What differences in values and traditions between his people and white people did he reveal in his speech? What similarities did he reveal? What did he believe about the destiny of each group?
3. Which parts of Seattle's speech made a particular impact on you? Why? What sense do you now have about the kind of man that Seattle was?

Writing Your Response to "The Indians' Night Promises to be Dark"

In your journal, write a list of questions you might ask Chief Seattle if you were a journalist interviewing him after hearing his speech. What ideas, events, and situations would you like to know more about?

Going Back Into the Text: Author's Craft

A **speech** is an oral presentation of ideas. It may be written down ahead of time and memorized, or put on note cards to be referred to during the presentation, or organized in the mind and presented from memory. A speaker may begin with a statement of a point of view or opinion and then offer details to support that viewpoint or opinion. Or a speaker may first use descriptions, cite some facts, and offer comments about a situation in order to build up to the crucial points to be made. Two important guidelines to keep in mind while presenting a speech are the purpose and the audience. A speaker adjusts tone of voice and facial expressions, and perhaps uses gestures, to capture an audience and keep its attention.

With a partner, exchange ideas about Chief Seattle's speech. Use the following questions to help guide your discussion.

1. How would you explain Chief Seattle's purpose? Do you think he planned what he was going to say?
2. How would you describe the structure of the speech? Do you think it caught people's attention and kept it? Why? Do you think it was a powerful speech?
3. What elements in the speech appealed to people's reason? To people's emotions?

MAKING CONNECTIONS

Native American Arts

When Europeans arrived in the Americas, they thought of Native Americans as a single people. Native Americans, however, belong to many different groups, each with its own language and culture. Yet these groups have much in common. In every Native American culture, people celebrate nature and stress the importance of living in harmony with the universe.

The Navajo celebrate their oneness with nature in their art. A weaver believes that her *hozho* (HUH-zoh), or spiritual harmony, enters a design during the weaving. So she always weaves a small imperfection into her work to let the hozho escape.

The people of the San Idefonso pueblo, or village, live on the upper Rio Grande River, not far from the Navajo. Although these groups have different ways of life, the Pueblo people also capture the power and beauty of the natural world in their art. They are master potters who still create works like the jar shown here.

The Navajo learned silversmithing in the 1800s and quickly adapted the art to their culture. Navajo silversmiths, like other artisans of this culture, draw their inspiration from nature. Typical of their work are the squash-blossom necklaces shown here.

LINKING
Literature, Culture, and Theme

Compare and contrast the traditional values represented in Native American art with the views expressed in the literature of this section.

▼ Beauty holds an important place in the Navajo view of the world. How is that value reflected both in Navajo art and in the literature of this section?

▼ What attitudes about nature are expressed in Native American art and literature? Why do you think Native Americans have valued nature so highly?

▼ What similarities do you see between the values and the attitudes reflected in the art shown on these pages and those expressed in the literature of this section?

They Are Taking the Holy Elements from Mother Earth

Reading the Author in a Cultural Context

The voice in the next selection is from the Navajo, a nation in what is now the southwestern United States. The essay expresses a strong reaction to the attitudes held by white people toward Native Americans and about what white people have done to the land and the Native Americans' way of life there.

The Navajo experience that Asa Bazhonoodah (aysah ba-zhoo-NOO-dah) tells about in "They Are Taking the Holy Elements from Mother Earth" describes the effects of massive strip mining during the late 1960s on the land and on her people. Strip mining removes the surface layers of earth in order to expose and extract the minerals. This type of mining leaves gaping holes in the earth, stirs up dust everywhere, and destroys plant life.

The Navajo Reservation extends over parts of Arizona, Utah, and New Mexico, an area rich in mineral deposits such as coal, oil, and uranium. When the mineral wealth of the reservation was first discovered in 1921, Standard Oil Company, a large U.S. corporation, gathered a council of Navajo elders and asked if it could strip mine the Navajo land. When the elders refused to give permission, the Bureau of Indian Affairs, an agency of the U.S. government, appointed another tribal council. This council agreed to the strip mining. Because of land disputes between the Navajo and the Hopi (HOH-pee), a Pueblo people whose reservation borders the Navajo reservation, strip mining did not begin until some years later. Large-scale mining by corporations created many problems for the Navajo people, and the Navajo eventually began to reconsider the policy of leasing their land for mining.

Focusing on the Selection

As you read the essay, think about the writer's voice. Is it a voice of praise, of protest, of sadness, or of something else? What does this writer reveal about the values of her people and the problems they must deal with? Also think about the essay form the writer has chosen to present her message. Do you think an essay is an appropriate form to use? Record your insights in your journal as you read.

They Are Taking the Holy Elements from Mother Earth

ASA BAZHONOODAH

IN ENGLISH THEY CALL ME "Kee Shelton's Mother." In Navajo my name is Asa Bazhonoodah, "Woman who had squaw dance." I am eighty-four years old.

I am originally from Black Mesa.[1] I was born and raised there. My parents and grandparents were all from that same area.

At present I live east and not far from the mining site. I was born in a hogan[2] which was still standing the last time I saw it. But now I don't know, maybe they have torn it down.

They tell me my parents used to live right down at the mining site at the time my mother was pregnant with me. Then when she was going to give birth to me they moved eastward to the place where I was born. This is not too far from the place they grind the coal. That is where I

---

1. **Black Mesa** (BLAK MAY-sah) Black Mesa is in northern Arizona. *Mesa* means "table" in Spanish. It is called Black Mesa because of the coal found there, which makes it look black from a distance.
2. **hogan** (HOH-gan) *n.* a six- or eight-sided traditional Navajo dwelling

Natural History Museum of Los Angeles. Photograph of Navajos and their hogans, or dwellings, taken in 1895. What do these dwellings suggest about the Navajo way of life?

was raised and after I got married my husband and I lived at the same place. During that time my husband cleared land and built a fence for a cornfield near where we lived. He used to move to the cornfield to plant and harvest the corn.

My mother died and was buried right there at our permanent home. Following that my husband died during the time people were killed by some kind of disease and he also is buried there. After this happened I moved to the cornfield which my husband had established. The cornfield is still there and I plant a little bit of corn every spring.

I strongly object to the strip mining for many reasons. . . .

The particles of coal dust that contaminate the water kill our animals. I know this for a fact because many of the sheep belonging to my children were killed. I have some cows and they started dying off. And now it has become too frequent, almost every day. We were asked to report every dead sheep or animal but it is impossible to do that because of the lack of communication. We don't have a trading post or a police station on Black Mesa where we could report these happenings.

We do not like the explosions at the mine because it scares our horses. Many of us herd sheep on horseback and every time an explosion goes off it scares the animals and they are afraid and try to run away.

The coal mine is destroying our grazing lands, because the grass is being put under the earth, and our sheep are getting thin, and not having many lambs. The mine also destroys our springs and water holes, so we have great trouble trying to water our livestock. My sheep are my life. Black Mesa is my "billfold," as the white man says. Black Mesa gives life to animals and these animals give us money. The stuff I prod my donkey with is like the pencil the whites use.

A long time ago the earth was placed here for us, the people, the Navajo. It gives us corn and we consider her our mother.

When Mother Earth needs rain we give pollen[3] and use the prayers that were given us when we came from the earth. That brings rain. Black Mesa area is used to ask for rain. And afterward (after the mining) we don't know what it will be like. We make prayers for all blessings for Mother Earth, asking that we may use her legs, her body, and her spirit to make ourselves more powerful and durable. After this the pollen is thrown into the water.

Air is one of the Holy Elements, it is important in prayer. Wooded areas are being cut down. Now the air is becoming bad, not working. The herbs that are taken from Mother Earth and given to a woman during childbirth no longer grow in the cut area. The land looks burned.

The Earth is our mother. The white man is ruining our mother. I don't know the white man's ways, but to us the Mesa, the air, the water, are Holy Elements. We pray to these Holy Elements in order for our people to flourish and perpetuate the well-being of each generation.

Even when we are small, our cradle is made from the things given to us from Mother Earth. We use these elements all of our lives and when we die we go back to Mother Earth.

When we were first put on Earth, the herbs and medicine were also put here for us to use. These have become part of our prayers to Mother Earth. We should realize it for if we forget these things we will vanish as the people. This is why I don't like it. The whites have neglected and misused the Earth. Soon the Navajo will resemble the Anasazi.[4] The wind took them away because they misused Earth. The white men wish that nothing will be left of us after his is over. They want us like the Anasazi.

Mother Earth is like a horse. We put out hay and grain to bring in the horse. So it is when we put out pollen to bring life from Mother Earth. We pray to Mother Earth to ask blessings from the water, the sun, and the moon. Why are they going up there (to the moon)? I'm also against this. This fooling around with the sacred elements.

---

 3. **pollen** (PAH-lihn) *n.* the powderlike substance formed by the flower; used in ceremonies and, when praying, as an offering to the spirits
 4. **Anasazi** (ah-nah-SAH-zee) *n.* a Navajo word meaning "the ancient ones"; an early southwest culture that thrived from 100 BC to 1300 AD

This pollution is what I'm especially against. When I first realized I had eyes, I saw that it was clear. Now it is getting hazy and gray outside. The coal mine is causing it. Because of the bad air, animals are not well, they don't feel well. They know what is happening and are dying. Peabody Coal Company is tampering with the Holy Elements, and this must be stopped.

I don't think Peabody Coal Company can replant the land. There is nothing but rocks, no soil. I don't see how they could replant. The soil is underneath. They advocate that this place will be beautiful when they finish. I don't believe that this place will be beautiful when they finish. If they replant, they will not replant our herbs. Even now our herbs are vanishing.

I have gone three times looking for herbs. I couldn't recognize the place where we find them. Finally I found some plants but they were scorched. I couldn't find my way around the mountain because it was so disturbed by the mining operation.

We have herbs that cure diseases that white medicine doesn't cure. Sometime the people come here to find medicine when the Public Health Service doesn't cure them. They pray and give Mother Earth something for curing them. This the white people do not know about.

Our prayer and healing have been tampered with and they don't work as well anymore.

How can we give something of value to Mother Earth to repay the damages that the mining had done to her. We still ask her for blessings and healing, even when she is hurt.

They are taking water and the other Holy Elements from her veins.

I don't want highways built because stock will be run over and the children hurt.

I see the cedar trees next to the ponds they built have turned red. The grasses are dying.

I want to see them stop taking water from inside the Mesa. The water underground, which works with that water that falls to the surface of Mother Earth, will wash away.

I want to see the burial grounds left alone. All of my relatives' graves are being disturbed.

How much would you ask if your mother had been harmed? There is no way that we can be repaid for the damages to our Mother. No amount of money we repay, money cannot give birth to anything. I want to see the mining stopped.

POSTREADING

Critical Thinking

1. What is the writer's attitude toward white people? Give examples from the essay that led you to understand her feelings.
2. What insights about the writer's culture have you gained from her choice of words and descriptions?
3. What attitudes expressed by Asa Bazhonoodah do you find similar to your own or to those of someone you know?

Writing Your Response to "They Are Taking the Holy Elements from Mother Earth"

In your journal, copy from the essay a phrase or statement that you feel is particularly interesting, powerful, truthful, or controversial. Then explain why you chose the words you did.

Going Back Into the Text: Author's Craft

An **essay** is a short work of nonfiction, usually focused on one topic. The purpose may be to inform, persuade, instruct, or amuse. If the topic and purpose are to inform or persuade, then the essay will be more **formal** and carefully structured. A statement at or near the beginning will let a reader know the topic very quickly. Then the writer will set forth his or her feelings and opinions in detail, supporting the main point of view with whatever facts are available.

If the topic is light and the purpose is to amuse, the essay will be more **informal** and loosely structured. The writer might include descriptions, stories, and anecdotes to give the essay a friendly, conversational tone.

With a partner, use the following questions to review the elements of an essay found in "They Are Taking the Holy Elements from Mother Earth."

1. What would you say are the topic and purpose of Asa Bazhonoodah's essay?
2. Is this essay an example of formal or informal structure? Give evidence from the essay to back up your answer.
3. Do you feel the essay is a good writing form for this topic? What topic might you consider for an essay?

Reviewing the Theme

1. Choose two of the speakers represented in the selections for the theme "Voices of the First Nations." Explain in what ways the experiences described by the speakers were similar and different.
2. What did you learn about Native Americans through these selections? Were your attitudes changed as a result of your reading? If so, how?
3. Which viewpoints expressed in this section do you agree with? Why? Are there any you disagree with? Explain.

Theme 5:
The Long Road from Slavery

THE AUTHORS represented in this theme deal with the subject of slavery and the enslaved Africans' and African Americans' struggle for freedom. However, the perspective from which each writer views the subject is quite different. In one selection, you will share songs that were a source of inspiration to and communication between enslaved African Americans in the United States. In another selection, you will read about the horrors of an ocean voyage on a slave ship from the perspective of a young African male. In a third selection, you will see slavery during the 1800s through the eyes of a popular African American writer of the 1800s. You will also take a broader look at the subject of slavery as two contemporary African American writers link the present with the past.

The writers represented in these selections explore both the brutality of slavery and the strength of the human spirit. Out of this strong human spirit rose a creative energy powerful enough for an oppressed people to produce new forms of music and literature. The spiritual and the slave narrative are two examples. Most spirituals were originally sung

Underground Railroad. Painting by African American artist Jerry Pinkney. Created for *National Geographic* magazine in 1984. The Underground Railroad was a secret system that helped thousands of African Americans escape from slavery in the South.

by African American slaves working in the fields. The narratives described the cruel experiences of enslavement. The narratives of former slaves were used to gain support from abolitionists and others opposed to slavery. Both forms of expression have become a part of U.S. culture.

The Drinking Gourd
Steal Away

Reading the Spirituals in a Cultural Context

Music has always played a large role in African culture. It has been part of celebrations and ceremonies, and also of everyday work activities. Music and dance remained a major link to African life for Africans brought to the Americas in slavery. Slave owners found that their slaves worked harder and faster if they sang while they worked. So singing in the fields was allowed, even encouraged. Singing also became a means of secret communication for African American slaves.

In the early 1800s, African American music took on a new character. At that time, religious revivalism was sweeping across the nation. Large outdoor meetings were held to stir religious spirit. Scripture readings and loud singing played a major role in these meetings. African American slaves were allowed to attend, and the Bible stories of Moses who, in the Old Testament, led the enslaved Jews out of Egypt, greatly interested them. African Americans began using the stories of the ancient Jews as lyrics, or words, for their own songs. They blended these lyrics with traditional African music to develop a unique style of music that became known as the spiritual.

Spirituals were called "sorrow songs" by W.E.B. Du Bois (1868-1963), an African American historian and civil rights leader. They expressed the frustration of oppression and a longing for freedom. The songs were passed down by word of mouth, and were often changed or added to over time by different individuals. As a result, some spirituals have several versions. Many also contained messages.

A particularly important message was communicated in "The Drinking Gourd." (A gourd is a hard-shelled fruit that can be scooped out and used as a cup or dipping object.) The words of "The Drinking Gourd" told enslaved African Americans that a star constellation called the Drinking Gourd, or the Big Dipper, was a marker they could rely upon to help them find the way north.

One interpretation of the lyrics of "Steal Away" emphasizes the Christian message in the call for religious salvation. However, disguised in the religious words is a message to the enslaved to steal away to freedom.

Focusing on the Selections

As you read the lyrics to "The Drinking Gourd" and "Steal Away," consider what you know about slavery. What kind of life were African American slaves fleeing? What obstacles did they have to overcome along the way? Also notice how the repetition of certain phrases in the songs creates a rhythm.

The Drinking Gourd

Follow the drinking gourd,
Follow the drinking gourd,
For the old man is a-waitin'
    for to carry you to freedom
Follow the drinking gourd.

When the sun comes back
    and the first quail[1] calls,
Follow the drinking gourd.
Then old man is a-waitin'
    for to carry you to freedom
Follow the drinking gourd.

The riverbank'll make a mighty good road.
The dead trees'll show you the way.
And the left foot, peg foot,[2] travelling on.
Just you follow the drinking gourd.

Now the river ends between two hills,
Follow the drinking gourd.
And there's another river on the other side.
Just you follow the drinking gourd.

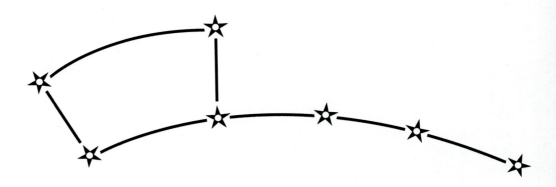

---

1. **quail** (KWAYL) *n.* a game bird
2. **peg foot** (PEG FUT) a wooden leg

Steal Away

Steal away, Steal away, Steal away to Jesus,
Steal away, Steal away home,
I ain't got long to stay here.

My Lord calls me, he calls me by the thunder;
The trumpet sounds within my soul,
I ain't got long to stay here.

Green trees bending, poor sinner stands a-trembling,
The trumpet sounds within my soul,
I ain't got long to stay here.

My Lord calls me, he calls me by the lightening,
The trumpet sounds within-a my soul,
I ain't got long to stay here.

Engraving of a fugitive enslaved African American by an unknown artist. What connections can you make between the spirituals and the picture?

Critical Thinking

1. What do the lyrics of these two songs tell you about the actual road from slavery and the people who traveled it?
2. What do you know about the conditions in which African American slaves lived that would make them want to "steal away" and "follow the drinking gourd"?
3. What emotional effect do the lyrics of these songs have on you today?

Writing Your Response to "The Drinking Gourd" and "Steal Away"

In your journal, write about the feeling or mood created in each song. Give examples from the songs to explain why you think as you do.

Going Back Into the Text: Author's Craft

Writers, especially lyricists and poets, use **repetition** to emphasize meaning, to link ideas, and to create rhythm in their writing. You know from your own writing experiences that unplanned and careless repetition is usually boring, but carefully planned repetition is often very effective.

A writer might choose to repeat a word, a phrase, a line, or a group of lines. If a line or a group of lines is repeated at regular intervals in a poem or song, it is called a **refrain.** Frequently, the refrain communicates the main idea or theme of the work.

With a partner, reread the lyrics to "The Drinking Gourd" and "Steal Away," paying attention to the repetitions. Then share your responses to the following questions.

1. How is repetition used to create rhythm in the songs?
2. Which repetitions create a refrain in each of the songs?
3. How is repetition used to emphasize meaning in each song?
4. What songs do you know that use repetitions to create rhythm? Which of these songs also convey meaning through refrain?

The Slave Auction
The Slave Ship

Reading the Authors in a Cultural Context

Frances Ellen Watkins Harper never personally experienced the trauma of a slave auction. Yet she was able to use the power of words to create the image of the auction in a reader's mind. This image, in turn, stirs strong emotion over the horror of human beings selling other human beings.

Frances E. W. Harper was born free in Baltimore, Maryland. Orphaned early in life, she was raised by an aunt and uncle. She attended school, where she developed a love for writing. Later on, in the 1850s, she put her love of writing to work for the abolitionist, or antislavery, movement.

Harper's work for human rights was not limited to a concern for racial justice. She was also involved in women's rights organizations and religious groups. Despite the tremendous demands on her time by these activities, Harper published several volumes of poetry, *Poems on Miscellaneous Subjects* (1854) and *Poems* (1871). "The Slave Auction" is from the first collection of poems. The passion in her writing made her a popular poet. Many fans considered hers to be a voice that spoke to the needs of the enslaved and the free alike.

Olaudah Equiano (oh-LOW-duh ek-wee-AH-noh) knew only too well the terror of being on an auction block. He was sold several times within his native Africa even before being shipped to Barbados, where he was sold to a Virginia plantation owner.

His autobiography, *The Interesting Narrative of the Life of Olaudah Equiano*, was published in England in 1789. In the book, Equiano described his childhood in Africa, his abduction around age 11, and his life after being sold into slavery. He bought his freedom in 1766 from his final owner, a British naval captain. Equiano then worked as a sailor, traveling as far as the Arctic. But he never was able to realize a dream of returning to Africa.

Equiano settled in England and intensified his fight against the slave trade. He helped bring the terrible conditions on board the slave ships to the attention of British naval authorities. In writing his autobiography, he gave a firsthand account of what being enslaved was like. It was one of the earliest books to be published in which African life was described by an African. Equiano's story is not just interesting, it is authentic. (The autobiography was later published under the title *Equiano's Travels*, from which "The Slave Ship" was taken.)

Focusing on the Selections

As you read "The Slave Auction" and "The Slave Ship," think about the emotions aroused in the people involved in slave trading. What were the feelings of the abducted Africans toward the traders? What were the attitudes of the traders toward the Africans? How might bystanders have felt as they observed the abductions and trading? Record your responses in your journal as you read.

The Slave Auction

FRANCES E. W. HARPER

The sale began—young girls were there,
　Defenceless in their wretchedness,
Whose stifled sobs of deep despair
　Revealed their anguish and distress.

And mothers stood with streaming eyes,
　And saw their dearest children sold;
Unheeded[1] rose their bitter cries,
　While tyrants bartered them for gold.

And woman, with her love and truth—
　For these in sable[2] forms may dwell—
Gaz'd on the husband of her youth,
　With anguish none may paint or tell.

And men, whose sole crime was their hue,[3]
　The impress[4] of their Maker's hand,
And frail and shrieking children, too,
　Were gathered in that mournful band.

Ye who have laid your love to rest,
　And wept above their lifeless clay,
Know not the anguish of that breast,
　Whose lov'd are rudely torn away.

Ye may not know how desolate
　Are bosoms[5] rudely forced to part,
And how a dull and heavy weight
　Will press the life-drops from the heart.

Photograph of the auction block in Fredericksburg, Virginia, where enslaved African Americans were sold before the Civil War. Why do you think the auction block was preserved?

---

1. **unheeded** (uhn-HEE-ded) *adj.* unnoticed; disregarded
2. **sable** (SAY-bul) *adj.* dark in color
3. **hue** (HYOO) *n.* color
4. **impress** (IHM-pres) *n.* an impression or mark
5. **bosoms** (BUZ-uhmz) *n.* the family, people who feel close to one another

The Slave Ship

from *Equiano's Travels*

OLAUDAH EQUIANO

THE FIRST OBJECT THAT SALUTED[1] MY EYES when I arrived on the coast was the sea, and a slave ship which was then riding at anchor and waiting for its cargo. These filled me with astonishment, which was soon converted into terror when I was carried on board. I was immediately handled and tossed up to see if I was sound by some of the crew, and I was now persuaded that I had gotten into a world of bad spirits and that they were going to kill me. Their complexions too differing so much from ours, their long hair and the language they spoke (which was very different from any I had ever heard) united to confirm me in this belief. Indeed such were the horrors of my views and fears at the moment that, if ten thousand worlds had been my own, I would have freely parted with them all to have exchanged my condition with that of the meanest slave in my own country. . . .

While we stayed on the coast I was mostly on deck, and one day, to my great astonishment, I saw one of these vessels coming in with the sails up. As soon as the whites saw it they gave a great shout, at which we were amazed; and the more so as the vessel appeared larger by approaching nearer. At last she came to an anchor in my sight, and when

1. **saluted** (suh-LOOT-ed) *v.* met

the anchor was let go I and my countrymen who saw it were lost in astonishment to observe the vessel stop, and were now convinced it was done by magic. Soon after this the other ship got her boats out, and they came on board of us, and the people of both ships seemed very glad to see each other. Several of the strangers also shook hands with us black people, and made motions with their hands, signifying I suppose we were to go to their country; but we did not understand them. At last, when the ship we were in had got in all her cargo, they made ready with fearful noises, and we were all put under deck so that we could not see how they managed the vessel. But this disappointment was the last of my sorrow. The stench of the hold while we were on the coast was so intolerably loathsome[2] that it was dangerous to remain there for any time, and some of us had been permitted to stay on the deck for the fresh air; but now that the whole ship's cargo were confined together it became absolutely pestilential.[3] The closeness of the place and the heat of the climate, added to the number in the ship, which was so crowded that each had scarcely room to turn himself, almost suffocated us. This produced copious perspirations, so that the air soon became unfit for respiration from a variety of loathsome smells, and brought on a sickness among the slaves, of which many died, thus falling victims to the improvident avarice,[4] as I may call it, of their purchasers. This wretched situation was again aggravated by the galling[5] of the chains, now become insupportable, and the filth of necessary tubs, into which the children often fell and were almost suffocated. The shrieks of the women and the groans of the dying rendered the whole a scene of horror almost inconceivable. Happily perhaps for myself I was soon reduced so low here that it was thought necessary to keep me almost always on deck, and from my extreme youth I was not put in fetters.[6] In this situation I expected every hour to share the fate of my companions, some of whom were almost daily brought upon deck at the point of death, which I began to hope would soon put an end to my miseries. Often did I think many of the inhabitants of the deep much more happy than myself. I envied them the freedom they enjoyed, and as often wished I could change my condition for theirs. Every circumstance I met with served only to render my state more painful, and heighten my apprehensions and my opinion of the cruelty of the whites. One day they had taken a number of fishes, and when they had killed and satisfied themselves with as many as they thought fit, to our astonishment who were on the

---

2. **loathsome** (LOH<u>TH</u>-sum) *adj.* disgusting enough to make one sick
3. **pestilential** (pes-tuh-LEN-shuhl) *adj.* carrying and spreading infection
4. **improvident avarice**(ihm-PRAHV-uh-duhnt AV-uhr-uhs) reckless greed
5. **galling** (GAWL-ihng) *adj.* making sore by rubbing
6. **fetters** (FET-uhrz) *n.* chains or shackles for the feet

deck, rather than give any of them to us to eat as we expected they tossed the remaining fish into the sea again, although we begged and prayed for some as well as we could, but in vain; and some of my countrymen, being pressed by hunger, took an opportunity when they thought no one saw them of trying to get a little privately; but they were discovered, and the attempt procured them some very severe floggings. One day, when we had a smooth sea and moderate wind, two of my wearied countrymen who were chained together, (I was near them at the time) preferring death to such a life of misery, somehow made through the nettings and jumped into the sea: immediately another quite dejected fellow, who on account of his illness was suffered to be out of irons, also followed their example; and I believe many more would very soon have done the same if they had not been prevented by the ship's crew, who were instantly alarmed. Those of us who were the most active were in a moment put down under the deck, and there was such a noise and confusion amongst the people of the ship as I never heard before, to stop her and get the boat out to go after the slaves. However two of the wretches were drowned, but they got the other and afterward flogged him unmercifully for thus attempting to prefer death to slavery. In this manner we continued to undergo more hardships than I can now relate, hardships which are inseparable from this accursed trade. Many a time we were near suffocation from the want of fresh air, which we were often without for whole days together. This and the stench of the necessary tubs carried off many. . . . At last we came in sight of the island of Barbados,[7] at which the whites on board gave a great shout and made many signs of joy to us. We did not know what to think of this, but as the vessel drew nearer we plainly saw the harbour and other ships of different kinds and sizes, and we soon anchored amongst them off Bridgetown.[8] Many merchants and planters now came on board, though it was in the evening. They put us in separate parcels and examined us attentively. They also made us jump, and pointed to the land, signifying we were to go there. We thought by this we should be eaten by these ugly men, as they appeared to us; and when soon after we were all put down under the deck again, there was much dread and trembling among us, and nothing but bitter cries to be heard all the night from these apprehensions, insomuch that at last the white people got some old slaves from the land to pacify us. They told us we were not to be eaten, but to work, and were soon to go on land where we should see many of our country people. This report eased us much; and sure enough soon after we landed there came to us Africans of all languages. We were conducted immediately to the merchant's yard, where we were

7. **Barbados** (bahr-BAY-dohs) an island country in the West Indies
8. **Bridgetown** (BRIHJ-town) Bridgetown, capital of Barbados

all pent up together like so many sheep in a fold without regard to sex or age. As every object was new to me everything I saw filled me with surprise. What struck me first was that the houses were built with bricks with storeys, and in every other respect different from those in Africa: but I was still more astonished on seeing people on horseback. I did not know what this could mean, and indeed I thought these people were full of nothing but magical arts. . . . We were not many days in the merchants' custody before we were sold after the usual manner, which is this: On a signal given, (as the beat of a drum) the buyers rush at once into the yard where the slaves are confined, and make choice of that parcel they like best. The noise and clamour[9] with which this is attended and the eagerness visible in the countenances[10] of the buyers serve not a little to increase the apprehensions of the terrified Africans, who may well be supposed to consider them as the ministers of that destruction to which they think themselves devoted. In this manner, without scruple, are relations and friends separated, most of them never to see each other again. I remember in the vessel in which I was brought over,

Portrait of Olaudah Equiano. *Royal Albert Memorial Museum, Exeter, England.* Oil painting in the style of Sir Joshua Reynolds.

---

9. **clamour** (KLAM-er) *n.* continual uproar and shouting
10. **countenances** (KOWN-tuh-nuhn-sez) *n.* facial expressions

in the man's apartment there were several brothers who, in the sale, were sold in different lots; and it was very moving on this occasion to see their distress and hear their cries at parting. . . . Surely this is a new refinement in cruelty which, while it has no advantage to atone[11] for it, thus aggravates distress and adds fresh horrors even to the wretchedness of slavery.

_____

11. **atone** (uh-TOHN) _v._ to make up for; to make amends

POSTREADING

Critical Thinking

1. What do the poem and the autobiography tell you about the attitudes of enslaved Africans toward slave traders?
2. Which events in Equiano's life do you think influenced him to write about his experiences?
3. As a result of reading the poem and the autobiography, what questions come to your mind about the nature of human beings?

Writing Your Response to "The Slave Auction" and "The Slave Ship"

In your journal, write about an event or an idea from the poem or the autobiography that aroused strong feelings in you. What was significant about the situation? How did you react to it? How does your reaction to the event or idea in the selection relate to your current life or the lives of people you know?

Going Back Into the Text: Author's Craft

Many different kinds of literature fall into the category of nonfiction. Autobiography, biography, diaries, journals, and letters give accounts of people's lives. If a life story is written by the person who actually lived the story, it is called an **autobiography**. An autobiography is written from the first-person point of view. While an autobiography may not present the most objective view, it nevertheless is often a good source of information about the subject's life and times. An autobiography is also valuable because it often reveals emotions that might not otherwise be known.

Use the following questions to review the elements of autobiography in "The Slave Ship."

1. What factual information about slavery does this excerpt from the autobiography include?
2. What does this portion of the autobiography reveal about Equiano's opinions and feelings?
3. How could a historian confirm the accuracy of Equiano's description of this period in history?
4. Compare the words and feelings in this piece with those in Harper's poem "The Slave Auction." How are they the same? How are they different?

The Slave who Dared to Feel like a Man.

Reading the Author in a Cultural Context

For over a century, the autobiographical writings of African American slaves were largely ignored as important American literature. This was true for all of the writings even though they were quite popular at the time of their publication. Today, this body of African American literature, called slave narratives, is recognized as a valuable source of information about slavery and about the personal experiences of the men and women who had been enslaved.

It is remarkable that some former slaves were able to write of their experiences themselves, instead of telling them to others who would then write them down. Slave owners recognized that slaves who became educated might also spread rebellion. As a result, in most states, slave owners had laws passed against teaching enslaved persons to read and write. Yet some slaves learned, despite the laws, because of the great dedication and courage of individuals.

Free African Americans and sympathetic whites risked severe penalties to teach in hidden schools. Children of plantation owners sometimes instructed enslaved children secretly at night. Free African Americans who remained in the South sometimes sent their children north. It was in the North that private, and later public, schooling for African Americans existed.

Harriet Jacobs was one of the courageous African Americans who worked very hard against slavery. Not only did she learn to read and write, but she also endured terrible hardship in order to escape the cruel treatment of her owner. Her ordeal involved hiding for seven years in the cramped attic of her freed grandmother's house. During these years, Jacobs endured the extreme heat, bitter cold, and cramped conditions of the attic.

When it was finally safe for her to leave the hiding place, Harriet Jacobs recorded her experiences in a narrative, *Incidents in the Life of a Slave Girl*. She fictionalized the characters, but the events of the narrative remained very real. The book was published in 1861 under the pen name of Linda Brent. A portion of it follows.

Focusing on the Selection

As you read this portion of Harriet Jacobs's narrative, think about the reactions of her family members to their circumstances. Why did they react differently from one another? What forces affected each person's decisions? What were the consequences of slavery on the family structure and unity? Record your responses in your journal as you read this autobiography.

The Slave who Dared to Feel like a Man.

from *Incidents in the Life of a Slave Girl*

HARRIET A. JACOBS

TWO YEARS HAD PASSED SINCE I entered Dr. Flint's family, and those years had brought much of the knowledge that comes from experience, though they had afforded little opportunity for any other kinds of knowledge.

My grandmother had, as much as possible, been a mother to her orphan grandchildren. By perseverance and unwearied industry, she was now mistress of a snug little home, surrounded with the necessaries of life. She would have been happy could her children have shared them with her. There remained but three children and two grandchildren, all slaves. Most earnestly did she strive to make us feel that it was the will of God: that He had seen fit to place us under such circumstances; and though it seemed hard, we ought to pray for contentment.

It was a beautiful faith, coming from a mother who could not call her children her own. But I, and Benjamin, her youngest boy, condemned it. We reasoned that it was much more the will of God that we should be situated as she was. We longed for a home like hers. There we always found sweet balsam[1] for our troubles. She was so loving, so sympathizing! She

---

1. **balsam** (BAWL-suhm) *n.* a soothing ointment, used here to mean "a healing"

Hampton University Museum, Hampton, Virginia. Panel painting depicting the living quarters of enslaved African Americans. From *The Frederick Douglass Series,* painted by African American artist Jacob Lawrence in 1938–1939. Tempera on hardwood.

always met us with a smile, and listened with patience to all our sorrows. She spoke so hopefully, that unconsciously the clouds gave place to sunshine. There was a grand big oven there, too, that baked bread and nice things for the town, and we knew there was always a choice bit in store for us.

But, alas! even the charms of the old oven failed to reconcile us to our hard lot. Benjamin was now a tall, handsome lad, strongly and gracefully made, and with a spirit too bold and daring for a slave. My brother William, now twelve years old, had the same aversion[2] to the word master that he had when he was an urchin of seven years. I was his confidant.[3] He came to me with all his troubles. I remember one instance in particular. It was on a lovely spring morning, and when I marked the sunlight dancing here and there, its beauty seemed to mock[4] my sadness. For my master, whose restless, craving, vicious nature roved about day and night, seeking whom to devour, had just left me, with stinging, scorching words; words that scathed ear and brain like fire. O, how I despised him! I thought how glad I should be, if some day when he walked the earth, it would open and swallow him up, and disencumber[5] the world of a plague.

2. **aversion** (ah-VER-shuhn) *n.* strong dislike
3. **confidant** (KAHN-fuh-dahnt) *n.* a person trusted with secrets
4. **mock** (MAHK) *v.* make fun of, ridicule
5. **disencumber** (dihs-ihn-KUM-buhr) *v.* free from a burden or a trouble

When he told me that I was made for his use, made to obey his command in *every* thing; that I was nothing but a slave, whose will must and should surrender to his, never before had my puny arm felt half so strong. . . .

I remember the first time I was punished. It was in the month of February. My grandmother had taken my old shoes, and replaced them with a new pair. I needed them; for several inches of snow had fallen, and it still continued to fall. When I walked through Mrs. Flint's room, their creaking grated harshly on her refined nerves. She called me to her, and asked what I had about me that made such a horrid noise. I told her it was my new shoes. "Take them off," said she; "and if you put them on again, I'll throw them into the fire."

I took them off, and my stockings also. She then sent me a long distance, on an errand. As I went through the snow, my bare feet tingled. That night I was very hoarse; and I went to bed thinking the next day would find me sick, perhaps dead. What was my grief on waking to find myself quite well!

I had imagined if I died, or was laid up for some time, that my mistress would feel a twinge of remorse that she had so hated "the little imp," as she styled me. It was my ignorance of that mistress that gave rise to such extravagant imaginings.

Dr. Flint occasionally had high prices offered for me; but he always said, "She don't belong to me. She is my daughter's property, and I have no right to sell her." Good, honest man! My young mistress was still a child, and I could look for no protection from her. I loved her, and she returned my affection. I once heard her father allude to[6] her attachment to me; and his wife promptly replied that it proceeded from fear. This put unpleasant doubts into my mind. Did the child feign[7] what she did not feel? or was her mother jealous of the mite[8] of love she bestowed on me? I concluded it must be the latter. I said to myself, "Surely, little children are true."

One afternoon I sat at my sewing, feeling unusual depression of spirits. My mistress had been accusing me of an offence, of which I assured her I was perfectly innocent; but I saw, by the contemptuous curl of her lip, that she believed I was telling a lie.

I wondered for what wise purpose God was leading me through such thorny paths, and whether still darker days were in store for me. As I sat musing[9] thus, the door opened softly, and William came in. "Well, brother," said I, "what is the matter this time?"

---

6. **allude to** (uh-LOOD TOO) *v.* mention
7. **feign** (FAYN) *v.* pretend or fake
8. **mite** (MEYET) *n.* very small amount
9. **musing** (MYOO-zihng) *v.* daydreaming, meditating

"O Linda, Ben and his master have had a dreadful time!" said he.

My first thought was that Benjamin was killed. "Don't be frightened, Linda," said William; "I will tell you all about it."

It appeared that Benjamin's master had sent for him, and he did not immediately obey the summons. When he did, his master was angry, and began to whip him. He resisted. Master and slave fought, and finally the master was thrown. Benjamin had cause to tremble; for he had thrown to the ground his master—one of the richest men in town. I anxiously awaited the result.

That night I stole to my grandmother's house, and Benjamin also stole thither[10] from his master's. My grandmother had gone to spend a day or two with an old friend living in the country.

"I have come," said Benjamin, "to tell you good by. I am going away."

I inquired where.

"To the north," he replied.

I looked at him to see whether he was in earnest. I saw it all in his firm, set mouth. I implored him not to go, but he paid no heed to my words. He said he was no longer a boy, and every day made his yoke[11] more galling. He had raised his hand against his master, and was to be publicly whipped for the offence. I reminded him of the poverty and hardships he must encounter among strangers. I told him he might be caught and brought back; and that was terrible to think of.

He grew vexed,[12] and asked if poverty and hardships with freedom, were not preferable to our treatment in slavery. "Linda," he continued, "we are dogs here; foot-balls, cattle, every thing that's mean. No, I will not stay. Let them bring me back. We don't die but once."

He was right; but it was hard to give him up. . . .

It is not necessary to state how he made his escape. Suffice it to say, he was on his way to New York when a violent storm overtook the vessel. The captain said he must put into the nearest port. This alarmed Benjamin, who was aware that he would be advertised in every port near his own town. His embarrassment was noticed by the captain. To port they went. There the advertisement met the captain's eye. Benjamin so exactly answered its description, that the captain laid hold on him, and bound him in chains. The storm passed, and they proceeded to New York. Before reaching that port Benjamin managed to get off his chains and throw them overboard. He escaped from the vessel, but was pursued, captured, and carried back to his master.

---

10. **thither** (THIH<u>TH</u>-uhr) *adv.* there
11. **yoke** (YOHK) *n.* a heavy wooden harness for work animals; used figuratively, to mean the pressures that held people in slavery
12. **vexed** (VEKSD) *adj.* annoyed; irritated

When my grandmother returned home and found her youngest child had fled, great was her sorrow; but, with characteristic piety, she said, "God's will be done." Each morning, she inquired if any news had been heard from her boy. Yes, news *was* heard. The master was rejoicing over a letter, announcing the capture of his human chattel.[13]

That day seems but as yesterday, so well do I remember it. I saw him led through the streets in chains, to jail. His face was ghastly pale, yet full of determination. He had begged one of the sailors to go to his mother's house and ask her not to meet him. He said the sight of her distress would take from him all self-control. She yearned to see him, and she went; but she screened herself in the crowd, that it might be as her child had said. . . .

Benjamin had been imprisoned three weeks, when my grandmother went to intercede[14] for him with his master. He was immovable. He said Benjamin should serve as an example to the rest of his slaves; he should be kept in jail till he was subdued, or be sold if he got but one dollar for him. However, he afterwards relented in some degree. The chains were taken off, and we were allowed to visit him.

As his food was of the coarsest kind, we carried him as often as possible a warm supper, accompanied with some little luxury for the jailer.

Three months elapsed, and there was no prospect of release or of a purchaser. One day he was heard to sing and laugh. This piece of indecorum[15] was told to his master, and the overseer[16] was ordered to re-chain him. He was now confined in an apartment with other prisoners, who were covered with filthy rags. Benjamin was chained near them, and was soon covered with vermin.[17] He worked at his chains till he succeeded in getting out of them. He passed them through the bars of the window, with a request that they should be taken to his master, and he should be informed that he was covered with vermin.

This audacity[18] was punished with heavier chains, and prohibition of our visits.

My grandmother continued to send him fresh changes of clothes. The old ones were burned up. The last night we saw him in jail his mother still begged him to send for his master, and beg his pardon. Neither persuasion nor argument could turn him from his purpose. He calmly answered, "I am waiting his time."

Those chains were mournful to hear.

---

13. **chattel** (CHAT-el) *n.* articles of property, except real estate
14. **intercede** (ihn-tuhr-SEED) *v.* plead on another person's behalf
15. **indecorum** (ihn-dih-KOHR-uhm) *n.* improper behavior
16. **overseer** (OH-vuhr-see-er) *n.* supervisor
17. **vermin** (VUR-mihn) *n.* fleas, lice, bedbugs
18. **audacity** (aw-DA-sih-tee) *n.* boldness

Another three months passed, and Benjamin left his prison walls. We that loved him waited to bid him a long and last farewell. A slave trader had bought him. You remember, I told you what price he brought when ten years of age. Now he was more than twenty years old, and sold for three hundred dollars. The master had been blind to his own interest. Long confinement had made his face too pale, his form too thin; moreover, the trader had heard something of his character, and it did not strike him as suitable for a slave. He said he would give any price if the handsome lad was a girl. We thanked God that he was not.

Could you have seen that mother clinging to her child, when they fastened the irons upon his wrists; could you have heard her heart-rending groans, and seen her bloodshot eyes wander wildly from face to face, vainly pleading for mercy; could you have witnessed that scene as I saw it, you would exclaim, *Slavery is damnable!*

Benjamin, her youngest, her pet, was forever gone! She could not realize it. She had had an interview with the trader for the purpose of ascertaining[19] if Benjamin could be purchased. She was told it was impossible, as he had given bonds not to sell him till he was out of the state. He promised that he would not sell him till he reached New Orleans.

. . . one morning, long before day, Benjamin was missing. He was riding over the blue billows, bound for Baltimore. . . .

Benjamin reached New York safely, and concluded to stop there until he had gained strength enough to proceed further. It happened that my grandmother's only remaining son had sailed for the same city on business for his mistress. Through God's providence,[20] the brothers met. You may be sure it was a happy meeting. "O Phil," exclaimed Benjamin, "I am here at last." Then he told him how near he came to dying, almost in sight of free land, and how he prayed that he might live to get one breath of free air. He said life was worth something now, and it would be hard to die. In the old jail he had not valued it; once, he was tempted to destroy it; but something, he did not know what, had prevented him; perhaps it was fear. He had heard those who profess to be religious declare there was no heaven for self-murderers; and as his life had been pretty hot here, he did not desire a continuation of the same in another world. "If I die now," he exclaimed, "thank God, I shall die a freeman!" . . .

---

19. ascertaining (ah-ser-TAYN-ihng) *v.* finding out
20. providence (PRAH-vu-dens) *n.* God's help

POSTREADING

Critical Thinking

1. What does Harriet Jacobs tell you about the struggle of African American slaves for freedom and dignity?
2. What does the narrative reveal about the strengths and weaknesses of the African American family under a system of slavery?
3. What similarities can you see between the author's family and U.S. families today? What differences can you see?

Writing Your Response to "The Slave who Dared to Feel like a Man."

Think about the people introduced in the narrative. Choose one character who impressed you to write about in your journal. Tell about that person and why he or she made an impact on you.

Going Back Into the Text: Author's Craft

A **narrative** is a story that is usually told in chronological order—the order in which the events happened. It can be fiction or nonfiction. When the narrator, the person telling the story, describes his or her own experience, it is called a *personal*, or *first-person*, *narrative*. A personal narrative is similar to an autobiography, but an autobiography gives an account of the narrator's entire life or a large portion of it. A personal narrative is much more brief—telling about one incident, or a limited number of incidents, in the person's life.

Sometimes what an author has chosen to leave out of an autobiography or personal narrative can reveal as much about the author's personality and values as what he or she has included. The exclusions may be planned and purposeful, or accidental and unmindful. Either way, reading with an awareness of what has been excluded can help a reader better understand the work and what is important to the author who created it.

With a partner, use the following questions to review the elements of personal narrative in "The Slave who Dared to Feel like a Man."

1. What factual information about slavery does this narrative provide?
2. What does this narrative reveal about the author's own personality and values?
3. How could a historian check the accuracy of Jacobs's description of the period?

The People Could Fly
Runagate Runagate

Reading the Authors in a Cultural Context

Virginia Hamilton is a 20th-century African American writer. She believes that an awareness of the past is necessary to understand the present. Hamilton's interest in African American history and folklore began by listening to stories told by her mother and grandmother. She collected these stories and others, from her extensive reading, into an anthology. Her collection of fables, supernatural tales, and slave narratives is meant to celebrate the rich African American literary heritage. The anthology *The People Could Fly: American Black Folktales* was published in 1985. "The People Could Fly," which you will read, is from that anthology.

Critics have honored the collection because it "makes these tales available to another generation of readers," and because "we are reminded . . . that the human spirit, however enslaved, still feels love and hope." Hamilton views the collection as her "personal tribute to the folklore" of her ancestors when they had to live under conditions very different from her own.

Virginia Hamilton is best known for her novels about African American children. She received awards for *Zeely* (1967), *The House of Dies Drear* (1974), *The Planet of Junior Brown* (1971), *MC Higgins the Great* (1974), and *Sweet Whispers, Brother Rush* (1982). Hamilton believes that the African American experience portrayed in her books is an important part of American culture. She thinks that it is essential for all Americans to know about and understand this experience.

Robert Hayden, whose poem "Runagate Runagate" you will also read, had a similar belief. In fact, Hayden devoted almost 35 years of study to African American history and literature. His anthology *Kaleidoscope* is the result of that study.

In creating a separate collection of African American poetry from the 1700s to the 1960s, Hayden was concerned that readers might misunderstand his intent. He did not want readers to view African American poets as spokespersons only for their own people and only as voices of protest. He asks readers to recognize that each poet has a different view and approach to the art of poetry.

Focusing on the Selections

As you read "The People Could Fly" and "Runagate Runagate," think about the different ways people resist and escape oppression. Why do some people flee and others stay? How do people help one another to flee or to endure staying? Also look for the theme or central message of the folktale and of the poem. Record your ideas in your journal as you read.

The People Could Fly

TOLD BY VIRGINIA HAMILTON

THEY SAY THE PEOPLE COULD FLY. Say that long ago in Africa, some of the people knew magic. And they would walk up on the air like climbing up on a gate. And they flew like blackbirds over the fields. Black, shiny wings flapping against the blue up there.

Then, many of the people were captured for Slavery. The ones that could fly shed their wings. They couldn't take their wings across the water on the slave ships. Too crowded, don't you know.

The folks were full of misery, then. Got sick with the up and down of the sea. So they forgot about flying when they could no longer breathe the sweet scent of Africa.

Say the people who could fly kept their power, although they shed their wings. They kept their secret magic in the land of slavery. They looked the same as the other people from Africa who had been coming over, who had dark skin. Say you couldn't tell anymore one who could fly from one who couldn't.

One such who could was an old man, call him Toby. And standin tall, yet afraid, was a young woman who once had wings. Call her Sarah. Now Sarah carried a babe tied to her back. She trembled to be so hard worked and scorned.

The slaves labored in the fields from sunup to sundown. The owner of the slaves callin himself their Master. Say he was a hard lump of clay. A hard, glinty coal. A hard rock pile, wouldn't be moved. His Overseer on horseback pointed out the slaves who were slowin down. So the one called Driver cracked his whip over the slow ones to make them move faster. That whip was a slice-open cut of pain. So they did move faster. Had to.

Sarah hoed and chopped the row as the babe on her back slept.

Say the child grew hungry. That babe started up bawling too loud. Sarah couldn't stop to feed it. Couldn't stop to soothe and quiet it down. She let it cry. She didn't want to. She had no heart to croon[1] to it.

"Keep that thing quiet," called the Overseer. He pointed his finger at the babe. The woman scrunched low. The Driver cracked his whip across the babe anyhow. The babe hollered like any hurt child, and the woman fell to the earth.

The old man that was there, Toby, came and helped her to her feet.

"I must go soon," she told him.

"Soon," he said.

Sarah couldn't stand up straight any longer. She was too weak. The sun burned her face. The babe cried and cried, "Pity me, oh, pity me," say it sounded like. Sarah was so sad and starvin, she sat down in the row.

"Get up, you black cow," called the Overseer. He pointed his hand, and the Driver's whip snarled around Sarah's legs. Her sack dress tore into rags. Her legs bled onto the earth. She couldn't get up.

Toby was there where there was no one to help her and the babe.

"Now, before it's too late," panted Sarah. "Now, Father!"

"Yes, Daughter, the time is come," Toby answered. "Go, as you know how to go!"

He raised his arms, holding them out to her. *"Kum...yali, kum buba tambe,"*[2] and more magic words, said so quickly, they sounded like whispers and sighs.

The young woman lifted one foot on the air. Then the other. She flew clumsily at first, with the child now held tightly in her arms. Then she felt the magic, the African mystery. Say she rose just as free as a bird. As light as a feather.

The Overseer rode after her, hollerin. Sarah flew over the fences. She flew over the woods. Tall trees could not snag her. Nor could the Overseer. She flew like an eagle now, until she was gone from sight. No one dared speak about it. Couldn't believe it. But it was, because they that was there saw that it was.

Say the next day was dead hot in the fields. A young man slave fell from the heat. The Driver come and whipped him. Toby come over and spoke words to the fallen one. The words of ancient Africa once heard are never remembered completely. The young man forgot them as soon

---

1. croon (KROON) *v.* hum, sing, or talk in a low tone
2. "Kum...yali, kum buba tambe" an ancient African chant

as he heard them. They went way inside him. He got up and rolled over on the air. He rode it awhile. And he flew away.

Another and another fell from the heat. Toby was there. He cried out to the fallen and reached his arms out to them. *"Kum kunka yali, kum ... tambe!"*[3] Whispers and sighs. And they too rose on the air. They rode the hot breezes. The ones flyin were black and shinin sticks, wheelin above the head of the Overseer. They crossed the rows, the fields, the fences, the streams, and were away.

"Seize the old man!" cried the Overseer. "I heard him say the magic *words*. Seize him!"

The one callin himself Master come runnin. The Driver got his whip ready to curl around old Toby and tie him up. The slaveowner took his hip gun from its place. He meant to kill old, black Toby.

But Toby just laughed. Say he threw back his head and said, "Hee, hee! Don't you know who I am? Don't you know some of us in this field?" He said it to their faces. "We are ones who fly!"

And he sighed the ancient words that were a dark promise. He said them all around to the others in the field under the whip, "... *buba yali ... buba tambe....*"

There was a great outcryin. The bent backs straightened up. Old and young who were called slaves and could fly joined hands. Say like they would ring-sing. But they didn't shuffle in a circle. They didn't sing. They rose on the air. They flew in a flock that was black against the heavenly blue. Black crows or black shadows. It didn't matter, they went so high. Way above the plantation, way over the slavery land. Say they flew away to *Free-dom*.

And the old man, old Toby, flew behind them, takin care of them. He wasn't cryin. He wasn't laughin. He was the seer.[4] His gaze fell on the plantation where the slaves who could not fly waited.

"Take us with you!" Their looks spoke it but they were afraid to shout it. Toby couldn't take them with him. Hadn't the time to teach them to fly. They must wait for a chance to run.

"Goodie-bye!" The old man called Toby spoke to them, poor souls! And he was flyin gone.

So they say. The Overseer told it. The one called Master said it was a lie, a trick of the light. The Driver kept his mouth shut.

The slaves who could not fly told about the people who could fly to their children. When they were free. When they sat close before the fire in the free land, they told it. They did so love firelight and *Free-dom*, and tellin.

---

3. *"Kum kunka yali, kum . . . tambe!"* an ancient African chant
4. **seer** (SEER) *n.* the overseer or slave driver, the often cruel person who drove the slaves to work harder and harder

They say that the children of the ones who could not fly told their children. And now, me, I have told it to you.

◆ ◆ ◆

"The People Could Fly" is one of the most extraordinary, moving tales in black folklore. It almost makes us believe that the people *could* fly. There are numerous separate accounts of flying Africans and slaves in the black folktale literature. Such accounts are often combined with tales of slaves disappearing. A plausible[5] explanation might be the slaves running away from slavery, slipping away while in the fields or under cover of darkness. In code language murmured from one slave to another, "Come fly away!" might have been the words used. Another explanation is the wish-fulfillment motif.[6]

The magic hoe variant[7] is often combined with the flying-African tale. A magic hoe is left still hoeing in an empty field after all the slaves have flown away. Magic with the hoe and other farm tools, and the power of disappearing, are often attributed to Gullah (Angolan) African slaves. Angolan slaves were thought by other slaves to have exceptional powers.

"The People Could Fly" is a detailed fantasy tale of suffering, of magic power exerted against the so-called Master and his underlings. Finally, it is a powerful testament to the millions of slaves who never had the opportunity to "fly" away. They remained slaves, as did their children. "The People Could Fly" was first told and retold by those who had only their imaginations to set them free.

Swing Low, Sweet Chariot. *National Museum of American Art, Smithsonian Institution, Washington, D.C.* Painted by African American artist William H. Johnson in 1944. Oil on paperboard. What similarities can you see between the images in this painting and those in the folktale?

5. **plausible** (PLAWZ-ihbuhl) *adj.* believable
6. **motif** (moh-TEEF) *n.* a main theme or subject
7. **variant** (VAR-eeuhnt) *n.* a symbol that is often used, but sometimes appears in different forms

Runagate Runagate

ROBERT HAYDEN

I.

Runs falls rises stumbles on from darkness into darkness
and the darkness thicketed[1] with shapes of terror
and the hunters pursuing and the hounds pursuing
and the night cold and the night long and the river
to cross and the jack-muh-lanterns beckoning beckoning
and blackness ahead and when shall I reach that somewhere
morning and keep on going and never turn back and keep on going

        Runagate
                Runagate
                    Runagate

Many thousands rise and go
many thousands crossing over

                     O mythic North
                 O star-shaped yonder Bible city

Some go weeping and some rejoicing
some in coffins and some in carriages
some in silks and some in shackles

        Rise and go or fare you well

No more auction block for me
no more driver's lash for me

      If you see my Pompey, 30 yrs of age,
      new breeches, plain stockings, negro shoes;
      if you see my Anna, likely young mulatto[2]
      branded E on the right cheek, R on the left,
      catch them if you can and notify subscriber.
      Catch them if you can, but it won't be easy.
      They'll dart underground when you try to catch them,
      plunge into quicksand, whirlpools, mazes,
      turn into scorpions when you try to catch them.

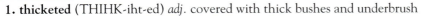

1. **thicketed** (THIHK-iht-ed) *adj.* covered with thick bushes and underbrush
2. **mulatto** (muh-LAH-toh) *n.* a person with some white and some black heredity

And before I'll be a slave
I'll be buried in my grave

North star and bonanza gold
I'm bound for the freedom, freedom-bound
and oh Susyanna don't you cry for me

Runagate

Runagate

II.
Rises from their anguish and their power,

Harriet Tubman,[3]

woman of earth, whipscarred,
a summoning, a shining

Mean to be free

And this was the way of it, brethren brethren,
way we journeyed from Can't to Can.
Moon so bright and no place to hide,
the cry up and the patterollers[4] riding,
hound dogs belling in bladed air.
And fear starts a-murbling, Never make it,
we'll never make it. *Hush that now,*
and she's turned upon us, levelled pistol
glinting in the moonlight:
Dead folks can't jaybird-talk,[5] she says;
you keep on going now or die, she says.

Wanted   Harriet Tubman   alias The General
alias Moses   Stealer of Slaves

---

3. **Harriet Tubman** (HAH-ree-uht TUB-muhn) helped enslaved African Americans escape to freedom through the Underground Railroad
4. **patterollers** (PAHT-uhr-ohl-erz) *n.* the train wheels
5. **jaybird-talk** (JAY-buhrd TAWK) chattering, gossipy talk

In league with Garrison Alcott Emerson
Garrett Douglass Thoreau John Brown[6]

Armed and known to be Dangerous

Wanted Reward Dead or Alive

      Tell me, Ezekiel,[7] oh tell me do you see
      mailed Jehovah[8] coming to deliver me?

Hoot-owl calling in the ghosted air,
five times calling to the hants[9] in the air.
Shadow of a face in the scary leaves,
shadow of a voice in the talking leaves:

      Come ride-a my train

      Oh that train, ghost-story train
      through swamp and savanna movering[10] movering,
      over trestles of dew, through caves of the wish,
      Midnight Special on a sabre track[11] movering movering,
      first stop Mercy and the last Hallelujah.

      Come ride-a my train

        Mean mean mean to be free.

---

6. Garrison, Alcott, Emerson, Garrett, Douglass, Thoreau, John Brown all were
famous abolitionists in the 1800s
7. Ezekiel (ee-ZEEK-ee-uhl) a Hebrew prophet
8. Jehovah (juh-HOH-vuh) the Hebrew name for God
9. hants (HANTS) *n.* haunts or ghosts
10. movering (MOOV-er-ihng) *v.* migrating
11. sabre track (SAY-buhr TRAK) railroad

Critical Thinking

1. What do the folktale and the poem tell you about the different ways African Americans escaped the horrors of slavery?
2. What do the folktale and the poem reveal about how African American slaves helped one another to flee or to endure their oppressors?
3. Do you think the message of the folktale is optimistic or pessimistic? What about the poem? Explain your thoughts.

Writing Your Responses to "The People Could Fly" and "Runagate Runagate"

In your journal, write your ideas and feelings about the selections. Which parts of each made the biggest impression on you as you read? Why do you think they impressed you so?

Going Back Into the Text: Author's Craft

Folktales are stories about common people or "folks." The stories usually teach a lesson or in some way involve a struggle between a character representing desirable qualities, such as honesty and a willingness to work hard, and a character representing undesirable qualities, such as greed or laziness. There is often a problem to be solved, and a resolution that includes some kind of magic.

Folktales explore universal themes, of interest to all people. Folktales often have uni-versal settings. "Once upon a time in a far-off land," is a common folktale setting.

Originally, folktales were handed down orally from generation to generation. This oral tradition, which depended upon the storytellers' memories, explains why there are so many different versions of some folktales.

With a partner, use the following questions to review why "The People Could Fly" is a folktale.

1. Who and what is the story about? What desirable and undesirable qualities are represented by the characters? What magic is involved?
2. What elements of this folktale can be considered universal?
3. What folktales do you know that have more than one version?

Reviewing the Theme

1. Review in your mind the horrors of slavery portrayed in this theme. What human rights were denied these people and other enslaved African Americans? What qualities would you say enabled them to endure and overcome such terrrible physical and emotional hardships? Explain your thinking.
2. How did the selections in the theme support or expand your knowledge about slavery?
3. Which selection in this theme made the greatest impact on you? Why?

Theme 6:
Stories of Newcomers

The Immigrants. *New York Public Library.* Woodcut print by Allen Lewis. Created in 1932 for the book *The Calico Bush* by Rachel Field, the story of a young French immigrant woman in the 1740s.

To MILLIONS OF PEOPLE in Europe and other parts of the world, the Americas—and later, the United States—represented the chance "to start all over again." The reasons they wanted that new start were often quite different. Some people fled from religious persecution. Others fled from political oppression. Still others hoped to escape an endless state of poverty. Some felt trapped by families or customs. Other people simply came for adventure. So, over the past 400 years, people have pulled up roots in their native lands. They have emigrated to the distant shores of the land of promise.

The newcomers brought with them their native languages. They also brought their ways of thinking and feeling, their stories, and their humor—their culture. For these immigrants, and their children born in the United States, trying to become "American" was a strange and unsettling experience. The stories of the newcomers you will read about in this theme share some of those unsettling, and even anxious, moments as they try to mix the old with the new. You will meet brides from Japan and Puerto Rico, a student-athlete from South Africa, and a teacher-poet of Native American and European ancestry who was born in the United States. Together, these people from many different parts of the world will help paint a picture of what it means to be a "newcomer."

Lali

Reading the Author in a Cultural Context

Nicholasa Mohr (nih-koh-LAH-suh MAWR) is a second-generation mainland Puerto Rican. She is called second-generation mainland because she was born, in 1935, in the continental United States—in the Bronx, New York. Her parents are called first-generation mainland because they were born in Puerto Rico, then emigrated to the U.S. mainland.

Puerto Rico was first a territory acquired by the United States in 1898. As a territory it was under U.S. rule and protection. Puerto Rico was made a commonwealth in 1952, with its own constitution and government. Many Puerto Ricans decided to move to the continental United States, though, in search of better jobs and a higher standard of living. Some spoke both English and Spanish, but since Puerto Rico is primarily a Spanish-speaking island, most spoke only Spanish.

Puerto Ricans represent many different cultures. Some live by the values and customs of their Spanish, or other European, ancestors. Others incorporate the culture of their African ancestors. Still others reflect their Indian heritage.

Puerto Ricans living in the continental United States today come from a variety of backgrounds. However, their families have some common features. Traditional Puerto Rican families often feel close ties not only with their parents and children, but also with distant relatives. Families can even include close friends. In fact, their warm, supportive relationships with these close friends, called *compadres* (kohm-PAH-drays) or *comadres* (kohm-AH-drays), are an important part of the family circle. Family needs are primary and are given a higher value than are individual needs.

Traditionally, Puerto Rican men are considered to be the heads of their families. A first-generation mainland Puerto Rican woman might hesitate to offer her opinions or to demand her rights. Second- and third-generation mainland family members are often bilingual. In addition, they have incorporated many new values from the mainstream U.S. culture with those of their original families.

In the selection that follows, Nicholasa Mohr explores the struggles of Puerto Rican girls and women in a male-dominated U.S. culture. Her writing also reflects the hardships of her economic circumstances.

Focusing on the Selection

As you read "Lali," think about what it must be like to move from a rural village to a big city where everything is very different. What obstacles might you have to overcome? Would your thoughts often drift back to that country setting? What feelings might you experience? Record your responses in your journal as you read.

Lali

from *In Nueva York*

NICHOLASA MOHR

THE ALARM CLOCK RANG. Lali opened her eyes, stretched out her arm, and pushed in the small knob that shut off the noise. She lay back staring at the ceiling. Off in a corner the paint was peeling and a large crack made that section buckle. Every day she cleaned the small chips of paint that fell on the dresser top and floor. She looked over at Rudi's side of the bed. He was gone. Each morning he awoke at five thirty and, except for Sunday, reset the alarm at seven thirty for Lali. On Sunday the store was closed, but Rudi got up at five-thirty anyway; he had been doing this for sixteen years. Since he always awoke before the alarm went off, Lali wondered why he bothered to set the clock, and had asked him about it.

"It's for that one time I might oversleep. Then what happens to the business and my customers, eh? All waiting for breakfast and no Rudi. No, I don't take chances."

Rudi was down in the luncheonette by six every morning, starting preparations for breakfast and waiting for the food deliveries. His customers would begin to come in after seven.

Lali pulled the covers tightly around her neck and shoulders. The old radiators hissed and clanked, sending out vaporous heat. In spite of

Casa con Arboles (House with Trees). *Institute of Puerto Rican Culture.* Painted by Puerto Rican artist Jose A. Torres Martino around 1950. Oil on canvas.

all the noise and steam, the room remained cold. The heat seemed to escape right through the walls of the tenement,[1] disappearing into the street, leaving behind cold moisture which framed the window panes with a smoky hue[2] and formed sweat drops on the walls.

Now that it was almost winter again, it was getting more difficult for Lali to get out of bed in the morning. At home it was always so easy; with the sound of the first rooster crowing, she would open her eyes and start the day.

---

1. tenement (TEN-uh-muhnt) *n.* apartment occupied by tenants
2. hue (HYOO) *n.* color

Lali sighed and closed her eyes; then half opening them, she squinted. There it was . . . coming into focus. She saw the morning mist settling like puffs of smoke scattered over the range of mountains that surrounded the entire countryside. Sharp mountainous peaks and curves covered with many shades of green foliage that changed constantly from light to dark, intense or soft tones, depending on the time of day and the direction of the rays of the brilliant tropical sun. Ah, the path, she smiled, following the road that led to her village. Lali inhaled the sweet and spicy fragrance of the flower gardens that sprinkled the countryside in abundance. In her mountain village, as well as in every mountain village on the island of Puerto Rico, country folk prided themselves on their flower gardens, which surrounded even the most modest and humble homes. Oh, Papi's flower garden! There were bright yellows, scarlet[3] and crimson hues, brilliant blues, wild purples; every color imaginable flourished on the plants and shrubbery that blossomed in her father's flower garden. Lali enjoyed the soft, cool, gentle morning breeze as she stood by the road and dug her bare feet into the dark moist earth.

"Lali! Lali, nena,[4] come here! What are you dreaming about? Always dreaming when there's work to be done. Papi wants to plant a row of four mango trees over by the chicken coop. Caramba![5] We have to prepare the earth . . ."

Her mother was always calling her, interrupting her dreams. Her private dreams. She used to wonder what was going on beyond the mountains, in other places far from her village. What were people like out there?

Outside in the street, Lali heard the trucks changing gears; buses and cars honked their horns. Lali opened her eyes and shivered, feeling a lump in her throat. She felt the tears coming to her eyes. I'm not gonna cry; it just makes me tired. Besides, she would be going home soon. In February, Rudi would close the luncheonette for two weeks. He had promised Lali that for their second wedding anniversary they would vacation in Puerto Rico and she could spend time with her family.

"This is the middle of November . . ." Lali whispered, "so, then December, January, and February! Thank God." She made the sign of the cross. Feeling better, she climbed out of bed, grabbed her bathrobe, and got ready to go to work.

Lali put on her uniform, brushed her hair, tied it back, and applied some lipstick. Quickly she reached in the dresser drawer and took out a pair of slacks and a blouse, slipping them on a plastic hanger. It was

---

3. scarlet (SCAHR-liht) *adj.* very bright red
4. nena (NAY-nah) *n.* child
5. Caramba (cah-RAHM-bah) *interj.* an exclamation of surprise or dismay

Thursday, and she had night school this evening. It saved time if she changed downstairs in the back room before going to class; and Rudi would have less to complain about. She locked the front door and realized she had forgotten her books. Going back into the apartment, Lali remembered she had been so excited about her trip home that she had not completed tonight's assignment. This had never happened before. School and homework were the two things she looked forward to. Well, it doesn't matter, Lali shrugged; Chiquitín[6] will help me finish my homework.

After a lifetime of separation from his mother and family, Chiquitín had been reunited with them over a year ago. That had been the happiest day of his life. He was introduced to his half-sister and half-brothers, stepfather, niece, nephew, and brother-in-law. It took some time for his family to get over the embarrassment of his dwarfishness. Chiquitín was used to people reacting in this way, and set out to prove he would be no burden. Once it was obvious that he would give more than he took, they accepted him completely. Immediately, he had been drawn to Lali, first by her sadness and then by her sense of helplessness.

They were both starting second year English together. Lali was fluent and when she spoke, she no longer planned her sentences ahead of time, or worried about her accent.

Lali walked into the luncheonette, and as usual Rudi had set out her breakfast on the counter. No matter how busy it was, Rudi insisted she have her breakfast undisturbed.

"What happened, Lali? You're fifteen minutes late."

"I'm sorry. I'll hurry up—"

"No," Rudi interrupted, "take your time. I was only worried that something happened . . . take your time. You feeling tired?"

"No." Lali turned away from Rudi and sat down to eat.

She finished breakfast and began the day's work. Lali worked at the grill during the early morning and late evening rush. The rest of the time she cooked the standard meals listed on the menu and the blue plate special[7] of the day.

Rudi had taught her how to cook quite a number of dishes, and how to prepare food for the restaurant business. Lali knew that his first wife had also done most of the cooking. Rudi had told her that they had both worked and saved their money until they were able to buy the luncheonette sixteen years ago. She had seen his first wife's picture in an old photograph album Rudi stored away in a suitcase. Lali had been surprised to see Rudi as a young man, with a full head of dark hair, lean and

---

6. **Chiquitín** (chih-kee-TEEN) a boy's name
7. **blue plate special** an inexpensive restaurant meal served on a large plate, which originally was blue

muscular in an army uniform. He stood with his arm around a young woman who smiled happily. A large orchid corsage was pinned on her brightly flowered print dress. On the back of the photo someone had written, *Carmin and Rudi Padillo on their wedding day—April 19, 1946, Brooklyn, N.Y.* That was the year she had been born; her birthday was a month later, May 3, 1946. Carmin Padillo had died of diabetes and heart complications five years ago. Three years after his first wife's death, Rudi went to Puerto Rico and brought back his second wife, Lali, a twenty-two-year-old bride.

Lali had suffered from shyness all her life, and even as an adult could not overcome the feeling that she must somehow stay out of other people's way. Except for a few trips to San Juan, the capital, she spent most of her life in the village where she was born. One younger brother was still home. All her other brothers and sisters were married. Most lived close to her parents and all of them were in Puerto Rico. Lali had graduated from first year high school and then worked at home helping her mother and father with their small farm and the younger children. Later she worked part-time, helping in the kitchen and waiting on tables in a small tourist road café near the state park a few miles from her home.

Rudi and his first wife had never had children. All his close relatives lived in Puerto Rico. Upon arriving in New York, Lali found herself in a strange environment without anyone to talk to except Rudi. Lali was unable to understand or speak the language she heard. Although they had taught English in the schools back home, it was almost impossible for her to understand what people said. They spoke so rapidly that she could barely make out a word now and then. She had begun her life in this new land in February; the weather was cold and bitter. Lali had never experienced such cold temperatures. Even the snow was a disappointment to her. In books and in the movies she remembered how beautiful everything looked: white, sparkling, and shiny. All her life she had wanted to see and touch snow, but as soon as the snow fell, traffic and pollution turned it to a brown and murky slush.

After almost two years of living and working together, the marriage still proved to be a strain on both Lali and Rudi. Although kind, Rudi was not an affectionate man by nature. He was hard-working and practical, unable to see beyond someone's most obvious need. He had been nervous with his young wife and responded to her shyness with confusion. As a result he developed a taciturn[8] manner with Lali, causing her to withdraw even further into herself. He hoped that a trip back home to Puerto Rico might help lessen the tension between them.

---

8. taciturn (TAS-uh-tern) *adj.* silent by habit, not talkative

Customers and people in the neighborhood had often kidded Rudi about overworking Lali. At first he had ignored them, but after a while, he wondered if that might not be the cause of the problem between them. When Old Mary's son had come looking for work, Rudi had given him a part-time job helping out during the evenings.

"Mira,[9] Lali, I'm getting extra help. . . . This way, you can take it a little easy now and then, eh?"

Lali had responded indifferently. The harder and longer she worked, the less homesick she felt. There was less time to think; the days were easier to live through and, at night, she was too tired to care.

But Chiquitín made a difference in Lali's life. He was interested in her and showed concern. Slowly she began to talk to Chiquitín, opening up about her loneliness.

"My parents didn't force me to marry him. It was all my idea. I was the one that said yes, even though Rudi was a lot older than me. In fact, he's a year younger than Papi. That's why they told me to think it over. But somehow, he was different, not like the boys I was used to dating. You know, to me he looked like he knew more about the world and all. And then, too, many people back home tell you how wonderful life is here. There's television and the movies; they give another impression. Anyway, I never been glamorous or anything like that, and when Rudi proposed, I couldn't believe it. I saw a chance to get away—to see what was going on in other places, to live in New York, another kind of life. It just seemed exciting to me. Now, Chiquitín, I have no life, except work and more work and church on Sunday, and nobody to talk to. I miss everybody. You know, I can't talk to people too easy. With you it's different because we are both from the countryside, I guess, but I don't understand what's going on around me."

"Come on, Lali, enroll in school with me," Chiquitín had said. "It's wonderful, you can learn the language and you won't feel like that, so left out . . ."

"But I was never a good student," she had protested.

"No matter. I'm not so good myself," he had insisted, "but I'll help you. Together we'll learn. What do you say? You are not doing nothing else. Why not try, eh?"...

---

9. Mira (MEE-rah) *v.* the Spanish word for *look*

Critical Thinking

1. In this story, what do you think Nicholasa Mohr is saying about the experiences of newcomers to the United States?
2. Which aspects of Mohr's culture do you think influenced her most in creating the character of Lali?
3. How are Lali's or Rudi's values and cultural experiences similar to and different from your own?

Writing Your Response to "Lali"

In your journal, write about one or two paragraphs in the selection that made an impression on you. Why were these particular words meaningful to you? Have you had a similar experience or did the passage remind you of something that happened to someone you know? Or, did you simply respond to Mohr's use of colorful language?

Going Back Into the Text: Author's Craft

Setting includes the time and the place in which the events of a story happen. Writers create setting by using words and phrases that act upon a person's senses to convey particular moods or feelings. Sometimes through the technique of **flashback**, a writer can contrast two very different settings. Usually a writer will use flashback to make a point and to support the theme or main idea.

With a partner, review "Lali" to see how Nicholasa Mohr uses flashback to make a point and to convey a particular mood. Use these questions as guidelines.

1. In the selection, which two settings does Mohr contrast using flashback?
2. How did the setting described in the flashback create a particular mood?
3. Explain why the setting is an important element in this story.

from Picture Bride

Reading the Author in a Cultural Context

Yoshiko Uchida's (yoh-shee-koh oo-chee-dah) many books for children and adults feature Japanese or Japanese American characters who use the values of their culture to try to understand themselves and the people around them. She explores how Japanese Americans react to the conflict of cultures that sometimes occurs within U.S. society, and to discrimination.

Uchida knew the cruelty of discrimination firsthand. In 1942, when she was a senior at the University of California at Berkeley, she and the rest of her family were imprisoned in the Topaz internment camp in Utah. Camps were set up in several states during World War II, when a widespread prejudice was that all Japanese Americans were possible spies for the Japanese government. People were rounded up, ordered to sell their homes, businesses, and belongings, and sent to the camps. There they were forced to live in terrible conditions. Uchida wrote about this experience directly in her book *Journey to Topaz*. (See *Farewell to Manzanar* in Theme 7 to find out more about these camps.)

Uchida's characters often have to face conflicts not only with mainstream U.S. society, but also with their families. Sometimes these conflicts are between the ways of the older generation and those of the younger one. In *Picture Bride*, for instance, the family of Hana (hah-nah), the main character in the story, believes in the old traditions that one owes obedience to elders.

Hana's family also believes in the custom of arranged marriages, a practice that has been followed in many cultures, and that survives in Japan to this day. Traditionally, Japanese couples did not marry for their own happiness, but to ensure the survival of their families. Today, the couple's consent is assumed to be necessary.

In the following selection, a Japanese woman, Hana Omiya, arrives in the United States through the Angel Island immigration center in San Francisco Bay. Hana, like thousands of other Asians, endures days of testing, questioning, and waiting before being allowed to enter the United States. The questioning could drag on for days and weeks, and even, in some cases, months and years. Even after this ordeal, some immigrants were refused entry.

Focusing on the Selection

As you read, think about Hana's expectations as a newcomer to the United States. What does her behavior tell you about her character? How does her mother see her? Her brother-in-law? Her uncle? How does she see herself? Record your responses in your journal.

from *Picture Bride*

YOSHIKO UCHIDA

1917–1918

HANA OMIYA[1] STOOD AT THE RAILING of the small ship that shuddered toward America in a turbulent November sea. She shivered as she pulled the folds of her silk kimono[2] close to her throat and tightened the wool shawl about her shoulders.

She was thin and small, her dark eyes shadowed in her pale face, her black hair piled high in a pompadour[3] that seemed too heavy for so slight a woman. She clung to the moist rail and breathed the damp salt air deep into her lungs. Her body seemed leaden and lifeless, as though it were simply the vehicle transporting her soul to a strange new life, and she longed with childlike intensity to be home again in Oka Village.

She longed to see the bright persimmon dotting the barren trees beside the thatched roofs, to see the fields of golden rice stretching to the mountains where only last fall she had gathered plump white mushrooms, and to see once more the maple trees lacing their flaming colors through the green pine. If only she could see a familiar face, eat a meal

---

1. **Hana Omiya** (hah-nah oo-mee-yah) a woman's name
2. **kimono** (kih-MOH-noh) *n.* a robe worn by Japanese women with short, wide sleeves, and a sash
3. **pompadour** (PAHM-puh-dawr) *n.* a hair style in which the hair is swept up high from the forehead and rolled backwards

Photograph of Japanese picture brides taken in 1931.
In the late 19th and early 20th centuries, it was common for
Japanese American men and Japanese women to have their
marriages arranged by a relative or matchmaker. Often, the
only information they would have about one another was a picture.

without retching, walk on solid ground and stretch out at night on a *tatami*[4] mat instead of in a hard narrow bunk. She thought now of seeking the warm shelter of her bunk but could not bear to face the relentless smell of fish that penetrated the lower decks.

Why did I ever leave Japan, she wondered bitterly. Why did I ever listen to my uncle? And yet she knew it was she herself who had begun the chain of events that placed her on this heaving ship. It was she who had first planted in her uncle's mind the thought that she would make a good wife for Taro Takeda,[5] the lonely man who had gone to America to make his fortune in Oakland, California.

It all began one day when her uncle had come to visit her mother.

"I must find a nice young bride," he had said, startling Hana with this blunt talk of marriage in her presence. She blushed and was ready to leave the room when her uncle quickly added, "My good friend Takeda has a son in America. I must find someone willing to travel to that far land."

This last remark was intended to indicate to Hana and her mother that he didn't consider this a suitable prospect for Hana who was the youngest daughter of what once had been a fine family. Her father, until his death fifteen years ago, had been the largest landholder of the village and one of its last *samurai*.[6] They had once had many servants and field hands, but now all that was changed. Their money was gone. Hana's three older sisters had made good marriages, and the eldest remained in

---

   4. *tatami* (tuh-TA-mee) *adj.* a floor mat woven of reeds or straw
   5. **Taro Takeda** (tah-roh tah-ke-dah) a man's name
   6. *samurai* (SAM-yoo-reye) *n.* a member of a landowner's army; in early Japan, each large landowner had his own army

their home with her husband to carry on the Omiya name and perpetuate the homestead. Her other sisters had married merchants in Osaka and Nagoya[7] and were living comfortably.

Now that Hana was twenty-one, finding a proper husband for her had taken on an urgency that produced an embarrassing secretive air over the entire matter. Usually, her mother didn't speak of it until they were lying side by side on their quilts at night. Then, under the protective cover of darkness, she would suggest one name and then another, hoping that Hana would indicate an interest in one of them.

Her uncle spoke freely of Taro Takeda only because he was so sure Hana would never consider him. "He is a conscientious, hard-working man who has been in the United States for almost ten years. He is thirty-one, operates a small shop and rents some rooms above the shop where he lives." Her uncle rubbed his chin thoughtfully. "He could provide well for a wife," he added.

"Ah," Hana's mother said softly.

"You say he is successful in this business?" Hana's sister inquired.

"His father tells me he sells many things in his shop—clothing, stockings, needles, thread and buttons—such things as that. He also sells bean paste, pickled radish, bean cake and soy sauce. A wife of his would not go cold or hungry."

They all nodded, each of them picturing this merchant in varying degrees of success and affluence. There were many Japanese emigrating to America these days, and Hana had heard of the picture brides who went with nothing more than an exchange of photographs to bind them to a strange man.

"Taro San[8] is lonely," her uncle continued. "I want to find for him a fine young woman who is strong and brave enough to cross the ocean alone."

"It would certainly be a different kind of life," Hana's sister ventured, and for a moment, Hana thought she glimpsed a longing ordinarily concealed behind her quiet, obedient face. In that same instant, Hana knew she wanted more for herself than her sisters had in their proper, arranged and loveless marriages. She wanted to escape the smothering strictures[9] of life in her village. She certainly was not going to marry a farmer and spend her life working beside him planting, weeding and harvesting in the rice paddies until her back became bent from too many years of stooping and her skin turned to brown leather by the sun and wind. Neither did she particularly relish the idea of marrying a merchant in a big city as her two sisters had done. Since her mother objected to her

---

7. **Osaka and Nagoya** (OH-sah-kah), (NAH-goh-yah) two seaports in Japan
8. **San** (SAHN) *n.* a word that shows respect
9. **strictures** (STRIHK-chers) *n.* restrictions

going to Tokyo to seek employment as a teacher, perhaps she would consent to a flight to America for what seemed a proper and respectable marriage.

Almost before she realized what she was doing, she spoke to her uncle. "Oji San, perhaps I should go to America to make this lonely man a good wife."

"You, Hana Chan?" Her uncle observed her with startled curiosity. "You would go all alone to a foreign land so far away from your mother and family?"

"I would not allow it." Her mother spoke fiercely. Hana was her youngest and she had lavished upon her the attention and latitude that often befall the last child. How could she permit her to travel so far, even to marry the son of Takeda who was known to her brother.

But now, a notion that had seemed quite impossible a moment before was lodged in his receptive mind, and Hana's uncle grasped it with the pleasure that comes from an unexpected discovery.

"You know," he said looking at Hana, "it might be a very good life in America."

Hana felt a faint fluttering in her heart. Perhaps this lonely man in America was her means of escaping both the village and the encirclement of her family.

Her uncle spoke with increasing enthusiasm of sending Hana to become Taro's wife. And the husband of Hana's sister, who was head of their household, spoke with equal eagerness. Although he never said so, Hana guessed he would be pleased to be rid of her, the spirited younger sister who stirred up his placid life with what he considered radical ideas about life and the role of women. He often claimed that Hana had too much schooling for a girl. She had graduated from Women's High School in Kyoto which gave her five more years of schooling than her older sister.

"It has addled[10] her brain—all that learning from those books," he said when he tired of arguing with Hana.

A man's word carried much weight for Hana's mother. Pressed by the two men she consulted her other daughters and their husbands. She discussed the matter carefully with her brother and asked the village priest. Finally, she agreed to an exchange of family histories and an investigation was begun into Taro Takeda's family, his education and his health, so they would be assured there was no insanity or tuberculosis[11] or police records concealed in his family's past. Soon Hana's uncle was devoting his energies entirely to serving as go-between for Hana's mother and Taro Takeda's father.

---

10. addled (AD-uhld) *v.* confused
11. tuberculosis (tuh-ber-kyoo-LOH-sihs) *n.* a disease of the lungs

When at last an agreement to the marriage was almost reached, Taro wrote his first letter to Hana. It was brief and proper and gave no more clue to his character than the stiff formal portrait taken at his graduation from Middle School. Hana's uncle had given her the picture with apologies from his parents because it was the only photo they had of him and it was not a flattering likeness.

Hana hid the letter and photograph in the sleeve of her kimono and took them to the outhouse to study in private. Squinting in the dim light and trying to ignore the foul odor, she read and reread Taro's letter, trying to find the real man somewhere in the sparse unbending prose.

By the time he sent her money for her steamship tickets, she had received ten more letters, but none revealed much more of the man than the first. In none did he disclose his loneliness or his need, but Hana understood this. In fact, she would have recoiled from a man who bared his intimate thoughts to her so soon. After all, they would have a lifetime together to get to know one another.

So it was that Hana had left her family and sailed alone to America with a small hope trembling inside of her. Tomorrow, at last, the ship would dock in San Francisco and she would meet face to face the man she was soon to marry. Hana was overcome with excitement at the thought of being in America and terrified of the meeting about to take place. What would she say to Taro Takeda when they first met, and for all the days and years after?

Hana wondered about the flat above the shop. Perhaps it would be luxuriously furnished with the finest of brocades[12] and lacquers,[13] and perhaps there would be a servant, although he had not mentioned it. She worried whether she would be able to manage on the meager[14] English she had learned at Women's High School. The overwhelming anxiety for the day to come and the violent rolling of the ship were more than Hana could bear. Shuddering in the face of the wind, she leaned over the railing and became violently and wretchedly ill.

By five the next morning Hana was up and dressed in her finest purple silk kimono and coat. She could not eat the bean soup and rice that appeared for breakfast and took only a few bites of the yellow pickled radish. Her bags, which had scarcely been touched since she boarded the ship, were easily packed for all they contained were her kimonos and some of her favorite books. The large willow basket, tightly secured

---

12. **brocades** (broh-KAYDZ) n. rich cloths with designs woven into them, often of silk, velvet, or gold
13. **lacquers** (LAHK-uhrz) n. fine boxes and ornaments made of wood and coated with a thick varnish
14. **meager** (MEE-guhr) adj. lacking in quality and/or quantity

by a rope, remained under the bunk, untouched since her uncle had placed it there.

She had not befriended the other women in her cabin, for they had lain in their bunks for most of the voyage, too sick to be company to anyone. Each morning Hana had fled the closeness of the sleeping quarters and spent most of the day huddled in a corner of the deck, listening to the lonely songs of some Russians also travelling to an alien land.

As the ship approached land, Hana hurried up to the deck to look out at the gray expanse of ocean and sky, eager for a first glimpse of her new homeland.

"We won't be docking until almost noon," one of the deck hands told her.

Hana nodded. "I can wait," she answered, but the last hours seemed the longest.

When she set foot on American soil at last, it was not in the city of San Francisco as she had expected, but on Angel Island, where all third-class passengers were taken. She spent two miserable days and nights waiting, as the immigrants were questioned by officials, examined for trachoma[15] and tuberculosis, and tested for hookworm by a woman who collected their stools on tin pie plates. Hana was relieved she could produce her own, not having to borrow a little from someone else, as some of the women had to do it. It was a bewildering, degrading beginning, and Hana was sick with anxiety, wondering if she would ever be released.

On the third day, a Japanese messenger from San Francisco appeared with a letter for her from Taro. He had written it the day of her arrival, but it had not reached her for two days.

Taro welcomed her to America and told her that the bearer of the letter would inform Taro when she was to be released so he could be at the pier to meet her.

The letter eased her anxiety for a while, but as soon as she was released and boarded the launch for San Francisco, new fears rose up to smother her with a feeling almost of dread.

The early morning mist had become a light chilling rain, and on the pier, black umbrellas bobbed here and there, making the task of recognition even harder. Hana searched desperately for a face that resembled the photo she had studied so long and hard. Suppose he hadn't come. What would she do then?

Hana took a deep breath, lifted her head and walked slowly from the launch. The moment she was on the pier, a man in a black coat, wearing a derby[16] and carrying an umbrella, came quickly to her side. He was of slight build, not much taller than she, and his face was

---

15. trachoma (truh-KOH-muh) *n.* an eye infection
16. derby (DER-bee) *n.* a stiff felt hat with a rounded top and brim

sallow[17] and pale. He bowed stiffly and murmured, "You have had a long trip, Miss Omiya. I hope you are well."

Hana caught her breath. "You are Takeda San?" she asked.

He removed his hat and Hana was further startled to see that he was already turning bald.

"You are Takeda San?" she asked again. He looked older than thirty-one.

"I am afraid I no longer resemble the early photo my parents gave you. I am sorry."

Hana had not meant to begin like this. It was not going well.

"No, no," she said quickly. "It is just that I . . . that is, I am terribly nervous . . ." Hana stopped abruptly, too flustered[18] to go on.

"I understand," Taro said gently. "You will feel better when you meet my friends and have some tea. Mr. and Mrs. Toda are expecting you in Oakland. You will be staying with them until . . ." He couldn't bring himself to mention the marriage just yet and Hana was grateful he hadn't.

He quickly made arrangements to have her baggage sent to Oakland and then led her carefully along the rain slick pier toward the streetcar that would take them to the ferry.

Hana shuddered at the sight of another boat, and as they climbed to its upper deck she felt a queasy tightening of her stomach.

"I hope it will not rock too much," she said anxiously. "Is it many hours to your city?"

Taro laughed for the first time since their meeting, revealing the gold fillings of his teeth. "Oakland is just across the bay," he explained. "We will be there in twenty minutes."

Raising a hand to cover her mouth, Hana laughed with him and suddenly felt better. I am in America now, she thought, and this is the man I came to marry. Then she sat down carefully beside Taro, so no part of their clothing touched. . . .

---

17. **sallow** (SAHL-oh) *adj.* a sickly, pale color
18. **flustered** (FLUS-terd) *adj.* nervous, confused

Critical Thinking

1. What does Uchida say through her characters about the expectations newcomers have of their new communities?
2. Why do you think Uchida chose to write about her culture through the subject of arranged marriages?
3. Marriage customs may vary a great deal from culture to culture. How are your culture's marriage customs similar to or different from those described in the story?

Writing Your Response to *Picture Bride*

In your journal, describe a scene, character, or dialogue that stood out while you were reading the selection. What made it memorable for you? Did it remind you of something in your own life?

Going Back Into the Text: Author's Craft

An author can reveal a great deal about a character by (1) telling you directly about the character; (2) describing what the character looks like; (3) revealing a character's thoughts and feelings; (4) showing what other characters say about or think about the character; (5) showing you the character's actions and letting you draw your own conclusions. The techniques that an author uses to develop a character are called **characterization.**

Reading literature can often help us understand ourselves, our culture, and some of the dilemmas we have to face. Evaluating a character's behavior, together with its effects on the character's life and on the lives of the other characters, can reveal implications for our own behavior.

With a partner, review the selection to see how Uchida develops the character of Hana. Use the questions below to guide your discussion.

1. Which of the five techniques listed above does Uchida use to develop the character of Hana?
2. How is Hana's personality different from that of the other characters in the selection? How is it similar?
3. How does Hana's nature affect the course of her life? Identify several examples in the selection.
4. In what ways might you be similar to or different from Hana? What might you have done?

I Leave South Africa

Reading the Author in a Cultural Context

Mark Mathabane was only 26 years old when he wrote *Kaffir Boy*, a book that exposed the horrors of apartheid (uh-PAHR-tayt). He was born in Alexandra, South Africa, in 1960. His parents were laborers. His family's life was a struggle with the poverty and oppression common to nonwhites under apartheid. Apartheid forced nonwhites and whites to live and work apart. Nonwhites could not choose where to live or go to school. They could not even choose whom to marry. They were made to live in the poorest houses and work at the lowest-paying jobs. They also were denied basic human rights.

Government censorship was severe. Criticism of apartheid was forbidden. Many writers and artists were forced to leave the country because their work was thought to be too political. Many continued to protest apartheid from outside their homeland. Some protested from within the country, too. They risked imprisonment or even death.

Mathabane's parents could not agree on the best way for Mark to escape poverty. His mother believed that education held the key. His father felt that a commitment to his African heritage was more important. Mark decided to go to school. At school, he also learned to play tennis. Many well-known tennis stars were impressed with his skill. One of these was U.S. player Stan Smith, who helped Mark win a scholarship to Limestone College, in South Carolina. Mark was glad to be able to "turn [his] anger into something positive."

Mathabane's autobiography, *Kaffir Boy*, talks about the struggle of living under apartheid. His second book, *Kaffir Boy in America*, from which the following selection is taken, continues his story.

Focusing on the Selection

As you read "I Leave South Africa," notice what Mark Mathabane tells you about his own culture and about his first impressions of the United States. What were his expectations? Which expectations were realized? Which were not? What did he find out about the United States through the eyes of one African American? Record your responses in your journal as you read.

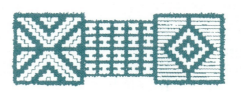

I Leave South Africa

from *Kaffir Boy in America*

MARK MATHABANE

THE PLANE LANDED at Atlanta's International Airport the afternoon of September 17, 1978. I double-checked the name and description of Dr. Killion's friend who was to meet me. Shortly after the plane came to a standstill at the gate, and I was stashing Dr. Killion's letter into my totebag, I felt a tap on my shoulder, and turning met the steady and unsettling gaze of the Black Muslim.[1]

"Are you from Africa?" he asked as he offered to help me with my luggage.

"Yes." I wondered how he could tell.

"A student?"

"Yes." We were aboard a jumbo jet, almost at the back of it. From the throng in front it was clear that it would be some time before we disembarked, so we fell into conversation. He asked if it was my first time in the United States and I replied that it was. He spoke in a thick American accent.

"Glad to meet you, brother," he said. We shook hands. "My name is Nkwame."[2]

---

1. **Black Muslim** (BLAK MUZ-luhm) a member of a predominantly African American sect of the Islamic faith
2. **Nkwame** (NKWAH-mee) a man's name

Photograph of
Mark Mathabane
taken in 1986.

"I'm Mark," I said, somewhat intimidated by his aspect.[3]

"Mark is not African," he said coolly. "What's your African name, brother?"

"Johannes."

"That isn't an African name either."

I was startled by this. How did he know I had an African name? I hardly used it myself because it was an unwritten rule among black youths raised in the ghettos to deny their tribal identity and affiliation, and that denial applied especially to names. But I didn't want to offend this persistent stranger, so I gave it to him. "Thanyani."[4]

"What does it stand for?"

How did he know that my name stood for something? I wondered in amazement. My worst fears were confirmed. Black Americans did indeed possess the sophistication to see through any ruse[5] an African puts up. Then and there I decided to tell nothing but the truth.

---

3. aspect (AS-pekt) *n.* appearance
4. Thanyani (tahn-EEAH-nee) a man's name
5. ruse (ROOZ) *n.* trick, or dodge

"The wise one," I said, and quickly added, "but the interpretation is not meant to be taken literally, sir."

We were now headed out of the plane. He carried my tennis rackets.

"The wise one, heh," he mused. "You Africans sure have a way with names. You know," he went on with great warmth, "one of my nephews is named after a famous African chief. Of the Mandingo tribe, I believe. Ever since I saw 'Roots' I have always wanted to know where my homeland is."

I found this statement baffling for I thought that as an American his homeland was America. I did not know about "Roots."

"Which black college in Atlanta will you be attending, Thanyani?" he asked. "You will be attending a black college, I hope?"

Black colleges? I stared at him. My mind conjured up images of the dismal tribal schools I hated and had left behind in the ghetto. My God, did such schools exist in America?

"No, sir," I stammered. "I won't be attending school in Atlanta. I'm headed for Limestone College in South Carolina."

"Is Limestone a black college?"

"No, sir," I said hastily.

"What a pity," he sighed. "You would be better off at a black college."

I continued staring at him.

He went on. "At a black college," he said with emphasis, "you can meet with your true brothers and sisters. There's so much you can teach them about the true Africa and the struggles of our people over there. And they have a lot to teach you about being black in America. And, you know, there are lots of black colleges in the South."

I nearly fainted at this revelation. Black schools in America? Was I hearing things or what? I almost blurted out that I had attended black schools all my life and wanted to have nothing to do with them. But instead I said, "Limestone College is supposed to be a good college, too, sir. It's integrated."

"That don't mean nothing," he snapped. "Integrated schools are the worst places for black folks. I thought you Africans would have enough brains to know that this integration business in America is a fraud. It ain't good for the black mind and culture. Integration, integration," he railed.[6] "What good has integration done the black man? We've simply become more dependent on the white devil and forgotten how to do things for ourselves. Also, no matter how integrated we become, white folks won't accept us as equals. So why should we break our backs trying to mix with them, heh? . . ."

---

6. **railed** (RAYLD) *v.* scolded

I was shaken by his outburst. I longed to be gone from him, especially since he had drawn me aside in the corridor leading toward customs. The Black Muslim must have realized that I was a complete stranger to him, that his bitter tone terrified and confused me, for he quickly recollected himself and smiled.

"Well, good luck in your studies, brother," he said, handing me my rackets. "By the way, where in Africa did you say you were from? Nigeria?"

"No. South Africa."

"South what!" he said.

"South Africa," I repeated. "That place with all those terrible race problems. Where black people have no rights and are being murdered every day."

I expected my statement to shock him; instead he calmly said, "You will find a lot of South Africa in this country, brother. Keep your eyes wide open all the time. Never let down your guard or you're dead. And while you're up there in South Carolina, watch out for the Ku Klux Klan. That's their home. And don't you ever believe that integration nonsense."

He left. I wondered what he meant by his warning. I stumbled my way to customs. There was a long queue[7] and when my turn came the white, somber-faced immigration official, with cropped reddish-brown hair, seemed transformed into an Afrikaner[8] bureaucrat. I almost screamed. He demanded my passport. After inspecting it, he asked to see my plane ticket. I handed it to him.

"It's a one-way ticket," he said.

"Yes, sir. I couldn't afford a return ticket," I answered, wondering what could be wrong.

"Under the student visa regulations you're required to have a return ticket," he said icily. "Otherwise how will you get back home? You intend returning home after your studies, don't you?"

"Yes, sir."

"Then you ought to have a return ticket."

I remained silent.

"Do you have relatives or a guardian in America?"

I speedily handed him a letter from Stan Smith, along with several completed immigration forms indicating that he had pledged to be my legal guardian for the duration of my stay in the States. The immigration officer inspected the documents, then left his cubicle and went to consult his superior. I trembled at the thought that I might be denied

---

7. **queue** (KYOO) *n.* line of people
8. **Afrikaner** (af-rih-KAHN-er) *adj.* a descendant of the Dutch who colonized South Africa in the 1600s

entry into the United States. But the one-way ticket, which created the impression that I was coming to America for good, was hardly my fault. Having had no money to purchase a ticket of my own, I had depended on the charity of white friends, and I was in no position to insist that they buy me a return ticket. The immigration officer came back. He stamped my passport and welcomed me to the United States. I almost fell on my knees and kissed the hallowed ground.

"Welcome to America, Mark," a tall, lean-faced white man greeted me as I came out of customs. It was Dr. Waller.

His kind voice and smiling face, as he introduced himself and asked me if I had a good flight, raised my spirits. As we walked toward the baggage claim area I stared at everything about me with childlike wonder. I scarcely believed I had finally set foot in *the* America. I felt the difference between South Africa and America instantly. The air seemed pervaded with freedom and hope and opportunity. Every object seemed brighter, newer, more modern, fresher, the people appeared better dressed, more intelligent, richer, warmer, happier, and full of energy— despite the profound impersonality of the place.

. . . In South Africa blacks adored Afros and often incurred great expense cultivating that curious hairdo, in imitation of black Americans. Those who succeeded in giving their naturally crinkly, nappy, and matted hair, which they loathed, that buoyant "American" look were showered with praise and considered handsome and "glamorous," as were those who successfully gave it the permanent wave or jerry-curl, and bleached their faces white with special creams which affected the pigmentation.

I remember how Uncle Pietrus, on my father's side, a tall, athletic, handsome man who earned slave wages, was never without creams such as Ambi to bleach his face, and regularly wore a meticulously combed Afro greased with Brylcreem. Many in the neighborhood considered him the paragon[9] of manly beauty, and women were swept away by his "American" looks.

From time to time he proudly told me stories of how, in the center of Johannesburg, whites who encountered black men and women with bleached faces, Afros, or straightened hair, and clad in the latest fashion from America, often mistook them for black Americans and treated them as honorary whites. A reasonable American accent made the masquerade almost foolproof. So for many blacks there were these incentives to resemble black Americans, to adopt their mannerisms and life-styles. And the so-called Coloureds (mixed race), with their naturally lighter skin and straightened hair, not only frequently took advantage of this deception but often passed for whites. But they were rarely

---

9. **paragon** (PAR-uh-gahn) *n.* model of perfection

secure in their false identity. And in their desperation to elude discovery and humiliation at being subjected to fraudulent race-determining tests like the pencil test (where the authorities run a pencil through one's hair: if the pencil slides smoothly through, one gets classified white; if it gets tangled, that's "positive" proof of being black), they often adopted racist attitudes toward blacks more virulent[10] than those of the most racist whites.

I had sense enough to disdain the practice of whitening one's skin. I considered it pathetic and demeaning to blacks. As for the companies which manufactured these popular creams, they are insidiously[11] catering to a demand created by over three hundred years of white oppression and domination. During that traumatic time the black man's culture and values were decimated[12] in the name of civilization, and the white man's culture and values, trumpeted as superior, became the standards of intelligence, excellence, and beauty. . . .

At the baggage-claim area I saw black and white people constantly rubbing shoulders, animatedly talking to one another, and no one seemed to mind. There were no ubiquitous[13] armed policemen.

"There truly is no apartheid here," I said to myself. "This is indeed the Promised Land."

I felt so happy and relieved that for the first time the tension that went with being black in South Africa left me. I became a new person.

---

10. **virulent** (VIHR-yoo-luhnt) *adj.* poisonous; full of hate
11. **insidiously** (ihn-SIHD-ee-uhs-lee) *adv.* treacherously
12. **decimated** (DES-uh-mayt-uhd) *v.* destroyed
13. **ubiquitous** (yoo-BIHK-wuh-tuhs) *adj.* present everywhere

Critical Thinking

1. What does Mark Mathabane tell you about his expectations for living in the United States? How were his expectations realized, and how were they challenged?
2. What does Mark Mathabane tell you about his own culture in South Africa?
3. How did reading this personal narrative support your understanding of racial discrimination?

Writing Your Response to "I Leave South Africa"

In your journal, write your reactions to the expectations and the realities presented in the selection. Which of Mark Mathabane's expectations were realistic and which were not? How did his experience match or not match his expectations? Which of Nkwame's comments are realistic and which are not? Explain your thinking.

Going Back Into the Text: Author's Craft

Irony is a term that describes a contrast between what is expected to happen and what really happens. For example, Mark Mathabane expected that African Americans would value anything considered "American" because the people of his culture did. Nkwame, though, seemed prouder of the African part of his heritage than he did of the American part. Their conversation is ironic because it contrasts with Mark's expectations.

Irony can also describe statements that mean the opposite of what they say. For example, if someone says, "that's a great plan," when he or she knows it will not work, we can say that is an **ironic** statement. This kind of irony is the basis of many jokes.

With a partner, spend some time talking about irony in the story. Use the following questions and directives to guide your discussion.

1. What is ironic about Nkwame's question: "You will be attending a black college, I hope?"
2. Find more examples of irony in the selection and explain why you identified them as irony.
3. What examples of irony can you give from the events in our world today? Think about different areas such as politics, the economy, the environment, education, and so on.

Ellis Island

Reading the Author in a Cultural Context

Joseph Bruchac (BROO-chak), like many other American writers, explores his ancestry in his work. Bruchac has two very different lines of ancestry—Abnaki (ahb-NAH-kee) Native American and Slovakian. His mother's family is Abnaki. The Abnaki are a part of the federation of Algonquian (al-GAHN-kee-uhn) peoples of the eastern United States. His grandparents on his father's side emigrated to the United States from Slovakia, the eastern part of modern-day Czechoslovakia. Often, Bruchac writes about both parts of his heritage, as he does in the poem you are about to read. Bruchac mainly writes poetry. However, he also collects and retells traditional Native American stories.

Bruchac understands the value that Native Americans place on the land. The value of land provides a consistent thread or theme in his work. In the introduction to *Iroquois Stories: Heroes and Heroines, Monsters and Magic*, he calls the land one of his teachers. He says of his own home area—Saratoga Springs, New York—"If it is true that all of our stories come first from the earth, then I have been blessed with good earth to listen to." Much of the land of his Abnaki ancestors was taken over first by the Iroquois Nation, as they became more powerful, and then by white settlers.

The white settlers represent the other side of Bruchac's heritage. When his grandparents emigrated to the United States, they came to escape the terrible poverty of Slovakia and to find a better life. Immigrants did not know that as they poured into the United States, they took away the land of Native Americans. This land had been passed from one Native American generation to the next.

Focusing on the Selection

As you read "Ellis Island," think about the two parts of the poet's ancestry. How does he describe his European ancestors' experience of coming to America? How does he describe his Native American ancestors' reaction to the European newcomers? In what way does Bruchac use the poem to reveal his own inner conflict? Record your responses in your journal as you read.

Ellis Island

JOSEPH BRUCHAC

Beyond the red brick of Ellis Island
where the two Slovak children
who became my grandparents
waited the long days of quarantine,[1]
after leaving the sickness,
the old Empires of Europe,
a Circle Line ship[2] slips easily
on its way to the island
of the tall woman, green
as dreams of forests and meadows
waiting for those who'd worked
a thousand years
yet never owned their own.
Like millions of others,
I too come to this island,
nine decades[3] the answerer
of dreams.

Yet only one part of my blood loves that memory.
Another voice speaks
of native lands
within this nation.
Lands invaded
when the earth became owned.
Lands of those who followed
the changing Moon,
knowledge of the season
in their veins.

Photograph of missionaries at work
with European immigrants on Ellis Island.
Why were immigrants willing to face the hardships of
leaving their homes and
coming to the United States?

---

1. **quarantine** (KWAHR-uhn-teen) *n.* separation
   and isolation, a waiting period imposed on travelers to keep disease from spreading.
2. **Circle Line ship** ferry that takes people to Liberty
   Island to visit the Statue of Liberty
3. **decades** (DEK-aydz) *n.* periods of ten years

Critical Thinking

1. What does Joseph Bruchac tell you about what immigration to the United States was like for millions of Europeans?
2. What does he tell you about the reaction of his Native American ancestors to European immigration?
3. What is your reaction to Joseph Bruchac's own inner conflict and to the conflict between the two cultures he tells about?

Writing Your Response to "Ellis Island"

In your journal, write about the parts of the poem that impressed you the most. Was it the particular words Bruchac used to create the imagery, or pictures, in your mind, or was it something else that moved you? Record your responses to the poem in your journal.

Going Back Into the Text: Author's Craft

Writers often use **figurative language** to help readers better understand ideas and feelings. Figurative expressions are not intended to be taken literally. They are used imaginatively and add color to writing by comparing and contrasting unlike things. *Simile* is one common figure of speech. A simile talks about one thing as if it were something very different. The words *like* or *as* are keys to finding similes. "I've been up and down this elevator so many times today, I feel like a yo-yo" is an example of a simile.

With a partner, reread the poem aloud. Then talk about Bruchac's use of figurative language. Use the following items to guide your discussion.

1. Identify at least one simile in the poem.
2. What comparison is Bruchac making in the simile?
3. How does the comparison create a clear picture in your mind? In what way does the picture give meaning to what Bruchac is trying to say?
4. What other similes might Bruchac have used in his poem? Brainstorm some ideas with your partner.

MAKING CONNECTIONS

The Immigrant Experience

Between 1866 and 1915, more than 25 million immigrants came to the United States seeking economic opportunity, political and religious freedom, or adventure. Many left villages where their families had lived for generations. Hundreds of thousands of immigrants still arrive in this country every year. Each has come with a dream of a better life—a dream both personal and universal.

Starting in 1892, most immigrants entered the United States through Ellis Island in New York Harbor. An immigration station for more than 60 years, Ellis Island was closed in 1954. In 1990, it reopened as a national monument and museum.

George Luks painted city life at the turn of the century. In works such as *Hester Street* (1905), Luks captured the spirit of immigrant neighborhoods like this one in New York City. In these neighborhoods, newcomers often settled among people who shared their language and customs.

From 1910 to 1940, most Asians who hoped to enter the United States passed through the immigration center at Angel Island in San Francisco Bay. Women and men were separated during immigration examinations. Today, Angel Island is a California state park.

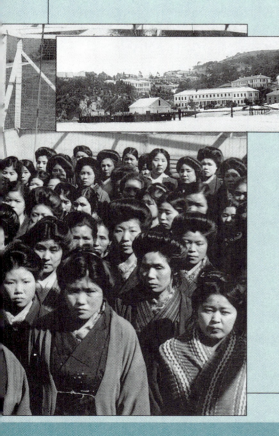

LINKING
Literature, Culture, and Theme

Compare the aspects of immigrant experience depicted on these pages with those expressed in Joseph Bruchac's poem "Ellis Island."

▼ Photographs focus on reality. George Luks also tried to picture the real world in his paintings. Joseph Bruchac, on the other hand, writes of dreams. How do the dreams he describes compare and contrast with the reality reflected in the pictures on these pages?

▼ What similar struggles do you think newcomers have faced after arriving in this country? What common goals do you think they have sought?

▼ Why do you think that both Angel Island and Ellis Island have been set aside as historical landmarks? Why do you think people visit them? What do these places represent?

Those Who Don't, No Speak English, and **The Three Sisters**

Reading the Author in a Cultural Context

Mexican American people can trace their roots in the southwestern United States back to the early 1600s. An area about the size of the present states of New Mexico, Arizona, California, Nevada, Utah, and Colorado was controlled by Mexico until 1848. Then, Mexico surrendered it as part of the treaty ending the Mexican-American War. The war was fought over Texas, which had also been part of Mexico. For 200 years, the dominant culture and language in the Mexican territory were Spanish. It seems odd, then, that Mexican Americans today face discrimination from people of other cultures who have more recently arrived in the United States.

Since then, Mexican Americans and newly arrived Mexican immigrants have moved to other parts of the United States, mostly to the cities. At present, about 85 percent of all Mexican Americans live in cities. Often, they are paid less than people of northern European ancestry for the same work. Poor wages have kept many Mexican Americans in poverty.

Some Mexican Americans have improved their lives despite discrimination. They have managed to do this without giving up ties to, or diluting, their cultural heritage.

Sandra Cisneros (SAHN-dra sihs-NAY-rohs) is one of those people.

Cisneros often writes about Mexican Americans. She was born in Chicago in 1954. Her father was born in Mexico and her mother was born in the United States. Cisneros knows firsthand what it is like to grow up in a poverty-stricken neighborhood. The stories that follow are from her first book of fiction, *The House on Mango Street*. In her stories, Cisneros tells about life in the Hispanic sections of Chicago. Her main character is Esperanza Cordero (es-payr-AHN-zah kawr-DAY-roh), a young Mexican American girl. In her stories, Cisneros talks about bias and tries to eliminate some Mexican American stereotypes.

Focusing on the Selections

As you read the three stories from *The House on Mango Street*, notice what Sandra Cisneros tells you about the Mexican American neighborhood on Mango Street. What is revealed here about living in a neighborhood whose culture is different from the mainstream culture? What mood or tone is created as a result of the experiences and the characters' reactions? Every neighborhood has characteristics that make it feel like home to its residents, just as this one does. What are some characteristics of your own neighborhood? Record your ideas in your journal as you read.

Those Who Don't

from *The House on Mango*[1] *Street*

SANDRA CISNEROS

THOSE WHO DON'T KNOW ANY BETTER come into our neighborhood scared. They think we're dangerous. They think we will attack them with shiny knives. They are stupid people who are lost and got here by mistake.

But we aren't afraid. We know the guy with the crooked eye is Davey the Baby's brother, and the tall one next to him in the straw brim, that's Rosa's Eddie V. and the big one that looks like a dumb grown man, he's Fat Boy, though he's not fat anymore nor a boy.

All brown all around, we are safe. But watch us drive into a neighborhood of another color and our knees go shakity-shake and our car windows get rolled up tight and our eyes look straight. Yeah. That is how it goes and goes.

---

1. **Mango** (MAHN-goh) *n.* a fruit

No Speak English

from *The House on Mango Street*

SANDRA CISNEROS

MAMACITA[2] IS THE BIG MAMA of the man across the street, third-floor front. Rachel says her name ought to be *Mamasota*, but I think that's mean.

The man saved his money to bring her here. He saved and saved because she was alone with the baby boy in that country. He worked two jobs. He came home late and he left early. Every day.

Then one day Mamacita and the baby boy arrived in a yellow taxi. The taxi door opened like a waiter's arm. Out stepped a tiny pink shoe, a foot soft as a rabbit's ear, then the thick ankle, a flutter of hips, fuchsia roses and green perfume. The man had to pull her, the taxicab driver had to push. Push, pull. Push, pull. Poof!

All at once she bloomed. Huge, enormous, beautiful to look at, from the salmon-pink feather on the tip of her hat down to the little rosebuds of her toes. I couldn't take my eyes off her tiny shoes.

Up, up, up the stairs she went with the baby boy in a blue blanket, the man carrying her suitcases, her lavender hatboxes, a dozen boxes of satin high heels. Then we didn't see her.

Somebody said because she's too fat, somebody because of the three flights of stairs, but I believe she doesn't come out because she is afraid to speak English, and maybe this is so since she only knows eight words. She knows to say: *He not here* for when the landlord comes, *No speak English* if anybody else comes, and *Holy smokes*. I don't know where she learned this, but I heard her say it one time and it surprised me.

My father says when he came to this country he ate hamandeggs for three months. Breakfast, lunch and dinner. Hamandeggs. That was the only word he knew. He doesn't eat hamandeggs anymore.

Whatever her reasons, whether she is fat, or can't climb the stairs, or is afraid of English, she won't come down. She sits all day by the window and plays the Spanish radio show and sings all the homesick songs about her country in a voice that sounds like a seagull.

Home. Home. Home is a house in a photograph, a pink house, pink as hollyhocks with lots of startled light. The man paints the walls of the apartment pink, but it's not the same you know. She still sighs for her pink house, and then I think she cries. I would.

Sometimes the man gets disgusted. He starts screaming and you can hear it all the way down the street.

---

2. **Mamacita** (mah-mah-SEE-tah) *n.* a pet name for mother

Ay, she says, she is sad.

Oh, he says, not again.

¡Cuándo,[3] cuándo, cuándo? she asks.

¡Ay, Caray![4] We *are* home. This *is* home. Here I am and here I stay. Speak English. Speak English. Christ!

¡Ay! Mamacita, who does not belong, every once in a while lets out a cry, hysterical, high, as if he had torn the only skinny thread that kept her alive, the only road out to that country.

And then to break her heart forever, the baby boy who has begun to talk, starts to sing the Pepsi commercial he heard on T.V.

No speak English, she says to the child who is singing in the language that sounds like tin. No speak English, no speak English, and bubbles into tears. No, no, no as if she can't believe her ears.

The Three Sisters

from *The House on Mango Street*

SANDRA CISNEROS

THEY CAME WITH THE WIND THAT BLOWS in August, thin as a spider web and barely noticed. Three who did not seem to be related to anything but the moon. One with laughter like tin and one with eyes of a cat and one with hands like porcelain. The aunts, the three sisters, *las comadres*,[5] they said.

The baby died. Lucy and Rachel's sister. One night a dog cried, and the next day a yellow bird flew in through an open window. Before the week was over, the baby's fever was worse. Then Jesus came and took the baby with him far away. That's what their mother said.

Then the visitors came . . . in and out of the little house. It was hard to keep the floors clean. Anybody who had ever wondered what color the walls were came and came to look at that little thumb of a human in a box like candy.

I had never seen the dead before, not for real, not in somebody's living room for people to kiss and bless themselves and light a candle for. Not in a house. It seemed strange.

They must've known, the sisters. They had the power and could sense what was what. They said, Come here, and give me a stick of gum.

---

3. ¡Cuándo (KWAN-doh) *adv.* the Spanish word for *When?*

4. ¡Ay, Caray! (EYE kah-RAY) *interj.* Oh, no!

5. *las comadres* (lahs kohm-AH-drays) *n.* the godmothers, or close family friends

Portrait of Nina Ibarra. Painted by Puerto Rican
American artist Rosa Ibarra in 1991. Oil on canvas.

They smelled like Kleenex or the inside of a satin handbag, and then I
didn't feel afraid.

    What's your name, the cat-eyed one asked.

    Esperanza,[6] I said.

    Esperanza, the old blue-veined one repeated in a high thin voice. Es-
peranza . . . a good good name.

    My knees hurt, the one with the funny laugh complained.

    Tomorrow it will rain.

    Yes, tomorrow, they said.

    How do you know? I asked.

    We know.

    Look at her hands, cat-eyed said.

---

6. **Esperanza** (ays-pay-RAHN-sah) *n.* a woman's name, meaning *hope*

And they turned them over and over as if they were looking for something.

She's special.

Yes, she'll go very far.

Yes, yes, hmmm.

Make a wish.

A wish?

Yes, make a wish. What do you want?

Anything? I said.

Well, why not?

I closed my eyes.

Did you wish already?

Yes, I said.

Well, that's all there is to it. It'll come true.

How do you know? I asked.

We know, we know.

Esperanza. The one with marble hands called me aside. Esperanza. She held my face with her blue-veined hands and looked and looked at me. A long silence. When you leave you must remember always to come back, she said.

What?

When you leave you must remember to come back for the others. A circle, understand? You will always be Esperanza. You will always be Mango Street. You can't erase what you know. You can't forget who you are.

Then I didn't know what to say. It was as if she could read my mind, as if she knew what I had wished for, and I felt ashamed for having made such a selfish wish.

You must remember to come back. For the ones who cannot leave as easily as you. You will remember? She asked as if she was telling me. Yes, yes, I said a little confused.

Good, she said rubbing my hands. Good. That's all. You can go.

I got up to join Lucy and Rachel who were already outside waiting by the door, wondering what I was doing talking to three old ladies who smelled like cinnamon. I didn't understand everything they had told me. I turned around. They smiled and waved in their smoky way.

Then I didn't see them. Not once, or twice, or ever again.

POSTREADING

Critical Thinking

1. What does Cisneros tell you about the experiences of Mexican Americans in a country in which the dominant language is English?
2. What does Cisneros tell you about the values and the culture of Mexican American people?
3. In what ways did reading these stories influence your thoughts about cultural stereotypes?

Writing Your Response to "Those Who Don't," "No Speak English," and "The Three Sisters"

In your journal, write about one event, character, idea, or issue that affected you as you read the selection. Tell what it was about the situation that touched you and how it relates to your own experience or to the experiences of people you know.

Going Back Into the Text: Author's Craft

Tone is the writer's attitude toward the subject, the characters, or his or her audience. The tone, or mood, of a literary work may be friendly or distant. It may be angry, humorous, or serious. Tone is usually revealed by the writer's choice of words. When you read a literary work, the emotions you feel are probably the result of the writer's tone. Paying attention to the words a writer chooses can sometimes help you to identify the tone of a literary work.

With a partner, review the selection to see how Cisneros uses words to create tone in each piece. Use the following questions to guide your discussion.

1. How would you describe the tone of each of the three stories?
2. Which words in particular provided clues that helped you to detect the writer's tone?
3. Explain how you think the tone of each story heightens or interferes with its message.

Reviewing the Theme

1. Choose two or more characters you read about in this section and compare their experiences as newcomers to the United States. What was similar and different about their reactions and about the obstacles they had to overcome?

2. Describe how an author's heritage can affect the characters, events, and theme of his or her work. Use examples from two or more selections in the section to support your answer.

3. Have you ever been a newcomer? How are your experiences similar to and different from those of some of the characters in this unit?

FOCUSING THE UNIT THEME

COOPERATIVE/COLLABORATIVE LEARNING

With three of your classmates, talk about the works presented in this unit as they relate to the theme and to your own lives. Below is a sample dialogue that one group of students used to start their discussion. You may wish to use it as a starting point in your discussion.

STUDENT 1: I know that each group that is a part of our country's history faced many difficulties in arriving and settling here. I now realize how terrible it was at times for these people. There were so many barriers to overcome—differences in language, in customs, and in accepting one another.

STUDENT 2: The lack of acceptance really hits home when you read Harper's poem "The Slave Auction." The sale of children before their mothers' eyes must have been heartbreaking. How could our country accept these injustices for so long?

STUDENT 3: In *Picture Bride*, Uchida describes arranged marriages. I can just imagine all the mixed feelings the man and the woman must have had. I wonder if arranged marriages are part of any other culture.

STUDENT 4: I'm not sure, but I really liked the way Bruchac conveyed the mixed feelings of newcomers in his poem "Ellis Island." I think we all at one time or another question our cultural backgrounds. We are not all the same. But like someone said, "We are many, we are one"—like the threads of the tapestry.

Writing Process

Review all the journal notes that you have made for the literature in this unit. Rethink your responses in terms of the unit theme, "Arrival and Settlement." Choose two or more of the selections that were the most helpful and meaningful to you in developing an understanding of the conditions under which the many groups arrived and settled here.

Write a personal essay based on the literature you have selected. Use the writing process described on pages 393-402 of the handbook to write your essay. If necessary, use the model personal essay provided.

Problem Solving

Analyze one or more of the challenges faced by newcomers presented in the unit. Explain how they are similar to or different from the challenges you or someone you know has experienced. In what ways can you relate the situation to an issue in your own life? How would you solve the problem if it affected you or your family? In the form of a skit, debate, dance, musical arrangement, news show, or art composition, express your reflections on the problem.

In your presentation, make sure to illustrate your insights about "Arrival and Settlement" in the United States. You may wish to work alone, with a partner, or in a small group.

Photograph of James Meredith in graduation procession at the University of Mississippi in 1963, taken by African American photographer Charles Moore. Meredith was the first African American to attend the university.

Photograph of Manzanar War Relocation Center, taken by Ansel Adams during the 1940s.

Photograph of Native Americans protesting unfair treatment by the U.S. government in front of the White House in 1978.

STRUGGLE AND RECOGNITION

The literature in Unit 3 depicts the continuing struggle for equality of various groups within U.S. society. The selections convey the quests these groups have undertaken to share fully in the nation's benefits. Sometimes this struggle for equality occurs on a very personal level. Individuals discover the need to break down walls of misunderstanding and mistrust and to appreciate people for who they are, not where they come from. At other times, the vision of equality has a greater scope. This larger goal is a nation in which groups of people overcome social barriers and share a common goal of building a multicultural society of diverse traditions.

The Declaration of Independence, written in 1776, proclaimed the ideals of freedom and equality. It states:

We hold these truths to be self-evident, that all men are created equal, that they are endowed by their Creator with certain unalienable Rights, that among these are Life, Liberty and the pursuit of Happiness.

We know, however, that the people who wrote that document did not mean to include enslaved African Americans, Native Americans, or women. During the 19th century, the United States opened its shores to increasing numbers of immigrants—but usually only to those immigrants who would go west to farm or who would carry on European traditions. Asians, for example, found themselves the target of discrimination and were denied their civil rights.

Prejudice against newcomers has sometimes made becoming an American a difficult and painful process. Throughout U.S. history, groups outside mainstream society have had to struggle for recognition and acceptance. The newcomer has usually been looked down upon and has often felt the fear and distrust of the groups who came before. Because of this feeling of being unwanted, newcomers put walls around themselves and their group to keep others out. They have tended to live together in neighborhoods, attend the same houses of worship, and socialize mainly within their own group.

People used to refer to the United States as the melting pot in which all the different groups would merge into one. Recently, however, other metaphors have replaced that symbol. Now the United States is often viewed as a kind of "salad bowl" containing a collection of different ingredients. The nation might also be seen as a mosaic or a tapestry. In a mosaic, each segment stands out from the others but adds to the complete picture. The individual threads in a tapestry weave together to make a cloth.

As you look around your school and your community, how would you describe the way in which different groups come together or stay apart? What metaphor would you use to

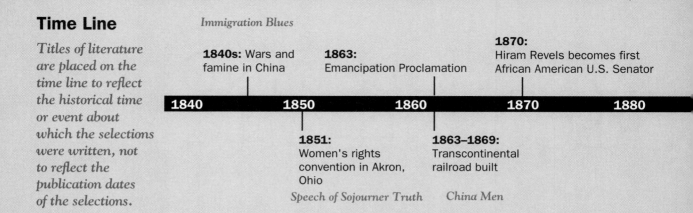

Time Line

Titles of literature are placed on the time line to reflect the historical time or event about which the selections were written, not to reflect the publication dates of the selections.

Immigration Blues

1840s: Wars and famine in China

1863: Emancipation Proclamation

1870: Hiram Revels becomes first African American U.S. Senator

1840   1850   1860   1870   1880

1851: Women's rights convention in Akron, Ohio

1863–1869: Transcontinental railroad built

Speech of Sojourner Truth   *China Men*

---

describe your community? How do individuals cross barriers that keep cultures apart? How does your school or community try to bring all the different groups together? What vision of a multicultural society do you have? What part do you play in making this vision a reality?

As you read the selections in this unit, think about how they relate to the section themes. What different attitudes and perspectives do the authors have on the quest for equality, on accepting differences, and on overcoming social barriers?

Consider whether the authors identify more with their own cultural groups or with some larger cross-cultural grouping or unity. What attitude do you think these writers have about the future of their cultures in the United States? Hopeful? Realistic? Distrustful? Enthusiastic? Do you think that the writers allow their cultural backgrounds to dominate their writing? Are the authors simply representatives of their cultures, or are they unique individuals with very personal attitudes? Or are they both? What similarities do you see among writers from different cultures? What common goals, values, and traditions do they have? How do these authors give voice to universal human hopes?

Historical Background and Thematic Organization

At different times in U.S. history, various groups have been forced to endure the injustices of second-class citizenship. These groups have fought hard to assert their rights as equal citizens.

During World War II, Japanese Americans were made to suffer because the United States was at war with the country that some of them had left three generations before. Those living on the West Coast were forced to leave their homes and businesses and were sent to internment camps. Only recently have their losses been recognized by the U.S. government.

In the 1950s, African Americans came to realize that unless they took firm action, they

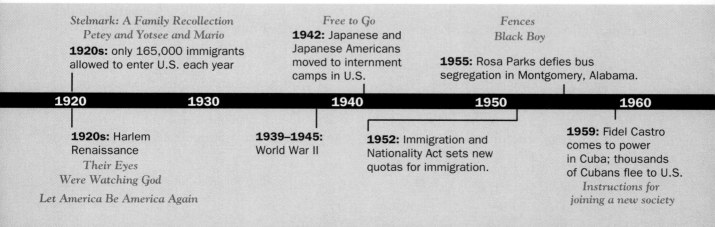

Stelmark: A Family Recollection
Petey and Yotsee and Mario

1920s: only 165,000 immigrants allowed to enter U.S. each year

Free to Go

1942: Japanese and Japanese Americans moved to internment camps in U.S.

Fences
Black Boy

1955: Rosa Parks defies bus segregation in Montgomery, Alabama.

1920   1930   1940   1950   1960

1920s: Harlem Renaissance
Their Eyes Were Watching God
Let America Be America Again

1939–1945: World War II

1952: Immigration and Nationality Act sets new quotas for immigration.

1959: Fidel Castro comes to power in Cuba; thousands of Cubans flee to U.S.
Instructions for joining a new society

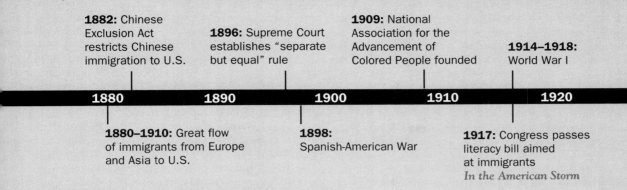

1882: Chinese Exclusion Act restricts Chinese immigration to U.S.

1896: Supreme Court establishes "separate but equal" rule

1909: National Association for the Advancement of Colored People founded

1914–1918: World War I

1880　1890　1900　1910　1920

1880–1910: Great flow of immigrants from Europe and Asia to U.S.

1898: Spanish-American War

1917: Congress passes literacy bill aimed at immigrants
In the American Storm

would never obtain the full civil rights promised by the U.S. Constitution. From the late 1950s through the 1970s, African Americans initiated a series of forceful actions in order to secure equal rights in education, employment, and housing. Boycotts, marches, and sit-ins dramatically captured the nation's attention and increased the pressure for federal action.

In addition to the quest for equality pursued by African Americans and Japanese Americans, Theme 7 also explores the discrimination and prejudice faced by early Chinese immigrants, Italian newcomers, and Mexican American migrant farm workers.

The selections in Theme 8 look at the ways in which people have dealt with cultural differences and misunderstandings. This struggle is often very personal and particular to the situation in which individuals find themselves. What happens, for example, when two people from different cultures fall in love and one or both families disapprove because of conflicting traditions and values? How does the couple solve its problem? Do you think that young people are able to move more easily across cultural barriers than adults? How do people come to understand and appreciate the similarities and differences among the ceremonies, customs, values, and beliefs of many cultures?

Theme 9 explores the desire to reach across social barriers and build unified communities. Often the first people to give voice to such a vision are writers and artists, those who would share their culture with the world. The literature in this section focuses on the idea of a multicultural society in which all groups have an equally valued place. In some cases, writers and artists have banded together to form cross-cultural groups. One such group, the Nuyorican school in New York City, is represented in this section. The diversity of ideas and attitudes expressed in the writings in Theme 9 is unified by the hope that people of all cultures can live together in harmony.

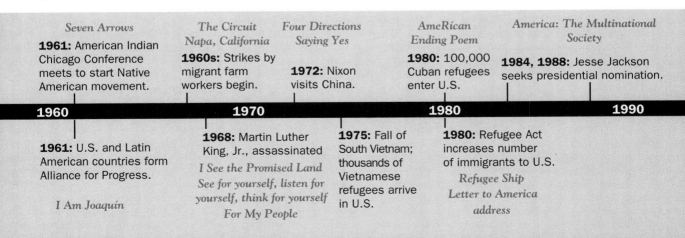

Seven Arrows
1961: American Indian Chicago Conference meets to start Native American movement.

The Circuit
Napa, California
1960s: Strikes by migrant farm workers begin.

Four Directions
Saying Yes
1972: Nixon visits China.

AmeRican
Ending Poem
1980: 100,000 Cuban refugees enter U.S.

America: The Multinational Society
1984, 1988: Jesse Jackson seeks presidential nomination.

1960　1970　1980　1990

1961: U.S. and Latin American countries form Alliance for Progress.

I Am Joaquín

1968: Martin Luther King, Jr., assassinated
I See the Promised Land
See for yourself, listen for yourself, think for yourself
For My People

1975: Fall of South Vietnam; thousands of Vietnamese refugees arrive in U.S.

1980: Refugee Act increases number of immigrants to U.S.
Refugee Ship
Letter to America address

Theme 7:
The Quest for Equality

ALTHOUGH THEY REPRESENT a variety of different cultures, the authors of the selections in this theme all focus on common goals: social, political, and economic equality. In their writing, they confront the prejudice and discrimination that have been aimed at their ethnic groups. They also expose the hypocrisy of a society that promises "liberty and justice for all," yet often fails to fulfill those promises for certain groups. You will read selections that describe the injustices that many Chinese immigrants experienced when they first arrived in the United States in the mid-1800s. Also included in this theme are speeches made by two well-known African American leaders of the Civil Rights Movement of the 1950s and 1960s. Other selections describe the economic exploitation of Mexican American migrant farm workers and Italian immigrants. One selection concerns the internment of Japanese Americans by the U.S. government during World War II. In addition, there is a historical document that discusses the discrimination women have faced throughout history.

The writers represented in this theme describe the hardships that they have endured. However, they also look to the traditions of their group as a way of gaining the human understanding needed to produce social change.

"Remember I *Had* a Dream . . ." Mural on a storefront security gate in Harlem, New York City. Painted in 1982 by an African American street artist named Franco. What messages are street artists able to communicate in murals like this one?

These writers offer insights into the customs and beliefs that make up their cultural heritages. At the same time, with strong voices, they express the personal values that define them as individuals.

I See the Promised Land

Reading the Author in a Cultural Context

Martin Luther King, Jr., became the most visible leader of the Civil Rights Movement of the 1950s and 1960s. In 1955, he was elected head of the Montgomery Improvement Association. This group organized a 381-day boycott against the Alabama city's bus companies because of their policy of segregation. At the time, King was only 26 years old, but he had already earned a doctorate and had become the pastor of a Baptist church in Montgomery.

The Montgomery bus boycott helped force the issue of segregation on Alabama buses to the Supreme Court. There the policy was found to be unconstitutional. The success of the boycott confirmed King's belief that nonviolent protest was the most effective method of achieving social change. To promote his policy of peaceful activism, King helped found the Southern Christian Leadership Conference in 1957. In 1963, his leadership qualities emerged during a month of protest marches in Birmingham, Alabama. The marches forced a most resistant community to agree to desegregate businesses and to hire African American workers. The protests helped prompt President John F. Kennedy to call for the passage of a new national civil rights bill.

Despite King's plea for peaceful coexistence among all races, civil rights workers frequently faced violence. After civil rights leader Medgar Evers was assassinated in the summer of 1963, more than 200,000 people marched on Washington, D.C. On that day, August 28, King delivered his famous "I Have a Dream" speech. In 1964, King became the youngest person in history to win the Nobel Peace Prize, for his nonviolent efforts to achieve desegregation.

King realized that poverty was often the reason for people's frustration and impatience with the slow pace of social change. In 1967, he began to organize a multiracial Poor People's Campaign for antipoverty legislation. In the spring of 1968, King stopped in Memphis, Tennessee, to show his support for the striking sanitation workers of that city. During a speech on the evening of April 3, he told his audience that because he believed his dream of freedom for all Americans would occur in the near future, he was not afraid to face death. The next day, as he stood on the balcony of his hotel room, King was shot and killed. Ironically, violence ended the life of one of our country's greatest pacifists.

Focusing on the Selection

As you read King's speech, think about the issues that King raises and the methods that he proposes to effect change. How do these issues apply specifically to the lives of African Americans? How do they relate to all humanity? Consider how King's references to the Bible enhance his message. Write your responses in your journal.

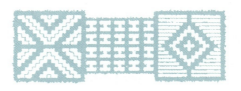

I See the Promised Land

MARTIN LUTHER KING, JR.

. . . TROUBLE IS IN THE LAND. Confusion all around. . . . But I know, somehow, that only when it is dark enough, can you see the stars. And I see God working in this period of the twentieth century in a way that men, in some strange way, are responding—something is happening in our world. The masses of people are rising up. And wherever they are assembled today, whether they are in Johannesburg, South Africa; Nairobi, Kenya; Accra, Ghana; New York City; Atlanta, Georgia; Jackson, Mississippi; or Memphis, Tennessee—the cry is always the same—"We want to be free."

. . . We have been forced to a point where we're going to have to grapple[1] with the problems that men have been trying to grapple with through history, but the demands didn't force them to do it. Survival demands that we grapple with them. Men, for years now, have been talking about war and peace. But now, no longer can they just talk about it. It is no longer a choice between violence and nonviolence in this world; it's nonviolence or nonexistence.

That is where we are today. And also in the human rights revolution, if something isn't done, and in a hurry, to bring the colored peoples

---

1. grapple (GRAP-puhl) *v.* to try to overcome or deal with

of the world out of their long years of poverty, their long years of hurt and neglect, the whole world is doomed. Now, I'm just happy that God has allowed me to live in this period, to see what is unfolding. And I'm happy that he's allowed me to be in Memphis.

I can remember, I can remember when Negroes were just going around as Ralph[2] has said, so often, scratching where they didn't itch, and laughing when they were not tickled. But that day is all over. We mean business now, and we are determined to gain our rightful place in God's world.

And that's all this whole thing is about. We aren't engaged in any negative protest and in any negative arguments with anybody. We are saying that we are determined to be men. We are determined to be people. We are saying that we are God's children. And that we don't have to live like we are forced to live.

Now, what does all of this mean in this great period of history? It means that we've got to stay together. We've got to stay together and maintain unity. You know, whenever Pharaoh wanted to prolong the period of slavery in Egypt,[3] he had a favorite, favorite formula for doing it. What was that? He kept the slaves fighting among themselves. But whenever the slaves get together, something happens in Pharaoh's court, and he cannot hold the slaves in slavery. When the slaves get together, that's the beginning of getting out of slavery. Now let us maintain unity.

Secondly, let us keep the issues where they are. The issue is injustice. The issue is the refusal of Memphis to be fair and honest in its dealings with its public servants, who happen to be sanitation workers. Now, we've got to keep attention on that. That's always the problem with a little violence. You know what happened the other day, and the press dealt only with the window-breaking. I read the articles. They very seldom got around to mentioning the fact that one thousand, three hundred sanitation workers were on strike, and that Memphis is not being fair to them, and that Mayor Loeb is in dire need of a doctor. They didn't get around to that.

Now we're going to march again, and we've got to march again, in order to put the issue where it is supposed to be. And force everybody to see that there are thirteen hundred of God's children here suffering, sometimes going hungry, going through dark and dreary nights wondering how this thing is going to come out. That's the issue. And we've got to say to the nation: we know it's coming out. For when people get caught up with that which is right and they are willing to sacrifice for it, there is no stopping point short of victory.

---

2. **Ralph** Ralph Abernathy, a civil rights leader and one of King's close associates
3. **Pharaoh** (FA-roh) . . . **slavery in Egypt** In ancient Egypt, the pharaoh, or king, enslaved the Jews.

We aren't going to let any mace stop us. We are masters in our non-violent movement in disarming police forces; they don't know what to do. I've seen them so often. I remember in Birmingham, Alabama, when we were in that majestic struggle there we would move out of the 16th Street Baptist Church day after day; by the hundreds we would move out. And Bull Connor[4] would tell them to send the dogs forth and they did come; but we just went before the dogs singing, "Ain't gonna let nobody turn me round." Bull Connor next would say, "Turn the fire hoses on." And as I said to you the other night, Bull Connor didn't know history. He knew a kind of physics that somehow didn't relate to the transphysics[5] that we knew about. And that was the fact that there was a certain kind of fire that no water could put out. And we went before the fire hoses; we had known water. If we were Baptist or some other denomination, we had been immersed. If we were Methodist, and some others, we had been sprinkled, but we knew water.

That couldn't stop us. And we just went on before the dogs and we would look at them; and we'd go on before the water hoses and we would look at it, and we'd just go on singing "Over my head I see freedom in the air." And then we would be thrown in the paddy wagons,[6] and sometimes we were stacked in there like sardines in a can. And they would throw us in, and old Bull would say, "Take them off," and they did; and we would just go in the paddy wagon singing, "We Shall Overcome."[7] And every now and then we'd get in the jail, and we'd see the jailers looking through the windows being moved by our prayers, and being moved by our words and our songs. And there was a power there which Bull Connor couldn't adjust to; and so we ended up transforming Bull into a steer, and we won our struggle in Birmingham.

Now we've got to go on to Memphis just like that. I call upon you to be with us Monday. Now about injunctions:[8] We have an injunction and we're going into court tomorrow morning to fight this illegal, unconstitutional injunction. All we say to America is, "Be true to what you said on paper." If I lived in China or even Russia, or any totalitarian country, maybe I could understand the denial of certain basic First Amendment privileges, because they hadn't committed themselves to that over there. But somewhere I read of the freedom of assembly. Somewhere I read of the freedom of speech. Somewhere I read of the freedom of the press. Somewhere I read that the greatness of America is

---

4. Bull Connor the Birmingham Chief of Police
5. transphysics (tranz-FIHZ-ihks) *n.* transcends laws of physics
6. paddy wagons (PAD-ee WAG-uhns) *n.* vans used by police for prisoners
7. "We Shall Overcome" the theme song of the civil rights movement
8. injunctions (in-JUHNK-shuhnz) *n.* court orders prohibiting an action

the right to protest for right. And so just as I say, we aren't going to let any injunction turn us around. We are going on.

We need all of you. . . . It's alright to talk about "streets flowing with milk and honey,"[9] but God has commanded us to be concerned about the slums down here, and his children who can't eat three square meals a day. It's alright to talk about the new Jerusalem, but one day, God's preacher must talk about the New York, the new Atlanta, the new Philadelphia, the new Los Angeles, the new Memphis, Tennessee. This is what we have to do.

Now the other thing we'll have to do is this: Always anchor our external direct action with the power of economic withdrawal. Now, we are poor people, individually, we are poor when you compare us with white society in America. We are poor. Never stop and forget that collectively, that means all of us together, collectively we are richer than all the nations in the world, with the exception of nine. Did you ever think about that? After you leave the United States, Soviet Russia, Great Britain, West Germany, France, and I could name the others, the Negro collectively is richer than most nations of the world. We have an annual income of more than thirty billion dollars a year, which is more than all of the exports of the United States, and more than the national budget of Canada. Did you know that? That's power right there, if we know how to pool it.

We don't have to argue with anybody. We don't have to curse and go around acting bad with our words. We don't need any bricks and bottles, we don't need any Molotov cocktails,[10] we just need to go around to these stores, and to these massive industries in our country, and say, "God sent us by here, to say to you that you're not treating his children right. And we've come by here to ask you to make the first item on your agenda—fair treatment, where God's children are concerned. Now, if you are not prepared to do that, we do have an agenda that we must follow. And our agenda calls for withdrawing economic support from you." . . .

But not only that, we've got to strengthen black institutions. I call upon you to take your money out of the banks downtown and deposit your money in Tri-State Bank—we want a "bank-in" movement in Memphis. So go by the savings and loan association. I'm not asking you something that we don't do ourselves at SCLC.[11] Judge Hooks[12] and others will tell you that we have an account here in the savings and loan association from the Southern Christian Leadership Conference.

---

9. **"streets flowing with milk and honey"** in the Bible, promised land of the Jews
10. **Molotov cocktails** (MAHL-ah-tahv KOK-taylz) *n.* bottles of explosive liquids
11. **SCLC** Southern Christian Leadership Conference, a civil rights organization founded in 1957 by Martin Luther King, Jr.
12. **Judge Hooks** Benjamin Hooks, an important figure in the Civil Rights Movement

Photograph of the Reverend Martin Luther King, Jr., speaking in 1960.

We're just telling you to follow what we're doing. Put your money there. You have six or seven black insurance companies in Memphis. Take out your insurance there. We want to have an "insurance-in."

Now these are some practical things we can do. We begin the process of building a greater economic base. And at the same time, we are putting pressure where it really hurts. I ask you to follow through here.

Now, let me say as I move to my conclusion that we've got to give ourselves to this struggle until the end. Nothing would be more tragic than to stop at this point, in Memphis. We've got to see it through. And when we have our march, you need to be there. Be concerned about your brother. You may not be on strike. But either we go up together, or we go down together. . . .

That's the question before you tonight. Not, "If I stop to help the sanitation workers, what will happen to all of the hours that I usually spend in my office every day and every week as a pastor?" The question is not, "If I stop to help this man in need, what will happen to me?" "If I do not stop to help the sanitation workers, what will happen to them?" That's the question.

Let us rise up tonight with a greater readiness. Let us stand with a greater determination. And let us move on in these powerful days, these days of challenge to make America what it ought to be. We have an opportunity to make America a better nation. And I want to thank God, once more, for allowing me to be here with you. . . .

Well, I don't know what will happen now. We've got some difficult days ahead. But it doesn't matter with me now. Because I've been to the mountaintop.[13] And I don't mind. Like anybody, I would like to live a long life. Longevity has its place. But I'm not concerned about that now. I just want to do God's will. And He's allowed me to go up to the mountain. And I've looked over. And I've seen the promised land. I may not get there with you. But I want you to know tonight, that we, as a people will get to the promised land. And I'm happy, tonight. I'm not worried about anything. I'm not fearing any man. Mine eyes have seen the glory of the coming of the Lord.[14]

---

13. **I've been to the mountaintop** After leading the Jews out of bondage in Egypt, Moses ascended a mountain (Deuteronomy 34:1-3) and surveyed Israel, the Promised Land where his people would forge a new life.
14. **Mine eyes have seen . . . the Lord** the first line of the "Battle Hymn of the Republic," a Civil War anthem written by Julia Ward Howe

POSTREADING

Critical Thinking

1. In this speech, what does King tell you about his attitudes toward African Americans' struggle for equal rights?
2. What aspects of King's life do you think most influenced these attitudes?
3. How do King's ideas about equal rights for African Americans relate to all humanity?

Writing Your Response to "I See the Promised Land"

In your journal, write about an idea, image, or issue in King's speech that is especially meaningful to you. Why is it memorable? How does it relate to an experience in your life or to the life of someone you know?

Going Back Into the Text: Author's Craft

An **allusion** in literature is a reference to a well-known person, place, event, literary work, or work of art. Writers often make allusions to the Bible, to Greek and Roman mythology, to Shakespearean plays, to historical events, and to other information they expect will be familiar to their readers. A writer may use allusions as a sort of shorthand to suggest specific ideas or views.

As a Baptist minister, King made many allusions to the Bible in order to emphasize important issues. With a partner, use the following guidelines to discuss allusions as you review King's speech.

1. List the biblical allusions you find in King's speech.
2. What point does King make with his allusion to the Egyptian pharaoh and the slaves? How does this allusion relate to African Americans and to the Civil Rights Movement?
3. Find an allusion in another selection in this book and discuss how it emphasizes one of the author's points.

See for yourself, listen for yourself, think for yourself

Reading the Author in a Cultural Context

Malcolm X was born Malcolm Little in Nebraska. Before he was 21 years old, he was arrested for burglary and served seven years in prison. In prison, Malcolm became a Muslim and a follower of The Nation of Islam. He changed his name to Malcolm X. Members of The Nation of Islam, then often called Black Muslims, call for separation from the white community. Malcolm's conversion motivated him to learn to read and write, in part so that he could communicate effectively with Elijah Muhammad, the founder of the Black Muslims. Malcolm spent his years in prison copying the dictionary, in order to increase his vocabulary and improve his writing.

Malcolm's self-education was very effective. He was released from prison in 1952, and two years later became the minister of a Black Muslim mosque in Harlem. He soon gained a substantial number of followers. During these years, Malcolm preached separatism for African Americans and a rejection of white society. However, on a visit to Mecca, in Saudi Arabia, the holiest city of the Muslim faith, Malcolm had a second conversion. He became critical of Elijah Muhammad's philosophy and formed his own Muslim group, the Organization of Afro-American Unity. He changed his name once again, to El-Hajj Malik El-Shabazz.

Continuing to affirm ethnic pride for African Americans, Malcolm's new message included the possibility of cooperation with whites. He emphasized, however, that African Americans should determine their own destinies, without depending on help from white society. In the following speech, "See for yourself, listen for yourself, think for yourself," Malcolm delivered this new message to a group of high school students from Mississippi who were visiting New York City. The students were members of the Student Nonviolent Coordinating Committee (SNCC), a civil rights organization that strove for political and economic equality for African Americans through local and regional action groups.

Because of his political positions, Malcolm X had a number of enemies in both the African American and the white communities. In February 1965, a little more than a month after his speech to the students from Mississippi, he was assassinated by three gunmen as he delivered a speech at the Audubon Ballroom in Harlem.

Focusing on the Selection

As you read the following speech, think about Malcolm X's attitudes toward fellow African Americans and toward white society. What values are important to him? Why do you think he tells the students to think for themselves? What is it about Malcolm X's language that makes his speech effective and persuasive? Write your responses in your journal.

See for yourself, listen for yourself, think for yourself

MALCOLM X

I WAS APPROACHED, I think we were at the United Nations, and I met Mrs. Walker, about two or three weeks ago, and she said that a group of students were coming up from McComb, Mississippi, and wanted to know if I would meet with you and speak with you. I told her frankly that it would be the greatest honor that I ever had experienced. Because I have never been in the state of Mississippi, number one—not through any fault of my own, I don't think—but it's been my great desire to either go there or meet someone from there.

To not take too much of your time, I would like to point out a little incident that I was involved in a short while ago that will give you somewhat of an idea of why I am going to say what I am.

I was flying on a plane from Algiers[1] to Geneva[2] about four weeks ago, with two other Americans. Both of them were white—one was a male, the other was a female. And after we had flown together for about forty minutes, the lady turned to me and asked me—she had looked at my briefcase and saw the initials M and X—and she said, "I would like

---

1. **Algiers** (al-JEERZ) the capital of Algeria, a country in North Africa
2. **Geneva** (je-NEE-vah) a city in southwestern Switzerland

to ask you a question. What kind of last name could you have that begins with X?"

So I told her, "That's it: X."

She was quiet for a little while. For about ten minutes she was quiet. She hadn't been quiet at all up to then, you know. And then finally she turned and she said, "Well, what's your first name?"

I said, "Malcolm."

She was quiet for about ten more minutes. Then she turned and she said, "Well, you're not *Malcolm X*?" [*Laughter*]

But the reason she asked that question was, she had gotten from the press, and from things that she had heard and read, she was looking for something different, or for someone different.

The reason I take time to tell you this is, one of the first things I think young people, especially nowadays, should learn how to do is see for yourself and listen for yourself and think for yourself. Then you can come to an intelligent decision for yourself. But if you form the habit of going by what you hear others say about someone, or going by what others think about someone, instead of going and searching that thing out for yourself and seeing for yourself, you'll be walking west when you think you're going east, and you'll be walking east when you think you're going west. So this generation, especially of our people, have a burden upon themselves, more so than at any other time in history. The most important thing we can learn how to do today is think for ourselves.

It's good to keep wide-open ears and listen to what everybody else has to say, but when you come to make a decision, you have to weigh all of what you've heard on its own, and place it where it belongs, and then come to a decision for yourself. You'll never regret it. But if you form the habit of taking what someone else says about a thing without checking it out for yourself, you'll find that other people will have you hating your own friends and loving your enemies. This is one of the things that our people are beginning to learn today—that it is very important to think out a situation for yourself. If you don't do it, then you'll always be maneuvered into actually—You'll never fight your enemies, but you will find yourself fighting your own self.

I think our people in this country are the best examples of that. Because many of us want to be nonviolent. We talk very loudly, you know, about being nonviolent. Here in Harlem,[3] where there are probably more Black people concentrated than any place else in the world, some talk that nonviolent talk too. And when they stop talking about how nonviolent they are, we find that they aren't nonviolent with each

---

3. **Harlem** (HAHR-luhm) a section of New York City, in northern Manhattan

Photograph of a mural of Malcolm X.

other. At Harlem Hospital, you can go out here on Friday night, which—today is what, Friday? yes—you can go out here to Harlem Hospital, where there are more Black patients in one hospital than any hospital in the world—because there's a concentration of our people here—and find Black people who claim they're nonviolent. But you see them going in there all cut up and shot up and busted up where they got violent with each other.

So my experience has been that in many instances where you find Negroes always talking about being nonviolent, they're not nonviolent with each other, and they're not loving with each other, or patient with each other, or forgiving with each other. Usually, when they say they're nonviolent, they mean they're nonviolent with somebody else. I think you understand what I mean. They are nonviolent with the enemy. A person can come to your home, and if he's white and he wants to heap some kind of brutality upon you, you're nonviolent. Or he can come put a rope around your neck, you're nonviolent. Or he can come to take your father out and put a rope around his neck, you're nonviolent. But now if another Negro just stomps his foot, you'll rumble with him in a minute. Which shows you there's an inconsistency there.

So I myself would go for nonviolence if it was consistent, if it was intelligent, if everybody was going to be nonviolent, and if we were going to be nonviolent all the time. I'd say, okay, let's get with it, we'll all be nonviolent. But I don't go along—and I'm just telling you how I think—I don't go along with any kind of nonviolence unless everybody's going to be nonviolent. If they make the Ku Klux Klan[4] nonviolent, I'll be nonviolent. If they make the White Citizens' Council[5] nonviolent, I'll be nonviolent. But as long as you've got somebody else not being nonviolent, I don't want anybody coming to me talking any kind of nonviolent talk. I don't think it is fair to tell our people to be nonviolent unless someone is out there making the Klan and the Citizens' Council and these other groups also be nonviolent.

Now I'm not criticizing those here who are nonviolent. I think everybody should do it the way they feel is best, and I congratulate anybody who can be nonviolent in the face of all that kind of action that I read about in that part of the world. But I don't think that in 1965 you will find the upcoming generation of our people, especially those who have been doing some thinking, who will go along with any form of nonviolence unless nonviolence is going to be practiced all the way around.

If the leaders of the nonviolent movement can go into the white community and teach nonviolence, good. I'd go along with that. But as long as I see them teaching nonviolence only in the Black community, then we can't go along with that. We believe in equality, and equality means you have to put the same thing over here that you put over there. And if just Black people alone are going to be the ones who are nonviolent, then it's not fair. We throw ourselves off guard. In fact, we disarm ourselves and make ourselves defenseless. . . .

---

4. **Ku Klux Klan** (KOO KLUX KLAN) a secret organization directed against African Americans, Catholics, Jews, and the foreign born
5. **White Citizens' Council** an organization similar to the KKK

POSTREADING

Critical Thinking

1. What does Malcolm X tell you about his positions on nonviolence and harmony between races?
2. Which experiences in Malcolm X's own life do you think most influenced these feelings?
3. How did reading this speech influence your attitudes about the issues of equality and cooperation?

Writing Your Response to "See for yourself, listen for yourself, think for yourself"

In your journal, write about one idea or question that occurred to you as you read Malcolm X's speech. What was it in the speech that provoked this thought? How does it relate to an experience in your life?

Going Back Into the Text: Author's Craft

The art of persuasive public speaking has always played a significant role in U.S. politics. Throughout history, talented speech-makers have spread messages, gained support for political parties and causes, and swayed public opinion.

A skilled speechmaker uses a variety of techniques to highlight the important concepts in his, or her speech. Some of these devices are **restatement, repetition,** and **parallelism.** A speaker uses restatement to convey an idea in a number of ways. When a speaker uses repetition, he or she simply restates an idea using the same words. Parallelism involves the repetition of phrase or sentence structures, as in, for example, "of the people, by the people, and for the people."

With a partner, review the excerpt from Malcolm X's speech to see how he applies these methods in his speech. Use the following questions as guidelines.

1. List two ideas that Malcolm X stresses through the use of repetition and restatement.
2. Find an example of parallelism. How does parallelism add to the effectiveness of the speech?
3. What other example of parallelism can you find in another selection in this book?

from China Men
Immigration Blues

Reading the Authors in a Cultural Context

Around 1848, stories carried by travelers and sailors about the gold rush in the United States reached the southern port cities of China. These stories, many of them exaggerated, so impressed the Chinese that they started calling California "the land of the Gold Mountain." Many Chinese decided to leave their country for California. Some traveled with the hope of settling permanently in California, while others planned to return home.

Upon arrival in California, Chinese immigrants usually needed to work long hours to repay the cost of their passage. Most of them worked as miners or as cooks and launderers in the mining camps. The greatest contribution of these workers came later, however. This was the backbreaking, and often dangerous, task of building the western section of the first U.S. transcontinental railroad. These Chinese laborers were praised by most employers for their diligence, their sense of duty, and their abilities. Unfortunately, they were also discriminated against by all levels of mainstream society. More and more discriminatory laws were passed. These included restrictions on owning property and businesses. The Exclusion Act of 1882 prohibited the immigration of Chinese laborers to the United States for ten years. This law was renewed in 1892 and remained in effect until 1943.

The selection by Maxine Hong Kingston comes from her book *China Men*. Kingston is a Chinese American writer who was born in California in 1940 to Chinese immigrant parents. In this book, she describes the physical hardships of some of the men in her family who worked on the railroad. She also describes the ways in which the workers applied their culture and beliefs to their new experiences, as a way of understanding U.S. society. She reveals the fears and concerns of a man named Ah Goong and his comrades about death and about their own ghosts after death. Kingston also describes the ghosts, spirits, demons, and dragons that they sense within the mountain, the railroad, and their employers.

The poems that follow the selection are from a collection called "The Gold Mountain Poems," which also explores the hardships of Chinese immigrants. This collection was written anonymously by some of the earliest Chinese immigrants in the 1800s. These poems express the discontent they felt with their homeland and the harsh realities they faced in the United States.

Focusing on the Selections

As you read the selections, think about the sacrifices and contributions of the Chinese immigrants in the United States. In what ways are the lives of the characters shaped by the conditions under which they live? What techniques does Kingston use in the story to develop the character of Ah Goong? Write your responses in your journal.

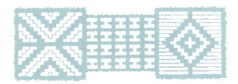

from *China Men*

MAXINE HONG KINGSTON

. . . THEN IT WAS AUTUMN, and the wind blew so fiercely, the men had to postpone the basketwork. Clouds moved in several directions at once. Men pointed at dust devils,[1] which turned their mouths crooked. There was ceaseless motion; clothes kept moving; hair moved; sleeves puffed out. Nothing stayed still long enough for Ah Goong to figure it out. The wind sucked the breath out of his mouth and blew thoughts from his brains. The food convoys[2] from San Francisco brought tents to replace the ones that whipped away. The baskets from China, which the men saved for high work, carried cowboy jackets, long underwear, Levi pants, boots, earmuffs, leather gloves, flannel shirts, coats. They sewed rabbit fur and deerskin into the linings. They tied the wide brims of their cowboy hats over their ears with mufflers. And still the wind made confusing howls into ears, and it was hard to think.

The days became nights when the crews tunneled inside the mountain, which sheltered them from the wind, but also hid the light and sky. Ah Goong pickaxed the mountain, the dirt filling his nostrils through a cowboy bandanna. He shoveled the dirt into a cart and pushed it to a

---

1. **dust devils** (DUST DEV-uhls) *n.* small whirlwinds common in dry regions on hot, calm afternoons and made visible by the dust, debris, and sand they pick up from the ground
2. **convoys** (KAHN-vois) *n.* groups of vehicles that travel together for protection

place that was tall enough for the mule, which hauled it the rest of the way out. He looked forward to cart duty to edge closer to the entrance. Eyes darkened, nose plugged, his windy cough worse, he was to mole a thousand feet and meet others digging from the other side. How much he'd pay now to go swinging in a basket. He might as well have gone to work in a tin mine. Coming out of the tunnel at the end of a shift, he forgot whether it was supposed to be day or night. He blew his nose fifteen times before the mucus cleared again.

The dirt was the easiest part of tunneling. Beneath the soil, they hit granite. Ah Goong struck it with his pickax, and it jarred his bones, chattered his teeth. He swung his sledgehammer against it, and the impact rang in the dome of his skull. The mountain that was millions of years old was locked against them and was not to be broken into. . . . "A man ought to be made of tougher material than flesh," he said. "Skin is too soft. Our bones ought to be filled with iron." He lifted the hammer high, careful that it not pull him backward, and let it fall forward of its own weight against the rock. Nothing happened to that gray wall; he had to slam with strength and will. He hit at the same spot over and over again, the same rock. Some chips and flakes broke off. The granite looked everywhere the same. It had no softer or weaker spots anywhere, the same hard gray. He learned to slide his hand up the handle, lift, slide and swing, a circular motion, hammering, hammering, hammering. He would bite like a rat through that mountain. His eyes couldn't see; his nose couldn't smell; and now his ears were filled with the noise of hammering. This rock is what is real, he thought. This rock is what real is, not clouds or mist, which make mysterious promises, and when you go through them are nothing. When the foreman measured at the end of twenty-four hours of pounding, the rock had given a foot. The hammering went on day and night. The men worked eight hours on and eight hours off. They worked on all eighteen tunnels at once. While Ah Goong slept, he could hear the sledgehammers of other men working in the earth. The steady banging reminded him of holidays and harvests; falling asleep, he heard the women chopping mincemeat[3] and the millstones striking.

The demons in boss suits came into the tunnel occasionally, measured with a yardstick, and shook their heads. "Faster," they said. "Faster. Chinamen too slow. Too slow." "Tell us we're slow," the China Men grumbled. The ones in top tiers of scaffolding let rocks drop, a hammer drop. Ropes tangled around the demons' heads and feet. The cave China Men muttered and flexed, glared out of the corners of their eyes. But

---

3. mincemeat (MIHNS-meet) *n.* a mixture composed of minced apples, suet, and sometimes meat, together with raisins, currants, candied citron, for filling a pie

Engraving of Chinese laborers at work on the Central Pacific Railroad in 1867. In what ways did newcomers like these struggle for equality in the United States?

usually there was no diversion—one day the same as the next, one hour no different from another—the beating against the same granite.

After tunneling into granite for about three years, Ah Goong understood the immovability of the earth. Men change, men die, weather changes, but a mountain is the same as permanence and time. This mountain would have taken no new shape for centuries, ten thousand centuries, the world a still, still place, time unmoving. He worked in the tunnel so long, he learned to see many colors in black. When he stumbled out, he tried to talk about time. "I felt time," he said. "I saw time. I saw world." He tried again. "I saw what's real. I saw time, and it doesn't move. If we break through the mountain, hollow it, time won't have moved anyway. You translators ought to tell the foreigners that." . . .

In the third year of pounding granite by hand, a demon invented dynamite. The railroad workers were to test it. They had stopped using gunpowder in the tunnels after avalanches, but the demons said that dynamite was more precise. They watched a scientist demon mix nitrate, sulphate, and glycerine, then flick the yellow oil, which exploded off his fingertips. Sitting in a meadow to watch the dynamite detonated in the open, Ah Goong saw the men in front of him leap impossibly high into the air; then he felt a shove as if from a giant's unseen hand— and he fell backward. The boom broke the mountain silence like fear breaking inside stomach and chest and groin. No one had gotten hurt; they stood up laughing and amazed, looking around at how they had fallen, the pattern of the explosion. Dynamite was much more powerful than gunpowder. Ah Goong had felt a nudge, as if something kind were moving him out of harm's way. "All of a sudden I was sitting next to you." "Aiya. If we had been nearer, it would have killed us." "If we were stiff, it would have gone through us." "A fist." "A hand." "We leapt like acrobats." Next time Ah Goong flattened himself on the ground, and the explosion rolled over him.

He never got used to the blasting; a blast always surprised him. Even when he himself set the fuse and watched it burn, anticipated the explosion, the bang—*bahng* in Chinese—when it came, always startled. It cleaned the crazy words, the crackling, and bing-bangs out of his brain. It was like New Year's, when every problem and thought was knocked clean out of him by firecrackers, and he could begin fresh. He couldn't worry during an explosion, which jerked every head to attention. Hills flew up in rocks and dirt. Boulders turned over and over. Sparks, fires, debris, rocks, smoke burst up, not at the same time as the boom (*bum*) but before that—the sound a separate occurrence, not useful as a signal.

The terrain changed immediately. Streams were diverted,[4] rock-scapes exposed. Ah Goong found it difficult to remember what land had looked like before an explosion. It was a good thing the dynamite was invented after the Civil War to the east was over.

The dynamite added more accidents and ways of dying, but if it were not used, the railroad would take fifty more years to finish. Nitroglycerine exploded when it was jounced on a horse or dropped. A man who fell with it in his pocket blew himself up into red pieces. Sometimes it combusted merely standing. Human bodies skipped through the air like puppets and made Ah Goong laugh crazily as if the arms and legs would come together again. The smell of burned flesh remained in rocks.

In the tunnels, the men bored holes fifteen to eighteen inches deep with a power drill, stuffed them with hay and dynamite, and imbedded the fuse in sand. Once, for extra pay, Ah Goong ran back in to see why some dynamite had not gone off and hurried back out again; it was just a slow fuse. When the explosion settled, he helped carry two-hundred-, three-hundred-, five-hundred-pound boulders out of the tunnel.

As a boy he had visited a Taoist[5] monastery where there were nine rooms, each a replica of one of the nine hells. Lifesize sculptures of men and women were spitted on turning wheels. Eerie candles under the

---

4. **diverted** (duh-VURT-ihd) *v.* to draw off to a different course; to turn aside
5. **Taoist** (DOW-ihst) *adj.* pertaining to the popular Chinese religion, Taoism, which advocates a life of complete simplicity, naturalness, and noninterference with the course of natural events to attain a happy and harmonious existence

suffering faces emphasized eyes poked out, tongues pulled, red mouths and eyes, and real hair, eyelashes, and eyebrows. Women were split apart and men dismembered. He could have reached out and touched the sufferers and the implements. He had dug and dynamited his way into one of these hells. "Only here there are eighteen tunnels, not nine, plus all the tracks between them," he said.

One day he came out of the tunnel to find the mountains white, the evergreens and bare trees decorated, white tree sculptures and lace bushes everywhere. The men from snow country called the icicles "ice chopsticks." He sat in his basket and slid down the slopes. The snow covered the gouged[6] land, the broken trees, the tracks, the mud, the campfire ashes, the unburied dead. Streams were stilled in mid-run, the water petrified. That winter he thought it was the task of the human race to quicken the world, blast the freeze, fire it, redden it with blood. He had to change the stupid slowness of one sunrise and one sunset per day. He had to enliven the silent world with sound. "The rock," he tried to tell the others. "The ice." "Time."

The dynamiting loosed blizzards on the men. Ears and toes fell off. Fingers stuck to the cold silver rails. Snowblind men stumbled about with bandannas over their eyes. Ah Goong helped build wood tunnels roofing the track route. Falling ice scrabbled on the roofs. The men stayed under the snow for weeks at a time. Snowslides covered the entrances to the tunnels, which they had to dig out to enter and exit, white tunnels and black tunnels. Ah Goong looked at his gang and thought, If there is an avalanche, these are the people I'll be trapped with, and wondered which ones would share food. A party of snowbound barbarians had eaten the dead. Cannibals, thought Ah Goong, and looked around. Food was not scarce; the tea man brought whiskey barrels of hot tea, and he warmed his hands and feet, held the teacup to his nose and ears. Someday, he planned, he would buy a chair with metal doors for putting hot coal inside it. The magpies[7] did not abandon him but stayed all winter and searched the snow for food.

The men who died slowly enough to say last words said, "Don't leave me frozen under the snow. Send my body home. Burn it and put the ashes in a tin can. Take the bone jar when you come down the mountain." "When you ride the fire car back to China, tell my descendants to come for me." "Shut up," scolded the hearty men. "We don't want to hear about bone jars and dying." "You're lucky to have a body to bury, not blown to smithereens." "Stupid man to hurt yourself," they bawled out the sick and wounded. How their wives would scold if they

---

6. **gouged** (GOWJD) *adj.* grooved, dug out
7. **magpies** (MAG-peyez) *n.* crow-like birds, having long, graduated tails, black and white feathers, and noisy, mischievous habits

brought back deadmen's bones. "Aiya. To be buried here, nowhere."
"But this is somewhere," Ah Goong promised. "This is the Gold Mountain. We're marking the land now. The track sections are numbered, and your family will know where we leave you." But he was a crazy man, and they didn't listen to him.

Spring did come, and when the snow melted, it revealed the past year, what had happened, what they had done, where they had worked, the lost tools, the thawing bodies, some standing with tools in hand, the bright rails. "Remember Uncle Long Winded Leong?" "Remember Strong Back Wong?" "Remember Lee Brother?" "And Fong Uncle?" They lost count of the number dead; there is no record of how many died building the railroad. Or maybe it was demons doing the counting and chinamen not worth counting. Whether it was good luck or bad luck, the dead were buried or cairned[8] next to the last section of track they had worked on. "May his ghost not have to toil," they said over graves. (In China a woodcutter ghost chops eternally; people have heard chopping in the snow and in the heat.) "Maybe his ghost will ride the train home." The scientific demons said the transcontinental railroad would connect the West to Cathay.[9] "What if he rides back and forth from Sacramento[10] to New York forever?" "That wouldn't be so bad. I hear the cars will be like houses on wheels." The funerals were short. "No time. No time," said both China Men and demons. The railroad was as straight as they could build it, but no ghosts sat on the tracks: no strange presences haunted the tunnels. The blasts scared ghosts away.

When the Big Dipper[11] pointed east and the China Men detonated nitroglycerine and shot off guns for the New Year, which comes with the spring, these special bangs were not as loud as the daily bangs, not as numerous as the bangs all year. Shouldn't the New Year be the loudest day of all to obliterate the noises of the old year? But to make a bang of that magnitude, they would have to blow up at least a year's supply of dynamite in one blast. They arranged strings of chain reactions in circles and long lines, banging faster and louder to culminate in a big bang. And most importantly, there were random explosions—surprise. Surprise. SURPRISE. They had no dragon, the railroad their dragon. . . .

---

8. **cairned** (KERND) *v.* buried in a landmark, tombstone, or monument
9. **Cathay** (ka-THAY) *n.* an antiquated name for China
10. **Sacramento** (sak-ruh-MEN-toh) *n.* a port and the capital city of California
11. **Big Dipper** *n.* the group of seven bright stars in Ursa Major resembling a dipper in outline

Immigration Blues

from *The Gold Mountain Poems*

In search of a pin-head gain,
I was idle in an impoverished village.
I've risked a perilous journey to come to the Flowery
       Flag Nation.
Immigration officers interrogated me:
And, just for a slight lapse of memory,
I am deported, and imprisoned in this barren
        mountain.
A brave man cannot use his might here,
And he can't take one step beyond the confines.

At home I was in poverty,
       constantly worried about firewood and rice.
I borrowed money
       to come to Gold Mountain.
Immigration officers cross-examined me;
       no way could I get through.
Deported to this island,
       like a convicted criminal.
Here—
Mournful sighs fill the gloomy room.
A nation weak; her people often humiliated
Like animals, tortured and destroyed at others'
       whim.

So, liberty is your national principle;
Why do you practice autocracy?
You don't uphold justice, you Americans,
You detain me in prison, guard me closely.
Your officials are wolves and tigers,
All ruthless, all wanting to bite me.
An innocent man implicated, such an injustice!
When can I get out of this prison and free
       my mind?

Critical Thinking

1. What do Kingston and the Gold Mountain poets tell you about the Chinese immigrants' quest for equality?
2. How are the writers' attitudes toward their cultural heritage conveyed in their works?
3. How did reading these works either support or change the way in which you think about your own freedom?

Writing Your Response to *China Men* and "Immigration Blues"

In your journal, describe a scene or image from either selection that is memorable to you. Why is it special to you? How did the author's use of descriptive words affect your choice?

Going Back Into the Text: Author's Craft

Characterization is the technique of creating a character in literature. There are two main methods of characterization—direct and indirect. In *direct characterization*, a writer simply states a character's traits. In *indirect characterization*, a character is revealed by one of the following means:

•by the words, thoughts, or actions of the character;

•by descriptions of the character's appearance or background;

•by what other characters say about the character;

•or by the ways in which other characters react to the character.

Work with a partner to look for the methods Kingston uses to depict the character of Ah Goong. Use the following questions as guidelines.

1. What techniques does Kingston use to develop the character of Ah Goong? Give examples.
2. How do these techniques contribute to the effectiveness of the characterization?
3. What techniques does the author use to develop the main character in another story you have enjoyed?

Arts of the Tapestry

On the next 16 pages you will see paintings, sculptures, drawings, collages, murals, folk art, ceramics, and other media that express the viewpoints of artists from many different cultures. These works of art illustrate the similarities and differences of the many cultures that make up the population of the United States. As you look at each piece, ask yourself: What do I see? What does each work show me about the artist and his or her culture? What does each piece say about the theme it illustrates?

Old Father Storyteller. Painted by Pablita Velarde, a native of the Santa Clara Pueblo in New Mexico. From her book *The Stars*. Old Father sits in the plaza pointing to constellations of stars that play a part in the story of his people.

El Museo del Barrio, New York City. Taino vessel (A.D. 1000–1500). Boat-shaped container made of fired clay with applied ornaments. The Taino were a Native American people who lived in what is now Puerto Rico, the Dominican Republic, and on other Caribbean islands at the time of Columbus's arrival.

Rice Eaters. *Asian American Society, New York City.* Etching with mixed media by Japanese American artist Tomie Arai.

 A2

The Holy Family. *Museum of International Folk Art, Santa Fe, New Mexico.*
Painted carving of Jesus, Mary, and Joseph created by José Benito Ortega in New
Mexico between 1875 and 1907. These carvings of saints and other Christian
figures are calles *santos*. Traditionally, they were produced in family workshops.

La Cama (The Bed).
El Museo del Barrio, New York City. Multimedia
installation created by Puerto Rican artist Pepón Osorio
in 1987. The bed is decorated with objects from everyday Puerto
Rican life and culture to celebrate the cycle of love, birth, and death.

Man sprouting leaves. Drawing in
charcoal and colored pencil by Bill
Traylor. Born into slavery in 1854,
Traylor worked on a plantation for most
of his life. When he was in his early 80s
he arrived penniless in Montgomery,
Alabama, and began sketching. Traylor
produced more than 1,000 works in
three years.

Celebrating Growth and Change

Apache Crown Dance. Painting by Chiricahua Apache artist Allan Houser. The Apache dance shown in the painting is performed to bless the young girls in the community and to pray for good crops. Allan Houser's family was interned by the U.S. government at Fort Sill in Oklahoma until 1912. His father, Sam Haozous, was a friend of and interpreter for Geronimo. Allan Houser was the first Chiricahua Apache in this century to be born out of captivity. He is now an internationally known sculptor and painter.

Dance apron. Made around 1890 by the Kwakiutl, a Native American people from British Columbia in northwestern Canada. Still worn for ceremonial purposes, these aprons are made of wool cloth and decorated with hanging rattles, beads, brass thimbles, and, in the past, with tufted puffin beaks.

National Museum of the American Indian, Smithsonian Institution, Washington, DC. Seneca (Iroquois) leather headdress.

Philbrook Art Center, Tulsa, Oklahoma. Speaker's staff. Painted cedarwood carving with abalone shell, dating from around 1890. Created by the frog clan of the Tlingit people, a Native American group from the coastal area of southern Alaska. The figures represent patrons and guardians of the family of the speaker, who was the political spokesperson for the community.

Jumper. Pastel drawing by Native American artist Jaune Quick-to-See Smith, 1986. An activist for Native American rights, the artist was born in Montana in 1940 and lived on several reservations. She is of Flathead, Shoshone, and French Cree ancestry.

Forward, 1967. *North Carolina Museum of Art, Raleigh, North Carolina.* Painted with tempera on wood by African American artist Jacob Lawrence.

 A8

Sunday Morning. Painting by African American artist Jonathan Green. Green's paintings reflect his roots in the "Gullah" culture of coastal South Carolina. The word *Gullah* is thought to have come from Angola, the West African homeland of many who were originally brought to the region as slaves.

Into Bondage. Oil painting on canvas, created in 1936 by African American artist Aaron Douglas. The painting depicts men and women from Africa being forced onto a slave ship.

Dinner. A family portrait by Puerto Rican artist J. Mejias. Acrylic on paper.

The Block. *Metropolitan Museum of Art, New York City.* Collage of cut and pasted paper on masonite created in 1971 by African American artist Romare Bearden (1914–1988). Bearden's vividly colored paintings and collages depict important aspects of the lives of many African Americans. These include the migration northward from the rural South and the expressiveness of jazz and blues. (Detail)

Young Bride. Oil painting on canvas by Bo Jia. The artist was born in China in 1962. From 1986 to 1989, Bo Jia was an exhibition designer and painter at the Museum of Chinese Revolution and History at Tian An Men Square in Beijing, China. Since 1989, the artist has exhibited throughout the eastern United States.

If You Believe in Woman. Oil painting on canvas by Jane Evershed, 1987. From her series of paintings entitled *The Power of Woman*.

Photograph of a painting on the wall of the old neighborhood center at 6th and Maclay Streets in Harrisburg, Pennsylvania.

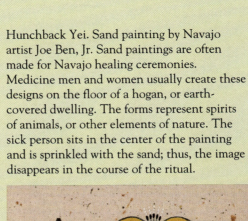

Hunchback Yei. Sand painting by Navajo
artist Joe Ben, Jr. Sand paintings are often
made for Navajo healing ceremonies.
Medicine men and women usually create these
designs on the floor of a hogan, or earth-
covered dwelling. The forms represent spirits
of animals, or other elements of nature. The
sick person sits in the center of the painting
and is sprinkled with the sand; thus, the image
disappears in the course of the ritual.

Sepia 1900. Painting using oils on canvas, plywood, and bowls by Hung Liu. The artist was born in China in 1948 and came to the United States in 1984. Having grown up under communism, she has used her new-found artistic freedom to comment on the historic oppression of Chinese women.

Under the Portal #1. Oil on canvas by Mexican American artist Elias Rivera.

Subway Graffitti #3. 600" x 800" painted canvas and pieced fabric by African American artist Faith Ringgold in 1987.

 A16

Napa, California
The Circuit

Reading the Authors in a Cultural Context

Ana Castillo and Francisco Jiménez often write about the experiences of Mexican American migrant farm workers. Because of California's large number of produce farms, many Mexicans and Mexican Americans have worked as farm laborers there. They often have little education and few job skills, and speak minimal English. Because of these conditions, many farm laborers have been exploited by the farm owners who hire them. Living in extreme poverty, working long hours, for low, unfair wages and receiving little or no medical care, these laborers move from farm to farm, following the crops of the season.

In her poem "Napa, California," Ana Castillo reveals the emotional and physical hardships migrant laborers have endured on the farms. Her work captures the heat, the hard work, and the humiliation of being treated unjustly by the farm owners. Notice that the poem is dedicated to César Chávez. Chávez, a Mexican American, worked as a migrant farm laborer for much of his childhood and young adulthood before committing himself to community service. In the early 1960s, Chávez began to organize migrant workers in California into the National Farm Workers Association. This union later merged with another to form the United Farm Workers. Chávez and his followers staged boycotts and strikes for better wages and living conditions. They also strove for recognition of their situation from mainstream society. As you read the poem, think about the images that Castillo uses to convey the inhumanity of life in the fields.

Born in Mexico, Francisco Jiménez moved to California with his family when he was 4 years old. By the time he was 6, he began to work in the California fields. Through the experiences of the narrator in "The Circuit," Jiménez captures the pain, shame, and uncertainty that come from living in poverty. At the same time, he emphasizes the importance of preserving traditional Mexican American values, such as family loyalty, a sense of dignity, and the strength to endure.

As you read "The Circuit," think about the problems the narrator confronts because of his family's constant moving from place to place.

Focusing on the Selections

As you read the following selections, think about the hardships that the farm laborers endure. What values do you think they possess that help them cope with their situation? What do these values reveal about Mexican American culture? How does the setting in both works emphasize the hard life the farm workers lead? Write your responses in your journal.

Napa, California

ANA CASTILLO

Dedicado al Sr. Chávez,[1] *sept. '75*

We pick
the bittersweet grapes
at harvest
one
    by
        one
with leather worn hands
    as they pick
        at our dignity
        and wipe our pride
        away
        like the sweat we wipe
        from our sun-beaten brows
        at midday

In fields
    so vast
    that our youth seems
    to pass before us
    and we have grown
    very
        very
            old

---

1. ***Dedicado al Sr. Chávez*** (day-dee-KAH-doh ahl say-NYOHR CHAH-vays) Dedicated to Mr. Chávez

by dusk . . .
(bueno pues, ¿qué vamos a hacer, Ambrosio?
¡bueno pues, seguirle, compadre, seguirle!
¡Ay, Mama!
Si pues, ¿qué vamos a hacer, compadre?
¡Seguirle, Ambrosio, seguirle!)[2]

We pick
    with a desire
    that only survival
    inspires
While the end
    of each day only brings
    a tired night
    that waits for the sun
    and the land
    that in turn waits
    for us . . .

---

2. *(bueno pues, ¿qué vamos a hacer, Ambrosio?/¡bueno pues, seguirle, compadre, seguirle!/¡Ay, Mama!/Si pues, ¿qué vamos a hacer, compadre?/¡Seguirle, Ambrosio, seguirle!)* (boo-AY-noh pways, kay VAH-mohs ah ah-SAIR, ahm-BROH-see-oh?/boo-AY-noh pways, say-GEER-lay, kohm-PAH-dray, say-GEER-lay/EYE, mah-MAH!/SEE pways, kay VAH-mohs ah ah-SAIR, kohm-PAH-dray?/say-GEER-lay, ahm-BROH-see-oh, say-GEER-lay!) Well, what are we going to do, Ambrosio?/Well, continue, my friend, continue!/Oh, Mother!/Yes, well, what else can we do?/Continue, Ambrosio, continue.

Photograph of César Chávez, labor union organizer and spokesperson for migrant farm workers. Chávez has said that "the truest act of courage . . . is to sacrifice ourselves for others in a totally nonviolent struggle for justice."

The Circuit

FRANCISCO JIMÉNEZ

IT WAS THAT TIME OF YEAR AGAIN. Ito, the strawberry sharecropper,[1] did not smile. It was natural. The peak of the strawberry season was over and the last few days the workers, most of them braceros,[2] were not picking as many boxes as they had during the months of June and July.

As the last days of August disappeared, so did the number of braceros. Sunday, only one—the best picker—came to work. I liked him. Sometimes we talked during our half-hour lunch break. That is how I found out he was from Jalisco,[3] the same state in Mexico my family was from. That Sunday was the last time I saw him.

When the sun had tired and sunk behind the mountains, Ito signaled us that it was time to go home. "Ya esora,"[4] he yelled in his broken Spanish. Those were the words I waited for twelve hours a day, every day, seven days a week, week after week. And the thought of not hearing them again saddened me.

---

1. **sharecropper** (SHAIR-crahp-per) *n.* a tenant farmer
2. **braceros** (brah-SAY-rohs) *n.* Mexicans who are brought into the United States and allowed to work temporarily on American farms
3. **Jalisco** (hah-LEES-koh) *n.* a state in west central Mexico
4. **Ya esora** (YAH ays-AW-rah) It's time (to stop working)

As we drove home Papá did not say a word. With both hands on the wheel, he stared at the dirt road. My older brother, Roberto, was also silent. He leaned his head back and closed his eyes. Once in a while he cleared from his throat the dust that blew in from outside.

Yes, it was that time of year. When I opened the front door to the shack, I stopped. Everything we owned was neatly packed in cardboard boxes. Suddenly I felt even more the weight of hours, days, weeks, and months of work. I sat down on a box. The thought of having to move to Fresno and knowing what was in store for me there brought tears to my eyes.

That night I could not sleep. I lay in bed thinking about how much I hated this move.

A little before five o'clock in the morning, Papá woke everyone up. A few minutes later, the yelling and screaming of my little brothers and sisters, for whom the move was a great adventure, broke the silence of dawn. Shortly, the barking of the dogs accompanied them.

While we packed the breakfast dishes, Papá went outside to start the "Carcanchita." That was the name Papá gave his old '38 black Plymouth. He bought it in a used-car lot in Santa Rosa in the winter of 1949. Papá was very proud of his little jalopy.[5] He had a right to be proud of it. He spent a lot of time looking at other cars before buying this one. When he finally chose the "Carcanchita," he checked it thoroughly before driving it out of the car lot. He examined every inch of the car. He listened to the motor, tilting his head from side to side like a parrot, trying to detect any noises that spelled car trouble. After being satisfied with the looks and sounds of the car, Papá then insisted on knowing who the original owner was. He never did find out from the car salesman, but he bought the car anyway. Papá figured the original owner must have been an important man because behind the rear seat of the car he found a blue necktie.

Papá parked the car out in front and left the motor running. "Listo,"[6] he yelled. Without saying a word, Roberto and I began to carry the boxes out to the car. Roberto carried the two big boxes and I carried the two smaller ones. Papá then threw the mattress on top of the car roof and tied it with ropes to the front and rear bumpers.

Everything was packed except Mamá's pot. It was an old large galvanized[7] pot she had picked up at an army surplus store in Santa María the year I was born. The pot had many dents and nicks, and the more dents

---

5. **jalopy** (jah-LAH-pee) *n.* an old, rickety automobile
6. **Listo** (LEES-toh) *adj.* ready
7. **galvanized** (GAL-van-eyezd) *adj.* plated or covered with zinc, by galvanic or electrical action

and nicks it acquired the more Mamá liked it. "Mi olla,"[8] she used to say proudly.

I held the front door open as Mamá carefully carried out her pot by both handles, making sure not to spill the cooked beans. When she got to the car, Papá reached out to help her with it. Roberto opened the rear car door and Papá gently placed it on the floor behind the front seat. All of us then climbed in. Papá sighed, wiped the sweat off his forehead with his sleeve, and said wearily: "Es todo."[9]

As we drove away, I felt a lump in my throat. I turned around and looked at our little shack for the last time.

At sunset we drove into a labor camp near Fresno. Since Papá did not speak English, Mamá asked the camp foreman[10] if he needed any more workers. "We don't need no more," said the foreman, scratching his head. "Check with Sullivan down the road. Can't miss him. He lives in a big white house with a fence around it."

When we got there, Mamá walked up to the house. She went through a white gate, past a row of rose bushes, up the stairs to the front door. She rang the doorbell. The porch light went on and a tall husky man came out. They exchanged a few words. After the man went in, Mamá clasped her hands and hurried back to the car. "We have work! Mr. Sullivan said we can stay there the whole season," she said, gasping and pointing to an old garage near the stables.

The garage was worn out by the years. It had no windows. The walls, eaten by termites, strained to support the roof full of holes. The dirt floor, populated by earth worms, looked like a gray road map.

That night, by the light of a kerosene lamp, we unpacked and cleaned our new home. Roberto swept away the loose dirt, leaving the hard ground. Papá plugged the holes in the walls with old newspapers and tin can tops. Mamá fed my little brothers and sisters. Papá and Roberto then brought in the mattress and placed it in the far corner of the garage. "Mamá, you and the little ones sleep on the mattress. Roberto, Panchito,[11] and I will sleep outside under the trees," Papá said.

Early next morning Mr. Sullivan showed us where his crop was, and after breakfast, Papá, Roberto, and I headed for the vineyard to pick.

Around nine o'clock the temperature had risen to almost one hundred degrees. I was completely soaked in sweat and my mouth felt as if I had been chewing on a handkerchief. I walked over to the end of the row, picked up the jug of water we had brought, and began drinking. "Don't drink too much; you'll get sick," Roberto shouted. No sooner had

---

8. **Mi olla** (mee OL-yah) My pot
9. **Es todo** (ays TOH-doh) That's everything
10. **foreman** (FOR-muhn) *n.* the person in charge of a department or group of workers
11. **Panchito** (pahn-CHEE-toh) *n.* nickname for Francisco

Chicano Farm Workers. Painted with acrylics on canvas by Mexican American artist Jesse Treviño. While Treviño was serving in Vietnam, his painting hand was lost to injury. The young artist painstakingly taught himself to paint with his remaining hand.

he said that than I felt sick to my stomach. I dropped to my knees and let the jug roll off my hands. I remained motionless with my eyes glued on the hot sandy ground. All I could hear was the drone[12] of insects. Slowly I began to recover. I poured water over my face and neck and watched the dirty water run down my arms to the ground.

———————

12. **drone** (DROHN) *n.* a continuous humming or buzzing sound

I still felt a little dizzy when we took a break to eat lunch. It was past two o'clock and we sat underneath a large walnut tree that was on the side of the road. While we ate, Papá jotted down the number of boxes we had picked. Roberto drew designs on the ground with a stick. Suddenly, I noticed Papá's face turn pale as he looked down the road. "Here comes the school bus," he whispered loudly in alarm. Instinctively, Roberto and I ran and hid in the vineyards. We did not want to get in trouble for not going to school. The neatly dressed boys about my age got off. They carried books under their arms. After they crossed the street, the bus drove away. Roberto and I came out from hiding and joined Papá. "Tienen que tener cuidado,"[13] he warned us.

After lunch we went back to work. The sun kept beating down. The buzzing insects, the wet sweat, and the hot dry dust made the afternoon seem to last forever. Finally the mountains around the valley reached out and swallowed the sun. Within an hour it was too dark to continue picking. The vines blanketed the grapes, making it difficult to see the bunches. "Vámonos,"[14] said Papá, signaling to us that it was time to quit work. Papá then took out a pencil and began to figure out how much we had earned our first day. He wrote down numbers, crossed some out, wrote down some more. "Quince,"[15] he murmured.

When we arrived home, we took a cold shower underneath a water hose. We then sat down to eat dinner around some wooden crates that served as a table. Mamá had cooked a special meal for us. We had rice and tortillas with "carne con chile,"[16] my favorite dish.

The next morning I could hardly move. My body ached all over. I felt little control over my arms and legs. This feeling went on every morning for days until my muscles finally got used to the work.

It was Monday, the first week of November. The grape season was over and I could now go to school. I woke up early that morning and lay in bed, looking at the stars and savoring the thought of not going to work and of starting sixth grade for the first time that year. Since I could not sleep, I decided to get up and join Papá and Roberto at breakfast. I sat at the table across from Roberto, but I kept my head down. I did not want to look up and face him. I knew he was sad. He was not going to school today. He was not going tomorrow, or next week, or next month. He would not go until the cotton season was over, and that was sometime in February. I rubbed my hands together and watched the dry, acid stained skin fall to the floor in little rolls.

---

13. **Tienen que tener cuidado** (tee-EN-en kay tay-NAIR kwee-DAH-doh) You have to be careful
14. **Vámonos** (VAH-moh-nohs) *v.* Let's go
15. **Quince** (KEEN-say) *n.* fifteen
16. **carne con chile** (KAHR-nay kohn CHEE-lay) *n.* a dish with beans and meat

When Papá and Roberto left for work, I felt relief. I walked to the top of a small grade next to the shack and watched the "Carcanchita" disappear in the distance in a cloud of dust.

Two hours later, around eight o'clock, I stood by the side of the road waiting for school bus number twenty. When it arrived I climbed in. Everyone was busy either talking or yelling. I sat in an empty seat in the back.

When the bus stopped in front of the school, I felt very nervous. I looked out the bus window and saw boys and girls carrying books under their arms. I put my hands in my pant pockets and walked to the principal's office. When I entered I heard a woman's voice say: "May I help you?" I was startled. I had not heard English for months. For a few seconds I remained speechless. I looked at the lady who waited for an answer. My first instinct was to answer her in Spanish, but I held back. Finally, after struggling for English words, I managed to tell her that I wanted to enroll in the sixth grade. After answering many questions, I was led to the classroom.

Mr. Lema, the sixth grade teacher, greeted me and assigned me a desk. He then introduced me to the class. I was so nervous and scared at that moment when everyone's eyes were on me that I wished I were with Papá and Roberto picking cotton. After taking roll, Mr. Lema gave the class the assignment for the first hour. "The first thing we have to do this morning is finish reading the story we began yesterday," he said enthusiastically. He walked up to me, handed me an English book, and asked me to read. "We are on page 125," he said politely. When I heard this, I felt my blood rush to my head; I felt dizzy. "Would you like to read?" he asked hesitantly. I opened the book to page 125. My mouth was dry. My eyes began to water. I could not begin. "You can read later," Mr. Lema said understandingly.

For the rest of the reading period I kept getting angrier and angrier with myself. I should have read, I thought to myself.

During recess I went into the restroom and opened my English book to page 125. I began to read in a low voice, pretending I was in class. There were many words I did not know. I closed the book and headed back to the classroom.

Mr. Lema was sitting at his desk correcting papers. When I entered he looked up at me and smiled. I felt better. I walked up to him and asked if he could help me with the new words. "Gladly," he said.

The rest of the month I spent my lunch hours working on English with Mr. Lema, my best friend at school.

One Friday during lunch hour Mr. Lema asked me to take a walk with him to the music room. "Do you like music?" he asked me as we entered the building.

"Yes, I like corridos,"[17] I answered. He then picked up a trumpet, blew on it and handed it to me. The sound gave me goose bumps. I knew that sound. I had heard it in many corridos. "How would you like to learn how to play it?" he asked. He must have read my face because before I could answer, he added: "I'll teach you how to play it during our lunch hours."

That day I could hardly wait to get home to tell Papá and Mamá the great news. As I got off the bus, my little brothers and sisters ran up to meet me. They were yelling and screaming. I thought they were happy to see me, but when I opened the door to our shack, I saw that everything we owned was neatly packed in cardboard boxes.

---

17. **corridos** (koh-REE-dohs) *n.* types of songs popular in Mexico

POSTREADING

Critical Thinking

1. What do the speakers in the poem and the story tell you about their attitudes toward equality and injustice?
2. What aspects of the writers' lives do you think most strongly shaped these attitudes?
3. How might you feel if you had to spend your childhood and teenage years working rather than in school? How do you think your feelings would compare to those of the narrator in "The Circuit?"

Writing Your Responses to "Napa, California" and "The Circuit"

In your journal, write about one scene, character, idea, or image in either the poem or the story that was meaningful to you. What did the passage make you think of? How can you relate it to something in your own life?

Going Back Into the Text: Author's Craft

The **setting** of a literary work is the time and place of the action. Setting serves a number of possible functions. It may simply provide a background for the action or it may be a crucial element in the plot or central conflict. It may help to create a certain *mood* or emotion. "Napa, California" and "The Circuit" share similar settings of migrant farming communities in California.

With a partner, review the function of setting in these works, using the following questions as guidelines.

1. What does the setting in "Napa, California" help to emphasize in the poem?
2. How does the setting in "The Circuit" convey a mood?
3. How does the setting add to the message or theme of both these works?

MAKING CONNECTIONS

Mexican American Heritage

In 1519, the Spanish conquered Mexico and then pushed north into what is now the southwestern part of the United States. By 1610, ten years before the Pilgrims reached Plymouth Rock, the Spanish had founded Santa Fe, New Mexico. Hispanic influence can still be seen there and in other cities throughout the region. Over the years, many people from Mexico have come to the United States. Thousands of them have settled in the Southwest, where they find much that is familiar.

Carmen Lomas Garza grew up in a Texas barrio. Her paintings evoke the vitality of life in the Mexican American community of her childhood. This painting is called *Cakewalk*.

Mexicans have been creating murals for generations. In the United States, that tradition lives on wherever Mexican Americans have settled. Many of these murals pay tribute to the Mexican American workers who have helped build the nation. This is a detail from a mural entitled *Tribute to the Chicano Working Class* by Emigdio Vasquez.

The Hispanic heritage of the Southwest is most visible in architecture, particularly in the missions that dot the region. These missions, like the Zia Mission shown in this painting, helped the Spanish spread Christianity and other aspects of their culture.

LINKING
Literature, Culture, and Theme

Compare the attitudes and values expressed in these images of Mexican American life with those in "The Circuit" by Francisco Jiménez and "Napa, California" by Ana Castillo.

▼ What values and attitudes are reflected in these works of art?

▼ How might Panchito's family (in "The Circuit") respond to the images in these pictures? Which picture do you think best reflects the family's sense of pride in its heritage? Explain your answer.

▼ In what ways are the attitudes and values expressed in Ana Castillo's poem similar to those reflected in the mural?

Speech of Sojourner Truth

Reading the Author in a Cultural Context

The abolitionist movement of the early to mid-1800s fought for the end of slavery. The campaign drew strength from a spirit of reform in the nation during this period. Various groups focused on women's rights, a renewed interest in religion, compulsory education, and other social and political reforms. The American Anti-Slavery Society, established in 1833, flooded the nation with abolitionist literature. In 1852, Harriet Beecher Stowe's novel *Uncle Tom's Cabin* became a best seller and turned many Americans against slavery.

Although sharing a common goal, abolitionists were divided over the method of achieving it. Some called for a strong moral appeal to Southern plantation owners to free their slaves. Others demanded direct political action by the federal government. After the outbreak of the Civil War, demands for an immediate end to slavery helped to prompt President Abraham Lincoln's Emancipation Proclamation of 1863.

Sojourner Truth, born Isabella in 1797 (enslaved people often had no last names), became one of the most effective speakers of the abolitionist movement. She gained her own freedom from slavery in 1827, when a New York law banned slavery. She then became strongly influenced by a preacher and began to experience visions. In one vision, she was given the name Sojourner Truth. She began to travel throughout the country, speaking out passionately against slavery and discrimination against women. Although she was unable to read or write, Truth financed her travels by selling copies of her autobiography, which Olive Gilbert had written down for her.

Wherever she went, people listened to Truth's powerful speeches against slavery. She also spoke out for women's rights, which was an unpopular issue at the time. As an African American woman, Truth experienced a double discrimination from the male-dominated white society. In 1851, she attended the Woman's Rights Convention in Akron, Ohio, where clergymen quoted the Bible as evidence that men were superior to women. As a response, Truth delivered the famous speech that follows.

As you read, think about the ways Truth connects the African American struggle for equality with the fight for equal rights for women. In what ways are the two similar? In what ways are they different? Consider why many of the people who were active in the antislavery movement were also active in the crusade for women's rights.

Focusing on the Selection

As you read, think about Truth's perspective on the issue of women's rights. How does she expose the falseness of discrimination? How does Truth use logic and humor to influence the audience's opinions? What other persuasive techniques does she use in her speech? Write your responses in your journal.

Speech of Sojourner Truth

"MAY I SAY A FEW WORDS?" Receiving an affirmative[1] answer, she proceeded; "I want to say a few words about this matter. I am a woman's rights. I have as much muscle as any man, and can do as much work as any man. I have plowed and reaped and husked[2] and chopped and mowed, and can any man do more than that? I have heard much about the sexes being equal; I can carry as much as any man, and can eat as much too, if I can get it. I am as strong as any man that is now. As for intellect, all I can say is, if woman have a pint and man a quart—why can't she have her little pint full? You need not be afraid to give us our rights for fear we will take too much, for we can't take more than our pint'll hold. The poor men seem to be all in confusion, and don't know what to do. Why children, if you have woman's rights give it to her and you will feel better. You will have your own rights, and they won't be so much trouble. I can't read, but I can hear. I have heard the bible and have learned that Eve caused man to sin. Well if woman upset the world, do give her a chance to set it right side up again. The Lady has spoken about Jesus, how he never spurned[3] woman from him, and she was right. When Lazarus died, Mary and Martha came to him with faith and love and besought him to raise their brother. And Jesus

---

1. **affirmative** (uh-FERM-uh-tihv) *adj.* agreeing
2. **husked** (HUSKT) *v.* removed outer layer, as with corn
3. **spurned** (SPERND) *v.* rejected

Sojourner Truth and Booker T. Washington. Charcoal drawing by African American artist Charles White. During the 1890s, Washington became a spokesperson for African Americans, urging them to gain practical skills through vocational education.

wept—and Lazarus came forth.[4] And how came Jesus into the world? Through God who created him and woman who bore him. Man, where is your part? But the women are coming up, blessed be God, and a few of the men are coming with them. But man is in a tight place, the poor slave is on him, woman is coming on him, and he is surely between a hawk and a buzzard."[5]

---

4. **and Lazarus came forth** In Christian religion, Jesus brought Lazarus back from death.

5. **between a hawk and a buzzard** in a difficult spot

POSTREADING

Critical Thinking

1. In this speech, what does Truth tell you about her attitudes concerning the struggle of women for equality?
2. What experiences in her own life do you think most influenced her decision to become a speaker for equality for women?
3. How does Truth's speech apply to other groups' struggle for equal rights?

Writing Your Response to "Speech of Sojourner Truth"

In your journal, write about one idea in the speech that is especially meaningful to you. In what ways is it significant? How does it relate to your own experience?

Going Back Into the Text: Author's Craft

Persuasive speeches attempt to convince listeners to think or act in a certain way. The effectiveness of a speech often depends on the techniques the speaker uses to convey his or her argument. In her speech, Sojourner Truth repeatedly uses such persuasive techniques as humor, logic, and rhetorical questions to refute the argument that men are superior to women. A *rhetorical question* is a question that is asked not to obtain information but rather to make a point in an indirect way. The speaker adds emphasis to an idea by putting it in the form of a question, the answer to which supports his or her argument.

With a partner, use the following points to review persuasive techniques in "Speech of Sojourner Truth."

1. Give an example of the way Truth uses humor in her speech to reject the idea that men are superior to women.
2. How does Truth use a rhetorical question to expose the falseness of the idea that women need to be treated with special consideration?
3. Find another example of a rhetorical question in this book. What point does it emphasize?

from I Am Joaquín

Reading the Author in a Cultural Context

The Chicano movement, like many other civil rights movements in the United States, gained strength in the 1960s. *Chicano* was the popular term that Mexican Americans used to identify themselves at the time. The movement rejected the idea of the United States as a great melting pot, in which all cultures blend together. Instead, it turned to the history and cultural traditions of Mexican Americans. The movement then used that heritage to promote solidarity among people of the Mexican American community.

The excerpt that follows is from a book-length poem called *I Am Joaquín*. It was written by Rodolfo Gonzales, a Mexican American civil rights leader. This poem became the proclamation of the entire Chicano movement, greatly influencing the thousands of people who read it. As you read the poem, think about how the Chicano movement is similar to other social or political movements.

Born in Denver, Colorado, to migrant workers, Gonzales took up boxing when he was 15 in an attempt to escape barrio life. After boxing competitively for many years, Gonzales launched his political career. He held numerous important positions in the Denver Democratic party during the 1960s. In the struggle for Mexican American rights, Gonzales began organizing protests against discrimination. In 1966, he founded the Crusade for Justice. This organization helped to give Mexican Americans the power to fight the social injustices they experienced and to regain pride in their Mexican heritage.

Gonzales's life as a writer is intertwined with his life as a political activist. With *I Am Joaquín*, Gonzales penetrates to the very core of the conflicts in Mexican American culture. The poem explores Mexican American history as a unique combination of influences—of the Spaniards who ruled Mexico, the Native American cultures that were oppressed by them, and finally the mainstream culture of the United States. Written in the aggressive language of a true fighter, *I Am Joaquín* challenges the Mexican American community to overcome the prejudice and exploitation that have plagued them in this country.

As you read, notice the language of the poem. What message does Gonzales convey through his imagery and word choice? Consider whether this poem reminds you of any other works you have read.

Focusing on the Selection

As you read the following excerpt from *I Am Joaquín*, think about the ways in which Joaquín represents his entire culture. What aspects of Mexican American life does Joaquín express? What are some of the conflicts Joaquín faces? How does he attempt to solve these conflicts? How does Gonzales use repetition to structure the poem? Write your responses in your journal.

from *I Am Joaquín*

RODOLFO GONZALES

I am Joaquín,[1]
lost in a world of confusion,
caught up in the whirl of a
        gringo[2] society.
confused by the rules,
scorned by attitudes,
suppressed by manipulation,
and destroyed by modern society.
My fathers
    have lost the economic battle
and won
    the struggle of cultural survival.
And now!
    I must choose
           between
    the paradox[3] of
victory of the spirit,
despite physical hunger,
        or
    to exist in the grasp
of American social neurosis,[4]
sterilization of the soul
    and a full stomach. . . .

I shed the tears of anguish
as I see my children disappear
behind the shroud of mediocrity,
never to look back to remember me.
I am Joaquín.
        I must fight
           and win this struggle
           for my sons, and they
           must know from me
           who I am.

El Pantalon Rosa. Woodblock print created by Mexican American artist Cesar Martinez in 1982. The title is Spanish for *the pink pants*.

---

1. **Joaquín** (hwah-KEEN) *n.* a man's name
2. **gringo** (GREEN-goh) *n.* a foreigner, especially someone from the U.S.
3. **paradox** (PAR-ah-dohks) *n.* a statement that seems self-contradictory
4. **neurosis** (noo-ROH-sihs) *n.* a mild personality disorder

Part of the blood that runs deep in me
could not be vanquished by the Moors.[5]
I defeated them after five hundred years,
and I endured.
      Part of the blood that is mine
      has labored endlessly four hundred
      years under the heel of lustful[6]
        Europeans.
            I am still here!

I have endured in the rugged mountains
    of our country.
I have survived the toils and slavery
    of the fields.
        I have existed
in the barrios[7] of the city
in the suburbs of bigotry
in the mines of social snobbery
in the prisons of dejection
in the muck of exploitation
and
in the fierce heat of racial hatred.

And now the trumpet sounds,
the music of the people stirs the
        revolution.
Like a sleeping giant it slowly
rears its head
to the sound of
            tramping feet
           clamoring voices
          mariachi[8] strains
         fiery tequila explosions
       the smell of chile verde[9] and
     soft brown eyes of expectation for a
                  better life.

---

5. Moors (MOORZ) *n.* a Muslim people from northwestern Africa who invaded Spain
6. lustful (LUST-fuhl) *adj.* full of or motivated by greed
7. barrios (BAH-ree-ohs) *n.* neighborhoods
8. mariachi (mah-ree-AH-chee) *n.* a type of Mexican dance music
9. chile verde (CHEE-lay VAIR-day) *n.* green peppers

And in all the fertile farmlands,
                         the barren plains,
the mountain villages,
smoke-smeared cities,
              we start to MOVE.
     La Raza!
Méjicano!
     Español!
       Latino!
          Hispano!
             Chicano![10]
or whatever I call myself,
          I look the same
          I feel the same
          I cry
                and
          sing the same.

I am the masses of my people and
I refuse to be absorbed.
          I am Joaquín.
The odds are great
but my spirit is strong,
                    my faith unbreakable,
                    my blood is pure.
I am Aztec[11] prince and Christian Christ.
              I SHALL ENDURE!
              I WILL ENDURE!

---

10. **La Raza!/Méjicano!/Español!/Latino!/Hispano!/Chicano!** (la RAH-sah!/may-
    hee-KAH-noh!/ays-pan-NYOHL!/lah-TEE-noh!/hees-PAH-noh!/chee-KAH-noh!)
    n. the Mexican people, Mexican, Spanish, Latin, Hispanic, Mexican American
11. **Aztec** (AZ-tek) *adj.* of a native people from central Mexico

POSTREADING

Critical Thinking

1. What does Gonzales tell you about Joaquín's attitudes toward his struggle for equality in U.S. society?
2. What experiences do you think prompted Gonzales to write this poem?
3. How did reading this poem influence your feelings about your cultural history? How are your attitudes similar to Joaquín's?

Writing Your Response to *I Am Joaquín*

In your journal, write about one idea, image, or situation in the poem that is especially memorable to you. How does it correspond to an experience in your own life or in the life of someone you know?

Going Back Into the Text: Author's Craft

Free verse is poetry that has no meter, or regular rhythmic pattern. A writer of free verse has few restrictions in creating a rhythm that is appropriate to the subject he or she is trying to convey. *Parallelism* is a form of repetition in which a writer uses phrases and/or sentences that are similar in structure or meaning. For instance, in the last stanza of the excerpt from *I Am Joaquín*, Gonzales uses a series of sentences that are structurally similar: "I look the same/I feel the same/I cry/and/sing the same." Poets often use parallelism in free verse to help create rhythm, emphasis, and unity in a poem.

With a partner, review the use of free verse and parallelism in *I Am Joaquín*. The following points can serve as guidelines.

1. Give two examples of parallelism in the poem.
2. Why do you think Gonzales uses free verse in this poem? Do you think it is appropriate? Explain.
3. What other examples of parallel structure can you find in this book? What effects do they help create?

Free to Go

Responding to Literature

Notice the sidenotes in the margins of the selection. These notes reflect one student's reading of "Free to Go," a selection from *Farewell to Manzanar*. The student points out elements such as chronological order, setting, and point of view in this personal narrative. The student also responds personally to experiences in Jeanne Wakatsuki Houston's life. Compare the student's responses to your own reactions.

Reading the Authors in a Cultural Context

At the beginning of World War II, rumors about possible acts of sabotage by Japanese Americans led U.S. officials to order 110,000 Japanese Americans from their West Coast homes. They were sent to one of ten internment camps. At the internment camps, Japanese Americans found themselves surrounded by barbed wire and armed guards. Over 35,000 Nisei—second-generation, or U.S.-born, Japanese—were able to leave the centers after being checked and cleared, provided that they moved eastward, away from the "Western Defense Area." Those who remained in the centers were assigned work, for which they received $16 dollars a month. This was hardly enough to replace the homes and possessions that had been lost, stolen, or sold at a loss after the evacuation order.

Even though she was only 8 years old and a U.S. citizen by birth, Jeanne Wakatsuki Houston was interned with the other members of her family at an internment camp in California during the war.

In the following excerpt from her book *Farewell to Manzanar*, she describes the fear and uncertainty of the internees once they were released from the camps. Like other ethnic groups in the United States, Japanese and Japanese Americans endured much prejudice in mainstream U.S. society, particularly on the West Coast. They were resented for their reluctance to give up their Japanese heritage and their failure to assimilate to, or blend in with, the dominant U.S. culture. They were also resented for their economic successes, even under discrimination and prejudice. Now, with their homes and assets gone, Japanese Americans were left with little more than the painful memories of the discrimination they had faced before their internment.

Focusing on the Selection

As you read "Free to Go," think about what the camps represent to the interned Japanese Americans. In what ways do the camps symbolize the prejudice they suffered? How do the camps protect them from this hatred? How does their release from the camps emphasize their lack of freedom?

Free to Go

from *Farewell to Manzanar*

JEANNE WAKATSUKI HOUSTON AND JAMES D. HOUSTON

THE ANSWERS BEGAN with a Supreme Court ruling that December, in the case called *Ex Parte*[1] *Endo*. It was the last of three key cases heard since the camps had opened.

In the first, Gordon Hirabayashi, a Nisei[2] student from the University of Washington, challenged the evacuation order.[3] He had also violated the army's curfew, imposed early in 1942 on all west-coast Japanese. He challenged the racial bias of these actions and the abuse of his civil rights. The court avoided the issue of the evacuation itself by ruling on the curfew. It upheld the army's decision to limit the movements of a racially select group of citizens. The reasoning: wartime necessity.

In the second case, the issue was the exclusion orders that removed us from our homes and sent us inland. Fred Korematsu, a young Nisei living in Oakland, had ignored the evacuation to stay with his Caucasian girlfriend. He had plastic surgery done on his face, he changed his name, and was posing as a Spanish Hawaiian when the FBI caught up with him. In court, the racial bias was challenged again. Why were no German Americans evacuated, it was asked, or Americans of Italian descent? Weren't these nations our enemies too? Due process had been violated, Korematsu claimed, along with other constitutional rights. But the army's decision to evacuate was also upheld by the Supreme Court.

The final case challenged the internment itself. Soon after she was evacuated, in April 1942, Mitsue Endo, a twenty-one-year-old Nisei and an employee of the California State Highway Commission, had filed a petition for habeus corpus,[4] protesting her detention at Topaz Camp in central Utah. She spent two and a half years awaiting the high court's decision, which was that she had been right: the government cannot detain loyal citizens against their will.

Anticipating this ruling, the army's Western Defense Command had already announced that the mass exclusion orders of 1942 were being rescinded. Next it was announced that all the camps would be closed within the coming twelve months and that internees now had the right to return to their former homes.

---

1. **Ex Parte** (eks PAR-tay) *adj.* a one-sided presentation of a court case
2. **Nisei** (NEE-SAY) *n.* a person of Japanese descent, born and educated in the U.S.
3. **evacuation order** the order by the U.S. army in 1942 to place all Japanese and Japanese Americans living on the West Coast in internment camps
4. **habeas corpus** (HAY-bee-uhs COR-puhs) *n.* order requiring a person to be in court

Photograph of the Mochida family, Japanese Americans being forced to move to an internment camp during World War II. How did citizens like these feel about being forced to leave their homes?

In our family the response to this news was hardly joyful. For one thing we had no home to return to. Worse, the very thought of going back to the west coast filled us with dread. What will they think of us, those who sent us here? How will they look at us? Three years of wartime propaganda—racist headlines, atrocity movies, hate slogans, and fright-mask posters—had turned the Japanese face into something despicable and grotesque. Mama and Papa knew this. They had been reading the papers. Even I knew this, although it was not until many years later that I realized how bad things actually were.

In addition to the traditionally racist organizations like the American Legion and The Native Sons of The Golden West, who had been agitating against the west-coast Japanese for decades, new groups had sprung up during the war, with the specific purpose of preventing anyone of Japanese descent from returning to the coast—groups like No Japs Incorporated in San Diego, The Home Front Commandoes in Sacramento, and The Pacific Coast Japanese Problem League in Los Angeles. Also, some growers' associations, threatened by the return of interned farmers, had been using the war as a way to foment[5] hostile feelings in the major farming areas.

What's more, our years of isolation at Manzanar had widened the already spacious gap between the races, and it is not hard to understand why so many preferred to stay where they were. Before the war one of the standard charges made against the Japanese was their clannishness, their standoffishness, their refusal to assimilate. The camps had made this a reality in the extreme. After three years in our desert ghetto, at least we knew where we stood with our neighbors, could live more or less at ease with them.

Yet now the government was saying we not only were free to go; like the move out of Terminal Island, and the move to Owens Valley,[6] we had to go. Definite dates were being fixed for the closing of the camp.

By January of '45 a few determined internees were already trying to recover former homes and farmlands. Ominous[7] reports of their reception began trickling back, to confirm our deepest fears. A Nisei man had been assaulted on the street in Seattle. A home was burned in San Jose. Nightriders carrying shotguns had opened fire on a farmhouse near Fresno, narrowly missing two sleeping children. Later on, in May, one of my sisters and her husband, leaving for the east, were escorted to the Southern Pacific depot in Los Angeles by armed guards, not because they were thought to be dangerous, but for their own protection.

Most of the Japanese returning to the coast resettled without suffering bodily harm. But gossip tends to thrive on bad news, not good. Stories such as these spread through the camp and grew in our minds like tumors. I remember hearing them discussed in our barracks, quietly, as if Ku Klux Klansmen lurked outside the window, the same way my brothers discussed our dilemma during the brief stay in Boyle Heights, before the evacuation.

---

5. **foment** (foh-MENT) *v.* to promote the growth or development of; to instigate or foster
6. **Terminal Island . . . Owens Valley** previous towns from which the family had been forced to move
7. **ominous** (AHM-ihn-uhs) *adj.* threatening

I would listen to the stories and I would cringe. And this was both odd and confusing to me, because ever since we'd arrived, the outside world had loomed in my imagination as someplace inaccessible yet wonderfully desirable. I would recall our days in Ocean Park. I would flip through the Sears, Roebuck catalogue, dreaming of the dresses and boots and coats that were out there somewhere at the other end of the highway beyond the gate. All the truly good things, it often seemed, the things we couldn't get, were outside, and had to be sent for, or shipped in. In this sense, God and the Sears, Roebuck catalogue were pretty much one and the same in my young mind.

Once, during a novena[8] at the Maryknoll chapel, I had asked for something I desperately longed for and had never seen inside the camp. We were told to ask for something we really wanted. We were to write it on a piece of paper, pray devoutly for nine days, and if we'd prayed well it would be answered. The nuns expected us to ask for purity of soul, or a holy life. I asked God for some dried apricots. I wrote this on a piece of paper, dropped it into the prayer box, and began to fantasize about how they would arrive, in a package from Sears, Roebuck. I knew how they would taste, and feel in my hands. I said my rosary, thirty times a day, for nine days, and for nine more days after that I waited. The dried apricots never came. My faith in God and in the Catholic church slipped several notches at that time. But not my faith in the outside, where all such good things could be found. I went back to flipping through the catalogue.

Those images, of course, had come from my past. What I had to face now, a year later, was the future. I was old enough to imagine it, and also old enough to fear it. The physical violence didn't trouble me. Somehow I didn't quite believe that, or didn't want to believe such things could happen to us. It was the humiliation. That continuous, unnamed ache I had been living with was precise and definable now. Call it the foretaste of being hated. I knew ahead of time that if someone looked at me with hate, I would have to allow it, to swallow it, because something in me, something about me deserved it. At ten I saw that coming, like a judge's sentence, and I would have stayed inside the camp forever rather than step outside and face such a moment.

I shared this particular paralysis with Mama and Papa, but not with my older brothers and sisters. The hostility worried them. But their desire to be rid of Manzanar outweighed that worry. They were in their twenties and had their lives to lead. They decided to take a chance on the east coast. It was 3,000 miles away, with no history of anti-Orientalism, in fact no Oriental history at all. So few people of Asian ancestry had settled there, it was like heading for a neutral country.

---

8. **novena** (noh-VEE-nah) *n.* in the Catholic Church, a devotion consisting of nine separate days of prayers or services

I don't blame her for being confused. She had always desired her freedom, but now the outside world had become more threatening than the internment camp.

Her desire for material things like dried apricots and dresses seems to be a suggestion of how "American" she really is.

I'm surprised the author and her family were Catholic. I thought that most Japanese Americans practice Eastern religions like Buddhism.

The author is starting to believe that she somehow deserves to be hated. Since she tells the story from her own point of view, I can understand her feelings more clearly.

I wonder if it's true that there was less prejudice against Japanese on the East Coast.

Bill was the first to make that move, with Tomi and their baby boy. He had lined up a job with Seabrook Farms in New Jersey, a new frozen-food enterprise that offered work to many Nisei at the end of the war. A few weeks later Frances and her husband joined them, followed by Martha and Kaz, then Lillian, who was just finishing her junior year in high school, and Ray.

As each cluster of relatives departed we'd say, "See you in New Jersey. Find us all a big house back there."

What we told each other was that Bill and Frances and the others would go on ahead, make sure things could be worked out, then they'd send for the rest of us. "See you in New Jersey," we would wave, as the bus pulled out taking someone else to the train station in L.A. But they all knew, even as they said it, that Papa would never move back east. As bad as the west coast sounded, it was still his home territory. He was too old to start over, too afraid of rejection in an unknown part of the world, too stubborn and too tired to travel that far, and finally too proud to do piecework on an assembly line. Like so many Issei,[9] he had, for better or worse, run his own businesses, been his own man for too long to tolerate the idea of working for someone else.

The truth was, at this point Papa did not know which way to turn. In the government's eyes a free man now, he sat, like those black slaves you hear about who, when they got word of their freedom at the end of the Civil War, just did not know where else to go or what else to do and ended up back on the plantation, rooted there out of habit or lethargy or fear.

---

9. Issei (EES-SAY) *n.* a Japanese who emigrated to the United States or Canada after 1907 and was not eligible for citizenship until 1952

POSTREADING

Critical Thinking

1. What does Jeanne Wakatsuki Houston tell you about her attitudes about being a Japanese American?
2. How did her experiences in the internment camp shape her attitudes?
3. Does prejudice against Japanese Americans or other groups exist in your community? What evidence can you offer to support your answer?

Writing Your Response to "Free to Go"

In your journal, write about one character, event, image, or idea that strongly affected you as you read the excerpt. Why was it memorable to you? How does it relate to an experience in your own life or in the life of someone you know?

Going Back Into the Text: Author's Craft

Irony is a contrast between what is stated and what is meant. It can also refer to the difference between what is expected to happen and what actually happens.

Three types of irony are used most often in writing. In *verbal irony*, a word or phrase can suggest the opposite of its usual meaning. Calling a traitor "an honorable man" is an example of verbal irony. In *dramatic irony*, there is a contradiction between what a character thinks and what the reader knows to be true. For example, a very trusting character may disbelieve another character who the reader knows is quite trustworthy. In *irony of situation*, an event occurs that directly contradicts the expectations of the characters or of the reader. For example, a disruptive character might help bring about a harmonious situation.

With a partner, review "Free to Go" to see the ways in which irony is used. The following questions can serve as guidelines.

1. What is ironic about the internment of Japanese American citizens in this country? Support your answer with reasons.
2. How does Houston's desire for dresses and other items from the Sears catalog emphasize the irony of her imprisonment?
3. How does the response of Houston's family to their approaching freedom reveal the irony of their situation?

In the American Storm

Reading the Author in a Cultural Context

Some European immigrants came to the United States to escape hunger, some to find religious or political freedom, and some to make money. Others came for adventure. But Constantine Panunzio did not even come to stay. Panunzio was an Italian sailor on the crew of a ship that arrived in Boston, Massachusetts, in 1902. The captain of his ship was a brutal man who sometimes beat Panunzio. The other sailors, who were from the northern part of Italy, teased Panunzio because he was from the south, which they looked down upon. When the ship docked in Boston, Panunzio decided that he was too miserable to continue living in such a situation. He then decided to leave the ship and look for work in order to pay for his passage back home to Italy.

Because of their harbors, Boston, New York City, and New Orleans have been centers of immigration since Colonial times. In the early 1900s, European immigrants to these cities often arrived with little but the clothes they wore. With limited English, it was difficult for them to find jobs. Besides, these immigrants had to fight several kinds of prejudice. Sometimes it was economic. Established groups would fight to deny jobs to newer immigrants because they believed that newcomers, desperately in need of money, would work for less pay. Sometimes the prejudice was religious, and sometimes it was cultural. Most of the time, it was a mix of these—in any case, the result was discrimination.

The great influx of immigrant groups into U.S. cities occurred in part because of the image of the United States as a land of opportunity. This idea included the belief that if a newcomer worked hard enough and learned to speak English, that person could leave poverty behind and rise upward in society. For some immigrants, this has been true. Constantine Panunzio managed not just to survive but to become accepted and succeed in the larger mainstream society. He studied, attended college, and earned a doctoral degree in theology. But he never forgot his experiences as a new immigrant. From 1915 to 1920, he worked with immigrants in settlement houses and at the YMCA. He also worked as an investigator of the causes of the 1919 Steel Strike.

The following excerpt is from Panunzio's book *The Soul of an Immigrant*, published in 1921. The book is generally optimistic in tone—a celebration of the American experience. However, like many of Panunzio's published works, this selection deals with the conflicts and struggles faced by many who have immigrated to the United States.

Focusing on the Selection

As you read the following selection from Panunzio's autobiographical work *The Soul of an Immigrant*, think about his attitude toward his struggle to find employment. What values help him through his hardships upon arriving in the United States? Notice the writer's tone as he describes his experiences. Write your responses in your journal.

In the American Storm

from *The Soul of an Immigrant*

CONSTANTINE M. PANUNZIO

. . . L ATE IN THE EVENING OF SEPTEMBER 8, 1902, when the turmoil
of the street traffic was subsiding, and the silence of the night
was slowly creeping over the city, I took my sea chest, my sailor bag and
all I had and set foot on American soil. I was in America. Of immigration laws I had not even a knowledge of their existence; of the English
language I knew not a word; of friends I had none in Boston or else-
where in America to whom I might turn for counsel or help. I had exactly fifty cents remaining out of a dollar which the captain had finally
seen fit to give me. But as I was soon to earn money and return to
Molfetta, I felt no concern. . . .

I roamed about the streets, not knowing where or to whom to turn.
That day and the next four days I had one loaf of bread each day for
food and at night, not having money with which to purchase shelter, I
stayed on the recreation pier on Commercial Street. One night, very
weary and lonely, I lay upon a bench and soon dozed off into a light
sleep. The next thing I knew I cried out in bitter pain and fright. A po-
liceman had stolen up to me very quietly and with his club had dealt me
a heavy blow upon the soles of my feet. He drove me away, and I think I
cried; I cried my first American cry. What became of me that night I
cannot say. And the next day and the next. . . . I just roamed aimlessly

about the streets, between the Public Garden with its flowers and the water-side, where I watched the children at play, even as I had played at the water's brink in old Molfetta.

Those first five days in America have left an impression upon my mind which can never be erased with the years, and which gives me a most profound sense of sympathy for immigrants as they arrive.

On the fifth day, by mere chance, I ran across a French sailor on the recreation pier. We immediately became friends. His name was Louis. Just to look at Louis would make you laugh. He was over six feet tall, lank, queer-shaped, freckle-faced, with small eyes and a crooked nose. I have sometimes thought that perhaps he was the "missing link" for which the scientist has been looking. Louis could not speak Italian; he had a smattering of what he called "italien," but I could not see it his way. On the other hand, I kept imposing upon his good nature by giving a nasal twang to Italian words and insisting on calling it "francese." We had much merriment. Two facts, however, made possible a mutual understanding. Both had been sailors and had traveled over very much the same world; this made a bond between us. Then too, we had an instinctive knowledge of "esperanto," a strange capacity for gesticulation[1] and facial contortion, which was always our last "hope" in making each other understand.

Not far from the recreation pier on which we met is located the Italian colony of "North End," Boston. To this Louis and I made our way, and to an Italian boarding house. How we happened to find it and to get in I do not now recall. It was a "three-room apartment" and the landlady informed us that she was already "full," but since we had no place to go, she would take us in. Added to the host that was already gathered there, our coming made fourteen people. At night the floor of the kitchen and the dining table were turned into beds. Louis and I were put to sleep in one of the beds with two other men, two facing north and two south. As I had slept all my life in a bed or bunk by myself this quadrupling did not appeal to me especially. But we could not complain. We had been taken in on trust, and the filth, the smells and the crowding together were a part of the trust.

We began to make inquiries about jobs and were promptly informed that there was plenty of work at "pick and shovel." We were also given to understand by our fellow-boarders that "pick and shovel" was practically the only work available to Italians. Now these were the first two English words I had heard and they possessed great charm. Moreover, if I were to earn money to return home and this was the only work available for Italians, they were very weighty words for me, and I must master

---

1. **gesticulation** (jes-tihk-yoo-LAY-shuhn) *n.* hand signals

them as soon and as well as possible and then set out to find their hidden meaning. I practised for a day or two until I could say "peek" and "shuvle" to perfection. Then I asked a fellow-boarder to take me to see what the work was like. He did. He led me to Washington Street, not far from the colony, where some excavation work was going on, and there I did see, with my own eyes, what the "peek" and "shuvle" were about. My heart sank within me, for I had thought it some form of office work; but I was game and since this was the only work available for Italians, and since I must have money to return home, I would take it up. After all, it was only a means to an end, and would last but a few days.

It may be in place here to say a word relative to the reason why this idea was prevalent among Italians at the time, and why so many Italians on coming to America find their way to what I had called "peek and shuvle." It is a matter of common knowledge, at least among students of immigration, that a very large percentage of Italian immigrants were "contadini" or farm laborers in Italy. American people often ask the question, "Why do they not go to the farms in this country?" This query is based upon the idea that the "contadini" were farmers in the sense in which we apply that word to the American farmer. The facts in the case are that the "contadini" were not farmers in that sense at all, but simply farm-laborers, more nearly serfs, working on landed estates and seldom owning their own land. Moreover, they are not in any way acquainted with the implements of modern American farming. Their farming tools consisted generally of a "zappa," a sort of wide mattock;[2] an ax and the wooden plow of biblical times. When they come to America, the work which comes nearest to that which they did in Italy is not farming, or even farm labor, but excavation work. This fact, together with the isolation which inevitably would be theirs on an American farm, explains, in a large measure, why so few Italians go to the farm and why so many go into excavation work. There is another factor to be considered, and that is that the "padrone"[3] perhaps makes a greater per capita percentage in connection with securing and managing workers for construction purposes than in any other line, and therefore he becomes a walking delegate about the streets of Italian colonies spreading the word that only "peek and shuvle" is available.

Now, though Louis and I had never done such work, because we were Italians we must needs adapt ourselves to it and go to work with "peek and shuvle." (I should have stated that Louis, desiring to be like the Romans while living with them, for the time being passed for an Italian.)

---

2. **mattock** (MAT-uhk) *n.* digging tool
3. **padrone** (pah-DROH-nay) In this sense, he is a person who recruited Italian immigrants to do low-paying jobs in the U.S.

So we went out to hunt our first job in America. For several mornings Louis and I went to North Square, where there were generally a large number of men loitering in groups discussing all kinds of subjects, particularly the labor market. One morning we were standing in front of one of those infernal institutions which in America are permitted to bear the name of "immigrant banks," when we saw a fat man coming toward us. "Buon giorno,[4] padrone," said one of the men. "Padrone?" said I to myself. Now the word "padrone" in Italy is applied to a proprietor, generally a respectable man, at least one whose dress and appearance distinguish him as a man of means. This man not only showed no signs of good breeding in his face, but he was unshaven and dirty and his clothes were shabby. I could not quite understand how he could be called "padrone." However, I said nothing, first because I wanted to get back home, and second because I wanted to be polite when I was in American society!

The "padrone" came up to our group and began to wax eloquent and to gesticulate (both in Sicilian dialect) about the advantages of a certain job. I remember very clearly the points which he emphasized: "It is not very far, only twelve miles from Boston. For a few cents you can come back any time you wish, to see 'i parenti e gli amici,'[5] your relatives and friends. The company has a 'shantee' in which you can sleep, and a 'storo' where you can buy your 'grosserie' all very cheap. 'Buona paga,' " he continued, "(Good pay), $1.25 per day, and you only have to pay me fifty cents a week for having gotten you this 'gooda jobba.' I only do it to help you and because you are my countrymen. If you come back here at six o'clock to-night with your bundles, I myself will take you out."

The magnanimity[6] of this man impressed Louis and me very profoundly; we looked at each other and said, "Wonderful!" We decided we would go; so at the appointed hour we returned to the very spot. About twenty men finally gathered there and we were led to North Station. There we took a train to some suburban place, the name of which I have never been able to learn. On reaching our destination we were taken to the "shantee" where we were introduced to two long open bunks filled with straw. These were to be our beds. The "storo" of which we had been told was at one end of the shanty. The next morning we were taken out to work. It was a sultry autumn day. The "peek" seemed to grow heavier at every stroke and the "shuvle" wider and larger in its capacity to hold the gravel. The second day was no better than the first, and the third was worse than the second. The work was heavy and monotonous to Louis and myself especially, who had never been

---

4. **Buon giorno** (BWOHN JOHR-noh) "good day"
5. **i parenti e gli amici** (EE pah-REN-tee AY LEE ah-MEE-chee)
6. **magnanimity** (mag-nah-NIM-ih-tee) *n.* generosity

"contadini" like the rest. The "padrone" whose magnanimity had so stirred us was little better than a brute. We began to do some simple figuring and discovered that when we had paid for our groceries at the "storo," for the privilege of sleeping in the shanty, and the fifty cents to the "padrone" for having been so condescending as to employ us, we would have nothing left but sore arms and backs. So on the afternoon of the third day Louis and I held a solemn conclave[7] and decided to part company with "peek and shuvle,"—for ever. We left, without receiving a cent of pay, of course.

_____

7. conclave (KAHN-klayv) *n.* meeting

Photograph of Italian immigrants arriving in the United States around 1900. What kinds of discrimination did Italian immigrants face after arriving in this country?

Going across country on foot we came to a small manufacturing village. We decided to try our luck at the factory, which proved to be a woolen mill, and found employment. Our work was sorting old rags and carrying them in wheelbarrows into a hot oven, in which the air was almost suffocating. Every time a person went in it he was obliged to run out as quickly as possible, for the heat was unbearable. Unfortunately for us, the crew was composed almost entirely of Russians, who hated us from the first day, and called us "dagoes." I had never heard the word before; I asked Louis if he knew its meaning, but he did not. In going in and out of the oven the Russians would crowd against us and make it hard for us to pass. One morning as I was coming out, four of the men hedged me in. I thought I would suffocate. I finally succeeded in pushing out, my hand having been cut in the rush of the wheelbarrows.

The superintendent of the factory had observed the whole incident. He was a very kindly man. From his light complexion I think he was a Swede. He came to my rescue, reprimanded the Russians, and led me to his office, where he bandaged my hand. Then he called Louis and explained the situation to us. The Russians looked upon us as intruders and were determined not to work side by side with "the foreigners," but to drive them out of the factory. Therefore, much as he regretted it, the superintendent was obliged to ask us to leave, since there were only two of us, as against the large number of Russians who made up his unskilled crew.

So we left. My bandaged hand hurt me, but my heart hurt more. This kind of work was hard and humiliating enough, but what went deeper than all else was the first realization that because of race I was being put on the road. And often since that day have I felt the cutting thrusts of race prejudice. They have been dealt by older immigrants, who are known as "Americans," as well as by more recent comers. All have been equally heart-rending and head-bending. I hold no grudge against any one; I realize that it is one of the attendant circumstances of our present nationalistic attitude the world over, and yet it is none the less saddening to the human heart. I have seen prejudice, like an evil shadow, everywhere. It lurks at every corner, on every street and in every mart. I have seen it in the tram and on the train; I have felt its dreaded power in school and college, in clubs and churches. It is an ever-present evil spirit, felt though unseen, wounding hearts, cutting souls. It passes on its poison like a serpent from generation to generation, and he who would see the fusion of the various elements into a truly American type must ever take into cognizance[8] its presence in the hearts of some human beings. . . .

---

8. **cognizance** (KAHG-nuh-zuhns) *n.* understanding

POSTREADING

Critical Thinking

1. What are Panunzio's feelings about his struggle to find work and overcome discrimination as a new immigrant in the United States?
2. What aspects of his personal or cultural background may have shaped his attitudes and values?
3. How do Panunzio's experiences in a new country compare with the experiences of your family, or a family you know, when they first arrived in the United States?

Writing Your Response to "In the American Storm"

In your journal, write about one incident, character, or image in the selection that is especially meaningful to you. Why does it stand out? How does it relate to an experience in your own life or in the life of someone you know?

Going Back Into the Text: Author's Craft

Tone in a piece of literature refers to the writer's attitude toward his or her subject, characters, or audience. The tone in a piece of nonfiction, such as Constantine Panunzio's autobiography, may be revealed through the writer's choice of words, the sentence struc-ture, and the portrayal of people and events. Sometimes the tone of a work is informal. It may be humorous or excited. In other works, the tone is more formal, restrained, or even somber.

With a partner, review the selection by Panunzio to analyze his tone. Use the following questions as guidelines.

1. How would you describe the tone of this excerpt?
2. How is the tone revealed?
3. Is the tone appropriate for its subject? Explain your answer.

Reviewing the Theme

1. Choose two authors represented in this theme and compare their ideas about freedom. What solutions does each writer propose to end the problems of racial and economic inequality?

2. Compare the personal perspectives of two writers in this theme who have the same cultural background. How are their attitudes similar? How are they different?

3. Which cultural conflict represented in this theme is most meaningful to you personally? How does it apply to your own life or to the life of someone you know?

Theme 8:
Recognizing Differences

DIFFERENCES AMONG groups of people may often seem obvious. However, the ability to accept these differences can be difficult. The authors of the following selections examine the conflicts that arise between their own cultures and mainstream U.S. society. Some also explore the internal struggles that can result when a person is caught between two cultures. Others portray the differences among generations.

In this theme, you will read about African Americans who must overcome prejudice, in society and even within themselves. Mexican American writers included portray the isolation many Hispanics feel living in the United States. Two Chinese American writers describe what it is like being a member of two very different cultures. A young Greek American learns valuable lessons about his heritage from a member of an older generation.

The authors represented here make clear that being different from the mainstream is rarely easy. It often requires having to overcome prejudice and injustice. However, by exploring the differences among cultural groups and the contradictions within themselves, these writers gain a better sense of who they are, where they come from, and what challenges they will face in the future.

Photograph of Chinese New Year celebration in Chinatown, New York City. How does this celebration compare with the way your family or community observes the New Year?

from Their Eyes Were Watching God

Reading the Author in a Cultural Context

When Zora Neale Hurston was young, her mother advised her to "jump at de sun," or to set high goals for herself. Hurston was raised in Eatonville, Florida, a rural Southern town whose population at the time was entirely African American. Her mother began encouraging her to learn to read at an early age. Hurston's autobiography, *Dust Tracks on a Road*, describes how the other children in Hurston's school were envious of her ability to read aloud with great skill. They called her "the smartaleck."

Hurston attended Howard University in Washington, D.C., and in 1928, graduated from Barnard College in New York City, where she studied anthropology. Her studies sparked an interest in folk traditions and led Hurston back to the South to gather the stories, songs, and proverbs of African Americans. She spent much of the late 1920s and early 1930s traveling through the back roads of Florida, Mississippi, and Louisiana in her Chevrolet coupe, exchanging tales with local people at roadside restaurants.

As fascinating as her personal story is, however, Hurston's influence arises from her writing. In New York City, Hurston, together with other African American writers such as Langston Hughes, Countee Cullen, and Claude McKay, participated in the Harlem Renaissance. This outpouring of creativity by African Americans in literature, theater, painting, sculpture, and music began around 1920. It established Harlem as a major U.S. cultural center. The poems and stories of the Harlem Renaissance writers showed a new pride, celebrating African American culture and exposing racism. In her writing, Hurston used the blues rhythms and authentic dialect she absorbed during her travels. These elements helped her capture the wide range of emotions, the courage, and the humor in the everyday lives of rural African Americans in the South during the early 1900s. (Notice Hurston's use of dialect, or regional pronunciations, in the following excerpt.)

The excerpt that follows is taken from Hurston's best-known novel, *Their Eyes Were Watching God*, published in 1937. Focusing on a character named Janie, Hurston conveys the complexity and richness of African American society. As you read, think about how the setting of the rural South influences Janie's feelings.

Focusing on the Selection

As you read the excerpt from *Their Eyes Were Watching God*, think about Janie's relationship to the other children portrayed in the novel. How is Janie treated by the white children? How does she see herself? Consider how Hurston's use of dialect adds to the portrayal of Janie's character. Write your responses in your journal.

from *Their Eyes Were Watching God*

ZORA NEALE HURSTON

JANIE SAW HER LIFE like a great tree in leaf with the things suffered, things enjoyed, things done and undone. Dawn and doom was in the branches.

"Ah know exactly what Ah got to tell yuh, but it's hard to know where to start at.

"Ah ain't never seen mah papa. And Ah didn't know 'im if Ah did. Mah mama neither. She was gone from round dere long before Ah wuz big enough tuh know. Mah grandma raised me. Mah grandma and de white folks she worked wid. She had a house out in de back-yard and dat's where Ah wuz born. They was quality white folks up dere in West Florida. Named Washburn. She had four gran'chillun[1] on de place and all of us played together and dat's how come Ah never called mah Grandma nothin' but Nanny, 'cause dat's what everybody on de place called her. Nanny used to ketch us in our devilment and lick every youngun on de place and Mis' Washburn did de same. Ah reckon dey never hit us ah lick amiss 'cause dem three boys and us two girls wuz pretty aggravatin', Ah speck.[2]

---

1. gran'chillun (GRAN-chihl-luhn) *n.* grandchildren
2. speck (SPEK) *v.* suspect

Jennie. *Howard University Gallery of Art, Washington, DC.*
Oil painting by African American artist Lois M. Jones, 1943.

"Ah was wid dem white chillun so much till Ah didn't know Ah wuzn't white till Ah was round six years old. Wouldn't have found it out then, but a man come long takin' pictures and without askin' anybody, Shelby, dat was de oldest boy, he told him to take us. Round a week later de man brought de picture for Mis' Washburn to see and pay him which she did, then give us all a good lickin'.

"So when we looked at de picture and everybody got pointed out there wasn't nobody left except a real dark little girl with long hair standing by Eleanor. Dat's where Ah wuz s'posed to be, but Ah couldn't recognize dat dark chile[3] as me. So Ah ast, 'where is me? Ah don't see me.'

---

3. chile (CHEYEL) *n.* child

"Everybody laughed, even Mr. Washburn. Miss Nellie, de Mama of de chillun who come back home after her husband dead, she pointed to de dark one and said, 'Dat's you, Alphabet, don't you know yo' ownself?'

"Dey all useter[4] call me Alphabet 'cause so many people had done named me different names. Ah looked at de picture a long time and seen it was mah dress and mah hair so Ah said:

" 'Aw, aw! Ah'm colored!'

"Den dey all laughed real hard. But before Ah seen de picture Ah thought Ah wuz just like de rest. . . ."

---

4. useter (YOOS-ter) *v.* used to

POSTREADING

Critical Thinking

1. In this passage, what does Hurston tell you about her attitudes concerning differences in skin color?
2. What experiences in Hurston's own life or historical period do you think may have influenced her decision to create the character of Janie?
3. How has reading this excerpt affected your thoughts or feelings about cultural differences? In what ways are your reactions similar to and different from Janie's?

Writing Your Response to *Their Eyes Were Watching God*

In your journal, write about a description or an idea in the excerpt that is especially meaningful to you. Discuss why it is memorable. Is it Hurston's use of dialect or something else? Does it relate to an experience in your own life?

Going Back Into the Text: Author's Craft

Dialect is the form of a language spoken by people of a particular region or cultural group. Dialect is frequently conveyed through *dialogue*, or conversations between characters. Each dialect is unique in its use of vocabulary, spelling, grammar, and pronunciation. Writers often use dialect to create realistic characters and to reveal the distinct characteristics, or "local color," of a region.

As you and a partner review dialect in the selection by Hurston, use the following questions as guidelines.

1. What examples of dialect can you find in the selection?
2. How does the use of dialect help to create characters and to establish the setting of the story?
3. What other examples of dialect can you give either from this book or from other stories or movies you know?

Refugee Ship
address
Letter to America

Reading the Authors in a Cultural Context

The following three poems give insight into the injustices that Mexican Americans have tried to overcome in the United States. In her poem "Refugee Ship," Lorna Dee Cervantes focuses on the hardships of being caught between two cultures. Born in San Francisco in 1954, Cervantes has Mexican ancestors who had settled in California by 1800. During her early childhood, she lived in poverty. As a way to cope with the harsh realities that surrounded her, she began writing poetry when she was 8 years old. Like many writers of her generation, Cervantes was involved in what was called the Chicano movement. This social and political movement, formed in the 1960s, demanded equal opportunity for Hispanics and encouraged ethnic pride among Mexican Americans. In reading "Refugee Ship," notice Cervantes's use of both English and Spanish, as well as concrete, vivid imagery. These elements help her explore her Hispanic roots and the conflicts that arise from trying to blend into the mainstream culture.

The poet Alurista also writes in both English and Spanish in his poem "address" to contrast the values of two different cultures. His use of Spanish sentences between impersonal English phrases suggests the isolation many Hispanics feel in the work world of mainstream society. Much of Alurista's poetry explores the intermingling of the Native American and Spanish cultures that forms his Mexican heritage. His poems also reflect aspects of Hispanic experience in the United States. Alurista was born in Mexico as Alberto Urista in 1947, and moved to California at age 13. He was also deeply involved in the Chicano movement.

Like Cervantes and Alurista, in "Letter to America" Francisco X. Alarcón writes of the discrimination and injustices Hispanics face. Notice how Alarcón uses a literary device called simile, the likening, or comparison of two unlike things using the word *like* or *as*. In the poem, Alarcón compares Hispanics to rugs, floors, and tables, suggesting that they have been stepped on, put upon, or used by mainstream society.

Focusing on the Selections

As you read the following poems, notice the unique perspective each poet has on cultural differences. How does Cervantes reveal her feelings of rootlessness? How does she express her womanhood? How do Alurista and Alarcón convey a sense of alienation or isolation in society? Consider what mood each writer creates in his or her poem. Write your responses in your journal.

Refugee Ship

LORNA DEE CERVANTES

Like wet cornstarch, I slide
past my grandmother's eyes. Bible
at her side, she removes her glasses.
The pudding thickens.

Mama raised me without language.
I'm orphaned from my Spanish name.
The words are foreign, stumbling
on my tongue. I see in the mirror
my reflection: bronzed skin, black hair.

I feel I am a captive
aboard the refugee ship.
The ship that will never dock.
El barco que nunca atraca.[1]

Portrait of Klavia. *Museo del Barrio, New York City.* Oil painting by Puerto Rican American artist Rosa Ibarra.

---

1. ***El barco que nunca atraca.*** (el BAHR-koh kay NOON-kah ah-TRAH-kah) The ship that will never dock.

address

ALURISTA

address
occupation
age
marital status
—perdone . . .
    yo me llamo pedro[1]
telephone
height
hobbies
previous employers
—perdone . . .
    yo me llamo pedro
    pedro ortega[2]
zip code
i.d. number
classification
rank
—perdone mi padre era
    el señor ortega
    (a veces don josé)[3]
race

---

1. **perdone . . . yo me llamo pedro** (pair-DOH-nay . . . yoh may YAH-moh PAY-droh) excuse me, my name is Pedro
2. **ortega** (awr-TAY-guh) *n.* a family name
3. **perdone mi padre era el señor ortega (a veces don josé)** (pair-DOH-nay, mee PAH-dray E-rah el se-NYOR awr-TAY-guh [ah VAY-says dohn hoh-SAY] excuse me, my father was Mr. Ortega (sometimes called Don José)

Letter to America

FRANCISCO X. ALARCÓN

pardon
the lag[1]
in writing you

we were left
with few
letters

in your home
we were cast
as rugs

sometimes
on walls
though we

were almost
always
on floors

we served
you as
a table

a lamp
a mirror
a toy

if anything
we made
you laugh

in your kitchen
we became
another pan

even now
as a shadow
you use us

you fear us
you yell at us
you hate us

you shoot us
you mourn us
you deny us

and despite
everything
we

continue
being
us

America
understand
once and for all:

we are
the insides
of your body

our faces
reflect
your future

---

1. **lag** (LAG) *n.* a period of delay

Critical Thinking

1. What do Cervantes, Alurista, and Alarcón tell you about their attitudes toward their cultural identity?
2. How do you think the personal and historical backgrounds of the poets influenced their writing of these works?
3. In seeking employment or in other situations, have you or someone you know faced difficulties because of cultural differences? If so, explain how. If not, how might you respond?

Writing Your Response to "Refugee Ship," "address," and "Letter to America"

In your journal, write about an image in one of the poems that is especially meaningful to you. Why is it special? In what ways does it relate to your own life?

Going Back Into the Text: Author's Craft

Mood is the feeling or atmosphere in a literary work or passage. Moods can include joy, fear, anger, sorrow, or hope. Elements that help create mood in literature include the author's tone, or attitude toward the subject; the setting; and diction or word choice. Elements such as these help to create an emotional atmosphere that influences the reader's expectations and attitudes.

With a partner, review "Refugee Ship," "address," and "Letter to America" to analyze the mood each poem expresses. Use the following questions as guidelines.

1. What is the mood in each poem?
2. What techniques does each poet use to create mood?
3. Describe the mood in another poem or story you have enjoyed.

from Black Boy

Reading the Author in a Cultural Context

Richard Wright overcame many obstacles to become a writer. Wright was 5 years old when his father deserted the family. When his mother became ill shortly afterward, the family went to live with a series of relatives in Mississippi, Arkansas, and Tennessee. As a result, Wright never completed a single full year of schooling before he was 12 years old, and the ninth grade was the last year he attended at all.

Despite these hardships, Wright was so determined to read that he once forged a permission note to borrow books from a library that served only whites. His resolve to write was even greater. Wright's first story was published in a local African American newspaper when he was in the eighth grade. He was very proud when the first installment of the story appeared but he soon learned that his family and friends did not share his excitement. They believed it was unrealistic to think that he could overcome the racial prejudice imposed on African Americans. However, the story awakened a dream in Wright to "accomplish something that would be recognized by others."

Wright's refusal to give in to discrimination did not mean that he could ignore it. In all of his writing, Wright uses his experiences as an African American in the South to try to eliminate excuses for racism. At the same time, his works expose the brutality that racism can cause. Consider Wright's political and social goals as you read the selection that follows.

In 1940, Wright published *Native Son*, a novel that severely criticized white society for the pressures it placed on African Americans. *Native Son* was highly successful among African American and white readers alike. It was a record-breaking best seller, and was chosen as a Book of the Month Club selection. More importantly, with this novel Wright encouraged African American writers to express their frustration and outrage with the conditions African Americans faced.

Though *Native Son* is Wright's best-known work, he also published a number of other novels, stories, and essays of equal merit. The selection that follows is from *Black Boy*, Wright's early autobiography. In this excerpt, Wright describes his childhood struggle to understand the differences between white Americans and African Americans.

Focusing on the Selection

As you read the following excerpt from *Black Boy*, think about how Wright arrives at an understanding of his racial identity. How does Wright portray himself as a young boy? Notice how he feels when his mother tells him that he will be considered a "colored man" when he grows up. In what ways does Wright suggest that his feelings about race will change as he matures? Write your responses in your journal.

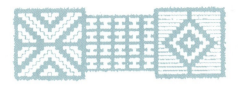

from *Black Boy*

RICHARD WRIGHT

...AT LAST WE WERE AT THE RAILROAD STATION with our bags, waiting for the train that would take us to Arkansas; and for the first time I noticed that there were two lines of people at the ticket window, a "white" line and a "black" line. During my visit at Granny's a sense of the two races had been born in me with a sharp concreteness that would never die until I died. When I boarded the train I was aware that we Negroes were in one part of the train and that the whites were in another. Naïvely I wanted to go and see how the whites looked while sitting in their part of the train.

"Can I go and peep at the white folks?" I asked my mother.

"You keep quiet," she said.

"But that wouldn't be wrong, would it?"

"Will you keep still?"

"But why can't I?"

"Quit talking foolishness!"

I had begun to notice that my mother became irritated when I questioned her about whites and blacks, and I could not quite understand it. I wanted to understand these two sets of people who lived side by side and never touched, it seemed, except in violence. Now, there was my grandmother . . . Was she white? Just how white was she? What did the whites think of her whiteness?

"Mama, is Granny white?" I asked as the train rolled through the darkness.

"If you've got eyes, you can see what color she is," my mother said.

"I mean, do the white folks think she's white?"

"Why don't you ask the white folks that?" she countered.

"But you know," I insisted.

"Why should I know?" she asked. "I'm not white."

"Granny looks white," I said, hoping to establish one fact, at least. "Then why is she living with us colored folks?"

"Don't you want Granny to live with us?" she asked, blunting[1] my question.

"Yes."

"Then why are you asking?"

"I want to *know*."

"Doesn't Granny live with us?"

"Yes."

"Isn't that enough?"

"But does she *want* to live with us?"

"Why didn't you ask Granny that?" my mother evaded[2] me again in a taunting voice.

"Did Granny become colored when she married Grandpa?"

"Will you stop asking silly questions!"

"But did she?"

"Granny didn't *become* colored," my mother said angrily. "She was *born* the color she is now."

Again I was being shut out of the secret, the thing, the reality I felt somewhere beneath all the words and silences.

"Why didn't Granny marry a white man?" I asked.

"Because she didn't want to," my mother said peevishly.

"Why don't you want to talk to me?" I asked.

She slapped me and I cried. Later, grudgingly, she told me that Granny came of Irish, Scotch, and French stock in which Negro blood had somewhere and somehow been infused. She explained it all in a matter-of-fact, offhand, neutral way; her emotions were not involved at all.

"What was Granny's name before she married Grandpa?"

"Bolden."

"Who gave her that name?"

"The white man who owned her."

"She was a slave?"

---

1. **blunting** (BLUN-tihng) *v.* dulling
2. **evaded** (ee-VAYD-ed) *v.* avoided answering directly

"Yes."

"And Bolden was the name of Granny's father?"

"Granny doesn't know who her father was."

"So they just gave her any name?"

"They gave her a name; that's all I know."

"Couldn't Granny find out who her father was?"

"For what, silly?"

"So she could know."

"Know for what?"

"Just to know."

"But for *what?*"

I could not say. I could not get anywhere.

"Mama, where did Father get his name?"

"From his father."

"And where did the father of my father get his name?"

"Like Granny got hers. From a white man."

"Do they know who he is?"

"I don't know."

"Why don't they find out?"

"For what?" my mother demanded harshly.

And I could think of no rational or practical reason why my father should try to find out who his father's father was.

"What has Papa got in him?" I asked.

"Some white and some red and some black," she said.

"Indian, white, and Negro?"

"Yes."

"Then what am I?"

"They'll call you a colored man when you grow up," she said. Then she turned to me and smiled mockingly and asked: "Do you mind, Mr. Wright?"

I was angry and I did not answer. I did not object to being called colored, but I knew that there was something my mother was holding back. She was not concealing facts, but feelings, attitudes, convictions which she did not want me to know; and she became angry when I prodded her. All right, I would find out someday. Just wait. All right, I was colored. It was fine. I did not know enough to be afraid or to anticipate in a concrete manner. True, I had heard that colored people were killed and beaten, but so far it all had seemed remote. There was, of course, a vague uneasiness about it all, but I would be able to handle that when I came to it. It would be simple. If anybody tried to kill me, then I would kill them first.

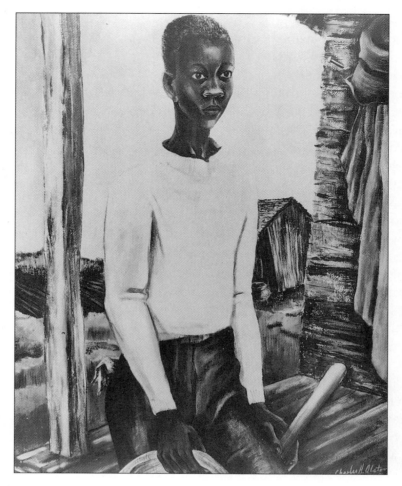

Farm Boy. *Atlanta University Collection of Afro-American Art, Atlanta, Georgia*. Painting by African American artist Charles Alston, 1941.

When we arrived in Elaine[3] I saw that Aunt Maggie lived in a bungalow[4] that had a fence around it. It looked like home and I was glad. I had no suspicion that I was to live here for but a short time and that the manner of my leaving would be my first baptism[5] of racial emotion.

A wide dusty road ran past the house and on each side of the road wild flowers grew. It was summer and the smell of clay dust was everywhere, day and night. I would get up early every morning to wade with my bare feet through the dust of the road, reveling[6] in the strange

---

3. Elaine (ee-LAYN) *n.* a town in eastern Arkansas, near the Mississippi border
4. bungalow (BUNG-guh-loh) *n.* a small house or cottage
5. baptism (BAP-tihz-uhm) *n.* a ceremonial immersion in water, or application of water, as an initiation
6. reveling (REV-uhl-ihng) *v.* taking great pleasure

mixture of the cold dew-wet crust on top of the road and the warm, sun-baked dust beneath.

After sunrise the bees would come out and I discovered that by slapping my two palms together smartly I could kill a bee. My mother warned me to stop, telling me that bees made honey, that it was not good to kill things that made food, that I would eventually be stung. But I felt confident of outwitting any bee. One morning I slapped an enormous bee between my hands just as it had lit upon a flower and it stung me in the tender center of my left palm. I ran home screaming.

"Good enough for you," my mother commented dryly.

I never crushed any more bees. . . .

POSTREADING

Critical Thinking

1. What does Wright tell you about his childhood awareness of racial differences? What is his attitude as a child toward being seen as "colored"?
2. What events in Wright's life do you think influenced these attitudes? What may have prompted changes in these attitudes as he matured?
3. How do the ways others perceive your own cultural identity affect the way you perceive yourself?

Writing Your Response to *Black Boy*

In your journal, write about an idea, feeling, or question you had as you read this selection. What does this excerpt make you think of? Does the excerpt relate to something in your own life? If so, describe how.

Going Back Into the Text: Author's Craft

An **autobiography** is a form of nonfiction in which a person tells his or her own life story. Most autobiographies are written in the first person, with the author speaking as "I." Because autobiographies present events as the writer views them, the portrayals are often influenced by his or her attitudes. As such, autobiographies provide insights into the writer's beliefs and perceptions. Autobiographies may also convey facts about the times and places described in the work.

With a partner, use these questions to review the selection by Wright.

1. What details does Wright use to portray himself as a young boy?
2. What does Wright reveal about his mother in this excerpt?
3. How might the passage be different if it was written by his mother?

from Four Directions
Saying Yes

Reading the Authors in a Cultural Context

Amy Tan is a Chinese American writer who was born in San Francisco, California, in 1952. Her parents emigrated to the United States shortly after the Communists came to power in China in 1949. It was a relatively good time for Chinese newcomers. In the United States, restrictions on Asian immigration had eased. The Immigration Act of 1924 had completely banned Chinese immigration. Chinese exclusion acts were repealed in 1943. In 1947, Chinese Americans living in the San Francisco area had become free legally to purchase land outside of Chinatown for the first time.

Through the latter half of the 20th century, racial conflicts between Chinese Americans and their neighbors decreased. However, tensions between the generations of Chinese American families grew. This was especially true of the relationship between Chinese-born women and their U.S.-born daughters. The second generation had little patience for the traditionally obedient role of women and attempted to become more "westernized."

This conflict defined the relationship between Amy Tan and her mother. Tan resisted her mother's plan for her to become a neurosurgeon and concert pianist. Tan wanted so badly to become "American," however, that she considered plastic surgery to change her appearance. It was not until her first visit to her parents' homeland in China, at the age of 35, that Tan accepted her Chinese heritage and started to think of herself as both Chinese and American.

The following selection is from *The Joy Luck Club*. This book weaves together eight different stories. It describes the lives of four Chinese women who emigrated to the United States as adults and the lives of their four U.S.-born daughters. In this excerpt, the narrator confronts the conflicting cultures of her Chinese family and her American fiancé.

Diana Chang was born in New York City in 1934 and returned there after spending most of her childhood in China. She attended Barnard College in New York City, graduating in 1959. Chang's poems often reflect her heritage, showing the influence of ancient Chinese poetry forms. In the poem included here, "Saying Yes," Chang embraces her Chinese American identity.

Focusing on the Selections

As you read the following selections by Amy Tan and Diana Chang, think about the cultural conflicts they suggest. In what ways does the narrator of Tan's novel reject her Chinese ancestry? In what ways does she embrace it? Consider how her fiancé represents mainstream U.S. culture and her mother embodies Chinese culture. Think about why the speaker in Chang's poem finds it difficult to explain her identity. What does she say yes to? Record your responses in your journal.

from *Four Directions*

from *The Joy Luck Club*

AMY TAN

. . . I'D NEVER KNOWN LOVE so pure, and I was afraid that it would become sullied[1] by my mother. So I tried to store every one of these endearments about Rich in my memory, and I planned to call upon them again when the time was necessary.

After much thought, I came up with a brilliant plan. I concocted[2] a way for Rich to meet my mother and win her over. In fact, I arranged it so my mother would want to cook a meal especially for him. I had some help from Auntie Suyuan. Auntie Su was my mother's friend from way back. They were very close, which meant they were ceaselessly tormenting each other with boasts and secrets. And I gave Auntie Su a secret to boast about.

After walking through North Beach one Sunday, I suggested to Rich that we stop by for a surprise visit to my Auntie Su and Uncle Canning. They lived on Leavenworth, just a few blocks west of my mother's apartment. It was late afternoon, just in time to catch Auntie Su preparing Sunday dinner.

"Stay! Stay!" she had insisted.

---

1. **sullied** (SUL-eed) *v.* soiled, tarnished
2. **concocted** (kuhn-KAHK-tuhd) *v.* devised, made up

"No, no. It's just that we were walking by," I said.

"Already cooked enough for you. See? One soup, four dishes. You don't eat it, only have to throw it away. Wasted!"

How could we refuse? Three days later, Auntie Suyuan had a thank-you letter from Rich and me. "Rich said it was the best Chinese food he has ever tasted," I wrote.

And the next day, my mother called me, to invite me to a belated birthday dinner for my father. My brother Vincent was bringing his girl-friend, Lisa Lum. I could bring a friend, too.

I knew she would do this, because cooking was how my mother ex-pressed her love, her pride, her power, her proof that she knew more than Auntie Su. "Just be sure to tell her later that her cooking was the best you ever tasted, that it was far better than Auntie Su's," I told Rich. "Believe me."

The night of the dinner, I sat in the kitchen watching her cook, wait-ing for the right moment to tell her about our marriage plans, that we had decided to get married next July, about seven months away. She was chopping eggplant into wedges, chattering at the same time about Aun-tie Suyuan: "She can only cook looking at a recipe. My instructions are in my fingers. I know what secret ingredients to put in just by using my nose!" And she was slicing with such a ferocity,[3] seemingly inattentive to her sharp cleaver, that I was afraid her fingertips would become one of the ingredients of the red-cooked eggplant and shredded pork dish.

I was hoping she would say something first about Rich. I had seen her expression when she opened the door, her forced smile as she scruti-nized[4] him from head to toe, checking her appraisal[5] of him against that already given to her by Auntie Suyuan. I tried to anticipate what criti-cisms she would have.

Rich was not only *not* Chinese, he was a few years younger than I was. And unfortunately, he looked much younger with his curly red hair, smooth pale skin, and the splash of orange freckles across his nose. He was a bit on the short side, compactly built. In his dark business suits, he looked nice but easily forgettable, like somebody's nephew at a funeral. Which was why I didn't notice him the first year we worked together at the firm. But my mother noticed everything.

"So what do you think of Rich?" I finally asked, holding my breath.

She tossed the eggplant in the hot oil and it made a loud, angry hiss-ing sound. "So many spots on his face," she said.

---

3. ferocity (fuh-RAHS-uh-tee) *n.* fierceness
4. scrutinized (SKROO-tihn-eyezd) *v.* examined in detail with careful or critical attention
5. appraisal (uh-PRAYZ-uhl) *n.* judging the value of someone

I could feel the pinpricks on my back. "They're freckles. Freckles are good luck, you know," I said a bit too heatedly in trying to raise my voice above the din[6] of the kitchen.

"Oh?" she said innocently.

"Yes, the more spots the better. Everybody knows that."

She considered this a moment and then smiled and spoke in Chinese: "Maybe this is true. When you were young, you got the chicken pox. So many spots, you had to stay home for ten days. So lucky, you thought."

I couldn't save Rich in the kitchen. And I couldn't save him later at the dinner table.

He had brought a bottle of French wine, something he did not know my parents could not appreciate. My parents did not even own wineglasses. And then he also made the mistake of drinking not one but two frosted glasses full, while everybody else had a half-inch "just for taste."

When I offered Rich a fork, he insisted on using the slippery ivory chopsticks. He held them splayed like the knock-kneed legs of an ostrich while picking up a large chunk of sauce-coated eggplant. Halfway between his plate and his open mouth, the chunk fell on his crisp white shirt and then slid into his crotch. It took several minutes to get Shoshana to stop shrieking with laughter.

And then he had helped himself to big portions of the shrimp and snow peas, not realizing he should have taken only a polite spoonful, until everybody had had a morsel.

He had declined the sautéed new greens, the tender and expensive leaves of the bean plants plucked before the sprouts turn into beans. And Shoshana refused to eat them also, pointing to Rich: "He didn't eat them! He didn't eat them!"

He thought he was being polite by refusing seconds, when he should have followed my father's example, who made a big show of taking small portions of seconds, thirds, and even fourths, always saying he could not resist another bite of something or other, and then groaning that he was so full he thought he would burst.

But the worst was when Rich criticized my mother's cooking, and he didn't even know what he had done. As is the Chinese cook's custom, my mother always made disparaging[7] remarks about her own cooking. That night she chose to direct it toward her famous steamed pork and preserved vegetable dish, which she always served with special pride.

"Ai! This dish not salty enough, no flavor," she complained, after tasting a small bite. "It is too bad to eat."

---

6. din (DIHN) *n.* continuous loud noise

7. disparaging (dihs-PAR-ihj-ihng) *adj.* showing disrespect for

This was our family's cue to eat some and proclaim it the best she had ever made. But before we could do so, Rich said, "You know, all it needs is a little soy sauce." And he proceeded to pour a riverful of the salty black stuff on the platter, right before my mother's horrified eyes.

And even though I was hoping throughout the dinner that my mother would somehow see Rich's kindness, his sense of humor and boyish charm, I knew he had failed miserably in her eyes.

Rich obviously had had a different opinion on how the evening had gone. When we got home that night, after we put Shoshana to bed, he said modestly, "Well. I think we hit it off *A-o-kay.*" He had the look of a dalmatian,[8] panting, loyal, waiting to be petted.

"Uh-hmm," I said. I was putting on an old nightgown, a hint that I was not feeling amorous.[9] I was still shuddering, remembering how Rich had firmly shaken both my parents' hands with that same easy familiarity he used with nervous new clients. "Linda, Tim," he said, "we'll see you again soon, I'm sure." My parents' names are Lindo and Tin Jong, and nobody, except a few older family friends, ever calls them by their first names.

"So what did she say when you told her?" And I knew he was referring to our getting married. I had told Rich earlier that I would tell my mother first and let her break the news to my father.

"I never had a chance," I said, which was true. How could I have told my mother I was getting married, when at every possible moment we were alone, she seemed to remark on how much expensive wine Rich liked to drink, or how pale and ill he looked, or how sad Shoshana seemed to be.

Rich was smiling. "How long does it take to say, Mom, Dad, I'm getting married?"

"You don't understand. You don't understand my mother."

Rich shook his head. "Whew! You can say that again. Her English was *so* bad. You know, when she was talking about that dead guy showing up on *Dynasty,* I thought she was talking about something that happened in China a long time ago."

That night, after the dinner, I lay in bed, tense. I was despairing over this latest failure, made worse by the fact that Rich seemed blind to it all. He looked so pathetic.[10] *So pathetic,* those words! My mother was

---

8. **dalmation** (dal-MAY-shuhn) *n.* short-haired dog with a white coat and black or brown spots
9. **amorous** (AM-uh-ruhs) *adj.* inclined or disposed to romantic love
10. **pathetic** (puh-THET-ihk) *adj.* pitiful; miserably inadequate

Self-Portrait. Acrylic painting by Asian American artist Heeyoung S. Kimm.

doing it again, making me see black where I once saw white. In her hands, I always became the pawn.[11] I could only run away. And she was the queen, able to move in all directions, relentless in her pursuit, always able to find my weakest spots.

I woke up late, with teeth clenched and every nerve on edge. Rich was already up, showered, and reading the Sunday paper. "Morning, doll," he said between noisy munches of cornflakes. I put on my jogging clothes and headed out the door, got into the car, and drove to my parents' apartment.

Marlene was right. I had to tell my mother—that I knew what she was doing, her scheming ways of making me miserable. By the time I arrived, I had enough anger to fend off a thousand flying cleavers.

My father opened the door and looked surprised to see me. "Where's Ma?" I asked, trying to keep my breath even. He gestured to the living room in back.

I found her sleeping soundly on the sofa. The back of her head was resting on a white embroidered doily. Her mouth was slack[12] and all the lines in her face were gone. With her smooth face, she looked like a young girl, frail, guileless,[13] and innocent. One arm hung limply down the side

---

11. pawn (PAWN) *n.* someone who is used or manipulated
12. slack (SLAK) *adj.* relaxed, loose
13. guileless (GEYEL-les) *adj.* sincere, honest, free from deception

of the sofa. Her chest was still. All her strength was gone. She had no weapons, no demons surrounding her. She looked powerless. Defeated.

And then I was seized with a fear that she looked like this because she was dead. She had died when I was having terrible thoughts about her. I had wished her out of my life, and she had acquiesced,[14] floating out of her body to escape my terrible hatred.

"Ma!" I said sharply. "Ma!" I whined, starting to cry.

And her eyes slowly opened. She blinked. Her hands moved with life. "*Shemma?* Meimei-ah? Is that you?"

I was speechless. She had not called me Meimei, my childhood name, in many years. She sat up and the lines in her face returned, only now they seemed less harsh, soft creases of worry. "Why are you here? Why are you crying? Something has happened!"

I didn't know what to do or say. In a matter of seconds, it seemed, I had gone from being angered by her strength, to being amazed by her innocence, and then frightened by her vulnerability.[15] And now I felt numb, strangely weak, as if someone had unplugged me and the current running through me had stopped.

"Nothing's happened. Nothing's the matter. I don't know why I'm here," I said in a hoarse voice. "I wanted to talk to you. . . . I wanted to tell you . . . Rich and I are getting married."

I squeezed my eyes shut, waiting to hear her protests, her laments, the dry voice delivering some sort of painful verdict.

"*Jrdaule*"—I already know this—she said, as if to ask why I was telling her this again.

"You know?"

"Of course. Even if you didn't tell me," she said simply.

This was worse than I had imagined. She had known all along, when she criticized the mink jacket, when she belittled his freckles and complained about his drinking habits. She disapproved of him. "I know you hate him," I said in a quavering voice. "I know you think he's not good enough, but I . . ."

"Hate? Why do you think I hate your future husband?"

"You never want to talk about him. The other day, when I started to tell you about him and Shoshana at the Exploratorium, you . . . you changed the subject . . . you started talking about Dad's exploratory surgery and then . . ."

"What is more important, explore fun or explore sickness?"

I wasn't going to let her escape this time. "And then when you met him, you said he had spots on his face."

---

14. **acquiesced** (ak-wee-EST) *v.* agreed, consented without protest
15. **vulnerability** (vuhl-nuhr-uh-BIHL-uh-tee) *n.* the susceptibility to being hurt

She looked at me, puzzled. "Is this not true?"

"Yes, but, you said it just to be mean, to hurt me, to . . ."

"Ai-ya, why do you think these bad things about me?" Her face looked old and full of sorrow. "So you think your mother is this bad. You think I have a secret meaning. But it is you who has this meaning. Ai-ya! She thinks I am this bad!" She sat straight and proud on the sofa, her mouth clamped tight, her hands clasped together, her eyes sparkling with angry tears.

Oh, her strength! her weakness!—both pulling me apart. My mind was flying one way, my heart another. I sat down on the sofa next to her, the two of us stricken by the other.

I felt as if I had lost a battle, but one that I didn't know I had been fighting. I was weary. "I'm going home," I finally said. "I'm not feeling too good right now."

"You have become ill?" she murmured, putting her hand on my forehead.

"No," I said. I wanted to leave. "I . . . I just don't know what's inside me right now."

"Then I will tell you," she said simply. And I stared at her. "Half of everything inside you," she explained in Chinese, "is from your father's side. This is natural. They are the Jong clan, Cantonese[16] people. Good, honest people. Although sometimes they are bad-tempered and stingy. You know this from your father, how he can be unless I remind him."

And I was thinking to myself, Why is she telling me this? What does this have to do with anything? But my mother continued to speak, smiling broadly, sweeping her hand. "And half of everything inside you is from me, your mother's side, from the Sun clan in Taiyuan."[17] She wrote the characters out on the back of an envelope, forgetting that I cannot read Chinese.

"We are a smart people, very strong, tricky, and famous for winning wars. You know Sun Yat-sen,[18] hah?"

I nodded.

"He is from the Sun clan. But his family moved to the south many centuries ago, so he is not exactly the same clan. My family has always live in Taiyuan, from before the days of even Sun Wei. Do you know Sun Wei?"

I shook my head. And although I still didn't know where this conversation was going, I felt soothed. It seemed like the first time we had had an almost normal conversation.

---

16. **Cantonese** (kan-tuh-NEEZ) *adj*. from Canton, a capital in southeast China
17. **Taiyuan** (teye-yoo-AHN) *n*. a capital city in northern China
18. **Sun Yat-sen** (SOON YAHT-SEN) *n*. (1866–1925) a Chinese leader

"He went to battle with Genghis Khan.[19] And when the Mongol[20] soldiers shot at Sun Wei's warriors—heh!—their arrows bounced off the shields like rain on stone. Sun Wei had made a kind of armor so strong Genghis Khan believed it was magic!"

"Genghis Khan must have invented some magic arrows, then," I said. "After all, he conquered China."

My mother acted as if she hadn't heard me right. "This is true, we always know how to win. So now you know what is inside you, almost all good stuff from Taiyuan."

"I guess we've evolved to just winning in the toy and electronics market," I said.

"How do you know this?" she asked eagerly.

"You see it on everything. Made in Taiwan."

"Ai!" she cried loudly. "I'm not from Taiwan!"

And just like that, the fragile connection we were starting to build snapped.

"I was born in China, in *Taiyuan*," she said. "Taiwan is not China."

"Well, I only thought you said 'Taiwan' because it sounds the same," I argued, irritated that she was upset by such an unintentional mistake.

"Sound is completely different! Country is completely different!" she said in a huff. "People there only dream that it is China, because if you are Chinese you can never let go of China in your mind."

We sank into silence, a stalemate.[21] And then her eyes lighted up. "Now listen. You can also say the name of Taiyuan is Bing. Everyone from that city calls it that. Easier for you to say. Bing, it is a nickname."

She wrote down the character, and I nodded as if this made everything perfectly clear. "The same as here," she added in English. "You call Apple for New York. Frisco for San Francisco."

"Nobody calls San Francisco that!" I said, laughing. "People who call it that don't know any better."

"Now you understand my meaning," said my mother triumphantly.

I smiled.

And really, I did understand finally. Not what she had just said. But what had been true all along.

I saw what I had been fighting for: It was for me, a scared child, who had run away a long time ago to what I had imagined was a safer place. And hiding in this place, behind my invisible barriers, I knew what lay on the other side: Her side attacks. Her secret weapons. Her uncanny ability to find my weakest spots. But in the brief instant that I had

---

19. Genghis Khan (GENG-ihs KAHN) *n.* (1162-1227) Mongol conqueror of Asia
20. Mongol (MAHNG-uhl) *adj.* a member of a people living in Mongolia
21. stalemate (STAYL-mayt) *n.* a standstill or deadlock

peered over the barriers I could finally see what was really there: an old woman, a wok[22] for her armor, a knitting needle for her sword, getting a little crabby as she waited patiently for her daughter to invite her in.

◆ ◆ ◆

Rich and I have decided to postpone our wedding. My mother says July is not a good time to go to China on our honeymoon. She knows this because she and my father have just returned from a trip to Beijing and Taiyuan.

"It is too hot in the summer. You will only grow more spots and then your whole face will become red!" she tells Rich. And Rich grins, gestures his thumb toward my mother, and says to me, "Can you believe what comes out of her mouth? Now I know where you get your sweet, tactful[23] nature."

"You must go in October. That is the best time. Not too hot, not too cold. I am thinking of going back then too," she says authoritatively. And then she hastily adds: "Of course not with you!"

I laugh nervously, and Rich jokes: "That'd be great, Lindo. You could translate all the menus for us, make sure we're not eating snakes or dogs by mistake." I almost kick him.

"No, this is not my meaning," insists my mother. "Really, I am not asking."

And I know what she really means. She would love to go to China with us. And I would hate it. Three weeks' worth of her complaining about dirty chopsticks and cold soup, three meals a day—well, it would be a disaster.

Yet part of me also thinks the whole idea makes perfect sense. The three of us, leaving our differences behind, stepping on the plane together, sitting side by side, lifting off, moving West to reach the East. . . .

---

22. **wok** (WAHK) *n.* a large, bowl-shaped pan used in Chinese cooking
23. **tactful** (TAKT-fuhl) *adj.* having a keen sense of what is appropriate or tasteful

Saying Yes

DIANA CHANG

"Are you Chinese?"
"Yes."

"American?"
"Yes."

"*Really* Chinese?"
"No . . . not quite."

"*Really* American?"
"Well, actually, you see . . ."

But I would rather say
yes

Not neither-nor,
not maybe,
but both, and not only

The homes I've had,
the ways I am

I'd rather say it
twice,
yes

Photograph of Chinese American boy holding a flag. How
does this photograph reflect the message in Chang's poem?

Critical Thinking

1. What does each writer tell you about the contradictions of her cultural identity? In what ways are Tan's and Chang's attitudes similar? In what ways are they different?
2. What aspects of each writer's personal and historical background do you think most influenced the writing of these works?
3. How has reading these selections helped you to resolve cultural conflicts in your life or the life of someone you know?

Writing Your Response to "Four Directions" and "Saying Yes"

In your journal, write about one scene, character, image, or idea from the novel or the poem that affects you most strongly. Why is it memorable to you? Does it relate to an experience or person in your own life? If so, explain how.

Going Back Into the Text: Author's Craft

Plot is the sequence of events in a literary work. In most novels, dramas, short stories, and narrative poems, the plot involves characters and a central conflict. A *conflict* is a struggle between opposing forces. Sometimes this struggle is *internal*, or within a character. At other times the struggle is *external*, or between a character and an outside force. The outside force is often another character in the story. Important events within the plot introduce the central conflict. The conflict then increases during plot *development* until it reaches a high point of interest or suspense called the *climax*. The climax is often followed by the *resolution*, or end, of the central conflict.

As you and your partner review the central conflicts in the selections by Amy Tan and Diana Chang, use the following questions as guidelines.

1. What conflict does the speaker in Chang's poem experience? How does she resolve the conflict?
2. What external conflicts does the narrator in Tan's novel experience? What internal conflicts does she experience?
3. When does the climax in the Tan selection occur? When does the resolution of the conflict occur?

from Stelmark: A Family Recollection

Reading the Author in a Cultural Context

Starting in the late 1800s and early 1900s, many Greek immigrants came to the United States as impoverished farmers seeking their fortunes in the United States. However, when they arrived in this country, these immigrants found few well-paying jobs. Settling in or near cities like Chicago, New York, and Boston, they worked in factories or mines or became street vendors, selling flowers and fruit. Eventually, many Greek Americans saved enough money to buy their own flower shops, restaurants, and grocery stores.

In order to ease the move from farm life to city life, many of these immigrants established Greek neighborhoods that encouraged close ties among the people living there. These ties resembled those in the villages of their rural homeland. In addition to maintaining a sense of community, these immigrants preserved their traditional values, such as individual achievement, self-reliance, and social responsibility. These values helped the immigrants, who were skilled farmers, adjust to the urban job market they found in the United States.

Harry Petrakis grew up in the Greek American community in Chicago, where his father served as a Greek Orthodox priest. The young Petrakis wrote to amuse himself during the two years he was confined to his home with tuberculosis. He learned to create an imaginative world of his own through writing. Petrakis credits his creative writing teacher, Marjorie Peters, for helping him find his distinctive voice as a writer, a voice that would best capture the Greek American immigrant experience.

Petrakis bases his stories on his recollections of people and events from the neighborhoods in which he was raised. Notice Petrakis's ability to convey universal human emotions through his own ethnic heritage and a local setting.

The excerpt that follows is from Petrakis's memoir, *Stelmark: A Family Recollection*. In this selection, Petrakis recalls an encounter he had as a young boy with a Greek grocer.

Focusing on the Selection

As you read the selection from *Stelmark: A Family Recollection*, think about the lessons Petrakis learns from the grocer. What differences does he see at first between himself and the older man? What does Petrakis value in the beginning of the excerpt? What does he come to appreciate at the end? Think about the ways that the food in the grocery store represents Greek culture. Why do the figs have special meaning for Petrakis? Consider what message or main idea Petrakis is trying to convey in this excerpt. Write your responses in your journal.

from *Stelmark: A Family Recollection*

HARRY MARK PETRAKIS

THERE WAS ONE STOREKEEPER I remember above all others in my youth. It was shortly before I became ill, spending a good portion of my time with a motley[1] group of varied ethnic ancestry. We contended with one another to deride[2] the customs of the old country. On our Saturday forays[3] into neighborhoods beyond our own, to prove we were really Americans, we ate hot dogs and drank Cokes. If a boy didn't have ten cents for this repast he went hungry, for he dared not bring a sandwich from home made of the spiced meats our families ate.

One of our untamed games was to seek out the owner of a pushcart or a store, unmistakably an immigrant, and bedevil him with a chorus of insults and jeers. To prove allegiance to the gang it was necessary to reserve our fiercest malevolence[4] for a storekeeper or peddler belonging to our own ethnic background.

---

1. **motley** (MAHT-lee) *adj*. diverse
2. **deride** (dih-REYED) *v*. laugh at in scorn or contempt
3. **forays** (FAWR-ayz) *n*. raids or attacks
4. **malevolence** (muh-LEV-uh-luhns) *n*. ill will, maliciousness

For that reason I led a raid on the small, shabby grocery of old Barba Nikos,[5] a short, sinewy[5] Greek who walked with a slight limp and sported a flaring, handlebar mustache.

We stood outside his store and dared him to come out. When he emerged to do battle, we plucked a few plums and peaches from the baskets on the sidewalk and retreated across the street to eat them while he watched. He waved a fist and hurled epithets[6] at us in ornamental Greek.

Aware that my mettle[7] was being tested, I raised my arm and threw my half-eaten plum at the old man. My aim was accurate and the plum struck him on the cheek. He shuddered and put his hand to the stain. He stared at me across the street, and although I could not see his eyes, I felt them sear my flesh. He turned and walked silently back into the store. The boys slapped my shoulders in admiration, but it was a hollow victory that rested like a stone in the pit of my stomach.

At twilight when we disbanded, I passed the grocery store on my way home. There was a small light burning in the store and the shadow of the old man's body outlined against the glass. Goaded[8] by remorse, I walked to the door and entered.

The old man moved from behind the narrow wooden counter and stared at me. I wanted to turn and flee, but by then it was too late. As he motioned for me to come closer, I braced myself for a curse or a blow.

"You were the one," he said, finally, in a harsh voice.

I nodded mutely.

"Why did you come back?"

I stood there unable to answer.

"What's your name?"

"Haralambos," I said, speaking to him in Greek.

He looked at me in shock. "You are Greek!" he cried. "A Greek boy attacking a Greek grocer!" He stood appalled at the immensity of my crime. "All right," he said coldly. "You are here because you wish to make amends." His great mustache bristled in concentration. "Four plums, two peaches," he said. "That makes a total of 78 cents. Call it 75. Do you have 75 cents, boy?"

I shook my head.

"Then you will work it off," he said. "Fifteen cents an hour into 75 cents makes"—he paused—"five hours of work. Can you come here Saturday morning?"

"Yes," I said.

---

5. **sinewy** (SIHN-yoo-ee) *adj.* tough, resilient, muscular
6. **epithets** (EP-uh-thets) *n.* words or phrases applied to a person or thing to describe an actual or attributed quality
7. **mettle** (MET-uhl) *n.* courage, spirit, quality of character
8. **goaded** (GOHD-ihd) *v.* prodded, driven

"Yes, Barba Nikos," he said sternly. "Show respect."

"Yes, Barba Nikos," I said.

"Saturday morning at eight o'clock," he said. "Now go home and say thanks in your prayers that I did not loosen your impudent[9] head with a solid smack on the ear." I needed no further urging and fled.

Saturday morning, still apprehensive, I returned to the store. I began by sweeping, raising clouds of dust in dark and hidden corners. I washed the windows, whipping the squeegee swiftly up and down the glass in a fever of fear that some member of the gang would see me. When I finished I hurried back inside.

For the balance of the morning I stacked cans, washed the counter, and dusted bottles of yellow wine. A few customers entered, and Barba Nikos served them. A little after twelve o'clock he locked the door so he could eat lunch. He cut himself a few slices of sausage, tore a large chunk from a loaf of crisp-crusted bread, and filled a small cup with a dozen black shiny olives floating in brine. He offered me the cup. I could not help myself and grimaced.

"You are a stupid boy," the old man said. "You are not really Greek, are you?"

"Yes, I am."

"You might be," he admitted grudgingly. "But you do not act Greek. Wrinkling your nose at these fine olives. Look around this store for a minute. What do you see?"

"Fruits and vegetables," I said. "Cheese and olives and things like that."

He stared at me with a massive scorn. "That's what I mean," he said. "You are a bonehead. You don't understand that a whole nation and a people are in this store."

I looked uneasily toward the storeroom in the rear, almost expecting someone to emerge.

"What about olives?" he cut the air with a sweep of his arm. "There are olives of many shapes and colors. Pointed black ones from Kalamata, oval ones from Amphissa,[10] pickled green olives and sharp tangy yellow ones. Achilles[11] carried black olives to Troy[12] and after a day of savage battle leading his Myrmidons,[13] he'd rest and eat cheese and ripe black olives such as these right here. You have heard of Achilles, boy, haven't you?"

---

9. **impudent** (IHM-pyoo-duhnt) *adj.* rude, disrespectful
10. **Kalamata** (kal-uh-MAHT-uh) . . . **Amphissa** (am-FIHS-uh) cities in southern Greece
11. **Achilles** (uh-KIHL-eez) *n.* a well-known Greek warrior in the Trojan War
12. **Troy** (TROI) *n.* an ancient city in Asia Minor
13. **Myrmidons** (MER-muh-dahnz) *n.* warriors of ancient Thessaly

"Yes," I said.

"Yes, Barba Nikos."

"Yes, Barba Nikos," I said.

He motioned at the row of jars filled with varied spices. "There is origanon there and basilikon and daphne and sesame and miantanos, all the marvelous flavorings that we have used in our food for thousands of years. The men of Marathon carried small packets of these spices into battle, and the scents reminded them of their homes, their families, and their children."

He rose and tugged his napkin free from around his throat. "Cheese, you said. Cheese! Come closer, boy, and I will educate your abysmal ignorance." He motioned toward a wooden container on the counter. "That glistening white delight is feta, made from goat's milk, packed in wooden buckets to retain the flavor. Alexander the Great demanded it on his table with his casks of wine when he planned his campaigns."

He walked limping from the counter to the window where the piles of tomatoes, celery, and green peppers clustered. "I suppose all you see here are some random vegetables?" He did not wait for me to answer. "You are dumb again. These are some of the ingredients that go to make up a Greek salad. Do you know what a Greek salad really is? A meal in itself, an experience, an emotional involvement. It is created deftly and with grace. First, you place large lettuce leaves in a big, deep bowl." He spread his fingers and moved them slowly, carefully, as if he were arranging the leaves. "The remainder of the lettuce is shredded and piled in a small mound," he said. "Then comes celery, cucumbers, tomatoes sliced lengthwise, green peppers, origanon, green olives, feta, avocado, and anchovies. At the end you dress it with lemon, vinegar, and pure olive oil, glinting golden in the light."

He finished with a heartfelt sigh and for a moment closed his eyes. Then he opened one eye to mark me with a baleful intensity. "The story goes that Zeus himself created the recipe and assembled and mixed the ingredients on Mount Olympus one night when he had invited some of the other gods to dinner."

He turned his back on me and walked slowly again across the store, dragging one foot slightly behind him. I looked uneasily at the clock, which showed that it was a few minutes past one. He turned quickly and startled me. "And everything else in here," he said loudly. "White beans, lentils, garlic, crisp bread, kokoretsi,[14] meat balls, mussels and clams." He paused and drew a deep, long breath. "And the wine," he went on, "wine from Samos, Santorini, and Crete,[15] retsina and

---

14. **kokoretsi** (koh-koh-RET-see) *n.* a roasted lamb dish
15. **Samos** (SAY-mahs) . . . **Santorini** (san-tor-EE-nee) . . . **Crete** (KREET) Greek islands

mavrodaphne,[16] a taste almost as old as water . . . and then the fragrant melons, the pastries, yellow diples and golden loukoumades, the honey custard galatobouriko. Everything a part of our history, as much a part as the exquisite sculpture in marble, the bearded warriors, Pan[17] and the oracles at Delphi, and the nymphs dancing in the shadowed groves under Homer's glittering moon." He paused, out of breath again, and coughed harshly. "Do you understand now, boy?"

He watched my face for some response and then grunted. We stood silent for a moment until he cocked his head and stared at the clock. "It is time for you to leave," he motioned brusquely[18] toward the door. "We are square now. Keep it that way."

I decided the old man was crazy and reached behind the counter for my jacket and cap and started for the door. He called me back. From a box he drew out several soft, yellow figs that he placed in a piece of paper. "A bonus because you worked well," he said. "Take them. When you taste them, maybe you will understand what I have been talking about."

I took the figs and he unlocked the door and I hurried from the store. I looked back once and saw him standing in the doorway, watching me, the swirling tendrils[19] of food curling like mist about his head.

I ate the figs late that night. I forgot about them until I was in bed, and then I rose and took the package from my jacket. I nibbled at one, then ate them all. They broke apart between my teeth with a tangy nectar, a thick sweetness running like honey across my tongue and into the pockets of my cheeks. In the morning when I woke, I could still taste and inhale their fragrance.

I never again entered Barba Nikos's store. My spell of illness, which began some months later, lasted two years. When I returned to the streets I had forgotten the old man and the grocery. Shortly afterwards my family moved from the neighborhood.

Some twelve years later, after the war, I drove through the old neighborhood and passed the grocery. I stopped the car and for a moment stood before the store. The windows were stained with dust and grime, the interior bare and desolate, a store in a decrepit group of stores marked for razing so new structures could be built.

I have been in many Greek groceries since then and have often bought the feta and Kalamata olives. I have eaten countless Greek salads

---

16. **retsina** (ret-SEE-nuh) **and mavrodaphne** (mav-ROH-daf-nee) Greek wines
17. **Pan** (PAN) *n.* the ancient Greek god of forests, pastures, flocks and shepherds
18. **brusquely** (BRUSK-lee) *adv.* roughly, abruptly, bluntly
19. **tendrils** (TEN-druhlz) *n.* threadlike, leafless parts of climbing plants

and have indeed found them a meal for the gods. On the holidays in our house, my wife and sons and I sit down to a dinner of steaming, buttered pilaf[20] like my mother used to make and lemon-egg avgolemono[21] and roast lamb richly seasoned with cloves of garlic. I drink the red and yellow wines, and for dessert I have come to relish the delicate pastries coated with honey and powdered sugar. Old Barba Nikos would have been pleased.

But I have never been able to recapture the halcyon[22] flavor of those figs he gave me on that day so long ago, although I have bought figs many times. I have found them pleasant to my tongue, but there is something missing. And to this day I am not sure whether it was the figs or the vision and passion of the old grocer that coated the fruit so sweetly I can still recall their savor and fragrance after almost thirty years.

Illustration of a fruit and vegetable market on a city street, by Beth Peck.
From the book *Matthew and Tilly* by Rebecca C. Jones.

---

20. **pilaf** (pih-LAHF) *n.* rice cooked in poultry or meat broth
21. **avgolemono** (ahv-goh-LEEM-uh-noh) *n.* a soup or sauce made with lemon juice
22. **halcyon** (HAL-see-uhn) *adj.* happy, peaceful, tranquil

Critical Thinking

1. In the beginning of the selection, what is Petrakis's attitude toward his Greek heritage? How does his attitude change?
2. What aspects of Petrakis's personal and cultural background do you think shaped his attitudes?
3. Have you ever met someone who greatly influenced your feelings about your cultural identity? Compare your experience with Petrakis's. If not, imagine such an encounter and describe the experience.

Writing Your Response to
Stelmark: A Family Recollection

In your journal, write about one person, event, image, or idea in the selection that stands out in your mind. What makes it special for you? In what ways does it relate to experiences in your own life?

Going Back Into the Text:
Author's Craft

To fully understand a piece of nonfiction, it is important to recognize the **main ideas** the writer wishes to convey. In effective writing, each paragraph contains a main idea that is either stated directly or suggested. Each main idea is supported and developed by the other sentences in the paragraph. The paragraphs work together to convey the main idea or ideas of the selection as a whole.

With a partner, review the excerpt from *Stelmark: A Family Recollection* to see how Petrakis conveys his main ideas. Use the following questions as guidelines.

1. What is the main idea of the first paragraph?
2. How does Petrakis sum up the main idea of the selection in the final paragraph?
3. Identify the main idea in two other paragraphs in the selection.

from Fences

Responding to Literature

Notice the sidenotes in the margins of this selection. These notes reflect one student's reading of the passage from *Fences*. The student points out how Wilson uses certain elements of drama, such as dialogue, conflict, character, and setting, as well as personally responding to the play. Compare these observations with your own critical reading.

Reading the Author in a Cultural Context

August Wilson emerged in the 1980s as an important voice in the theater in the United States. His plays often center on conflicts between older African Americans who embrace their cultural heritage and younger African Americans who reject it. As a group, his plays work together to convey a broad scope of African American experience in the 20th century.

Wilson grew up in a poor section of Pittsburgh, Pennsylvania, called "the Hill." At an early age he was proud of his African American heritage because of his mother, who worked hard to support her six children. Wilson dropped out of school when he was in the ninth grade. Ending his formal education, he continued to learn through books at the local library. He discovered African Ameri-

can writers such as Ralph Ellison, Langston Hughes, and Arna Bontemps.

The following selection is a scene from Wilson's Pulitzer-Prize-winning play *Fences*. Wilson focuses this play on a character named Troy Maxson, formerly an outstanding high school athlete who was excluded from major league baseball because he is African American. Set in the 1950s, *Fences* contrasts Troy's bitterness over his failed career with the hopes of his son, Cory, whose chances of attaining his dream are more realistic.

Wilson's goal is to write plays about African Americans living in each decade of the 20th century. He hopes to help African American audiences become fully conscious of their identity through their history and culture. Yet because he expresses the sufferings and joys that come with being human, his plays continue to reach all people. As you read the excerpt from *Fences*, think about how Troy's values represent African American culture and universal human values.

Focusing on the Selection

In the following scene from *Fences*, think about the conflicts in Troy's family. Why doesn't Troy want his son to pursue a career in sports? In what ways are Troy's values different from Cory's? How does the dialogue reveal these conflicts and the personalities of the characters in the play? Write your responses in your journal.

from *Fences*

AUGUST WILSON

Act One
Scene Three

*. . . (*CORY *takes the saw and begins cutting the boards.* TROY *continues working. There is a long pause.)*

CORY: Hey, Pop . . . why don't you buy a TV?

TROY: What I want with a TV? What I want one of them for?

CORY: Everybody got one. Earl, Ba Bra . . . Jesse!

TROY: I ain't asked you who had one. I say what I want with one?

CORY: So you can watch it. They got lots of things on TV. Baseball games and everything. We could watch the World Series.

TROY: Yeah . . . and how much this TV cost?

CORY: I don't know. They got them on sale for around two hundred dollars.

TROY: Two hundred dollars, huh?

CORY: That ain't that much, Pop.

TROY: Naw, it's just two hundred dollars. See that roof you got over your head at night? Let me tell you something about that roof. It's been over ten years since that roof was last tarred. See now . . . the snow come this winter and sit up there on that roof like it is . . . and it's gonna seep inside. It's just gonna be a little bit . . . ain't gonna hardly notice it. Then the next thing you know, it's gonna be leaking all over the house. Then the wood rot from all that water and you gonna need a whole new roof. Now, how much you think it cost to get that roof tarred?

CORY: I don't know.

TROY: Two hundred and sixty-four dollars . . . cash money. While you thinking about a TV, I got to be thinking about the roof . . . and whatever else go wrong around here. Now if you had two hundred dollars, what would you do . . . fix the roof or buy a TV?

CORY: I'd buy a TV. Then when the roof started to leak . . . when it needed fixing . . . I'd fix it.

TROY: Where you gonna get the money from? You done spent it for a TV. You gonna sit up and watch the water run all over your brand new TV.

CORY: Aw, Pop. You got money. I know you do.

TROY: Where I got it at, huh?

CORY: You got it in the bank.

TROY: You wanna see my bankbook? You wanna see that seventy-three dollars and twenty-two cents I got sitting up in there.

CORY: You ain't got to pay for it all at one time. You can put a down payment on it and carry it on home with you.

TROY: Not me. I ain't gonna owe nobody nothing if I can help it. Miss a payment and they come and snatch it right out your house. Then what you got? Now, soon as I get two hundred dollars clear, then I'll buy a TV. Right now, as soon as I get two hundred and sixty-four dollars, I'm gonna have this roof tarred.

CORY: Aw . . . Pop!

TROY: You go on and get you two hundred dollars and buy one if ya want it. I got better things to do with my money.

CORY: I can't get no two hundred dollars. I ain't never seen two hundred dollars.

TROY: I'll tell you what . . . you get you a hundred dollars and I'll put the other hundred with it.

CORY: Alright, I'm gonna show you.

TROY: You gonna show me how you can cut them boards right now.

(CORY *begins to cut the boards. There is a long pause.*)

CORY: The Pirates won today. That makes five in a row.

TROY: I ain't thinking about the Pirates. Got an all-white team. Got that boy . . . that Puerto Rican boy . . . Clemente. Don't even half-play him. That boy could be something if they give him a chance. Play him one day and sit him on the bench the next.

Troy and Cory have very different priorities. Troy has a strong sense of responsibility. He feels that his family is safe and protected. Cory is a teenager who doesn't understand those things yet.

Troy's family is poor. Even when this play was set, in the 1950s, I bet 73 dollars didn't go very far. No wonder he worries about the leaky roof.

Troy seems to be softening. At first I thought he was a stubborn man and strict father, but it looks like he's going to give in.

CORY: He gets a lot of chances to play.

TROY: I'm talking about playing regular. Playing every day so you can get your timing. That's what I'm talking about.

CORY: They got some white guys on the team that don't play every day. You can't play everybody at the same time.

TROY: If they got a white fellow sitting on the bench . . . you can bet your last dollar he can't play! The colored guy got to be twice as good before he get on the team. That's why I don't want you to get all tied up in them sports. Man on the team and what it get him? They got colored on the team and don't use them. Same as not having them. All them teams the same.

CORY: The Braves got Hank Aaron and Wes Covington. Hank Aaron hit two home runs today. That makes forty-three.

TROY: Hank Aaron ain't nobody. That's what you supposed to do. That's how you supposed to play the game. Ain't nothing to it. It's just a matter of timing . . . getting the right follow-through. Hell, I can hit forty-three home runs right now!

CORY: Not off no major-league pitching, you couldn't.

TROY: We had better pitching in the Negro leagues. I hit seven home runs off of Satchel Paige. You can't get no better than that!

CORY: Sandy Koufax. He's leading the league in strike-outs.

TROY: I ain't thinking of no Sandy Koufax.

CORY: You got Warren Spahn and Lew Burdette. I bet you couldn't hit no home runs off of Warren Spahn.

TROY: I'm through with it now. You go on and cut them boards. (*Pause.*)
Your mama tell me you done got recruited by a college football team? Is that right?

CORY: Yeah. Coach Zellman say the recruiter[1] gonna be coming by to talk to you. Get you to sign the permission papers.

TROY: I thought you supposed to be working down there at the A&P. Ain't you suppose to be working down there after school?

---

1. recruiter (rih-KROOT-uhr) *n.* a person who discovers and enlists new members

Photograph of 1985 Yale Repertory production of *Fences*, with Mary Alice as Rose,
Ray Aranha as Cory, and James Earl Jones as Troy.

CORY: Mr. Stawicki say he gonna hold my job for me until after the football season. Say starting next week I can work weekends.

TROY: I thought we had an understanding about this football stuff? You suppose to keep up with your chores and hold that job down at the A&P. Ain't been around here all day on a Saturday. Ain't none of your chores done . . . and now you telling me you done quit your job.

CORY: I'm gonna be working weekends.

TROY: You damn right you are! And ain't no need for nobody coming around here to talk to me about signing nothing.

CORY: Hey, Pop . . . you can't do that. He's coming all the way from North Carolina.

TROY: I don't care where he coming from. The white man ain't gonna let you get nowhere with that football noway. You go on and get your book-learning so you can work yourself up in that A&P or learn how to fix cars or build houses or something, get you a trade. That way you have something can't nobody take away from you. You go on and learn how to put your hands to some good use. Besides hauling people's garbage.

CORY: I get good grades, Pop. That's why the recruiter wants to talk with you. You got to keep up your grades to get recruited. This way I'll be going to college. I'll get a chance . . .

TROY: First you gonna get your butt down there to the A&P and get your job back.

CORY: Mr. Stawicki done already hired somebody else 'cause I told him I was playing football.

TROY: You a bigger fool than I thought . . . to let somebody take away your job so you can play some football. Where you gonna get your money to take out your girlfriend and whatnot? What kind of foolishness is that to let somebody take away your job?

CORY: I'm still gonna be working weekends.

TROY: Naw . . . naw. You getting your butt out of here and finding you another job.

CORY: Come on, Pop! I got to practice. I can't work after school and play football too. The team needs me. That's what Coach Zellman say . . .

TROY: I don't care what nobody else say. I'm the boss . . . you understand? I'm the boss around here. I do the only saying what counts.

CORY: Come on, Pop!

TROY: I asked you . . . did you understand?

CORY: Yeah . . .

TROY: What?!

CORY: Yessir.

TROY: You go on down there to that A&P and see if you can get your job back. If you can't do both . . . then you quit the football team. You've got to take the crookeds with the straights.

CORY: Yessir.
(Pause.)
Can I ask you a question?

TROY: What . . . you wanna ask me? Mr. Stawicki the one you got the questions for.

CORY: How come you ain't never liked me?

TROY: Liked you? Who . . . say I got to like you? What law is there say I got to like you? Wanna stand up in my face and ask a . . . question like that. Talking about liking somebody. Come here, boy, when I talk to you.
(CORY comes over to where TROY is working. He stands slouched over and TROY shoves him on his shoulder.)
Straighten up, . . . I asked you a question . . . what law is there say I got to like you?

CORY: None.

TROY: Well, alright then! Don't you eat every day?
(Pause.)
Answer me when I talk to you! Don't you eat every day?

CORY: Yeah.

TROY: Nigger, as long as you in my house, you put that sir on the end of it when you talk to me!

CORY: Yes . . . sir.

TROY: You eat every day.

CORY: Yessir!

TROY: Got a roof over your head.

This passage of dialogue helps develop the central conflict in the play. Cory reveals that he thinks his father doesn't like him.

I guess Troy has a hard time showing his feelings toward Cory, but it seems like he cares about him and is looking out for his best interests.

CORY: Yessir!

TROY: Got clothes on your back.

CORY: Yessir.

TROY: Why you think that is?

CORY: Cause of you.

TROY: Aw, hell I know it's cause of me . . . but why do you think that is?

CORY: (Hesitant.) Cause you like me.

TROY: Like you? I go out of here every morning . . . bust my butt . . . putting up with them crackers every day . . . cause I like you? You about the biggest fool I ever saw.
(Pause.)
It's my job. It's my responsibility! You understand that? A man got to take care of his family. You live in my house . . . sleep you behind on my bedclothes . . . fill you belly up with my food . . . cause you my son. You my flesh and blood. Not cause I like you! Cause it's my duty to take care of you. I owe a responsibility to you! Let's get this straight right here . . . before it go along any further . . . I ain't got to like you. Mr. Rand don't give me my money come payday cause he likes me. He gives me cause he owe me. I done give you everything I had to give you. I gave you your life! Me and your mama worked that out between us. And liking . . . wasn't part of the bargain. Don't you try and go through life worrying about if somebody like you or not. You best be making sure they doing right by you. You understand what I'm saying, boy?

CORY: Yessir.

TROY: Then get . . . out of my face, and get on down to that A&P.

(ROSE *has been standing behind the screen door for much of the scene. She enters as* CORY *exits.*)

ROSE: Why don't you let the boy go ahead and play football, Troy? Ain't no harm in that. He's just trying to be like you with the sports.

TROY: I don't want him to be like me! I want him to move as far away from my life as he can get. You the only decent thing that ever happened to me. I wish him that. But I don't wish him a thing else from

Troy thinks the most important thing about being a parent is providing for his family. Maybe he didn't have those things when he was a kid.

The stage directions give important information about the movements of characters on stage. Without this stage direction, we wouldn't know about Rose's position behind the door.

Photograph of 1985 Yale Repertory production of *Fences*, with James Earl Jones as Troy and Mary Alice as Rose. In what ways does the play illustrate the theme of recognizing differences?

my life. I decided seventeen years ago that boy wasn't getting involved in no sports. Not after what they did to me in the sports.

ROSE: Troy, why don't you admit you was too old to play in the major leagues? For once . . . why don't you admit that?

TROY: What do you mean too old? Don't come telling me I was too old. I just wasn't the right color. Hell, I'm fifty-three years old and can do better than Selkirk's[2] .269 right now!

ROSE: How's was you gonna play ball when you were over forty? Sometimes I can't get no sense out of you.

TROY: I got good sense, woman. I got sense enough not to let my boy get hurt over playing no sports. You been mothering that boy too much. Worried about if people like him.

ROSE: Everything that boy do . . . he do for you. He wants you to say "Good job, son." That's all.

TROY: Rose, I ain't got time for that. He's alive. He's healthy. He's got to make his own way. I made mine. Ain't nobody gonna hold his hand when he get out there in that world.

ROSE: Times have changed from when you was young, Troy. People change. The world's changing around you and you can't even see it.

TROY: (Slow, methodical.) Woman . . . I do the best I can do. I come in here every Friday. I carry a sack of potatoes and a bucket of lard. You all line up at the door with your hands out. I give you the lint from my pockets. I give you my sweat and my blood. I ain't got no tears. I done spent them. We go upstairs in that room at night . . . I get up Monday morning . . . find my lunch on the table. I go out. Make my way. Find my strength to carry me through to the next Friday.
(Pause.)
That's all I got, Rose. That's all I got to give. I can't give nothing else.

(TROY exits into the house. The lights go down to black.) . . .

---

2. **Selkirk's** refers to George Selkirk, an outfielder for the New York Yankees

POSTREADING

Critical Thinking

1. What does this passage from *Fences* tell you about August Wilson's attitude toward racism?
2. What experiences do you think influenced Wilson's decision to write this play?
3. What universal human values does this passage from *Fences* express?

Writing Your Response to *Fences*

In your journal, write about a feeling, idea, or question you had while reading the selection. How does this scene relate to an experience in your own life or in the life of someone you know?

Going Back Into the Text: Author's Craft

A **dialogue** is a conversation between characters. In *drama*, which is a story meant to be performed by actors on a stage, dialogue becomes the playwright's primary method for developing character. Costume, scenery, and physical movements and gestures give insight into a character. However, it is most often through dialogue that the characters in a play convey their personalities, values, and beliefs to the audience.

With a partner, review the scene from *Fences* to see how Wilson uses dialogue to reveal character. The following questions can serve as guidelines.

1. What aspects of Troy's character are revealed through his dialogue with Cory?
2. What aspects of Troy's character are revealed through his dialogue with Rose?
3. How do your conversations with a friend reveal your friend's personality? What aspects are not revealed by conversations?

Reviewing the Theme

1. Choose two selections in this theme that depict relationships among members of different generations. Compare and contrast the ideas about cultural differences expressed by the older and younger generations.

2. Compare the issues and attitudes presented by two writers from different cultural groups. How are their perspectives on their cultural identities similar? How are they different?

3. In what ways are cultural differences valuable? What are the advantages of preserving these differences? Support your answers with details from the selections in this theme and from your own life.

Theme 9:
Breaking Down Barriers and Building Communities

Photograph of children from different cultural backgrounds.

THE LITERATURE in this theme focuses on breaking down social and political barriers among groups in the United States. The authors included here offer ideas about building communities that represent such ideals of democracy as justice and equality for all people.

The section begins with an essay that defines a new kind of society. The author of this selection describes a multicultural society that is a harmonious combination of all groups within it. This society is in contrast to one in which a dominant culture suppresses the rights and needs of other groups. In addition, you will read selections by African American and Hispanic American writers who describe both their cultural pride and their dream of understanding among social groups in the United States. Two other writers—a Native American and a Jewish American—also explore the possibility of a future of social harmony. Through a variety of literary forms, these writers express their ideas about communities where cultural pride and human understanding flourish.

The writers in this theme recognize that in order to break down barriers, people must accept and respect differences. More important, acceptance will help people recognize the common threads that link them together.

America: The Multinational Society

Reading the Author in a Cultural Context

African American author Ishmael Reed believes that one of the liberties African Americans need to fight for is freedom of expression. For Reed, that means the freedom to criticize any problem, no matter who created it. For example, he has written works in which he attacks racism. However, he has also criticized the emotional writing style of protest that was popular among some African American writers in the 1960s. Some African Americans saw this criticism as a betrayal. But Reed said he was trying to point out that the writers were following a particular style too closely. This style, he said, prevented the personal voice of the writer from emerging.

Reed's writing style is distinctive and personal. He plays with language and punctuation. His invented forms give life and original meaning to his ideas. Reed's goal has been to develop an aesthetic (es-THET-ihk)—a philosophy of creativity and a standard for quality—for African American writing. His method combines aspects of African American history, art, folklore, and oral tradition in written texts. The text can take many forms. Reed has written novels, poems, essays, plays, and short stories.

Another of Reed's literary goals has been to publish the works of writers from many nations. In the 1970s, Reed helped to found the Yardbird Publishing Company to publish works by writers from a variety of ethnic backgrounds.

Ishmael Reed's ideas about literature and society suggest the universal nature of human existence. Reed addresses more than the experiences of African Americans in his writings. He explores the common bond of humanity that unites all people.

Focusing on the Selection

As you read Ishmael Reed's essay, think about his attitudes concerning the United States as a multicultural society. What evidence does he give to support his ideas? How strong, do you think, is his argument that the United States is a unique blend of many cultures? What future does Reed see for the United States? Record your responses in your journal.

America: The Multinational Society

ISHMAEL REED

At the annual Lower East Side Jewish Festival yesterday, a Chinese woman ate a pizza slice in front of Ty Thuan Duc's Vietnamese grocery story. Beside her a Spanish-speaking family patronized a cart with two signs: "Italian Ices" and "Kosher by Rabbi Alper." And after the pastrami[1] ran out, everybody ate knishes.[2]

(New York Times, 23 June 1983)

O N THE DAY BEFORE MEMORIAL DAY, 1983, a poet called me to describe a city he had just visited. He said that one section included mosques,[3] built by the Islamic people who dwelled there. Attending his reading, he said, were large numbers of Hispanic people, forty thousand of whom lived in the same city. He was not talking about a fabled city located in some mysterious region of the world. The city he'd visited was Detroit.

A few months before, as I was leaving Houston, Texas, I heard it announced on the radio that Texas's largest minority was Mexican

---

1. **pastrami** (puh-STRAH-mee) *n.* smoked beef
2. **knishes** (kuh-NIHSH-uhz) *n.* pastries stuffed with potatoes or cheese
3. **mosques** (MAHSKS) *n.* Moslem places of worship

Main Street. Collage by Mick Wooten depicting the multicultural landscape of the United States. How does our nation benefit by being a mixture of many cultures, as suggested by this collage?

American, and though a foundation recently issued a report critical of bilingual education, the taped voice used to guide the passengers on the air trams connecting terminals in Dallas Airport is in both Spanish and English. If the trend continues, a day will come when it will be difficult to travel through some sections of the country without hearing commands in both English and Spanish; after all, for some western states, Spanish was the first written language and the Spanish style lives on in the western way of life.

Shortly after my Texas trip, I sat in an auditorium located on the campus of the University of Wisconsin at Milwaukee as a Yale professor—whose original work on the influence of African cultures upon those of the Americas has led to his ostracism[4] from some monocultural intellectual circles—walked up and down the aisle, like an old-time southern evangelist,[5] dancing and drumming the top of the lectern, illustrating his points before some serious Afro-American intellectuals

---

4. **ostracism** (AHS-truh-sihz-uhm) *n.* exclusion; being shut out
5. **evangelist** (ih-VAN-juh-luhst) *n.* a traveling preacher of the Gospel

and artists who cheered and applauded his performance and his mastery of information. The professor was "white." After his lecture, he joined a group of Milwaukeeans in a conversation. All of the participants spoke Yoruban,[6] though only the professor had ever traveled to Africa.

One of the artists told me that his paintings, which included African and Afro-American mythological symbols and imagery, were hanging in the local McDonald's restaurant. The next day I went to McDonald's and snapped pictures of smiling youngsters eating hamburgers below paintings that could grace the walls of any of the country's leading museums. The manager of the local McDonald's said, "I don't know what you boys are doing, but I like it," as he commissioned the local painters to exhibit in his restaurant.

Such blurring of cultural styles occurs in everyday life in the United States to a greater extent than anyone can imagine and is probably more prevalent than the sensational conflict between people of different backgrounds that is played up and often encouraged by the media. The result is what the Yale professor, Robert Thompson, referred to as a cultural bouillabaisse,[7] yet members of the nation's present educational and cultural Elect still cling to the notion that the United States belongs to some vaguely defined entity they refer to as "Western civilization," by which they mean, presumably, a civilization created by the people of Europe, as if Europe can be viewed in monolithic[8] terms. Is Beethoven's Ninth Symphony, which includes Turkish marches, a part of Western civilization, or the late nineteenth- and twentieth-century French paintings, whose creators were influenced by Japanese art? And what of the cubists,[9] through whom the influence of African art changed modern painting, or the surrealists,[10] who were so impressed with the art of the Pacific Northwest Indians that, in their map of North America, Alaska dwarfs the lower forty-eight in size?

Are the Russians, who are often criticized for their adoption of "Western" ways by Tsarist dissidents[11] in exile, members of Western civilization? And what of the millions of Europeans who have black African and Asian ancestry, black Africans having occupied several countries for hundreds of years? Are these "Europeans" members of Western civilization, or the Hungarians, who originated across the Urals

---

6. **Yoruban** (YOHR-uh-buhn) *n.* language of a West African people
7. **bouillabaisse** (boo-yuh-BAYS) *n.* fish soup
8. **monolithic** (mahn-uh-LIHTH-ihk) *adj.* single; uniform; having no differences
9. **cubists** (KYOO-bihsts) *n.* artists whose work represents geometric figures
10. **surrealists** (suh-REE-uhl-ihsts) *n.* artists who use images from the unconscious
11. **Tsarist dissidents** (ZAHR-ihst DIHS-uh-duhnts) followers of the Russian emperor who disagree with a political policy

in a place called Greater Hungary, or the Irish, who came from the Iberian Peninsula?

Even the notion that North America is part of Western civilization because our "system of government" is derived from Europe is being challenged by Native American historians who say that the founding fathers, Benjamin Franklin especially, were actually influenced by the system of government that had been adopted by the Iroquois hundreds of years prior to the arrival of large numbers of Europeans.

Western civilization, then, becomes another confusing category like Third World, or Judeo-Christian culture, as man attempts to impose his small-screen view of political and cultural reality upon a complex world. Our most publicized novelist recently said that Western civilization was the greatest achievement of mankind, an attitude that flourishes on the street level as scribbles in public restrooms: "White Power," . . . or "Hitler was a prophet," the latter being the most telling, for wasn't Adolf Hitler the archetypal[12] monoculturalist who, in his pigheaded arrogance, believed that one way and one blood was so pure that it had to be protected from alien strains at all costs? Where did such an attitude, which has caused so much misery and depression in our national life, which has tainted even our noblest achievements, begin? An attitude that caused the incarceration of Japanese-American citizens during World War II, the persecution of Chicanos and Chinese Americans, the near-extermination of the Indians, and the murder and lynchings of thousands of Afro-Americans.

Virtuous, hardworking, pious, even though they occasionally would wander off after some fancy clothes, or rendezvous in the woods with the town prostitute, the Puritans are idealized in our schoolbooks as "a hardy band" of no-nonsense patriarchs whose discipline razed[13] the forest and brought order to the New World (a term that annoys Native American historians). Industrious, responsible, it was their "Yankee ingenuity" and practicality that created the work ethic. They were simple folk who produced a number of good poets, and they set the tone for the American writing style, of lean and spare lines, long before Hemingway. They worshiped in churches whose colors blended in with the New England snow, churches with simple structures and ornate[14] lecterns.

The Puritans were a daring lot, but they had a mean streak. They hated the theater and banned Christmas. They punished people in a cruel and inhuman manner. They killed children who disobeyed their parents. When they came in contact with those whom they considered

---

12. **archetypal** (ahr-kuh-TEYEP-uhl) *adj.* original
13. **patriarchs . . . razed** (PAY-tree-ahrks) . . . (RAYZD) *n.* rulers . . . destroyed
14. **ornate** (ohr-NAYT) *adj.* much decorated

heathens or aliens, they behaved in such a bizarre and irrational manner that this chapter in the American history comes down to us as a late-movie horror film. They exterminated the Indians, who taught them how to survive in a world unknown to them, and their encounter with the calypso culture of Barbados resulted in what the tourist guide in Salem's Witches' House refers to as the Witchcraft Hysteria.

The Puritan legacy of hard work and meticulous[15] accounting led to the establishment of a great industrial society; it is no wonder that the American industrial revolution began in Lowell, Massachusetts, but there was the other side, the strange and paranoid[16] attitudes toward those different from the Elect.

The cultural attitudes of that early Elect continue to be voiced in everyday life in the United States: the president of a distinguished university, writing a letter to the *Times*, belittling the study of African civilizations; the television network that promoted its show on the Vatican art with the boast that this art represented "the finest achievements of the human spirit." A modern up-tempo state of complex rhythms that depends upon contacts with an international community can no longer behave as if it dwelled in a "Zion Wilderness" surrounded by beasts and pagans.[17]

When I heard a schoolteacher warn the other night about the invasion of the American educational system by foreign curriculums, I wanted to yell at the television set, "Lady, they're already here." It has already begun because the world is here. The world has been arriving at these shores for at least ten thousand years from Europe, Africa, and Asia. In the late nineteenth and early twentieth centuries, large numbers of Europeans arrived, adding their cultures to those of the European, African, and Asian settlers who were already here, and recently millions have been entering the country from South America and the Caribbean, making Yale Professor Bob Thompson's bouillabaisse richer and thicker.

One of our most visionary[18] politicians said that he envisioned a time when the United States could become the brain of the world, by which he meant the repository[19] of all of the latest advanced information systems. I thought of that remark when an enterprising[20] poet friend of mine called to say that he had just sold a poem to a computer magazine and that the editors were delighted to get it because they

---

15. **meticulous** (muh-TIHK-yoo-luhs) *adj.* extremely careful
16. **paranoid** (PAR-uh-noid) *adj.* very suspicious
17. **pagans** (PAY-guhnz) *n.* people with no religion
18. **visionary** (VIHZH-uhn-air-ee) *adj.* imaginative
19. **repository** (rih-PAHZ-uh-tawr-ee) *n.* place where things are stored
20. **enterprising** (EN-tuhr-preye-zihng) *adj.* ready to try something new

didn't carry fiction or poetry. Is that the kind of world we desire? A humdrum homogeneous[21] world of all brains and no heart, no fiction, no poetry; a world of robots with human attendants bereft[22] of imagination, of culture? Or does North America deserve a more exciting destiny? To become a place where the cultures of the world crisscross. This is possible because the United States is unique in the world. The world is here.

---

21. **homogeneous** (hoh-muh-JEE-nee-uhs) *adj.* similar; of the same kind
22. **bereft** (bih-REFT) *adj.* deprived of; loss

POSTREADING

Critical Thinking

1. What does this essay tell you about Ishmael Reed's ideas and attitudes concerning a multicultural society in the United States?
2. What life experiences or historical factors do you think may have influenced Reed in writing this essay?
3. Has Reed's essay affected the way you feel about living in a multicultural society? If so, how? How do Reed's ideas about overcoming cultural barriers compare or contrast with your own?

Writing Your Response to "America: The Multinational Society"

In your journal, write about an idea in the essay that particularly interests you or about a question the essay provokes. What is it about this idea or question that is meaningful to you? How does it relate to an experience that you have had?

Going Back Into the Text: Author's Craft

When one event brings about another event, the first is said to be the **cause** and the second the **effect**. In fiction, the plot is a series of causes and effects. In political or historical writing, such as Ishmael Reed's essay, writers often explain aspects of history or society by describing causes and effects.

With a partner, review Reed's essay to see how he describes causes and effects. Use the following questions as guidelines.

1. How does Reed use cause and effect to show that U.S. society is a type of "cultural bouillabaisse"?
2. According to Reed, what was the cause of Japanese American internment, the near-extermination of Native Americans, and the lynching of thousands of African Americans in this country?
3. Find another cause-and-effect relationship in the essay. How does Reed use it to strengthen his position?

For My People
Let America Be America Again

Reading the Authors in a Cultural Context

Margaret Walker is a writer of many "firsts." Her novel *Jubilee* was the first historical African American novel to call for the social liberation of African American women.

She was also one of the youngest African American writers to publish a full volume of poetry. When she won the Yale Younger Poets Award in 1942 for *For My People*, from which this poem was taken, she was the first African American woman honored in a national poetry competition. Her purpose in writing these poems was to express cultural unity for African Americans. Most are about folk heroes who struggle against terrible obstacles—as many African Americans do today. The figures portrayed overcome their problems with great style.

Walker did exactly that in her own life. Even though she earned a doctoral degree from the University of Iowa, she faced discrimination in her teaching career there. Despite this, she was eventually able to direct an African American studies program at Jackson State University.

Margaret Walker succeeded, as her characters do, because of hope—hope she said all people should feel. "Writers should not write exclusively for black or white audiences . . . it is the business of all writers to write about the human condition," Walker said.

The African American poet Langston Hughes had the same view. He celebrated humanity's great diversity of people, beliefs, and cultures. His early poetic works made him a leading figure of the Harlem Renaissance. Like Walker, Hughes envisioned a world in which people of different cultural and ethnic backgrounds would live together peacefully. This philosophy alienated him from some African Americans who believed in separation of African Americans and whites.

Like Walker, Hughes also wrote about heroes, although these are not superhuman characters. They are everyday people—individuals who daily face losing their jobs and having their furniture repossessed, but who have the courage to venture out again to find new jobs and create new lives. Hughes was criticized for writing about ordinary African Americans and for using dialect. Some African Americans wanted to see only successful role models portrayed. Hughes responded by saying "I knew only the people I had grown up with, and they weren't people whose shoes were always shined . . . . But they seemed to me good people, too."

Focusing on the Selections

As you read the following poems, consider the values and beliefs shared by the speakers in the poems. How do the poems speak to all people, in addition to African Americans? How does each poet use lists to help shape his or her poem? Write your responses in your journal.

For My People

MARGARET WALKER

For my people everywhere singing their slave songs
        repeatedly: their dirges and their ditties and their blues
        and jubilees,[1] praying their prayers nightly to an
        unknown god, bending their knees humbly to an
        unseen power;

For my people lending their strength to the years, to the
        gone years and the now years and the maybe years,
        washing ironing cooking scrubbing sewing mending
        hoeing plowing digging planting pruning patching
        dragging along never gaining never reaping never
        knowing and never understanding;

For my playmates in the clay and dust and sand of Alabama
        backyards playing baptizing and preaching and doctor
        and jail and soldier and school and mama and cooking
        and playhouse and concert and store and hair and Miss
        Choomby and company;

For the cramped bewildered years we went to school to learn
        to know the reasons why and the answers to and the
        people who and the places where and the days when, in
        memory of the bitter hours when we discovered we
        were black and poor and small and different and nobody
        cared and nobody wondered and nobody understood;

For the boys and girls who grew in spite of these things to
        be man and woman, to laugh and dance and sing and
        play and drink their wine and religion and success, to
        marry their playmates and bear children and then die
        of consumption and anemia and lynching;[2]

---

1. **dirges** (DERJ-uhz) . . . **ditties** (DIHT-eez) . . . **jubilees** (joo-buhl-EEZ) *n.* African
   American songs: funeral songs; short, simple songs; and folk songs about a happy
   time in the future
2. **consumption** (kuhn-SUMP-shuhn) . . . **anemia** (ah-NEEM-eeuh) . . . **lynching**
   (LIHNCH-ihng) a lung disease . . . a blood condition. . . murder by a mob

Yesterday, Today and Tomorrow. Ink drawing by
African American artist Charles White, 1968.

For my people thronging 47th Street in Chicago and Lenox
      Avenue in New York and Rampart Street in New
      Orleans, lost disinherited dispossessed[3] and happy
      people filling the cabarets and taverns and other
      people's pockets needing bread and shoes and milk and
      land and money and something—something all our own;

For my people walking blindly spreading joy, losing time
      being lazy, sleeping when hungry, shouting when
      burdened, drinking when hopeless, tied, and shackled
      and tangled among ourselves by the unseen creatures
      who tower over us omnisciently[4] and laugh;

---

3. dispossessed (dihs-poh-ZEST) *adj.* forced to give up possessions such as a house
   or land
4. omnisciently (ahm-NIHSH-uhnt-lee) *adv.* having complete knowledge

For my people blundering and groping and floundering in
the dark of churches and schools and clubs and
societies, associations and councils and committees and
conventions, distressed and disturbed and deceived and
devoured by money-hungry glory-craving leeches,[5]
preyed on by facile[6] force of state and fad and novelty, by
false prophet and holy believer;

For my people standing staring trying to fashion a better way
from confusion, from hypocrisy and misunderstanding,
trying to fashion a world that will hold all the people,
all the faces, all the adams and eves and their countless
generations;

Let a new earth rise. Let another world be born. Let a
bloody peace be written in the sky. Let a second
generation full of courage issue forth; let a people
loving freedom come to growth. Let a beauty full of
healing and a strength of final clenching be the pulsing
in our spirits and our blood. Let the martial songs be
written, let the dirges disappear. Let a race of men now
rise and take control.

---

5. **leeches** (LEECH-uhz) *n.* people who try to get what they want without earning it
6. **facile** (FAS-uhl) *adj.* easily managed

Let America Be America Again

LANGSTON HUGHES

Let America be America again.
Let it be the dream it used to be.
Let it be the pioneer on the plain
Seeking a home where he himself is free.

(America never was America to me.)

Let America be the dream the dreamers dreamed—
Let it be that great strong land of love
Where never kings connive nor tyrants scheme
That any man be crushed by one above.

(It never was America to me.)

O, let my land be a land where Liberty
Is crowned with no false patriotic wreath,
But opportunity is real, and life is free,
Equality is in the air we breathe.

(There's never been equality for me,
Nor freedom in this "homeland of the free.")

Say who are you that mumbles in the dark?
And who are you that draws your veil across the stars?

I am the poor white, fooled and pushed apart,
I am the Negro bearing slavery's scars.
I am the red man driven from the land,
I am the immigrant clutching the hope I seek—
And finding only the same old stupid plan
Of dog eat dog, of mighty crush the weak.

I am the young man, full of strength and hope,
Tangled in that ancient endless chain
Of profit, power, gain, of grab the land!
Of grab the gold! Of grab the ways of satisfying need!
Of work the men! Of take the pay!
Of owning everything for one's own greed!

I am the farmer, bondsman[1] to the soil.
I am the worker sold to the machine.
I am the Negro, servant to you all.
I am the people, worried, hungry, mean—
Hungry yet today despite the dream.
Beaten yet today—O, Pioneers!
I am the man who never got ahead,
The poorest worker bartered[2] through the years.

Yet I'm the one who dreamt our basic dream
In that Old World while still a serf[3] of kings,
Who dreamt a dream so strong, so brave, so true,
That even yet its mighty daring sings
In every brick and stone, in every furrow[4] turned
That's made America the land it has become.
O, I'm the man who sailed those early seas
In search of what I meant to be my home—
For I'm the one who left dark Ireland's shore,
And Poland's plain, and England's grassy lea,
And torn from Black Africa's strand[5] I came
To build a "homeland of the free."
The free?

A dream—
Still beckoning to me!

---

1. bondsman (BAHNDZ-muhn) *n.* slave
2. bartered (BAHR-tuhrd) *v.* traded
3. serf (SERF) *n.* slave
4. furrow (FUHR-oh) *n.* a groove cut in the land by a plow
5. strand (STRAND) *n.* shore

O, let America be America again—
The land that never has been yet—
And yet must be—
The land where *every* man is free.
The land that's mine—
The poor man's, Indian's, Negro's, ME—
Who made America,
Whose sweat and blood, whose faith and pain,
Whose hand at the foundry, whose plow in the rain,
Must bring back our mighty dream again.

Sure, call me any ugly name you choose—
The steel of freedom does not stain.
From those who live like leeches on the people's lives,
We must take back our land again,
America!

O, yes,
I say it plain,
America never was America to me,
And yet I swear this oath—
America will be!
An ever-living seed,
Its dream
Lies deep in the heart of me.

We, the people, must redeem
Our land, the mines, the plants, the rivers,
The mountains and the endless plain—
All, all the stretch of these great green states—
And make America again!

POSTREADING

Critical Thinking

1. What do Walker and Hughes tell you about their ideas and attitudes concerning the hardships many groups, particularly African Americans, have endured in this country?
2. What values, beliefs, and goals do the poets share? What differences can you find between their ideas?
3. Evaluate the solutions these poets suggest for overcoming tension in the United States. Do you agree with their solutions? Why or why not?

Writing Your Response to "For My People" and "Let America Be America Again"

In your journal, write about an idea, image, or description in one of the poems that is especially striking or memorable to you. Why is it meaningful? How does it relate to something in your own life? Do either of these poems express goals or values that are important in your own life? If so, in what ways?

Going Back Into the Text: Author's Craft

Free verse is poetry that does not use regular rhyme or fixed rhythm. Instead, poets often use techniques such as repetition to structure their poems and to achieve certain effects. Another structuring technique often used in free verse is **cataloging**. A catalog is a list of things, people, places, or events. Poets use catalogs to suggest diversity, to establish a setting, or to develop a theme.

With a partner, review the poems by Margaret Walker and Langston Hughes to see how they use cataloging. The following questions can serve as guidelines.

1. What idea does the catalog in the second stanza of "For My People" help to convey? How is this catalog linked to the larger meaning of the poem?
2. How do the catalogs in "Let America Be America Again" suggest inclusion?
3. What other example of a catalog can you identify in a poem or song? How does this catalog develop the theme of the work?

MAKING CONNECTIONS

African American Traditions

In the 1920s, many African American writers, artists, and musicians were drawn to Harlem, a section of New York City. There, they encouraged and influenced one another's work. This outpouring of creativity was called the Harlem Renaissance.

The 1920s is a period often called the golden age of jazz. Jazz has its roots in the rhythms of West Africa, gospel songs and spirituals, and work songs from the days of enslavement. African Americans such as Jelly Roll Morton, shown here at the piano, helped to create and popularize this form of music.

Rise shine for thy light has come!

In the 1700s, an African said of his homeland, "We are almost a nation of dancers, musicians, and poets." Artists like Aaron Douglas remind viewers of that legacy by using music as a symbol of African American pride. The piece by Douglas shown here is called *Rise, Shine for Thy Light Has Come*.

LINKING
Literature, Culture, and Theme

Compare the roles of music and art in African American culture with the views about community expressed in Margaret Walker's "For My People" and Langston Hughes's "Let America Be America Again."

▼ What kinds of songs does Margaret Walker mention? How does she view their role in the African American community?

▼ What elements of African music can you find in Langston Hughes's poem? What effects do these elements help create in the poem? How do they contribute to the theme of the poem?

▼ Youssou N'Dour, a singer from Senegal in Africa, has said: "Music has no language—it has no frontiers. It's a message that people receive directly. And they get the message of African music through the rhythm, the groove." How do music and art break down barriers and create unity among peoples? Which writer or artist represented in this section best achieves these goals?

Richmond Barthe, whose portrait is shown here, is best known as a sculptor. His work expresses the grace, strength, and affirmation of African Americans in their cultural traditions. Musicians and dancers figure prominently in his work.

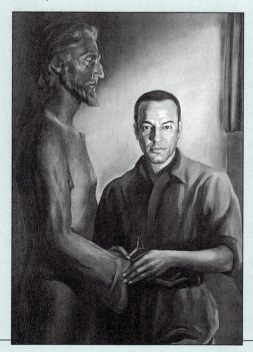

Petey and Yotsee and Mario

Reading the Author in a Cultural Context

Henry Roth grew up in the crowded tenements of New York City. Like most of his neighbors, who also lived in the tiny apartments, Roth was an immigrant. He was born in Austria-Hungary, which was then an empire in central Europe. In 1908, he came with his parents to the United States and settled on the Lower East Side of New York, an immigrant community described as one of the most crowded places on earth.

The Roths, like other Jewish immigrants, emigrated to escape the economic hardships and religious persecution that existed in Eastern Europe. Even though they had lived in the region for centuries, Jews were viewed as outsiders, and had no rights or opportunities. In some countries, Jews were not allowed to own land. They could be expelled at a moment's notice. Thousands were killed in pogroms (poh-GRAHMZ)—government-sponsored massacres—such as those in Poland and Russia.

Most Eastern European Jews settled in the industrial cities of the East and Midwest of the United States. In New York City, many found work in clothing factories. Immigrant workers often worked 13 hours a day, sometimes earning as little as five or six dollars a week. They knew they were being treated unfairly, but were grateful for the work and inspired by the freedoms and opportunities available.

The Roths were eager to take full advantage of those opportunities. Within a few years, the family moved to a better neighborhood in Harlem. But to young Henry, the move was terrifying. He left the safety of a mostly Jewish neighborhood for one that was ethnically mixed. During Roth's early years, he discovered that anti-semitism was not limited to Eastern Europe. It also existed in the United States.

Roth, like other young immigrants, was caught between two cultures. At home, his family spoke Yiddish (YIHD-ihsh), a dialect spoken by many Eastern European Jews that includes words from German, Hebrew, Russian, Polish, and English. They also followed the traditions they learned in Europe. At school, everyone spoke English and had different customs and traditions. Roth wanted to be like the other students, but he also wanted to please his parents. This conflict is reflected in his famous novel *Call It Sleep*. Published in 1934, the book explores the Jewish immigrant experience through the eyes of a frightened young boy. In 1956, he wrote "Petey and Yotsee and Mario." This story offers another perspective on the struggles that shaped Henry Roth's life.

Focusing on the Selection

As you read the following story, think about Fat's feelings about his heritage. What do you think Roth is saying about breaking down cultural barriers? What solution does the story suggest for developing a sense of community? What is the advantage of telling the story from Fat's point of view? Write your responses in your journal.

Petey and Yotsee and Mario

July 14, 1956

HENRY ROTH

THERE WAS A DOCK that stretched out into the Harlem River at about 130th Street, a few blocks north of the New York Central and New Haven station; the trestle[1] of the railroad crossed the river only a short distance from where we swam. To the west was the Madison Avenue turn bridge, and across the river were the freight yards and a large lumberyard. Below us, the big bucket of a coal company crane pounded monotonously into the hold of a scow[2] and issued dripping lumps of coal. Tugs wallowed[3] by, solitary sometimes, or towing barges, their bow mats like brown mustaches over foam. We went in when the tide was high; the water looked cleaner then and covered the mud flats. We sat on the torrid,[4] splintery dock and slipped into our trunks[5]— tights, we called them—and dived off.

I had just learned to swim that summer, and was already considered a fair swimmer, though nothing in comparison with Petey and Yotsee

---

1. **trestle** (TRES-uhl) *n.* railroad bridge
2. **scow** (SKOW) *n.* a large, flat-bottom boat used to carry freight
3. **wallowed** (WAHL-ohd) *v.* rolled with pleasure
4. **torrid** (TAWR-uhd) *adj.* very hot
5. **trunks** (TRUNKS) *n.* short pants worn by athletes

and Mario, who were there from my block. They swam with a special Sunday stroke, an overhand that slapped the water with a kind of strict flip of the wrist, and they kept their chests above the surface. I hadn't mastered that yet.

One day, I swam out into the river. It looked inviting. And whether the changing tide pulled me out farther than I realized or I allowed myself to be lured[6] out farther, I don't know, but when I turned back, I found myself at a considerable distance from the dock, and also found that I was tired. And then the inevitable unforeseen happened: a passing tug sent a following wave over me that left me gasping and gagging. I tried to regulate my breathing again and move those leaden arms. But if I was gaining on the dock, it wasn't apparent; it seemed in motion itself, away from me. And now the rebound from the original wave slapped me in the face, and I was really beginning to flounder.[7] Consciousness became an alternation between glimpses of sunlight on weathered dock and somewhat longer glimpses of pale-green water. I heard the cry go up from the dock: "Hey, Fat's drownin'!"

They came splashing toward me, all three of them—Petey and Yotsee and Mario.

"I'm all right," I gasped when they reached me. I could feel hands under me as I labored forward. I could hear their laughter. They towed me in toward the dock, swimming on their backs and screaming with laughter. And then they gave me a final shove toward the slimy piles and I climbed up the makeshift ladder. I sat panting on the dock while they climbed, too. "Gee, I must have been drowning," I said.

"You musta been," Petey said.

"You wasn't drownin'. You was just fetchin' way down," Yotsee said.

"He wasn't drownin'," said Mario. "He was just tryin' to dive to the bottom and run like hell for the shore!"

And, overcome with mirth,[8] they bellywhopped off the dock.

When I got home, I told my mother and my sister what had happened.

"Thank God!" said my mother. "Blessed Gentile children to save you! May the Almighty bestow[9] on them that joy they bestow on me!"

"You're a dope to go out so far," said my sister.

"I didn't know I was out that far," I protested.

"Why didn't you look back?"

"I know," said my mother. "I'm going to bake them a cake."

"What?"

---

6. **lured** (LOORD) *v.* tempted
7. **flounder** (FLOWN-duhr) *v.* struggle awkwardly
8. **mirth** (MERTH) *n.* joy
9. **bestow** (bee-STOH) *v.* give as a gift

"I'm going to bake them a cake. Now. A big one." She was already clearing a space on the covered washtubs for her earthenware mixing bowl.

"Aw, Mom," I said. "That ain't what—" I couldn't express it. "Don't bake them no cake."

"Why not?"

"Aw, you bake Jewish cakes."

"And what kind of cakes are not Jewish cakes?"

"Oh, you know. Like in the store. Ward's. Tip-Top. Golden Queen. Like that."

"Go, go," she said. "I'll bake them a spicecake."

"It's Jewish."

"Don't be a fool," said my mother.

She baked them a spicecake. It was embossed[10] with walnuts, dark with crystallized honey, and full of raisins—our typical holiday spicecake.

"Well," she said, exhibiting it when it had cooled. "Who needs to be ashamed of this? Will you give it to them or not?"

"Aw, Mom, they don't understand cakes like that."

"Are they in the street?"

"Yes."

"Then come with me." She slipped the cake carefully into a paper bag, and I followed her reluctantly down the stairs and into the street. "Where are they?"

"There. There's Petey—with the handball. There's Yotsee. Mario is by the cellar. Those three."

"Come."

I trailed her across the street. The three boys were lolling[11] in front of the candy store, just east of the corner.

"You, Petey. You, Mario," she said, and they lifted their tough lean faces.

"And what is the other's name?" she asked, turning to me.

"Yotsee. Yotsee Hunt."

"And you. Yotsee. You should be blessed for saving my son."

"Oh," Petey said. They understood.

"That's nothin'," Yotsee said.

"Fat's—I mean, he's from the block." Mario sent his finger through a curve of explanation.

"You—If I could talk better," she said, "I would tell you. You all got mamas. They understand. Sometime you ask them, they'll explain you."

---

10. **embossed** (ihm-BAWSD) *v.* decorated with a design that stands out from the surface

11. **lolling** (LAHL-ihng) *v.* hanging around

What does this photograph tell you about "Breaking Down Barriers and Building Communities"?

"Aw, we won't tell 'em. What's the difference?" said Yotsee.

"Here's from me a cake."

They stared at her. "For us?" Petey asked.

"It's for you. You should remember."

They took it from her—Petey took it. "Thanks," he said.

"You're welcome," my mother said.

I followed her back to the stoop,[12] and there we stood a little while, watching them. Petey was brandishing[13] the cake aloft. "Hey, Weasel! Look!" The rest of the gang converged on them. We could hear their avid[14] cries: "What about us?" "Hey, what about a hunk?" The cake was broken and divided and eaten with gusto. Still munching, Mario pointed us out. My mother nodded in acknowledgment.

"You see?" She turned to me. "What were you afraid of?"

"I don't know."

"You were afraid they wouldn't like Jewish cake. What kind of people would they be if they didn't like Jewish cake? Would they have even saved you?" she said, and went into the house.

---

12. stoop (STOOP) *n.* a porch at the entrance of a house

13. brandishing (BRAN-dihsh-ihng) *v.* waving

14. avid (AV-ihd) *adj.* greedy

POSTREADING

Critical Thinking

1. What does this story tell you about Henry Roth's attitude toward embracing one's heritage?
2. What aspects of Roth's personal experiences and background do you think influenced his writing of this story?
3. Has reading this story influenced your attitude toward religious or other cultural differences between you and your friends? If so, explain how.

Writing Your Response to "Petey and Yotsee and Mario"

In your journal, write about an idea, question, or feeling you had while reading Henry Roth's story. What aspect of the story made you think or feel this way? Does the story relate to an experience in your own life? If so, how?

Going Back Into the Text: Author's Craft

A **short story** is a brief work of fiction. Unlike longer forms of fiction, such as the novel, short stories usually have a simple plot and a single setting and do not develop all aspects of the characters fully. In many short stories, as in "Petey and Yotsee and Mario," a single aspect of a character's personality is revealed or is changed as a result of the central conflict.

In discussions about literature, the term *point of view* refers to the angle from which a story is told. The most commonly used points of view are *first-person*, *limited third-person*, and *omniscient third-person*. When the first-person point of view is used, the narrator, or teller of the story, is a character in the story and refers to himself or herself with the first-person pronoun *I* or *me*.

The two types of third-person points of view use third-person pronouns such as *he* and *she* to refer to the characters. The third-person limited narrator conveys the thoughts and feelings of only one character. All the events in the story are viewed from that character's perspective. The third-person omniscient narrator knows and reveals what each character in the story thinks and feels.

With a partner, review "Petey and Yotsee and Mario" to see how Henry Roth uses point of view. The following questions can serve as guidelines.

1. What point of view is used in the story?
2. Why is this point of view effective for the story?
3. How do you think the story would be different if it were told from the point of view of Fat's mother?

AmeRícan
Ending Poem
Instructions for joining a new society

Reading the Authors in a Cultural Context

The three poems that follow were written by Hispanic poets from islands in the Caribbean Sea. Tato Laviera (TAH-toh lah-VEEAI-rah) was born in Puerto Rico. He arrived in New York City in 1960 at the age of 10 and spent his adolescent years in a Spanish-speaking neighborhood, or barrio. Like many immigrants, he suffered from poverty and a sense of alienation from mainstream U.S. society. In much of his poetry, Laviera depicts the people of the barrio. These communities survive by making a place for the Hispanic and Afro-Caribbean traditions of their homeland within the dominant U.S. culture. His poem "AmeRícan" conveys a sense of reconciliation with mainstream society and a new generation that celebrates the many cultures that form U.S. society.

Aurora Levins Morales was also born in Puerto Rico. She is the daughter of a Jewish American father and a Puerto Rican mother. Levins Morales describes herself as raised on "books and social justice." "Ending Poem" is from a book called *Getting Home Alive*, which Morales wrote with her mother, Rosario. Born in New York City, Rosario Morales moved to Puerto Rico with her husband, who was trying to avoid the draft during the Korean War. The couple, enthusiastic antiwar activists, settled on a piece of an abandoned coffee plantation and learned about the land.

Getting Home Alive is an exploration of the lives of two Puerto Rican women who were born in very different places but share the same complex cultural heritage. Notice how "Ending Poem" examines the mixing of Puerto Rican and mainstream U.S. cultures, as well as the Jewish, African, and European influences that make up the Morales family.

"Instructions for joining a new society" was written by Cuban poet Heberto Padilla. Padilla was arrested, imprisoned, and finally banished from Cuba by Fidel Castro's Communist regime. He now lives in exile in the United States. Padilla's poetry often explores the relationship of the individual to society, capturing the estrangement he himself experienced—first in Castro's Cuba and then in the United States. Observe how Padilla conveys both his reluctance and his desire to become an American in "Instructions for joining a new society."

Focusing on the Selections

As you read the following poems, think about each poet's perspective on cultural barriers. What are the writers' thoughts on building communities in the United States? What similarities can you see among the ideas conveyed in these poems? How do the poets use the repetition of sounds to emphasize ideas? Write your responses in your journal.

AmeRícan[1]

TATO LAVIERA

we gave birth to a new generation,
AmeRícan, broader than lost gold
never touched, hidden inside the
puerto rican mountains.

we gave birth to a new generation,
AmeRícan, it includes everything
imaginable you-name-it-we-got-it
society.

we gave birth to a new generation,
AmeRícan salutes all folklores,
european, indian, black, spanish,
and anything else compatible:

AmeRícan,   singing to composer pedro flores'[2] palm
                  trees high up in the universal sky!

AmeRícan,   sweet soft spanish danzas[3] gypsies
                  moving lyrics la española cascabelling[4]
                  presence always singing at our side!

AmeRícan,   beating jíbaro modern troubadours
                  crying guitars romantic continental
                  bolero love songs!

---

1. **AmeRícan** (ah-may-REE-kahn) *n.* a word made up of *American* and *Puerto Rican*
2. **pedro flores** (PAY-droh FLOH-rays) *n.* a Puerto Rican composer
3. **danzas** (DAHN-sahs) *n.* dances
4. **la española cascabelling** (lah ays-pahn-NYOH-lah kahs-kah-BEL-lihng) the
   Spanish woman ringing (Spanish word combined with English suffix)

AmeRícan,   across forth and across back
back across and forth back
forth across and back and forth
our trips are walking bridges!

it all dissolved into itself, the attempt
was truly made, the attempt was truly
absorbed, digested, we spit out
the poison, we spit out the malice,
we stand, affirmative in action,
to reproduce a broader answer to the
marginality that gobbled us up abruptly!

AmeRícan,   walking plena-rhythms[5] in new york,
strutting beautifully alert, alive,
many turning eyes wondering,
admiring!

AmeRícan,   defining myself my own way any way many
ways Am e Rícan, with the big R and the
accent on the í!

AmeRícan,   like the soul gliding talk of gospel
boogie music!

AmeRícan,   speaking new words in spanglish[6] tenements,
fast tongue moving street corner "que
corta"[7] talk being invented at the insistence
of a smile!

---

5. plena-rhythms (PLAY-nah) *n.* a kind of music invented in Puerto Rico
6. spanglish (SPAN-glihsh) *n.* combination of Spanish and English
7. que corta (kay KOR-tah) *adj.* sharp

AmeRícan,   abounding inside so many ethnic english
people, and out of humanity, we blend
and mix all that is good!

AmeRícan,   integrating in new york and defining our
own destino,[8] our own way of life,

AmeRícan,   defining the new america, humane america,
admired america, loved america, harmonious
america, the world in peace, our energies
collectively invested to find other civilizations, to touch God, further and further,
to dwell in the spirit of divinity!

AmeRícan,   yes, for now, for i love this, my second
land, and i dream to take the accent from
the altercation,[9] and be proud to call
myself american, in the u.s. sense of the
word, AmeRícan, America!

---

8. **destino** (days-TEE-noh) *n.* destiny
9. **altercation** (awl-ter-CAY-shuhn) *n.* quarrel

Ending Poem

AURORA LEVINS MORALES AND ROSARIO MORALES

I am what I am.
A child of the Americas.
A light-skinned mestiza[1] of the Caribbean.
A child of many diaspora, born into this continent at a crossroads.
I am Puerto Rican. I am U.S. American.
I am New York Manhattan and the Bronx.
A mountain-born, country-bred, homegrown jíbara[2] child,
up from the shtetl,[3] a California Puerto Rican Jew.
A product of the New York ghettos I have never known.
I am an immigrant
and the daughter and granddaughter of immigrants.
We didn't know our forbears' names with a certainty.
They aren't written anywhere.
First names only, or mija, negra, ne,[4] honey, sugar, dear.

I come from the dirt where the cane was grown.
My people didn't go to dinner parties. They weren't invited.
I am caribeña, island grown.
Spanish is in my flesh, ripples from my tongue, lodges in my hips,
the language of garlic and mangoes.
Boricua. As Boricuas come from the isle of Manhattan.
I am of latinoamerica, rooted in the history of my continent.
I speak from that body. Just brown and pink and full of drums inside.

I am not African.
Africa waters the roots of my tree, but I cannot return.

I am not Taína.
I am a late leaf of that ancient tree,
and my roots reach into the soil of two Americas.
Taíno is in me, but there is no way back.

---

1. **mestiza** (may-STEE-sah) *n.* woman of mixed race
2. **jíbara** (HEE-bah-rah) *n.* Puerto Rican peasant woman
3. **shtetl** (SHTET-uhl) *n.* small Jewish village formerly found in eastern Europe
4. **mija, negra, ne** (MEE-hah, NAY-grah, NAY) *n.* my daughter (a shortened form of *mi hija*), black woman, baby (a shortened form of *nena*)

I am not European, though I have dreamt of those cities.
Each plate is different,
wood, clay, papier mâché, metal, basketry, a leaf, a coconut shell.
Europe lives in me but I have no home there.

The table has a cloth woven by one, dyed by another,
embroidered by another still.
I am a child of many mothers.
They have kept it all going
All the civilizations erected on their backs.
All the dinner parties given with their labor.

We are new.
They gave us life, kept us going,
brought us to where we are.
Born at a crossroads.
Come, lay that dishcloth down. Eat, dear, eat.
History made us.
We will not eat ourselves up inside anymore.

And we are whole.

Instructions for joining a new society

HEBERTO PADILLA

One: Be optimistic.
Two: Be well turned out, courteous, obedient.
(Must have made the grade in sports.)
And finally, walk
as every member does:
one step forward
and two or three back;
but always applauding, applauding.

POSTREADING

Critical Thinking

1. What do these poets tell you about their attitudes toward the diversity of their cultural backgrounds? What are their feelings about breaking down cultural barriers?
2. What events in each poet's life do you think most influenced these attitudes?
3. How has reading these poems influenced your own attitudes about the joining of cultures in U.S. society?

Writing Your Response to "AmeRícan," "Ending Poem," and "Instructions for joining a new society"

What idea, image, or description in one of the poems has special meaning for you? Write about it in your journal. Why is it special? How does it relate to your own life?

Going Back Into the Text: Author's Craft

Alliteration is the repetition of similar sounds, usually consonants, in a group of words. For example, notice the repetition of the *s* sound in "The sun sank slowly over the sea." When alliteration occurs at the beginning of words, which it most often does, it is called *initial alliteration*. When alliteration occurs within words, it is called *internal* or *hidden alliteration*. An example is the repetition of the *t* sound in "little white buttons." Poets and other writers use alliteration to link and to emphasize ideas, as well as to create musical sounds and pleasing rhythms. The use of alliteration is also a way for poets to make their poems easier for readers to memorize.

With a partner, review the poems to see how each poet uses alliteration. The following questions can serve as guidelines during your discussion.

1. In "Ending Poem," find an example of initial alliteration and an example of internal alliteration.
2. What ideas does alliteration link or emphasize in this poem?
3. Find an example of alliteration in one of the other two poems. What effect does it help create?

from Seven Arrows

Reading the Author in a Cultural Context

Throughout their history, the Native American nations of the Great Plains, such as the Cheyenne, the Crow, and the Lakota, have told tales as a way of understanding themselves and the world around them. Because these nations did not have a written language, their stories were memorized and passed down orally. Their conversational tone reflects the fact that they were spoken and listened to, rather than read. Part of the art of telling a story includes emphasizing certain words to signal symbolic or multiple meanings. As you read, try to imagine you are hearing the story being told aloud. What words might be emphasized?

The Plains nations' system of belief centers on certain symbols that represent the many facets of life. For instance, the circle of the Medicine Wheel represents all the people, animals, rocks, rivers, and religions in the entire universe. Each part of the circle is connected to all other parts. The philosophy, or way of perceiving life, of the Plains nations focuses on gaining understanding—of yourself, of your fellow human beings, of the natural wonders of the world, and of your place in that world. The way to achieve this understanding is to experience all life as part of the circle of the Medicine Wheel. All peoples and creatures are equally important in this perfect circle of understanding, growth, and connectedness.

The stories of the Plains nations are part of this understanding. As a way of preserving the traditional stories of his childhood and of teaching the philosophy of his people, Hyemeyohsts (heye-yem-EYE-yoh) Storm, a Cheyenne shield maker, wrote down many of the tales in a book called *Seven Arrows*. The tales have symbolic meanings that are intended to teach lessons about life. Storm emphasizes that no matter how well you know the stories, you never finish learning. Like the Medicine Wheel, which represents life itself, learning is a continuous, ever-changing process of growth.

In the following excerpt from *Seven Arrows*, a woman named White Rabbit, a wise teacher, explains the nature of the Medicine Wheel to a girl named Red Star. White Rabbit hopes that by learning about the traditional beliefs of their ancestors, Red Star will gain a deeper understanding of her place in her culture as well as in the universe. Think about the different levels of meaning the story contains.

Focusing on the Selection

As you read the excerpt from *Seven Arrows*, think about the traditional beliefs the story illustrates. Why are these beliefs important? How is understanding the Medicine Wheel a way to bring all people together? What attitudes about nature does the tale express? What symbols does the tale contain? Write your responses in your journal.

from **Seven Arrows**

HYEMEYOHSTS STORM

"FIRST, I WILL DRAW YOU this Medicine Wheel," White Rabbit began.

"As you see, I have drawn Eagle Lodges at all Four of the Directions," explained White Rabbit, "one to the North, one to the South, one to the East, and one to the West. When we are born into this world, we always enter into it from one of these Ways.

"Of course there are many Ways and many Medicines. I will begin with the example of the Eagle first. Some people are born with the Medicine of the Eagle. When they reach adulthood, at about nine years of age, they begin to experience this Medicine. If a person was born Yellow Eagle, he would wear the Yellow Robe of the East. This would be his Gift of Perceiving. He would be able to See Far in the things of Illumination. If this Eagle were instead to wear the Green Robe, he would still Perceive Far, but from within the Innocence of Heart of the South. If he were to wear the Black Robe, he would Perceive Far from the West, from Looks-Within. If he wore the White Robe, he would Perceive Far in the things of Knowledge. Each one of these people would be given the Beginning Medicine of the Eagle, but each one would be different. Each one would Perceive Far from whatever point he was Given as his starting Gift on the Medicine Wheel. But no person should be content with Perceiving from only One Way. It is for each person to seek the Other Ways in all that he does. It is through this seeking that he then will Grow."

"Then within these Ways are found the Names of the People!" Red Star exclaimed.

"Yes," answered White Rabbit. "We are given our beginning names almost at birth. But these are only our beginning names, and they are always names from our Clan.[1] For instance, a man or woman may be born into the Clan of Water, or Rattling Hoof, or even Kit Fox, and they will be given a beginning name of this Clan. But this name will not be who they truly are. They must then seek their true Name. This is done through the Vision Quest[2] and the Sun Dance. Through the Ways of the Brotherhood."

"Then," Red Star broke in, "the man who visited our camp who was called Night Bear had another beginning name."

"Yes, he did," White Rabbit answered. "His Clan beginning name was Bull Looks Around. He was born in the Brotherhood of the Buffalo Clan, and his uncles were all those men born into this same Clan. I spoke to him about this and discovered that he was one of my Clan uncles. Even though his language was both that of the Little Black Crow and also that of the Painted Arrow, I never knew which of these was his first tongue. He was my Clan uncle, even though I was from the People of another tongue. I was as you are, born of the Little Medicine Bird People."

"Then that handsome one was my uncle, too?" Red Star asked excitedly.

White Rabbit laughed. "I cannot know this of you, little sister. I do not know to which of the Clans your mother belonged. If your mother was of the Clan of the Buffalo, then he was your uncle."

"But then how was he given the Name of Night Bear?" asked Red Star, frowning again.

"He learned of his Name through the Vision Quest," White Rabbit answered as she began beading on some moccasins. "He spoke with the Power and was taught by Seven Arrows. He not only discovered that his Name was Bear, but he discovered that he was the Looks-Within Bear of the Four Star Colors."

"Then are his uncles of the Buffalo still his uncles?" asked Red Star.

"Yes," answered the woman, smiling. "This will never change. But what is more important is this. He discovered his Perceiving and his Brotherhood."

---

1. **Clan** (KLAN) *n.* a division within a nation; a group of several families with a common ancestor
2. **Vision Quest** a message received from the spirit world (see "Humaweepi, the Warrior Priest" in Theme 3 and "Wasichus in the Hills" in Theme 4 for more information)

"Brotherhood?" asked Red Star. "Is this Brotherhood of which you speak the one of the Shields?"

"Yes," White Rabbit answered. "Now not only does he have uncles of many tongues, but he has Brothers of many tongues. His Brothers are of the Four Stars."

"Is there more?" asked Red Star.

"Yes, there is much more," answered White Rabbit. "This is only the beginning. The next Teaching is of the *Masuam*[3], or Animal Dance. The Animal Dance is the Give-Away. Let me draw you another of these Wheels for explanation.

"Each dot I have made with my finger in the dirt is an animal," said White Rabbit. "There is no one of any of the animals in this world that can do without the next. Each whole tribe of animals is a Medicine Wheel, in that it is the One Mind. Each dot on the Great Wheel is a tribe of animals. And parts of these tribes must Give-Away in order that they all might grow. The animal tribes all know of this. It is only the tribes of People who are the ones who must learn it. It is this Way because the People were placed here upon the Earth to learn. The Power gave each person a Beginning Way to learn. That is his Medicine. And the Medicine is given to us from one of the animal tribes, because we too are animals."

"How is it you say that we are animals?" asked Red Star. "That is hard for me to believe."

"No," White Rabbit laughed. "We are not really animals. But we are of this Earth and therefore we are Medicine Animals. It is an Understanding, this Medicine Way. Those of the People who are Buffalo wish to Give-Away. That is their nature. Your own mother was one of these Medicine Gifts. The shame is that the whitemen never understood this. They used her, instead of receiving her as a Gift. It is a pity."

"Then why did she not stop giving?" Red Star asked. "Why did she take such punishment?"

"Why does one person feel almost no desire?" answered White Rabbit. "And why do others have great desire? These questions are the same with everything, and are equal. Why does one person eat more than another? Why is one more frightened? Another more greedy? Still another more shy? These questions are equal and are the same. What we must each ask ourselves is, who am I? What is my Medicine? In what Way do I Perceive? Why? Because some of us are given the Gift of Perceiving as Mice, some as Buffalo, some as Eagles, some as Foxes, and on and on and on. Each person is born with a different animal Medicine, from which he receives his own Medicine Way. But often, even when two

---

3. *Masuam* (mah-soo-AHM)

people are of the same animal Medicine, they may still Perceive differently. This depends upon where they were born on the Medicine Wheel, to the East, the South, the North, or the West. Within these many Medicine Ways we must seek our Name and our Perceiving. Now naturally, a person born with the Medicine of Wolf will not eat his brother or sister who is Buffalo. No! That would be silly. It is the Understanding that is the Gift."

"Then the girl who is a little She-Wolf is able to receive the same things Buffalo wishes to give?" Red Star asked.

"Yes," White Rabbit answered. "These people who are Buffalo have an overwhelming desire to give. If a Buffalo had married me, I no doubt would have loved him. But there is not much a Buffalo can offer to me, a Rabbit. Our Understandings are different. It is the little She-Wolf who is Hungry for Buffalo. And this little Wolf is the one who can accept her Buffalo's Gifts."

"But then how is it that the Buffalo too can be Full?" asked Red Star.

"Those who walk together are like the Twin Medicine Lakes. They are Two Mirrors. She-Wolf is Hungry for Buffalo, and Buffalo Hungers to Give-Away to the She-Wolf. They both Give in this manner. It is a Way of Understanding. It is the perfect Circle. It is a Way for all People to come together in Brotherhood, Wolves with Rabbits, Birds, Mice, and Weasels. All are beautiful and all are equal in the great Give-Away Dance. This Dance is the Sun Dance. There we learn of our Perceiving, and also of the Ways of our brothers and sisters. This Brotherhood is found among all the tongues of the People. The most powerful Sign of these things is the Understanding of the Medicines. Whenever you hear a Story, my little sister, all the Names you hear within it are Signs. These Signs are of the Medicine Wheel and its Growing. Each one is a part of the Universe. Each one is Sweet Medicine." . . .

Photograph of a medicine wheel in Boynton Canyon near Sedona, Arizona. What values and beliefs do medicine wheels like this one represent for Native Americans?

Critical Thinking

1. What does the story tell you about Storm's attitude toward the traditions and beliefs of his people?
2. Why do you think Storm used story-telling to convey information about the Medicine Wheel? How else do people pass on traditions?
3. How do you think an understanding of the Medicine Wheel can be a way of bringing all people together?

Writing Your Response to *Seven Arrows*

In your journal, write about one scene, image, character, or idea in the story that is especially meaningful to you. Can you relate any part of the tale to your own life or to the life of someone you know? If so, explain how. How do your own views about life and nature compare with the philosophy expressed in the story?

Going Back Into the Text: Author's Craft

Seven Arrows contains many allegories, such as the story about the Medicine Wheel. An **allegory** is a story with two or more levels of meaning—a literal level and one or more symbolic levels. A *symbol* is anything that stands for or represents something else. For example, a rose might be used as a symbol for love or beauty. The events, setting, and characters in an allegory are symbols for ideas or qualities. Writers use symbols to reveal the theme, or central message of their work.

With a partner, review the selection from *Seven Arrows* to see how Storm uses symbols. These questions can serve as guidelines.

1. What do the colored robes symbolize?
2. What other symbols does Storm use? What do these symbols represent?
3. How do Storm's symbols reveal the theme of the allegory?

Reviewing the Theme

1. Choose two authors in this theme and compare their ideas about breaking down barriers in a multicultural society. What is each writer's vision or hope for the future?

2. Compare the attitudes of two writers who share the same cultural heritage. How are their perspectives on building communities similar? How are they different? What does each writer propose as a possible solution to culture-based discrimination and injustice?

3. Which selection in this theme most closely expresses your ideas or opinions about social equality and harmony among different groups? Explain your answer.

FOCUSING THE UNIT THEME

COOPERATIVE/COLLABORATIVE LEARNING

With three of your classmates, discuss the works presented in this unit as they relate to the unit theme and to your own lives. Below is a sample dialogue that one group of students used to start their discussion. You may wish to use it as a starting point for your discussion. At the end of the allotted time, summarize the main ideas expressed by your group and share them with the rest of the class.

Student 1: Some of these writers talked about the conflicts within themselves. I know how they feel. As a Jewish American, I sometimes feel torn between two cultures.

Student 2: Yes, but until the dominant culture in the United States treats the different cultural groups fairly, nothing is going to change. As Malcolm X said, nonviolence on the part of African Americans isn't going to accomplish anything unless everyone practices it too.

Student 3: Not much has changed. Take the prejudice against Japanese Americans during World War II. I think a similar kind of discrimination is on the rise in this country today.

Student 4: I was interested in the different techniques the writers used to convey the same idea. For instance, Margaret Walker and Langston Hughes used cataloging to help express ideas about cultural diversity and social harmony. Henry Roth used the symbol of a spice cake to emphasize the same points.

Writing Process

Review your journal entries for this unit. Rethink your responses in terms of the unit theme. From different sections, choose two or more selections that were especially helpful to you in developing an understanding of this theme.

Write a persuasive essay that attempts to show a certain audience how a particular group has struggled against discrimination. Your audience might be a group of classmates, a political organization, or the President of the United States. Use the selections you have chosen from this unit to illustrate the problem, to strengthen your argument, and to support your proposals for change. Refer to the handbook at the back of the book to help you with the writing process, using the model essays as necessary.

Problem Solving

The combination of many cultures within one society can sometimes create a sense of disunity. Choose one or more of the authors included in this unit and analyze their insights into this problem. How are their solutions similar? How are they different? What are your ideas for a solution to the problem? How do your solutions compare to the ideas of the writers? In the form of a skit, dance, musical arrangement, art composition, news show, debate, or poem, express your thoughts and feelings about the problem and a solution. You may wish to work alone, with a partner, or in a small group.

CHINUA ACHEBE (1930–   ) is best known for his novel *Things Fall Apart*. Achebe, who was born in Ogidi, Nigeria, was nominated for the Booker Prize in 1987 for *Ant Hills of the Savannah*.

FRANCISCO X. ALARCÓN (1954–   ) grew up in Mexico. His first book of poetry, *Body in Flames/Cuerpo en Llamas*, which contains "Letter to America," was nominated for a Lambda Award in Poetry. His next poetry collection, *Snake Poems*, includes translations from Nahuatl, an Aztec language, and from Spanish, as well as his own poems about Aztec traditions.

ALURISTA (ALBERTO URISTA) (1947–   ) is often considered the leading Mexican American poet of the 1960s. His poetry has sought to raise people's awareness about the struggles of Mexican Americans for equality. Born in Mexico City, Alurista has lived in the United States since 1959.

RUDOLFO A. ANAYA (1937–   ) was born in Pastura, New Mexico, of Mexican American parents. Awards such as the Quinto Sol literary award, which he received after the publication of his novel *Bless Me, Ultima,* have brought him recognition as a leading Hispanic writer.

BLACK ELK (1863–1950) was a holy man of the Oglala Lakota nation. His people were relocated to the Dakota reservations created in 1867. Black Elk's spoken memoirs, which were written down and published as *Black Elk Speaks,* tell about his life as a warrior and priest, as well as his efforts to preserve the traditional ways of his people.

JOSEPH BRUCHAC (1942–   ) was born in Saratoga Springs, New York, and is of Abnaki Native American and Slovakian heritage. In his poem "Ellis Island," Bruchac focuses on both immigrant and Native American experiences. In his other poetry and fiction, he explores the sometimes conflicting concerns of both of these heritages. Bruchac has also written a number of works about Native American issues.

ANA CASTILLO (1953–   ) has written poetry, fiction, and literary criticism. Her novel *The Mixquiahala Letters* explores the changing role of Hispanic women in the United States and Mexico. She is of Aztec and Mexican American heritage and re-creates in some of her poetry traditional Native American ways of life. Castillo was born in Chicago.

VIRGINIA CERENIO is a second-generation Filipino–American who was raised in San Francisco. A member of the Kearny Street Workshop, Cerenio writes both poetry and fiction.

LORNA DEE CERVANTES (1954–   ) was born in San Francisco into an old Californio family. (The Californios were the original Hispanic settlers of California.) In the 1960s, she became active in the Chicano Movement and the American Indian Movement. Her poetry has been published in Mexico and England, and she is one of only a few Mexican American poets to be published by the mainstream press in the United States.

DIANA CHANG (1934–   ) was born in New York City and raised primarily in China by her Eurasian mother. In addition to poetry, Chang has written several novels including *The Frontiers of Love* and *Eye to Eye*.

CHIEF SEATTLE (1786–1866) was born near present-day Seattle, Washington. The chief of the Suquamish and Duwamish people, he was the first signer of the Port Elliott Treaty in 1855, which gave a reservation to the Native American peoples of what is now the state of Washington. The city of Seattle was named after him.

SANDRA CISNEROS (1954–   ) was born in Chicago to a Mexican father and a Mexican American mother. She has received two National Endowment for the Arts fellowships for her poetry and fiction. Her other books include *Woman Hollering Creek*, a collection of stories, and *My Wicked Wicked Ways*, a volume of poetry.

MARY CROW DOG (1953–   ) has spent her life seeking equal rights for herself and her fellow Native Americans. Born and raised on the Rosebud Reservation in South Dakota, Crow Dog is of Lakota heritage.

VICTOR HERNANDEZ CRUZ (1949–   ) is a member of the Nuyorican school of poets. He blends the spirit of his early years in Aguas Buenas, Puerto Rico, where he was born, with the experiences of his later life in New York. "ALONE/december/night" is taken from his collection of poetry *Snaps*.

OLAUDAH EQUIANO (1745?–1797) was born in Essaka, in what is now eastern Nigeria in Africa. Enslaved at the age of 10 and brought to the Americas, Equiano obtained his freedom in 1766. He spent the rest of his life writing and working against slavery.

RODOLFO GONZALES (1929–   ) was born in a Mexican American barrio of Denver, Colorado. His parents were seasonal farm workers. He became involved in the Chicano movement of the 1960s, founding the Crusade for Justice and organizing annual Chicano youth conferences. He is well known for his epic poem *I Am Joaquín*, which focuses on the Mexican American struggle for self–determination.

ALEX HALEY (1921–1992) is best known for his Pulitzer Prize-winning novel *Roots*, which blends history and fiction to explore Haley's African American heritage. Born in Ithaca, New York, Haley grew up in Henning, Tennessee.

VIRGINIA HAMILTON (1936–   ) is best known for her novel M.C. *Higgins, the Great*, for which she won the Newbery Medal and a National Book Award. This novel, like her other novels for young adults, centers on the life and emerging self–awareness of an African American teenager.

FRANCES E. W. HARPER (1825–1911), an African American, was born of free parents in Baltimore, Maryland. As a teenager, Harper began producing volumes of both poetry and prose. Her work explores the lives of African Americans of her day and advocates the abolitionist cause.

ROBERT E. HAYDEN (1913–1980) was a well-known African American poet and scholar. He won several awards for his poetry, including the Jule and Avery Hopwood Prize. In 1975, he was named Fellow of the Year by the Academy of American Poets.

JAMES D. HOUSTON (1933–   ) was born in San Francisco, California. In addition to his collaboration with his wife, Jeanne Wakatsuki Houston, on the book *Farewell to Manzanar*, he has published a number of collections of short stories and essays, as well as several novels. He is a recipient of the Joseph Henry Jackson Award for Fiction.

JEANNE WAKATSUKI HOUSTON (1934–   ) and her Japanese American family spent three-and-a-half years in Manzanar, an internment camp, during World War II. With her husband, James D. Houston, she tells the story of that life in *Farewell to Manzanar*, from which "Free to Go" is taken. Houston was born in Inglewood, California.

LANGSTON HUGHES (1902–1967) is one of the most popular African American writers in U.S. literature. His large volume of work, including poetry, plays, short stories, and journalism, focuses on the complexities of African American life. Hughes was born in Joplin, Missouri, and was raised in Lawrence, Kansas, and Cleveland, Ohio.

NORA ZEALE HURSTON (1891–1960), an African American writer and anthropologist, was born in Eatonville, Florida. In both her fiction and nonfiction, she writes mainly about the rural African American culture in which she grew up. *Their Eyes Were Watching God* is often cited as the first African American feminist novel of the 20th century.

HARRIET A. JACOBS (1813–1897) published the narrative of her life as an enslaved African American under the pseudonym Linda Brent. Born in Edenton, North Carolina, Jacobs escaped slavery as an adult and went into hiding for seven years. After finally reaching the North in 1842, she worked as a housekeeper and recorder of her experiences. Later, she helped African Americans during the Civil War, nursing soldiers and working with the homeless.

FRANCISCO JIMÉNEZ (1943–   ) is best known for his short stories such as "Cajas de carton" (the original title of "The Circuit"). This story won the *Arizona Quarterly* annual award in 1973. Jiménez was born in a small town near Guadalajara, Mexico, and was raised in Santa Maria, California, where his parents were migrant farm workers.

DANG MANH KHA was born in Vietnam. After emigrating to the United States, he attended college. He has worked as a teacher and as an administrator of programs to help Vietnamese refugees.

MARTIN LUTHER KING, JR. (1929–1968) was a central figure in the Civil Rights Movement of the 1950s and 1960s. This African American leader, a minister like his father, advocated peaceful protest against racism. In 1964, King became the youngest person ever to receive the Nobel Peace Prize. He was assassinated in 1968.

MAXINE HONG KINGSTON (1940–   ) was born in California to Chinese parents who spoke little English. Her work explores the tension between her traditional family and the modern world. Her autobiographical novels include *The Woman Warrior: Memoirs of a Girlhood Among Ghosts* (1976) and *China Men* (1980).

TATO LAVIERA (1950–   ) is a member of the Nuyorican school of writing. Born in Santurce, Puerto Rico, Laviera emigrated to New York City in 1960. He is active in the Hispanic community as a writer, dramatist, and teacher.

MALCOLM X (1925–1965) was an African American political activist who at one point promoted the idea of a separate African American society. Born Malcolm Little in Omaha, Nebraska, he changed his name when he became a Muslim. He was assassinated in 1965, possibly because he had opened the door to cooperation with whites. *The Autobiography of Malcolm X*, written with Alex Haley, was published in 1965.

PAULE MARSHALL (1929–   ) was born in Brooklyn, New York, to parents who had emigrated from Barbados, an island in the Caribbean Sea. In novels such as *Brown Girl, Brownstones*, she focuses on the lives of African American women, primarily of West Indian heritage, and the conflict between ethnic and mainstream influences.

MARK MATHABANE (1960–   ) was born in the shantytown of Alexandra, South Africa, to poor black South African parents. In 1978, Mathabane came to the United States, where he has written autobiographical books such as *Kaffir Boy* and *Kaffir Boy in America*, as well as articles about the struggle to overcome apartheid.

NICHOLASA MOHR (1935–   ) is an author and illustrator of Puerto Rican heritage. Her fiction for young adults focuses mainly on the Puerto Rican community in New York City. For her first novel, *Nilda*, Mohr won the Merit Award from the Society of Illustrators. *In Nueva York* is her second novel.

N. SCOTT MOMADAY (1934–   ) was born in Oklahoma and raised on reservations in the U.S. Southwest. His work has focused on his Kiowa heritage and on Kiowa folklore. Momaday's first novel, *House Made of Dawn* (1968), won a Pulitzer Prize. He also writes poetry.

AURORA LEVINS MORALES (1954–   ) began writing poetry at the age of 7. Her work explores and celebrates her mixed Puerto Rican, U.S., and Jewish heritages.

ROSARIO MORALES (1930–) rediscovered her childhood gift for poetry in her 40s. Her collaboration with her daughter is a shared dialogue about many issues, including feminism. In 1990, she won the Boston Contemporary Writers Award for her poetry.

SÉAMUS Ó CATHÁIN is a collector of Irish and Scandinavian folktales. He has written and presented radio and television programs on folklore. He has also edited and written books and critical studies of folktales. His books include *The Living Landscape* (1975), *Fairy Legends from Donegal* (1977), and *The Bedside Book of Irish Folklore* (1980).

HEBERTO PADILLA (1932–) was born in Pinar del Rio, Cuba. After the Cuban Revolution, he worked for the Cuban press agency in London and Moscow. In 1968, he was recalled to Cuba and arrested because a controversial book of his had been awarded a prize. This arrest led to Cuban leader Fidel Castro's loss of credibility with writers and artists. Padilla later emigrated to the U.S. and began translating his poetry into English.

CONSTANTINE M. PANUNZIO (1884–1964) was born in Apulia in southeastern Italy. After coming to the United States in 1902, he became passionately attached to his adopted country. His autobiography, *The Soul of an Immigrant*, explores, among other issues, the conflict between his attachment to the United States and his love for his native Italy.

HARRY MARK PETRAKIS (1923–) was born in St. Louis, Missouri, to parents of Greek heritage. He has twice been nominated for a National Book Award, for the novels *Pericles on 31st Street* and *Dream of Kings*, which focus on the immigrant experience in America.

ISHMAEL REED (1938–) was born in Chattanooga, Tennessee, and raised in Buffalo, New York. He has been active in the African American cultural movement, using his novels and poetry to comment on the roles whites and African Americans play in the world's problems. His work has been nominated for the National Book Award.

HENRY ROTH (1906?–) emigrated with his parents from eastern Europe to the Lower East Side of New York City as a very small child. His novel, *Call It Sleep*, which focuses on the Jewish immigrant experience, is considered a key part of Jewish American literature.

RICARDO SÁNCHEZ (1941–) was born in El Paso, Texas, and grew up in the Mexican barrio. In his many collections of poetry and nonfiction, such as his best-known work, *The Liberation of a Chicano Mind*, Sánchez has spoken out against discrimination against Mexican Americans. He was awarded a Ford Foundation fellowship to work on his doctorate.

LESLIE MARMON SILKO (1948–) was born in Albuquerque, New Mexico, and raised on the Laguna Pueblo Reservation. Her work explores the relationship of traditional Laguna folklore to modern experience. She was awarded a MacArthur Foundation Fellowship in 1981 to pursue her writing.

GARY SOTO (1952–) is is a poet and writer whose works often focus on elements of his Mexican American heritage. Soto, who was born in Fresno, California, has written several books for children including *Baseball in April and Other Stories*, an ALA Best Book for Young Adults, published in 1990.

HYEMOYOHSTS STORM (1935–) is a Northern Cheyenne, born and raised in Montana on the Cheyenne and Crow reservations. In addition to *Seven Arrows*, for which he is best known, Storm is the author of *Song of Heyoehkah*. He has taught at the University of Iowa and has lectured widely.

AMY TAN (1952–　) was born in Oakland, California, to parents who had recently emigrated from China. She received a National Book Critics Circle Award for *The Joy Luck Club* and was also a National Book Award finalist for that book. Her second book is titled *The Kitchen God's Wife*.

SOJOURNER TRUTH (1797?–1883) was born into slavery in Ulster County, New York. After escaping to freedom in 1827, just before New York freed all enslaved African Americans, she took refuge with the Van Wagener family. Later, she worked in New York City. In 1843, she took the name Sojourner Truth and began to travel about the country speaking against slavery and for women's rights.

YOSHIKO UCHIDA (1921–1992) was born in Alameda, California. She wrote about both traditional Japanese culture and modern Japanese American society. A recipient of a Ford Foundation Fellowship, she wrote more than 20 books.

PABLITA VELARDE (1918–　) is a member of the Tewa nation, born at Santa Clara Pueblo in New Mexico. She is best known as a painter of Native American life and culture, for which she has received awards such as the French government's Palmes des Academiques.

MARGARET WALKER (1915–　), an African American, was recognized for celebrating African American identity in her first poetry collection, *For My People*. She is best known, however, for her historical novel *Jubilee*, which was based on her great-grandmother's life. Walker was born in Birmingham, Alabama.

AUGUST WILSON (1945–　) has received two Pulitzer Prizes, for his plays *Fences* and *The Piano Lesson*. He has also won the New York Drama Critics Circle Best New Play award several times. Wilson, an African American, was born in Pittsburgh, Pennsylvania.

RICHARD WRIGHT (1908–1960) is best known for his novel *Native Son* (1940). Selected by The Book-of-the-Month Club, it was the first book by an African American to become a best seller. Wright also received a Guggenheim Fellowship. Born near Natchez, Mississippi, Wright grew up moving about the South. In later life he lived in Chicago, New York City, and Paris.

HISAYE YAMAMOTO (1921–　) was born in Redondo Beach, California, to Japanese immigrant parents. She and her family were sent to the Poston, Arizona, internment camp during World War II. Her work has appeared in publication since she was 14 years old and has received many awards, including the 1986 American Book Award for Lifetime Achievement from the Before Columbus Foundation.

Accent is the force or stress given to some words or syllables in speech. In this book, accent is indicated by the use of upper-case letters. Words of one syllable are always shown as accented. Thus, if the word *hand* were pronounced, the pronunciation would be printed (HAND). In words of more than one syllable, the syllable that gets the main accent is printed in upper-case letters. The other syllable or syllables are printed in lower-case letters. If the word *handbag* were pronounced, the pronunciation would be printed (HAND-bag). The phonetic respellings are based on the pronunciations given in *Webster's New World Dictionary*.

This glossary defines important terms used in this book. The page on which a term first appears is given in parentheses at the end of the definition.

Vowel Sound	Symbol	Respelling
a as in *hat*	a	HAT
a as in *day, date, paid*	ay	DAY, DAYT, PAYD
vowels as in *far, on*	ah	FAHR, AHN
vowels as in *dare, air*	ai	DAIR, AIR
vowels as in *saw, call, pour*	aw	SAW, KAWL, PAWR
e as in *pet, debt*	e	PET, DET
e as in *seat, chief*; **y** as in *beauty*	ee	SEET, CHEEF, BYOO-tee
vowels as in *learn, fur, sir*	er	LERN, FER, SER
i as in *sit, bitter*; **ee** as in *been*	ih	SIHT, BIHT-uhr, BIHN
i as in *mile*; **y** as in *defy*; **ei** as in *height*	eye	MEYEL, dee-FEYE, HEYET
o as in *go*	oh	GOH
vowels as in *boil, toy*	oi	BOIL, TOI
vowels as in *foot, could*	oo	FOOT, KOOD
vowels as in *boot, rule, suit*	o͞o	BO͞OT, RO͞OL, SO͞OT
vowels as in *how, out, bough*	ow	HOW, OWT, BOW
vowels as in *up, come*	u	UP, KUM
vowels as in *use, use, few*	yoo	YOOZ, YOOS, FYOO
vowels in unaccented syllables (*schwas*):		
again, upon, sanity	uh	uh-GEN, uh-PAHN, SAN-uh-tee

Consonant Sound	Symbol	Respelling
ch as in *choose, reach*	ch	CHOOZ, REECH
g as in *go, dig*	g	GOH, DIHG
j as in *jar*; **dg** as in *fudge*; and **g** as in *gem*	j	JAHR, FUJ, JEM
k as in *king*; **c** as in *come*; and **ch** as in *Christmas*	k	KIHNG, KUM, KRIHS-muhs
s as in *treasure*; **g** as in *bourgeois*	zh	TRE-zhuhr, boor-ZHWAH
sh as in *ship*	sh	SHIHP
th as in *thin*	th	THIHN
<u>**th**</u> as in *this*	<u>th</u>	<u>TH</u>IHS
z as in *zero*; **s** as in *chasm*	z	ZEE-roh, KAZ-uhm
x as in *fix, axle*	ks	FIHKS, AK-suhl
x as in *exist*	gz	ihg-ZIHST
s as in *this, sir*	s	<u>TH</u>IS, SER
wh as in *white*	wh	WHEYET
h as in *who, whole*	h	HOO, HOHL
gh as in *rough, laugh*	f	RUF, LAF
ph as in *telephone*	f	TEL-uh-fohn

GLOSSARY

A

a ti y a tu familia (ah TEE ee ah TOO fah-MEE-lee-ah) Spanish for *to you and your family*, 53

a-waitin' waiting, in "The Drinking Gourd," 154

Achilles (uh-KIHL-eez) *n.* a well-known Greek warrior in the Trojan War, 316

acquiesced (ak-wee-EST) *v.* agreed, consented without protest, 306

addled (AD-uhld) *v.* confused, 194

admonished (ad-MAHN-ihshd) *v.* warned, 65

adobe (uh-DOH-bee) *n.* a house built from sundried mud bricks, 22, 49

Adodarhoh (ah-doh-DAR-hoh) *n.* Iroquois Chief of Chiefs, 132

advances (ad-VAN-sez) *n. pl.* efforts to court or win the love of, 59

affirmative (uh-FER-muh-tihv) *adj.* agreeing, 261

Afrikaner (af-rih-KAHN-er) *adj.* a descendant of the Dutch who colonized South Africa in the 1600s, 203

Alcott Amos Bronson Alcott, a famous philosopher and abolitionist in the 1800s, 179

Alexander the Great king of Macedonia from 336-323 B.C.; conqueror of Greek city-states and of the Persian empire from Asia Minor and Egypt to India, 317

Algiers (al-JEERZ) the capital of Algeria, a country in North Africa, 233

allies (AL-eyez) *n. pl.* people or groups united for a purpose, 133

allude to (uh-LOOD TOO) *v.* mention, 167

Alt an Torr (AHLT ahn TOWR) a small wooded area in "The Man Who Had No Story," 39

altar (AWL-tuhr) *n.* a raised platform usually used for religious purposes, 116

altercation (awl-ter-CAY-shuhn) *n.* quarrel, 359

AmeRícan (ah-may-REE-kahn) *n.* a shortened form of *American* and *Puerto Rican*, 357

amigos (ah-MEE-gohs) *n. pl.* Spanish for *friends*, 47

amorous (AM-uh-ruhs) *adj.* inclined or disposed to romantic love, 304

Amphissa (am-FEE-sah) *n.* a city in southern Greece, 316

Anasazi (ah-nah-SAH-zee) *n.* a Navajo word meaning *the ancient ones*; an early southwest culture that thrived from 100 B.C. to A.D. 1300, 149

and Lazarus came forth in the Christian religion, Jesus brought Lazarus back from death, 263

anemia (ah-NEEM-eeuh) *n.* a blood condition, 341

ang guapo lalake (AHNG GWAHP-oh lah-LAHK-ay) a Tagalog (a language spoken in the Philippines) phrase meaning *a handsome man*, 85

anvil's edge edge of the iron block on which a blacksmith hammers metal, 76

áo-dài (ow-DEYE) *n. pl.* Vietnamese word for *long robes*, 33

apartheid (uh-PAHRT-hayt) *n.* the South African policy of strict racial segregation of, and discrimination against, nonwhite people, 205

appraisal (uh-PRAYZ-uhl) *n.* judging the value of someone, 302

apprehensive (ap-ruh-HEN-sihv) *adj.* worried, fearful, 65

archetypal (ahr-kuh-TEYEP-uhl) *adj.* original, 337

argumentative (ahr-gyoo-MEN-tuh-tihv) *adj.* ready to fight, 60

ascertaining (ah-ser-TAYN-ihng) *v.* finding out, 170

aspect (AS-pekt) *n.* appearance, 201

aspens (AS-penz) *n.* slender-trunked trees, 105

assail (uh-SAYL) *v.* attack physically or assault, 84

assimilate (uh-SIHM-uh-layt) *v.* to lose one's identity and become part of a group, 272

asthmatic (az-MAT-ihk) *adj.* wheezy, as if coughing, 66

atole (ah-TOH-lay) *n.* Spanish for *cornmeal porridge*, 50

atone (uh-TOHN) *v.* to make up for; to make amends, 163

audacity (aw-DA-sih-tee) *n.* boldness, 169

avarice (AV-uhr-uhs) *n.* greed, 160

Ave María Purísima (AH-vay mah-REE-ah poor-EES-ee-mah) Spanish for *Hail Mary, most pure*; a reference to the Immaculate Conception, 47

aversion (ah-VER-shuhn) *n.* strong dislike, 166

avgolemono (ahv-goh-LEEM-uh-noh) *n.* a Greek soup or sauce made with lemon juice, 319

avid (AV-ihd) *adj.* greedy, 352

awful (AW-fuhl) *adj.* full of deep respect, 78

¡Ay, Caray! (EYE kah-RAY) *interj.* Spanish for *Oh, no!*, 215

¡Ay Dios Mio! (AI DEE-ohs MEE-oh) *interj.* Spanish for *Oh, my God!*, 51

Aztec (AZ-tek) *adj.* of a Native American people from central Mexico, 267

B

balsam (BAWL-suhm) *n.* a soothing ointment, used in "The Slave who Dared to Feel like a Man." to mean *healing*, 165

band (BAND) *n.* a group made up of several families who lived and traveled together; similar to clans; often identified by its leader, as in Crazy Horse's band, 126

baobab (BAH-oh-bab) *n.* kind of tree with a broad trunk, 57

baptism (BAP-tihz-uhm) *n.* a ceremonial immersion in water, or application of water, as an initiation, 298

Barbadian cast (bahr-BAY-dee-uhn KAST) looking like someone from Barbados, 65

Barbados (bahr-BAY-dohs) an island country in the West Indies, 161

Barr an Ghaoith (BAWR ahn GWEE-hah) a town in "The Man Who Had No Story," 39

barrios (BAH-ree-ohs) *n.* Spanish for *neighborhoods*, 84, 266

bartered (BAHR-tuhrd) *v.* traded, 345

bedevil (bee-DE-vuhl) *v.* to torment or harass maliciously, 314

Benin mask (be-NEEN MASK) mask from Benin, a kingdom in West Africa that existed during the years 1350-1680, 72

benjo (BEN-joh) *n.* a Japanese word for an outdoor toilet in a small shed, 93

Berbice chair (BER-bihs CHAIR) kind of lounge chair, 72

bereft (bih-REFT) *adj.* deprived of; loss, 339

bestow (bee-STOH) *v.* give as a gift, 352

betrothed (bih-TROTHD) *n.* person one is engaged to marry, 97

between a hawk and a buzzard in a difficult spot, 263

Big Chief at Washington a phrase used in "The Indians' Night Promises to be Dark" to refer to President Franklin Pierce, the 14th President of the United States, 139

Big Dipper a constellation that looks like a cup with a long handle, 13, 244

birthright (BERTH-reyet) *n.* what a person is entitled to from birth, 79

Black Mesa (BLAK MAY-sah) in northern Arizona; the coal found there makes it look black from a distance; *mesa* means *table* in Spanish, 147

Black Muslim (BLAK MUZ-luhm) a member of a predominantly African American sect of the Islamic faith, 200

Blue Clouds Arapaho Native Americans, 129

blue plate special an inexpensive restaurant meal served on a large plate, which originally was blue, 186

blundering (BLUN-duhr-ihng) *v.* moving clumsily, making a foolish mistake, 343

blunting (BLUN-tihng) *v.* dulling, 296

bo (BOH) *interj.* an expression in Barbados meaning *you see* or *you understand*, 67

bodice (BAHD-ihs) *n.* top part of a dress, 64

bolero (boh-LAY-roh) *n.* a kind of dance music, 357

bondsman (BAHNDZ-muhn) *n.* slave, 345

bonnet (BAHN-iht) *n.* a war bonnet, or Native American headdress with feathers, 10

Boricua (boh-REE-kwah) *n.* Puerto Rican, 360

bosoms (BUZ-uhms) *n.* the family, people who feel close to one another, 158

bouillabaisse (boo-yuh-BAYS) *n.* a French fish soup, 336

braceros (brah-SAY-rohs) *n.* Mexicans who are brought into the United States and allowed to work temporarily on farms, 251

brandishing (BRAN-dihsh-ihng) *v.* waving, 354

breadfruit (bred-FROOT) a fruit tree common to Barbados in the West Indies, 67

breeches (BREECH-uhz) *n.* knickers, or trousers that reach only to the knee, 177

Brian Ó Braonacháin (BREEN oh BRAYN-uh-kahn) an Irish man's name, 39

Bridgetown (BRIHJ-town) the capital of Barbados, 161

bridles (BREYE-duhls) *n. pl.* leather gear used to lead or guide horses, 50

brocades (broh-KAYDZ) *n.* rich cloths with designs woven into them, often of silk, velvet, or gold, 195

bronzed (BRAHNZD) *adj.* reddish brown in color, 290

brooding (BROOD-ihng) *adj.* worrying, 49

browsed (BROWZD) *v.* nibbled plants or grass, 20

brujas (BROO-hahs) *n. pl.* Spanish for *witches*, 48

brusquely (BRUSK-lee) *adv.* roughly, abruptly, bluntly, 318

brutality (broo-TAL-uh-tee) *n.* the quality of being cruel, unfeeling, and often violent, 236

(bueno pues, ¿qué vamos a hacer, Ambrosio?/¡bueno pues, seguirle, compadre, seguirle!/¡Ay, Mama!/Se pues, ¿qué vamos a hacer, compadre?/¡Seguirle, Ambrosio, seguirle!) (boo-AY-noh pways, kay VAH-mohs ah ah-SAIR, ahm-BROH-see-oh?/boo-AY-noh pways, say-GEER-lay, kohm-PAH-dray, say-GEER-lay/EYE, mah-MAH!/SEE pways, kay VAH-mohs ah ah-SAIR, kohm-PAH-dray?/say-GEER-lay, ahm-BROH-see-oh, say-GEER-lay!) Spanish for *Well, what are we going to do, Ambrosio?/Well, continue, my friend, continue!/Oh, Mother!/Yes, well, what else can we do?/Continue, Ambrosio, continue.* 249

Buenos días le de Dios, Grande (BWAY-nohs DEE-ahs lay day DEE-ohs, GRAHN-day) Spanish for *God grant you a good day, Grande,* 53

Bull Connor the Birmingham, Alabama, Chief of Police, 228

bungalow (BUNG-guh-loh) *n.* a small house or cottage, 298

bunions (BUN-yuhns) *n.* inflamed swellings on the big toes, 104

Buon giorno (BWOHN JOHR-noh) an Italian expression meaning *good day,* 280

C

C'dear (kuh-DEER) a fond expression in Barbados, *Come, dear* or *Good dear,* 67

cairned (KERND) *v.* buried in a landmark, tombstone, or monument, 244

calligraphy (kuh-LIHG-ruh-fee) *n.* beautiful, ornamental writing or script, 95

calloused (KAL-uhst) *adj.* hardened by work, 65

caló (kah-LOH) *n.* the Spanish dialect spoken in a Mexican American neighborhood, 84

calypso (kuh-LIHP-soh) *adj.* A kind of song common to the people of the West Indies, containing irregular rhythms and satire. 338

Cám (CAM) a Vietnamese girl's name, 30

Cancer (KAN-ser) *n.* a constellation in the shape of a crab; also a sign of the zodiac, 10

candidate (KAN-duh-dayt) *n.* a person who seeks or is nominated for an office or award, 134

canes (KAYNZ) *n. pl.* tall, thin stems of sugar cane plants, 66

Cante Ishta (KAHN-tay IHSH-tah) Lakota for *the eye of the heart,* 108

Cantonese (kan-tuh-NEEZ) *adj.* from Canton, a capital in southeast China, 307

Caramba (cah-RAHM-bah) *interj.* a Spanish exclamation of surprise or dismay, 185

caribeña (kah-ree-BAY-nyah) *adj.* Spanish for *a Caribbean woman,* 360

carne con chile (KAHR-nay kohn CHEE-lay) *n.* a dish with beans and meat, 255

Cathay (ka-THAY) *n.* an old name for China, 244

ceremoniously (ser-uh-MOHN-ee-uhs-lee) *adj.* formally, 49

chapas (CHAH-pahs) *n. pl.* Spanish for *chaps,* leather leg protectors worn by cowboys, 50

chattel (CHAT-uhl) *n.* articles of property, except real estate, 169

chestnut wood Chestnut wood in burning throws out sparks, which would disturb the Iroquois council. 133

chicano (chih-KAH-noh) *adj.* pertaining to someone of Mexican heritage, 84

chide (CHEYED) *v.* scold, 136

chile (CHEYEL) *n.* child, 287

chile verde (CHEE-lay VAIR-day) *n.* Spanish for *green peppers,* 266

Chiquitín (chih-kee-TEEN) *Spanish,* a boy's name, 186

Circle Line ship ferry that takes people to Liberty Island to visit the Statue of Liberty, 208

clamour (KLAM-er) *n.* continual uproar and shouting, 162

Clan *n.* a division within a nation; a group of several families with a common ancestor, 365

cognizance (KAHG-nuh-zuhns) *n.* understanding, 282

colonized (KAHL-uh-neyezd) *v.* In "To Da-duh, In Memoriam," Da-duh means *civilized.* 66

comme il faut (KUM EEL FOH) a French phrase meaning *as I must,* 90

compadres (kohm-PAH-drays) *n. pl.* Spanish for *close friends,* 46

compound (KAHM-pownd) *n.* yard, walled-in area around a house and other buildings, 27

conclave (KAHN-klayv) *n.* meeting, 281

concocted (kuhn-KAHK-tuhd) *v.* devised, made up, 301

Confederate (kuhn-FED-er-et) *adj.* a person or group united with others for a common purpose, 132

confidant (KAHN-fuh-dahnt) *n.* a person trusted with secrets, 166

consummate (KAHN-suh-mayt) *adj.* complete, 79

consumption (kuhn-SUMP-shuhn) a lung disease, 341

contaminate (kuhn-TAM-uh-nayt) *v.* to make dirty or impure, 148

contumacious (kahn-too-MAY-shuhs) *adj.* disobedient, 135

convoys (KAHN-vois) *n.* groups of vehicles that travel together for protection, 239

copious (KOH-pee-uhs) *adj.* plentiful, overflowing, 160

coral (KAWR-uhl) *n.* shell-like substance formed from the skeletons of tiny sea animals, used in jewelry, 103

corns (KAWRNZ) *n.* thick, hard, sometimes painful growths on the toes, 104

corrective (kuh-REK-tihv) *adj.* intended to fix, 59

corridos (koh-REE-dohs) *n.* types of songs popular in Mexico, 256

countenances (KOWN-tuh-nuhn-sez) *n.* facial expressions, 162

countered (KOWN-tuhrd) *v.* to say or do something in reply, or in retaliation, 296

countryside a rural area, 185

coyote (keye-OHT-ee) *n.* a small wolf, 11

Crazy Horse a chief of the Oglala Lakota people, 128

cremation (kree-MAY-shuhn) *n.* burning to ashes, 96

Crete (KREET) a Greek island, 317

crimson (KRIHM-zuhn) *adj.* a deep red, 185

croon *v.* hum, sing, or talk in a low tone, 174

crudo (KROO-doh) *adj.* Spanish for *feeling ill*, 47

cruelty *n.* trying to inflict pain on someone, 160

crystallized (KRIHS-tuh-leyezd) *adj.* something that looks like a crystal, with a solid structure and a regularly repeated pattern, 353

¿Cuándo (KWAN-doh) *adv.* the Spanish word for *When?*, 215

cubists (KYOO-bihsts) *n.* artists whose work represents geometric figures, 336

cuentos (KWEN-tohs) *n. pl.* Spanish for *stories*, 48

cunning (KUN-ihng) *n.* cleverness, trickiness, 25

curandera (koor-ahn-DAI-rah) *n.* Spanish for *healer*, 48

cured hides *n. pl.* animal skins prepared for use as blankets, 57

curfew (KUR-fyoo) *n.* the time by which people must be home, and not on the streets, 270

D

dalmation (dal-MAY-shuhn) *n.* short-haired dog with a white coat and black or brown spots, 304

danzas (DAHN-sahs) *n.* dances, 357

decades (DEK-aydz) *n.* periods of ten years, 208

deceived (dih-SEEVD) *v.* misled or tricked, 343

decimated (DES-uh-mayt-uhd) *v.* destroyed, 205

decrease (dih-KREES) *v.* to lessen or get smaller, 58

Dedicado al Sr. Chávez (day-dee-KAH-doh ahl say-NYOHR CHAH-vays) Spanish for *dedicated to Mr. Chávez*, 249

deftly (DEFT-lee) *adv.* skillfully, 317

deicide (DEE-ih-seyed) *n.* killing of a god, 79

delectable (dih-LEK-tuh-buhl) *adj.* delightful or delicious, 27, 94

Delphi (DEL-feye) *n.* ancient Greek city where Apollo delivered an oracle, 318

derby (DER-bee) *n.* a stiff felt hat with a rounded top and brim, 196

deride (dih-REYED) *v.* laugh at in scorn or contempt, 314

destination (des-tuh-NAY-shuhn) *n.* the place someone would like to go, 9

destino (days-TEE-noh) *n.* Spanish for *destiny*, 359

diaspora (deye-AS-puh-ruh) *n.* a scattering of people with a common background or beliefs, often a kind of exile, 360

din (DIHN) *n.* continuous loud noise, 303

dirges (DERJ-uhz) *n. pl.* funeral songs, 341

discontented (dihs-kuhn-TENT-ihd) *adj.* restless or unsatisfied, 30

disdain (dihs-DAYN) *v.* to regard as unworthy or reject with scorn, 205

disembarkation shed (dihs-em-bahr-KAY-shuhn SHED) *n.* a building in Barbados through which passengers arriving by ship go ashore, 63

disencumber (dihs-ihn-KUM-buhr) *v.* free from a burden or a trouble, 166

disinherited (dihs-ihn-HER-iht-ihd) *adj.* having gifts from one's ancestors taken away, 342

disparaging (dihs-PAR-ihj-ihng) *adj.* showing disrespect for, 303

disposition (dihs-poh-ZISH-uhn) *n.* intention, 133

dispossessed (dihs-poh-ZEST) *adj.* forced to give up possessions such as a house or land, 342

dissonant (DIHS-uh-nuhnt) *adj.* clashing, lacking harmony, 66

ditties (DIHT-eez) *n. pl.* short, simple songs, 341

diverted (duh-VURT-ihd) *v.* to draw off to a different course; to turn aside, 242

Don José Vigil (DOHN hoh-SAY VEE-hil) *n. don* is a title of respect in Spanish; José Vigil is the man's name, 17

Douglass Frederick Douglass, originally an enslaved African American who became a writer and speaker for African American rights in the 1800s, 179

drags (DRAGZ) *n.* sledlike platforms that held loads and could be pulled by horses or humans, 127

dreams *n.* wishes and hopes, 208

drinking gourd (GAWRD) a ladle; another name for the Big Dipper, the constellation that enslaved African Americans used to find the way north in "The Drinking Gourd," 154

drone (DROHN) *n.* a continuous humming or buzzing sound, 254

drumtalked (DRUM-tawkd) *v.* communicated using drums, 58

dubious (DOO-bee-uhs) *adj.* doubtful or suspicious, 92

Dunloe (duhn-LOH) a town in "The Man Who Had No Story," 39

dusk (DUSK) *n.* the beginning of darkness in the evening, 249

dust devils (DUST DEV-uhls) *n.* small whirlwinds common in dry regions on hot, calm afternoons and made visible by the dust, debris, and sand they pick up from the ground, 239

dynamite (DEYE-nuh-meyet) *n.* a powerful explosive, 241

E

ebbing (EB-ihng) *v.* declining or receding, 140

ebony (EB-uhn-ee) *n.* black wood, 57

Ekwefi (ek-WEE-fee) *n.* an African woman's name, 25

El barco que nunca atraca. (el BAHR-koh kay NOON-kah ah-TRAH-kah) Spanish for *The ship that will never dock*, 290

Elaine (ee-LAYN) *n.* a town in eastern Arkansas, near the Mississippi border, 298

elders (EL-derz) *n. pl.* older people; in *Roots*, the honored men who govern the village, 57

Ellis Island the island in New York harbor on which many immigrants first landed in the United States; the immigration center there was open from 1892 to 1954, 208

eloquent (EL-uh-kwunt) *adj.* forceful or expressive, 27

emaciated (ih-MAY-shee-ay-tihd) *adj.* very thin, 21

embossed (ihm-BAWSD) *v.* decorated with a design that stands out from the surface, 353

Emerson Ralph Waldo Emerson, a famous writer and abolitionist in the 1800s, 179

emissary (EM-uh-ser-ee) *n.* messenger, 70

engender (ihn-JEN-der) *v.* cause to grow, 78

enmities (EN-me-teez) *n.* hatreds, 80

enraptured (en-RAP-cherd) *v.* filled with delight, 109

enterprising (EN-tuhr-preye-zihng) *adj.* ready to try something new, 338

epithets (EP-uh-thets) *n.* words or phrases applied to a person or thing to describe an actual or attributed quality, 315

Es todo (ays TOH-doh) Spanish for *That's everything*, 253

Es verdad (AYS bair-DAHD) Spanish for *it is true*, 48

Esperanza (ays-pay-RAHN-sah) *Spanish*, a woman's name, meaning *hope*, 216

Está bien (ay-STAH BEE-yen) Spanish for *it's all right*, 49

Está sola, ya no queda gente en el pueblito de Las Pasturas (ay-STAH SO-lah, YAH NO KAY-dah HEN-tay AYN EL POOAY-bleeto DAY LAHS pahs-TOO-rahs) (Spanish) She is alone, there is no one left in the little town of Las Pasturas. 46

evacuation order in 1942, the order to place all Japanese and Japanese Americans living on the West Coast in internment camps, 270

evaded (ee-VAYD-ed) *v.* avoided answering directly, 296

evangelist (ih-VAN-juh-luhst) *n.* a traveling preacher of the Gospel, 335

Eve According to the Old Testament in the Bible, the first woman created by God, 261

evolved (ih-VAHLVD) *v.* developed gradually, 308

ewe (YOO) *n.* female sheep, 20

Ex Parte (eks PAR-tay) *adj.* a one-sided presentation of a court case, 270

excavation (eks-kuh-VAY-shuhn) *n.* a hole made by digging, 279

Ezekiel (ee-ZEEK-ee-uhl) a Hebrew prophet, 179

Ezinma (e-ZIHN-mah) *n.* an African girl's name, 25

F

facile (FAS-uhl) *adj.* easily managed, 343

fagots (FAG-uhtz) *n. pl.* bundles of sticks, 30

fairy tale *n.* a story about a human's adventures with the "little people," called fairies. A magical world inhabited by little people and other beings is part of Irish folklore. 40

famine (FAM-ihn) *n.* a great shortage of food, 25

fatuous (FACH-oo-us) *adj.* silly, foolish, 17

feign (FAYN) *v.* pretend or fake, 167

Felipa (fay-LEE-pah) *Spanish*, a woman's name, 16

fell (FEL) *adj.* fierce, terrible, 141

Fenian (FEE-nee-uhn) *adj.* pertaining to the struggle for Irish independence and its supporters, 39

ferocity (fuh-RAHS-uh-tee) *n.* fierceness, 302

feta (FET-uh) a Greek cheese made from goat's milk, 317

fetters (FET-uhrz) *n.* chains or shackles for the feet, 160

firmament (FER-muh-muhnt) *n.* sky, 141

First Amendment the amendment to the U.S. Constitution that guarantees freedom of speech, 228

flaunting (FLAWNT-ihng) *v.* showing off, 71

floundering (FLOWN-duhr-ihng) *v.* struggling awkwardly, 343, 352

flustered (FLUS-terd) *adj.* nervous, confused, 197

fog (FAHG) *n.* a thick mist that makes it hard to see, 40

foment (foh-MENT) *v.* to promote the growth or development of; to instigate or foster, 272

for seven hakes turned-around version of the common expression *for heaven's sakes*, 93

forage (FOHR-ihj) *v.* look for food, 50

forays (FAWR-ayz) *n.* raids or attacks, 314

foreign (FAWR-ihn) *adj.* from another country, 290

foreman (FOR-muhn) *n.* the person in charge of a department or group of workers, 253

forgiving (fawr-GIHV-ihng) *adj.* giving up the desire for revenge, 236

formidable (FAWR-mihd-uh-buhl) *adj.* frightening, powerful, 64

fronds (FRAHNDZ) *n. pl.* leaves of palm trees, 71

funereal (fyoo-NIHR-ee-uhl) *adj.* like a funeral, slow, 66

furrow (FUHR-oh) *n.* a groove cut in the land by a plow, 345

G

galling (GAWL-ihng) *adj.* making sore by rubbing, 160

galvanized (GAL-van-eyezd) *adj.* plated or covered with zinc, by galvanic or electrical action, 252

Garrett Thomas Garrett, an abolitionist who assisted in the escape of more than 2,700 enslaved African Americans in the 1800s, 179

Garrison William Lloyd Garrison, a famous editor and abolitionist in the 1800s, 179

Gayanashagowa (geye-ahn-ah-shah-GOW-uh) the Iroquois name for *The Great Binding Law*, 132

Gemini (JEM-ihn-eye) *n.* a constellation; in Roman mythology, it represents twins who sit across the Milky Way from Orion; Native Americans called them stars of decision, 9

Geneva (je-NEE-vah) a city in southwestern Switzerland, 233

Genghis Khan (GENG-ihs KAHN) *n.* (1162-1227) Mongol conqueror of Asia, 308

Gentile (JEN-teyel) *adj.* a person who is not Jewish, 352

gesticulation (jes-tihk-yoo-LAY-shuhn) *n.* hand signals, 278

giddy (GIHD-ee) *adj.* feeling dizzy, 94

Gimpachi (geem-PAH-chee) Rosie's uncle in "Seventeen Syllables," 92

glen (GLEN) *n.* a valley, 40

Glenties (GLEN-teez) a town in "The Man Who Had No Story," 39

goaded (GOHD-ihd) *v.* prodded, driven, 315

God in religions that worship one god, the name of the creator and ruler of the universe, 263

gouged (GOWJD) *adj.* grooved, dug out, 243

gourd (GAWRD) *n.* a hard-shelled fruit that can be scooped out and used as a cup or bowl, 154

gran'chillun (GRAN-chihl-luhn) *n.* grandchildren, 286

grapple (GRAP-puhl) *v.* to try to overcome or deal with, 226

grave (GRAYV) *adj.* very serious, 94

gringo (GREEN-goh) *n.* Spanish for *foreigner*, especially someone from the United States, 265

grudgingly (GRUJ-ihng-lee) *adv.* giving something reluctantly, 65, 296

guava (GWAH-vuh) a fruit tree common to Barbados in the West Indies, 67

guileless (GEYEL-les) *adj.* sincere, honest, free from deception, 305

H

habeas corpus (HAY-bee-uhs COR-puhs) *n.* a Latin phrase used in the legal system; order requiring a person to be in court, 270

hai (HEYE) *n. pl.* Vietnamese word for *shoes*, 32

haiku (HEYE-koo) *n.* a traditional Japanese poetic form consisting of three unrhymed lines with 5, 7, and 5 syllables in each line, respectively, 89

halcyon (HAL-see-uhn) *adj.* happy, peaceful, tranquil, 319

hallowed (HAL-ohd) *adj.* sacred, 141

Hana Omiya (hah-nah oo-mee-yah) *Japanese*, a woman's name, 191

hants (HANTS) *n.* haunts or ghosts, 179

Harlem (HAHR-luhm) a section of New York City, in northern Manhattan, 234

Harriet Tubman (HAH-ree-uht TUB-muhn) helped enslaved African Americans escape to freedom through the Underground Railroad, 178

harvest (HAHR-vihst) *n.* the time of year when ripe fruits, vegetables, and grains are picked, 248

Hayano (HEYE-yah-noh) a Japanese family name, 91

Hayashi (HEYE-yah-shee) a Japanese family name, 90

helplessness (HELP-luhs-nuhs) *n.* the state of being weak or needing protection, 94

herbs (ERBZ) *n. pl.* plants often used as seasonings or medicines, 149

hied (HEYED) *v.* hurried, 81

Hiroshiges (HEE-roh-shee-gayz) *n. pl.* beautiful block prints by the famous Japanese artist Hiroshige, 95

hogan (HOH-gan) *n.* a six- or eight-sided traditional Navajo dwelling, 147

hold (HOHLD) *n.* the interior of a ship below the decks, 160

Holy Elements Among Native Americans, all parts of the earth are believed to be sacred. 147

Homer (HOH-mer) *n.* 8th-century B.C. Greek epic poet; author of the *Iliad* and the *Odyssey*, 318

homogeneous (hoh-muh-JEE-nee-uhs) *adj.* similar; of the same kind, 339

hue (HYOO) *n.* color, 158, 184

human rights privileges belonging to everyone, 226

humiliating (hyoo-MIHL-ee-ay-tihng) *v.* hurting someone's pride; making someone feel foolish, 282

husked (HUSKT) *v.* removed the outer layer, as with corn, 261

Hydas (HEYE-dahz) *n.* literally means *people*; Native Americans of the Pacific Northwest, 140

I

i parenti e gli amici (EE pah-REN-tee AY LEE ah-MEE-chee) an Italian expression meaning *parents and friends*, 280

I've been to the mountaintop After leading the Jews out of bondage in Egypt, Moses ascended a mountain (Deuteronomy 34:1-3) and surveyed Israel, the Promised Land where his people would forge a new life. 231

ill-provisioned (ihl-pruh-VIHZH-uhnd) *adj.* poorly supplied, 77

impress (IHM-pres) *n.* an impression or mark, 158

improvident (ihm-PRAHV-uh-duhnt) *adj.* reckless, 160

impudent (IHM-pyoo-duhnt) *adj.* rude, disrespectful, 316

in a body *prep. phrase* all together, 26

incarceration (ihn-kahr-ser-AY-shuhn) *n.* imprisonment, 337

incredulous (ihn-KREJ-oo-luhs) *adj.* unbelieving, 71

indecorum (ihn-dih-KOHR-uhm) *n.* improper behavior, 169

indigent (IN-duh-juhnt) *adj.* poor, 19

indiscretion (ihn-dihs-KRESH-uhn) *n.* an unwise act, 97

indolent (IHN-duh-luhnt) *adj.* idle or lazy, 30

infinitum (ihn-fuh-NEYET-uhm) *n.* forever, without limit, 84

inflicting (ihn-FLIHKT-ihng) *v.* bringing down on, 59

injunctions (in-JUHNK-shuhnz) *n.* court orders prohibiting an action, 228

injustice the quality of being unfair, 227

insidiously (ihn-SIHD-ee-uhs-lee) *adv.* treacherously, 205

intellectualism (ihn-tuhl-EK-choo-wuhl-ihzum) *n.* focus on logical thought, 109

intercede (ihn-tuhr-SEED) *v.* plead on another person's behalf, 169

internment camps (ihn-TERN-muhnt KAMPS) During World War II, the U.S. government forced

Japanese Americans living on the West Coast to move to armed camps in the western deserts because it feared that all Japanese Americans might be spies for Japan. 269

irate (eye-RAYT) *adj.* angry, 59

irrevocable (ih-REV-uh-kuh-buhl) *adj.* not able to be called back or changed, 96

irritable (IHR-ih-tuh-buhl) *adj.* easily annoyed, 60

Issei (EES-SAY) *n.* a Japanese who emigrated to the United States or Canada after 1907 and was not eligible for citizenship until 1952, 274

J

Jalisco (hah-LEES-koh) *n.* a state in west central Mexico, 251

jalopy (jah-LAH-pee) *n.* an old, rickety automobile, 252

jarred (JAHRD) *v.* shaken or vibrated from a sudden impact, 240

jaybird-talk (JAY-buhrd TAWK) chattering, gossipy talk, 178

Jehovah (jih-HOH-vuh) the Hebrew name for God, 179

jerked venison dried deer meat, 101

Jesus (JEE-zuhs) according to the Christian religion, the son of God, 261

Jesus Carrasco (HAY-soos kah-RAHS-koh) *Spanish*, a man's name, 92

Jewish cake a cake that is traditional to Jewish families and celebrations, 353

jíbara (HEE-bah-rah) *n.* Puerto Rican peasant woman, 360

jíbaro (HEE-bah-roh) *n.* Puerto Rican peasant, 357

Joaquín (hwah-KEEN) *Spanish*, a man's name, 265

John Brown the leader of a raid on the arsenal at Harpers Ferry to get arms for abolitionists, 179

journey (JER-nee) *n.* a trip, 9

jubilees (joo-buhl-EEZ) *n. pl.* African American folk songs about a happy time in the future, 341

Judge Hooks Benjamin Hooks, an important figure in the Civil Rights Movement, 229

Juffure's (joo-FOO-rahz) *n.* belonging to the village of Juffure in present-day The Gambia, in Africa, 57

K

kafo (KAH-foh) *n.* a group of young men who have reached manhood at the same time, 57

Kalamata (kal-uh-MAHT-uh) a city in southern Greece, 316

kimono (kih-MOH-noh) *n.* a robe worn by Japanese women with short, wide sleeves, and a sash, 191

kintango (kin-TANG-goh) *n.* leader who supervised the training of young men in what is now The Gambia, in Africa, 58

kiva (KEE-vuh) *n.* structure used for religious and other purposes by some Native American groups, 100

knishes (kuh-NIHSH-uhz) *n.* pastries stuffed with potatoes or cheese, 334

knoll (NOHL) *n.* small hill, 76

kokoretsi (koh-koh-RET-see) *n.* a Greek roasted lamb dish, 317

Ku Klux Klansmen (KOO KLUX KLANZ-men) members of the Ku Klux Klan, a secret organization directed against African Americans, Catholics, Jews, and the foreign-born, 236, 272

"Kum kumka yali, kum . . . tambe" an ancient African chant, 175

"Kum . . . yali, kum buba tambe" an ancient African chant, 174

Kuroda (KOO-roh-dah) *Japanese*, a man's name, 96

L

La Bajada (LAH bah-HAH-dah) *n.* name of a town in "The Sheep of San Cristóbal," 21

la española cascabelling (lah ays-pahn-NYOH-lah kahs-kah-BEL-ihng) the Spanish woman ringing (Spanish word combined with English suffix), 357

la familia (lah fah-MEE-lee-ah) *n.* Spanish for *the family*, 49

La Raza!/Méjicano!/Español!/Latino!/Hispano!/ Chicano! (la RAH-sah!/MAY-hee-kah-noh!/ays-pan-NYOHL!/lah-TEE-noh!/hees-PAH-noh!/chee-KAH-noh!) Spanish for *the Mexican people, Mexican, Spanish, Latin, Hispanic, Mexican American*, 267

lacquers (LAHK-uhrz) *n.* fine boxes and ornaments made of wood and coated with a thick varnish, 195

lag (LAG) *n.* a period of delay, 291

Lame Deer a medicine man of the Oglala people, 108

languishing (LANG-gwihsh-ihng) *v.* lying weakly, 73

Las Colonias (LAHS koh-LOH-nee-ahs) *n.* the name of a town in "The Sheep of San Cristóbal," 16

las comadres (lahs kohm-AH-drays) *n.* the Spanish expression for *the godmothers*, or close family friends, 215

Later he got rubbed out for doing that a reference to the Battle of the Little Bighorn (June 25, 1876), in which the Lakota, under the leadership of Chief Crazy Horse and Chief Sitting Bull, killed Custer and his men, 127

latinoamerica (la-TEE-noh-uh-MER-ee-ka) *n.* the area of land that includes Mexico, Central and South America, and the West Indies, where Spanish, Portuguese, and French are the offical languages, 360

lazo (LAH-soh) *n.* Spanish for *lasso*, 47

leeches (LEECH-uhz) *n.* people who try to get what they want without earning it, 343

lender's slave *n.* In Africa, a debtor who had to work off the debt to the lender, 59

lentils (LEN-tihlz) *n. pl.* flat seeds used as food, from the legume family, 317

Leo (LEE-oh) *n.* a constellation in the shape of a lion; also a sign of the zodiac, 10

lichen-covered (LEYE-kuhn KUV-erd) covered with gray or greenish plant growth, 103

lined (LEYEND) *v.* made line drives, or hard hits that travel close to the ground in baseball, 116

Listo (LEES-toh) *adj.* Spanish for *ready*, 252

llaneros (yahn-AY-rohs) *n. pl.* Spanish for *plainsmen*, 47

llano (YAHN-oh) *n.* Spanish for *a flat area*, like a prairie, 46

loathsome (LOH<u>TH</u>-sum) *adj.* disgusting enough to make one sick, 160

lolling (LAHL-ihng) *v.* hanging around, 353

Long Sash the name of the guide in "The Stars," also the Native American name for Orion, 8

lorry (LAWR-ee) *n.* a British word for *truck*, 65

Luna (LOO-nah) *n.* the mother's family name in *Bless Me, Ultima*, 49

luncheonette (lun-chuh-NET) *n.* a restaurant that serves lunches and other light meals, 183

lured (LOORD) *v.* tempted, 352

lustful (LUST-fuhl) *adj.* full of or motivated by greed, 266

lynching (LIHNCH-ihng) *n.* murder by a mob, 341

M

machetes (muh-SHET-eez) *n. pl.* heavy knives used for cutting sugar cane and underbrush, or as weapons, 27

Madre de Dios (MAHD-ray day DEE-ohs) Spanish for *Mother of God*; Mary, the mother of Jesus Christ, 52

magnanimity (mag-nah-NIM-ih-tee) *n.* generosity, 280

magpies (MAG-peyez) *n.* crow-like birds, having long, graduated tails, black and white feathers, and noisy, mischievous habits, 243

Mainichi Shimbun (MEYE-een-nee-chee SHEEM-boon) a Japanese-language newspaper published in San Francisco, 90

malevolence (muh-LEV-uh-luhns) *n.* ill will, maliciousness, 314

Mamacita (mah-mah-SEE-tah) *n.* a Spanish pet name for *mother*, 214

man-training *n.* formal preparation for becoming a man, 58

Mango (MAHN-goh) *n.* a kind of fruit, 67, 213, 360

Manuel (mahn-WEL) *Spanish*, a man's name, 22

Marathon (MAR-uh-thon) *n.* a plain in southeast Greece in the province of Attica, where the Athenians defeated the Persians in 490 B.C., 317

Márez (MAH-rays) *n.* Márez is the family name of the father's relatives in *Bless Me, Ultima*, 51

María Luna (mah-REE-ah LOO-nuh) the mother's name in *Bless Me, Ultima*, 52

mariachi (mah-ree-AH-chee) *n.* a type of Mexican dance music, 266

marl (MAHRL) *n.* mixture of dirt and shell fragments, 67

Mary in the Christian religion, the mother of Jesus, 261

master *n.* a ruler, someone who has control over others, 166

Masuam (mah-soo-AHM) Animal Dance of the Plains people, 366

match (MACH) *n.* arranged marriage, 97

mattock (MAT-uhk) *n.* a digging tool, 279

mavrodaphne (mav-ROH-daf-nee) a Greek wine, 318

meager (MEE-guhr) *adj.* lacking in quantity and/or quality, 195

medicine man (MED-uh-sihn MAN) *n.* a priestly healer, 28

Medicine of the Eagle According to the Plains Native Americans, some people are born with the ability to "see far," or perceive things or ideas with great depth. 364

Medicine Wheel in the Plains nations' belief system, the circle that represents all the people, animals, rocks, rivers, and religions in the universe, 364

mesa (MAY-suh) *n.* land formation that looks like a hill or mountain with a flat top, 17, 101

mestiza (may-STEE-sah) *n.* a woman of mixed European and Native American descent, 360

meticulous (muh-TIHK-yoo-luhs) *adj.* extremely careful, 338

mettle (MET-uhl) *n.* courage, spirit, quality of character, 315

Mi olla (mee OL-yah) Spanish for *My pot*, 253

mija, negra, ne (MEE-hah, NAY-grah, NAY) *n.* Spanish for *my daughter* (a shortened form of *mi hija*), *black woman*, *baby* (a shortened form of *nena*), 360

Milky Way a wide band of milky light across the night sky; it is caused by the light of thousands of faint stars, 13

mincemeat (MIHNS-meet) *n.* a mixture composed of minced apples, suet, and sometimes meat, together with raisins, currants, candied citron, for filling a pie, 240

Mine eyes have seen the glory of the coming of the Lord the first line of the "Battle Hymn of the Republic," a Civil War anthem written by Julia Ward Howe, 231

Mira (MEE-rah) *v.* the Spanish word for *look*, 187

mirth (MERTH) *n.* joy, 352

Mitakuye oyasin (mee-tah-kee AH-SAY) Lakota for *All my relatives!*, 113

mite (MEYET) *n.* very small amount, 167

mock (MAHK) *v.* make fun of, ridicule, 166

mole (MOHL) *n.* a small animal that burrows in the soil, 11

molestation (moh-les-TAY-shun) *n.* interference, 142

molino (moh-LEE-noh) *n.* Spanish for *a mill*, 50

Molotov cocktails (MAHL-ah-tahv KOK-taylz) *n.* bottles of explosive liquids, 229

Mongol (MAHNG-uhl) *adj.* a member of a people living in Mongolia, 308

monolithic (mahn-uh-LIHTH-ihk) *adj.* single; uniform; having no differences, 336

monsoon (mahn-SOON) *adj.* referring to the rainy season of southeast Asia, 34

moon (MOON) *n.* month, 57, 142

Moors (MOORZ) *n.* a Muslim people from northwestern Africa who invaded Spain, 266

mosques (MAHSKS) *n.* Moslem places of worship, 334

motif (moh-TEEF) *n.* a main theme or subject, 176

motley (MAHT-lee) *adj.* diverse, 314

Mount Olympus (MOWNT oh-LIHM-pus) *n.* home of the Greek gods, 317

movering (MOOV-er-ihng) *v.* migrating, 179

mulatto (muh-LAH-toh) *n.* a person with some white and some black heredity, 177

musing (MYOO-zihng) *v.* daydreaming, meditating, 167

Myrmidons (MER-muh-dahnz) *n.* warriors of ancient Thessaly in eastern Greece, 316

N

Nagoya (NAH-goh-yah) a seaport in Japan, 193

Nâng Tien (NAHNG TIHN) a fairy who helps T'âm in "In the Land of Small Dragon," 32

Navajo (NAH-vah-hoh) *n.* name of a Native American people of the southwestern United States, 22

Negrita (nay-GREE-tah) *n.* in Spanish, *little black one*; the name Felipa gives a sheep in "The Sheep of San Cristóbal," 20

nena (NAY-nah) *n.* Spanish word for *child*, 185

neurosis (noo-ROH-sihs) *n.* a mild personality disorder, 265

new men *n. pl.* young men formally accepted into the adult male African community, 57

nightriders *n. pl.* people who try to frighten others by performing acts of terror and violence at night, 272

Nisei (NEE-SAY) *n.* a person of Japanese descent, born and educated in the U.S., 270

Nkwame (NKWAH-mee) an African man's name, 200

nocturnal (nahk-TER-nuhl) *adj.* night-time, 80

nomadic (noh-MAD-ihk) *adj.* wandering, 77

nonviolent (nahn-VEYE-uh-luhnt) *adj.* not using physical force, 234

North Star name for a star used to find direction, 13

notes of a white man's scale specific musical notes of European musical tradition, 110

novena (noh-VEE-nah) *n.* in the Catholic Church, a devotion consisting of nine separate days of prayers or services, 273

Nuestra Señora de los Dolores (noo-AYS-trah say-NYOR-ah DAY LOHS doh-LOH-rays) *Spanish* for *Our Lady of Sorrows*, a name for Mary, the mother of Jesus Christ, 18

O

obdurate (AHB-duhr-uht) *adj.* stubbornly persistent in behaving improperly or wrongly, 136

obsidian (ahb-SIHD-ee-uhn) *n.* a hard volcanic glass, 102

oinikaga tipi (oi-NEE-kah-gah TEE-pee) a Lakota sweat lodge, 112

old Empires countries ruled by one ruler; for centuries, the countries of Europe were ruled by kings and queens; in "Ellis Island," the immigrants are leaving these countries for the United States, 208

old man another name for God in "The Drinking Gourd," 154

old Wasichu's road, the the Bozeman Trail, which ran from Fort Laramie, Colorado, to the mining town of Virginia City, Montana: Native Americans objected to settlers' use of this road by gold prospectors because it crossed their main hunting grounds, 129

omen (OH-men) *n.* a sign, something that tells about the future, 10

ominous (AHM-ihn-uhs) *adj.* threatening, 272

omnisciently (ahm-NIHSH-uhnt-lee) *adv.* having complete knowledge, 342

opaque (oh-PAYK) *adj.* not clear; not letting light go through, 80

oracles (OR-ah-kuhls) *n. pl.* the ambiguous and wise pronouncements of ancient Greek gods, goddesses, priests, and priestesses, 318

orator (AWR-uht-uhr) *n.* a speaker or giver of formal speeches, 26

Orion (oh-REYE-uhn) *n.* a constellation; in Roman mythology, Orion was a great hunter, 8

ornate (ohr-NAYT) *adj.* much decorated, 337

ortega (awr-TAY-guh) *Spanish*, a family name, 292

Osaka (OH-sah-kah) a seaport in Japan, 193

ostracism (AHS-truh-sihz-uhm) *n.* exclusion; being shut out, 335

Our Lady Mary, the mother of Jesus Christ, 17

out of hand *prep. phrase* at once, 59

overseer (OH-vuhr-see-er) *n.* supervisor, 169

ow ilaw sa gabing madilim wangis mo'y bituin sa langit (OH EE-low SAH GAHB-ihng mah-dih-LEEM WAHNG-ees MOI bih-TWEEN SAH LAHNG-iht) Tagalog (a language spoken in the Philippines) for *Light in the middle of the night/your face like stars in the sky*, 85

Owens Valley a town from which the Wakatsuki family had been forced to move, 272

P

paddy wagons (PAD-ee WAG-uhns) *n.* vans used by police for prisoners, 228

Padre (PAH-dray) *n.* Father; priest's title in Spanish, 18

padrone (pah-DROH-nay) in "In the American Storm," a person who recruited Italian immigrants to do low-paying jobs in the United States, 279

pagans (PAY-guhnz) *n.* people with no religion, 338

Pahuska (pa-HUS-kah) Lakota for *Long Hair*, a name for U.S. General George Custer, 127

Pan (PAN) *n.* the ancient Greek god of forests, pastures, flocks, and shepherds, 318

Panama money (PAN-uh-mah MUN-ee) money earned from working on the Panama Canal, 67

Panchito (pahn-CHEE-toh) *n.* a Spanish nickname for *Francisco*, 253

papaw (PAW-paw) *n.* also called *papaya*, a fruit tree common to Barbados in the West Indies, 67

paradox (PAR-ah-dohks) *n.* a statement that seems self-contradictory, 265

paragon (PAR-uh-gahn) *n.* model of perfection, 204

paranoid (PAR-uh-noid) *adj.* very suspicious, 338

particles (PAHR-tih-kuhlz) *n. pl.* tiny pieces, 148

pase, Grande, pase. Nuestra casa es su casa (PAH-say GRAHN-day, PAH-say. noo-AYS-trah

CAH-sah ays soo CAH-sah) Spanish for *Come in Grande, come in. Our home is your home.* 54

pastrami (puh-STRAH-mee) *n.* smoked beef, 334

paterollers (PAHT-uhr-ohl-erz) *n.* the train wheels, 178

pathetic (puh-THET-ihk) *adj.* pitiful; miserably inadequate, 304

patriarchs (PAY-tree-ahrks) *n. pl.* rulers, 337

pawn (PAWN) *n.* someone who is used or manipulated, 305

pedro flores (PAY-droh FLOH-rays) *n.* a Puerto Rican composer, 357

peevishly (PEEV-ihsh-lee) *adv.* in a way that shows annoyance, 296

peg foot a wooden leg, 154

penance (PEN-uhns) *n.* an act done to show that one is sorry for doing wrong, 18

perdone . . . yo me llamo pedro (pair-DOH-nay . . . yoh may YAH-moh PAY-droh) Spanish for *excuse me, my name is Pedro,* 291

perdone mi padre era el señor ortega (a veces don josé) (pair-DOH-nay, mee PAH-dray E-rah el se-NYOR awr-TAY-guh [ah VAY-says dohn hoh-SAY]) Spanish for *excuse me, my father was Mr. Ortega (sometimes called Don José),* 291

perennial (puh-REN-ee-uhl) *adj.* every year, everlasting, 70

pestilential (pes-tuh-LEN-shuhl) *adj.* carrying and spreading infection, 160

peta owihankeshni (pay-TAH oh-wee-HAHNK-shnee) the Lakota "fire without end" passed down through generations, 112

petitioners (puh-TIHSH-uhn-erz) *n. pl.* people asking for help, 57

peyote (pay-OHT-ee) *n.* drug that comes from cactus buttons, 108

Pharaoh (FA-roh) **wanted to prolong the period of slavery in Egypt** In ancient Egypt, the pharaoh, or king, enslaved the Jews. 227

pick and shovel hard, physical work, usually involving digging, 278

pickaxed (PIHK-akst) *v.* hit with a pickax; a pickax is a tool with a two-sided head: one end of its head has a point and the other has a chisel edge; used for digging in hard soil or rock, 239

piki bread (PEE-kee BRED) crisp flat bread made from cornmeal, 101

pilaf (pih-LAHF) *n.* rice cooked in poultry or meat broth, 319

pillage (PIHL-ihj) *n.* theft, 77

Plain of Pine Trees the name of a flat, treeless area of land in "Wasichus in the Hills," 129

plausible (PLAWZ-ihbuhl) *adj.* believable, 176

plena-rhythms (PLAY-nah) *n.* a kind of music invented in Puerto Rico, 358

plumage (PLOO-mihj) *n.* feathers, 27

pollen (PAH-lihn) *n.* the powderlike substance formed by the flower; used in ceremonies and, when praying, as an offering to the spirits, 149

pollution (puh-LOO-shuhn) *n.* contamination, dirt, 187

pompadour (PAHM-puh-dawr) *n.* a hair style in which the hair is swept up high from the forehead and rolled backwards, 191

praise (PRAYZ) *n.* approval or admiration, 204

prayed (PRAYD) *v.* asked for help or guidance from God, 18

priest (PREEST) *n.* the leader of a church or religious group, 18

privy (PRIHV-ee) *n.* outdoor toilet in a small shed, 93

Promised Land a name for *heaven* in the Christian religion, 226

propaganda (prahp-uh-GAN-duh) *n.* information that is supposed to mislead people and to make them think in a particular way, 271

prophet (PROF-iht) *n.* a person who tells what will happen in the future, 343

prophetic (proh-FET-ihk) *adj.* telling the future, 11

proprietary right (pruh-PREYE-uh-ter-ee REYET) right of ownership, 134

protracted (proh-TRAKT-ed) *adj.* long and drawn out, 73

providence (PRAH-vu-dens) *n.* God's help, 170

Ptesan Win (TAY-sah WEE) another name for the White Buffalo Woman, a character in "Cante Ishta—The Eye of the Heart," 109

pueblo (PWEB-loh) *n.* type of village built by some Native American peoples, 100

purification (pyoor-ih-fih-KAY-shuhn) *n.* making pure, clearing of guilt or imperfections, 113

purled (PERLD) *v.* rippled, moved gently, 81

pushcart (PUHSH-kahrt) *n.* any of various types of wheeled light cart to be pushed by hand, as one used by a street vendor, 314

Q

quail (KWAYL) *n.* a game bird, 154

quarantine (KWAHR-uhn-teen) *n.* separation and isolation; a waiting period imposed on immigrants to keep disease from spreading into the United States, 208

que corta (kay KOR-tah) *adj.* Spanish for *sharp*, 358

¡Qué lástima! (kay LAHS-tee-mah) the Spanish expression, *What a pity!*, 46

"¿qué tal, hermano?" (KAY TAHL uhr-MAH-noh) Spanish for *how goes it, brother?*, 84

queue (KYOO) *n.* line of people, 203

Quince (KEEN-say) *n.* Spanish for *fifteen*, 255

R

race (RAYS) *n.* a group of people whose members are regarded as having a common ancestry or origin and similar physical traits, 291

railed (RAYLD) *v.* scolded, 202

rains (RAYNZ) *n. pl.* years. Since there is one rainy season a year in The Gambia, counting rainy seasons is the same as counting years. 58

Ralph Ralph Abernathy, a civil rights leader and one of Dr. King's close associates, 227

rambunctiously (ram-BUNK-shuhs-lee) *adv.* uncontrollably, 92

rancheros (rahn-CHAY-rohs) *n. pl.* Spanish for *ranchers*, 46

range (RAYNJ) *n.* a row, line, or series, 76

ravishing (RAV-ihsh-ihng) *adj.* very beautiful, 34

razed (RAYZD) *v.* destroyed, 337

red brick in "Ellis Island," the poet is referring to the buildings through which the immigrants had to pass to enter the United States, 208

Red Cloud an Oglala chief, 127

relentless (rih-LENT-lihs) *adj.* unyieldingly severe, strict, or harsh, 305

rendered (REN-duhrd) *v.* caused to become or made, 160

repercussions (ree-puhr-KUSH-uhnz) *n. pl.* reactions to an event, 91

repository (rih-PAHZ-uh-tawr-ee) *n.* place where things are stored, 338

reproachful (rih-PROHCH-fuhl) *adj.* blaming, disappointed, 18

reproved (rih-PROOVD) *v.* spoken to in disapproval, 64

retsina (ret-SEE-nuh) a Greek wine, 318

revelation (rev-uh-LAY-shuhn) *n.* telling of previously unknown information, 97

reveling (REV-uhl-ihng) *v.* taking great pleasure, 298

revenge (rih-VENJ) *n.* the act of hurting or getting back at someone, 30

rice paddy *n.* wet land on which rice is grown, 30

ring of heat summer heat, 116

rods (RAHDZ) *n.* straight, slender sticks growing on trees or bushes, 39

roguish (ROH-gihsh) *adj.* playfully mischievous, 67

rose *v.* went to a higher place, the past tense of *rise*, 116

royaneh (LOY-ah-nee) *n.* Iroquois lords, 136

rumble *v.* fight, 236

ruse (ROOZ) *n.* trick, or dodge, 201

S

sable (SAY-bul) *adj.* dark in color, 158

sabre track (SAY-buhr TRAK) railroad, 179

sachems (SAY-chemz) *n.* leaders or chiefs of the Suquamish people, 141

Sacramento (sak-ruh-MEN-toh) *n.* a port and the capital city of California, 244

sacred (SAY-krihd) *adj.* holy, 77

sage (SAYJ) *n.* a plant with grayish, spicy-smelling leaves, 112

sala (SAH-lah) *n.* Spanish for *living room*, 46

sallow (SAHL-oh) *adj.* a sickly, pale color, 197

saluted (suh-LOOT-ed) *v.* met, 159

Samos (SAY-mahs) a Greek island, 317

sampans (SAM-panz) *n. pl.* small boats used in China and Japan, 95

samurai (SAM-yoo-reye) *n.* a member of a landowner's army; in early Japan, each large landowner had his own army, 192

San (SAHN) *n.* a word that shows respect in Japanese, 193

San Cristóbal (SAHN krees-TOH-bahl) *n.* the Spanish name for Saint Christopher and a town in "The Sheep of San Cristóbal," 16

Sancho (SAHN-choh) *Spanish,* a man's name, 17

Sandoval (SAHN-doh-vahl) *n.* Felipa's family name in "The Sheep of San Cristóbal," 22

Santorini (san-tor-EE-nee) a Greek island, 317

scarlet (SCAHR-liht) *adj.* very bright red, 185

scathed (SKAY<u>TH</u>d) *v.* burned or injured, 166

scissortail (SIHZ-er-tayl) *n.* a bird with a deeply forked tail, 81

SCLC Southern Christian Leadership Conference, a civil rights organization founded in 1957 by Martin Luther King, Jr., 229

scow (SKOW) *n.* a large, flat-bottom boat used to carry freight, 351

scowling (SKOWL-ihng) *v.* making an angry or unhappy face, 30

scrutinized (SKROO-tihn-eyezd) *v.* examined in detail with careful attention, 302

seer (SEER) *n.* the overseer or slave driver, the often cruel person who drove the slaves to work harder and harder, 175

self-immolation (self-ihm-uh-LAY-shuhn) *n.* self-sacrifice or self-destruction, 73

sentinels (SEN-tih-nuhlz) *n.* watchers or guards, 80

sequestered (see-KWES-terd) *adj.* hidden, 141

serf (SERF) *n.* slave, 345

shackled (SHAK-uhld) *v.* restrained by metal bands around wrists or ankles, 342

sham (SHAM) *adj.* false, 108

sharecropper (SHAIR-crahper) *n.* a tenant farmer who works the landowner's farm for a share of the crops, 251

shoveled (SHUV-uhld) *v.* dug out with a broad, deep scoop, 239

shtetl (SHTET-uhl) *n.* small Jewish village formerly found in eastern Europe, 360

Shyelas (SHEYE-las) Cheyenne Native Americans, 129

Sí, mamá (SEE mah-MAH) Spanish for *yes, mother,* 51

sinewy (SIHN-yoo-ee) *adj.* tough, resilient, muscular, 315

sinisterness (SIHN-ihs-tuhr-nes) *n.* hint of evil or danger, 93

Sioux (SOO) *n.* a Native American nation that lives on the plains, 109

sipapu (see-PAH-poo) *n.* the hole in the floor of a council meeting room from which the Hopis' ancestors were thought to have first emerged, 11

sipo-pede (see-POH-pay-day) *n.* the hole in the floor of a council meeting room from which the Tewas' ancestors were thought to have first emerged, 11

slack (SLAK) *adj.* relaxed, loose, 305

slave ship a boat used to bring enslaved Africans to the United States, 159

sledgehammer (SLEJ-ham-uhr) *n.* a large hammer used to break up heavy objects, usually used with both hands, 240

slurred (SLERD) *v.* stirred up, disturbed, 66

Smoky Earth River the name of a river in "Wasichus in the Hills," 127

Socorro (soh-KOH-roh) *n.* name of a town in present-day New Mexico, 22

Soldiers' Town Fort Robinson, in western South Dakota, 127

solitudes (SAHL-uh-toodz) *n. pl.* secluded or lonely places, 142

somber (SAHM-ber) *adj.* dark or gloomy, 142

Songe-de-ho (sahn-gah-DAY-hoh) the Hopi word for *goodbye,* 13

soul (SOHL) *n.* a way of addressing a person in Barbados, similar to *child* or *girl,* 65

spanglish (SPAN-glihsh) *n.* combination of Spanish and English, 358

speck (SPEK) *v.* suspect, 286

spicecake a traditional Jewish cake often baked for special occasions, 353

spurned (SPERND) *v.* rejected, 59, 261

stalemate (STAYL-mayt) *n.* a standstill or deadlock, 308

steal away escape quietly; in "Steal Away," the singer hopes to escape slavery and to find God, 155

stench (STENCH) *n.* foul smell, 160

stiletto (stih-LET-oh) *adj.* thin and sharp, like a dagger, 67

stillborn (STIHL-bawrn) *adj.* born dead, 97

stolidly (STAH-lihd-lee) *adv.* showing no emotion, 141

stoop (STOOP) *n.* a porch at the entrance of a house, 354

strand (STRAND) *n.* shore, 345

"streets flowing with milk and honey" in the Bible, the promised land of the Jews, 229

strictures (STRIHK-chers) *n.* restrictions, 193

succession (suhk-SESH-uhn) *n.* a number of people or things coming after one another in line, 59

succulent (SUK-yoo-luhnt) *adj.* juicy, 102

suffice (suh-FEYES) *adj.* sufficient, 168

sugar apple (SHUG-er AP-puhl) a fruit tree common to Barbados in the West Indies, 67

sullied (SUL-eed) *v.* soiled, tarnished, 301

Sun Dance In the Plains nations' belief system, people should choose whom they will marry by comparing their medicines, or inborn ways of seeing the world. Those who choose wisely are said to be equal in the great Give-Away Dance, or Sun Dance. 365

Sun Yat-sen (SOON YAHT-SEN) *n.* (1866-1925) a Chinese leader, 307

sun-beaten (SUN-beet-uhn) *adj.* being very tired and hot from being in the sun a long time, 248

surrealists (suh-REE-uhl-ihsts) *n.* artists who use images from the unconscious, 336

sweat (SWET) *n.* perspiration, often caused by heat or hard work, 248

sweat tepee (SWET TEE-pee) also sweat lodge. A structure used by many Native American peoples for prayer and cleansing. 126

T

T'âm (TAHM) a Vietnamese girl's name, 30

tables of stone the Ten Commandments in the Old Testament of the Bible, 141

taciturn (TAS-uh-tern) *adj.* silent by habit, not talkative, 187

tactful (TAKT-fuhl) *adj.* having a keen sense of what is appropriate or tasteful, 309

Tai-me (teye-MEE) sacred Kiowa and Crow Sun Dance doll, 77

Taína (teye-EE-nah) *n.* a female member of an extinct Puerto Rican people, 360

Taíno (teye-EE-noh) *n.* a male member of an extinct Puerto Rican people, 360

tainted (TAYNT-uhd) *adj.* spoiled; contaminated, 337

Taiwan (TEYE-WAHN) *n.* an island off the coast of China. In 1949, Taiwan became an independent state called the Republic of China. 308

Taiyuan (teye-yoo-AHN) *n.* a capital city in northern China, 307

Taka (TAH-kah) Rosie's aunt in "Seventeen Syllables," 92

tangled (TANG-uhld) *v.* confused or caught in a net, 342

Taoist (DOW-ihst) *adj.* pertaining to the popular Chinese religion, Taoism, which advocates a life of complete simplicity, naturalness, and noninterference with the course of natural events to attain a happy and harmonious existence, 242

Taro Takeda (tah-roh tah-ke-dah) *Japanese,* a man's name, 192

tatami (tuh-TA-mee) *adj.* a Japanese floor mat woven of reeds or straw, 192

taunting (TAWNT-ihng) *adj.* mocking or teasing, 296

tejanos (tay-HAH-nohs) *n. pl.* Spanish for *Texans,* 46

tenaciously (tuh-NAY-shuhs-lee) *adv.* strongly, not letting go, 46

tendrils (TEN-druhlz) *n.* threadlike, leafless parts of climbing plants, 318

tenement (TEN-uh-muhnt) *n.* apartment occupied by tenants; often meaning a building that is overcrowded and in poor condition, 184

tenuous (TEN-yoo-uhs) *adj.* shaky, 79

Terminal Island a place from which the Wakatsuki family had been forced to move, 272

Tesúque (tay-SOO-kay) *n.* name of a town in "The Sheep of San Cristóbal," 21

Thanyani (tahn-EEAH-nee) an African man's name, 201

the trumpet sounds a religious belief that God will signal the end of the world with the sound of a trumpet, 155

thicketed (THIHK-iht-ed) *adj.* covered with thick bushes and underbrush, 177

'37 strike in 1937, economic conditions in Barbados, in the West Indies, were so severe that riots broke out. 73

thither (THI<u>TH</u>-uhr) *adv.* there, 168

Thoreau Henry David Thoreau, a famous writer and abolitionist in the 1800s, 179

thrill (THRIHL) *v.* to shiver with excitement, 142

throng (THRAWNG) *v.* to fill with a large crowd, 142

thronging (THRAWNG-ihng) *v.* crowding around, 342

Tienen que tener cuidado (tee-EN-en kay tay-NAIR

kwee-DAH-doh) Spanish for *You have to be careful*, 254

tolerance (TAHL-er-uhnz) *n.* allowing and accepting differences, 10

Tome Hayashi (TOH-may HEYE-yah-shee) *Japanese,* a woman's name, 91

torrid (TAWR-uhd) *adj.* very hot, 351

tortilla (tawr-TEE-yah) *n.* Spanish for *cornmeal pancake,* 50, 255

totalitarian (toh-tal-uh-TER-ee-uhn) *adj.* having one political party or group that maintains complete control under a dictatorship and bans all others, 228

trachoma (truh-KOH-muh) *n.* an eye infection, 196

trade cloth *n.* cheap cloth offered by European traders to Native Americans, whose clothing was made from animal skins, 112

transphysics (tranz-FIHZ-ihks) *n.* transcends laws of physics, 228

traumatic (trow-MAT-ihk) *adj.* hurtful or shocking, 205

trestle (TRES-uhl) *n.* railroad bridge, 351

Troy (TROI) *n.* an ancient city in Asia Minor, 316

truculent (TRUK-yoo-luhnt) *adj.* fierce, 65

trunks (TRUNKS) *n.* short pants worn by athletes, 351

truth *n.* the state of being honest, 201

Tsarist dissidents (ZAHR-ihst DIHS-uh-duhnts) followers of the Russian emperor who disagreed with a political policy, 336

Tsimpsians (TSIMP-see-unz) *n.* literally means *people of the Skeena River;* Native Americans of the Pacific Northwest, 140

tuberculosis (tuh-ber-kyoo-LOH-sihs) *n.* a disease of the lungs, 194

tumbleweeds (TUM-buhl-weedz) *n. pl.* large plants that break off at the soil, become dry, and roll about in the wind, 47

Tunka (toon-KAH) the rock, the oldest Lakota god, 112

Tunkashila (toon-KAH-shee-lah) the Lakota Grandfather Spirit, 110

turned *adj.* well-shaped, 116

turquoise (TER-koiz) *n.* a greenish blue, semiprecious stone, 102

Tutsi (TUHT-see) *adj.* referring to a specific African tribe, 74

U

ubiquitous (yoo-BIHK-wuh-tuhs) *adj.* present everywhere, 205

uli (OO-lee) *n.* an African word for *dye,* 25

Ultima (OOL-tee-mah) *Spanish,* a woman's name, 46

Ume Hanazono (OO-may HAH-nah-zoh-noh) *Japanese,* Rosie's mother's pen name in "Seventeen Syllables," 91

Unci (OONG-SHEE) *n.* a Lakota name for *Grandmother Earth,* 112

underground a hiding place; in "Runagate Runagate," a reference to the Underground Railroad, which helped enslaved African Americans escape to the North and to freedom, 177

unheeded (uhn-HEE-ded) *adj.* unnoticed; disregarded, 158

unnervingly (un-NERV-ihng-lee) *adv.* disturbingly, 64

unorthodox (uhn-AWR-thuh-dahks) *adj.* unconventional, out of the ordinary, 95

unrelenting (uhn-rih-LEN-tihng) *adj.* not letting up, 63, 77

urchin (ER-chihn) *n.* a small, ragged boy, 166

useter (YOOS-ter) *v.* used to, 288

Ute (YOOT) *n.* a Native American people of the southwestern United States, 16

V

vacillating (VAS-uh-layt-ihng) *adj.* wavering back and forth, undecided, 96

vales (VAYLZ) *n. pl.* valleys, 141

Vámonos (VAH-moh-nohs) *v.* Spanish for *Let's go,* 255

Van Gogh (van GOH) *n.* a Dutch painter known for using vivid colors, 74

vaquero (bah-KAY-roh) *n.* Spanish for *cowboy,* 46

variant (VAR-eeuhnt) *n.* a symbol that is often used, but sometimes appears in different forms, 176

verdant (VER-dent) *adj.* green, 141

vermin (VUR-mihn) *n.* fleas, lice, bedbugs, 169

vernaculars (vuhr-NAK-yuh-luhrz) *n. pl.* newspapers written in everyday language, 90

vexed (VEKSD) *adj.* annoyed; irritated, 168

vileness (VEYEL-nes) *n.* ugliness, horror, 97

violent (VEYE-uh-luhnt) *adj.* using physical force, 235

virulent (VIHR-yoo-luhnt) *adj.* poisonous; full of hate, 205

vision (VIH-zhun) *n.* a dream or experience a person has that communicates with the spirit world, 126

Vision Quest a message received from the spirit world (see "Humaweepi, the Warrior Priest" in Theme 3 and "Wasichus in the Hills" in Theme 4 for more information), 365

visionary (VIHZH-uhn-air-ee) *adj.* imaginative, 338

voluble (VAHL-yoo-buhl) *adj.* talkative, 26

vulnerability (vuhl-nuhr-uh-BIHL-uh-tee) *n.* the susceptibility to being hurt, 306

W

wake-house *n.* a house in which a wake, or watch over a dead person, is taking place, 41

wallowed (WAHL-ohd) *v.* rolled with pleasure, 351

wariness (WER-ee-nihs) *n.* watchfulness, 79

washte wikcemna (wah-SHTAI week-CHEM-nah) a Lakota sweet-smelling herb, 112

Wasichus (wah-SEE-choos) literally *stealers of the fat* in Lakota (Sioux); the name Lakota and Dakota people call white people, 126

wax (WAKS) *v.* grow in strength or number, 140

"We Shall Overcome" the theme song of the Civil Rights Movement, 228

when the hundred were rubbed out may refer to the Battle of the Hundred Slain, 127

White Chief a phrase used in "The Indians' Night Promises to be Dark" to refer to Governor Isaac Stevens of Washington, 139

White Citizens' Council a racist organization similar to the Ku Klux Klan, 236

without peer superior, without equal, 96

wives' Having more than one wife is an ancient, although uncommon, practice in Africa. Usually, a man must prove he can afford to marry another woman before he does so. Many African women accept this arrangement because they can then share household and child-rearing chores. 25

wok (WAHK) *n.* a large, bowl-shaped pan used in Chinese cooking, 309

wont (WAWNT) *n.* custom, usual way of behaving, 91

wunna (WUN-nah) *pron.* an expression in Barbados meaning *everybody* or *all of you*, 66

Y

Ya esora (YAH ays-AW-rah) the Spanish expression *It's time* (to stop working), 251

yoke (YOHK) *n.* a heavy wooden harness for work animals; sometimes meaning the pressures that held people in slavery, 168

Yoruben (YOHR-uh-buhn) *n.* language of a West African people, 336

youngun (YUNG-uhn) *n.* young one, 286

yucca fiber (YUK-kuh FEYE-ber) threadlike parts of the yucca plant, 102

yuwipi (yoo-WEE-pee) *n.* a healing ceremony done by Lakota and other Plains medicine men, 109

Z

Zeus (ZOOS) *n.* the supreme deity or god of the ancient Greeks, 317

THE WRITING PROCESS

When you are asked to write, do you feel that you are supposed to produce a perfect stream of words in your first attempt? Few good writers create a finished composition in a single draft, or version. Good writing is often the result of a process, or series of steps, that takes place over a period of time. These steps, or stages, are prewriting, drafting, revising, proofreading, and publishing. The steps follow a logical order. Good writers, however, often return to an earlier stage to adjust or refine some of their ideas. As a writer, you can use the process in a way that is most effective for you personally.

PREWRITING

The process of writing frequently begins long before putting pen to paper or fingers to keyboard. Writers must first decide what they are going to write about, for whom they are writing, and why they are writing. Deciding these three things is the main goal of the prewriting stage. Remember, however, that you can change or adjust any of them as you move through the writing process.

Choosing a Topic. In school, you are often asked to write in response to a specific assignment and occasionally to choose your own topic. In either case, you need to figure out what you already know about your subject and what you must find out. For instance, if your assignment is to write about your ancestors, you might begin by thinking about your family. You may recall a moving story that your grandfather told you about having to leave his homeland. You may realize that you never quite understood the details behind his decision to leave. In this case, you need to find out more about your grandfather's life. If your topic seems too large to cover adequately, narrow it down by focusing on one aspect of your subject. At this point you may find that your original subject is changing.

Determining Audience and Purpose. After you have a topic, you need to decide who is going to read what you write, your audience. You also must identify your purpose for writing, the effect you want your writing to have on your readers. Your audience for most school assignments will be your teacher and your classmates. Your audience might also be friends, family members, the readers of your school newspaper or a possible employer.

Your purpose for writing can vary widely. You may want to inform, amuse, persuade, shock, or incite your readers to action. To achieve your purpose, you must ask yourself what your audience knows about your topic and how they are likely to feel about it.

Developing Writing Ideas. Once you know your topic, audience, and purpose for writing, you can begin developing your ideas and gathering information. Your writing ideas may come from your own knowledge and experiences or from outside sources.

Several prewriting strategies can help you develop your writing ideas. *Making lists* is a good way to help you choose a topic and generate useful ideas. *Clustering* is another method of generating ideas that has the added benefit of indicating relationships among details. When you cluster, you write your topic in a circle in the middle of a piece of paper. Then you surround it with related ideas that you connect to the topic with diagonal lines, like the spokes of a wheel. Another prewriting strategy is *freewriting*. This technique involves simply writing down, for a set period of time, whatever comes into your mind about your topic without concern for logic or correct form. *Brainstorming*, which is best done in a group, is another spontaneous method of associating ideas. In a brainstorming session, group members share ideas about a topic, allowing one person's idea to trigger another person's thoughts.

If you need information about your topic that you do not have personally, there are many *outside sources* that you can consult. These resources include textbooks and reference books, newspapers, magazines, computer data banks, and knowledgeable people. Choose the best sources for the type of information you need. What sources might you suggest for a student who is going to write about his grandfather's immigration from the Dominican Republic?

Making a Writing Plan. After you have developed ideas about your topic, you need to think about how you are going to arrange your material. What order seems to grow naturally out of your ideas? Do you want to tell a story in the sequence in which the events happened? Do you want to organize a number of arguments in the order of their increasing importance? You may wish to indicate your order of presentation in outline form. You can always change your outline, or add or drop an idea at any point. Remember that the writing process is a flexible method of composition, not a lock step series of rules to follow in the same way each time you decide to write.

DRAFTING AND REVISING

After you develop and organize your ideas, you are ready to write. However, you still should not expect to create a polished composition in one version. Use your outline to begin a *first draft* in which you put your thoughts down on paper as completely and freely as you can. Do not stop your writing flow to perfect sentence structure, paragraph organization, spelling, or punctuation. If you think of additional information about your topic or discover a better order of presentation, add your new ideas to your draft. Much creative thinking can occur as you revise your writing.

Revising a Draft. Once you have completed your first draft, the *revision* stage gives you the opportunity to evaluate your draft and improve its content and organization. Before you begin revising, it is a good idea to let some time pass and then go back to your draft with a fresh perspective.

Using a checklist of questions such as the following can help you evaluate your draft in a systemic way.

TOPIC, AUDIENCE, PURPOSE

> Have I stayed focused on my topic?
> Is my writing geared to my audience?
> Have I achieved my purpose for writing?
> Have I used language appropriate to my topic, audience, and purpose?

CONTENT AND DEVELOPMENT

> Have I presented my main ideas clearly?
> Have I supported my main ideas with sufficient details, examples, or evidence?
> Is my attitude toward my subject consistent?
> Are my sources of information reliable and properly identified?

ORGANIZATION

> Have I organized my ideas effectively?
> Have I used transitions to connect ideas?
> Do I have a clear beginning, middle, end?

Peer evaluation is another invaluable revising tool. This method is a collaborative process in which you work with another student or group of students, reading one another's writing and offering responses or suggestions for improvement. Sometimes a reader's comments or questions might reveal that essential information is lacking, or that the sequence of ideas in the draft is confusing. These comments will help you identify areas in which you need more research or clearer reasoning. You should expect to revise and edit at any point in the writing process. Remember, however, that it is you the writer who has the final say on any changes in your own work.

PROOFREADING AND PUBLISHING

You are now ready to read through your writing one last time to look for errors in spelling, sentence structure, usage, and the mechanics of capitalization and punctuation. Proofread your work carefully because errors distract readers from the important ideas you are trying to communicate.

When you are unsure about a matter of form, check a dictionary or a grammar and writing handbook. The chart below shows some common editing and proofreading symbols to use as you check your work.

SYMBOL	MEANING	SYMBOL	MEANING
(story) ⌐	move text	⌣	add apostrophe
~~almost~~ e	delete	`` `` ⌣ ⌣	add quotation marks
∧	insert	⫠H	begin paragraph
⌒	no space		
⊙	add period	/	lower case
⌃	add comma	≡	capitalize

Sharing Your Writing. The final stage in the writing process is *publishing.* Since writing is meant to communicate, the process is not complete until writing is shared with an audience. Below are a few ways you can share your writing with others. Brainstorm with your classmates for other ways to share your writing.

1. Create a class magazine or anthology of student writing.
2. Submit your writing to the school newspaper or yearbook.
3. Send an editorial, or opinion piece, to your local newspaper.
4. Give copies of your writing to anyone you interviewed when gathering information.
5. Enter writing contests.

MODEL ESSAYS

THE EXPOSITORY ESSAY

Most essays that you are asked to write in school are **expository** in nature. Their purpose is to explain a topic or inform an audience about a subject. The model essay that follows was written in response to the Unit 1 writing assignment on page 119. The essay explains how authors from different cultural backgrounds value the past in similar and in different ways.

THE PAST HELPS GUIDE US INTO THE FUTURE

1 Many of the selections in Unit 1 suggest that the past is often a guide to the present and the future. 2 The writers convey this theme by their choice of characters and events. 3 For example, in "The Stars," by Pablita Velarde, in Bless Me, Ultima, by Rudolfo Anaya, and in many other selections, older characters act as guides and teachers of the young. 4 In "The Stars," Old Father tells his young listeners about the origin of their Pueblo ancestors. 5 In Bless Me, Ultima, the young narrator's encounter with an old Mexican woman helps him to clarify the contrasting influences in his ancestry and to find his own true course.

6 The main events Old Father relates in "The Stars" concern the ancestors' long and difficult journey to find their true home. 7 He reminds his listeners that Long Sash, the mythic ancestral leader, "taught his followers how to talk from their hearts, how to find happiness in their misery, and how to read signs." 8 The purpose of Old

1-2. An introductory topic sentence expresses the thesis, or main idea, of the essay.

3-5. Specific selections are cited to illustrate the thesis.

6-9. The second paragraph examines how the events in one selection reveal the theme. An exact quotation is used for support.

STUDENT HANDBOOK ■ 397

Father's storytelling is to give his people a sense of where they came from, how they have survived, and what values from the past they can carry into the future. 9 The treasure he offers them is their cultural identity as a people.

10-12. The third paragraph examines how the events in another selection illustrate the thesis. A second quotation is used for support.

10 The central event of _Bless Me, Ultima_ is the arrival of Ultima, an old woman who brings knowledge of the past, and perhaps special powers that come with such knowledge. 11 Before her arrival, the narrator, Antonio, has a dream about his birth in which he sees Ultima as the midwife. 12 He suspects that she alone understands his unique destiny, and his intuition is confirmed when they meet and Ultima says to his mother: "This was the last child I pulled from your womb, Maria. I knew there would be something between us."

13. The attitudes of one character toward the past are contrasted with those of other characters in the same selection. 14. A quotation is provided to illustrate a character's attitude.

13 Unlike his sisters, Antonio neither fears nor dismisses the past represented by Ultima. 14 On the contrary, he carries thoughts of Ultima with him into the future: "Many years later, long after Ultima was gone and I had grown to be a man, I would awaken sometimes at night and think I caught a scent of her fragrance in the cool-night breeze."

15. The last paragraph summarizes the similarities and differences in the way each writer views the past.

15 Although _Bless Me, Ultima_ deals primarily with the origin and identity of a single person and "The Stars" with the beginnings of an entire people, both writers present the past as a means of understanding the present and charting a course for the future.

THE PERSONAL ESSAY

One of the best resources that every writer can call upon is personal experience. A **personal essay** focuses on a writer's experience to support or illustrate a main idea. The model essay that follows is a response to the Unit 2 writing assignment on page 219. In the essay, a student has used the story of her grandmother's emigration to broaden her understanding of the immigrant experience in general and of the selections in the unit.

THE TRUE IMMIGRANT

1 Reading the selections in Unit 2 brought back the stories my grandmother told me about her emigration to the United States from Ireland in 1929. *2* I always loved hearing about her experiences, but I never fully appreciated the courage she had until I read <u>Picture Bride</u>, by Yoshiko Uchida, and "No Speak English," by Sandra Cisneros. *3* Now I realize how much courage and faith it takes to leave what is secure, familiar, and loved to face a totally unknown future.

4 Like the Omiya family in <u>Picture Bride</u>, Irish farming families traditionally arranged marriages that would bring them dowries, or marriage gifts, which often included land or possessions. *5* In my grandmother's case, a go-between, or matchmaker, approached my great-grandfather with a proposal that his daughter be married to an older man with a good-sized farm on fertile land. *6* My great-grandfather thought it was a perfect match and urged my grandmother to accept it. *7* She was appalled. *8* The man was seventeen years older than she was, and she would be living not only with him but also with his aging parents and sisters, who were ill.

1-2. The first two sentences relate the writer's grandmother's experience to the unit selections.

3. The third sentence expresses the thesis or main idea.

4. The writer points out a similarity between the cultural background of her grandmother and that of a character in a selection.

5-9. These sentences elaborate the grandmother's experiences that support the thesis.

9 It was then that she decided to follow her older brother to the United States. *10* She loved her parents dearly and her six younger brothers and sister, but, like Hana Omiya, "She certainly was not going to marry a farmer and spend her life working beside him planting, weeding, and harvesting . . . until her back bent. . . ." *11* She would take the risks involved in moving to an unfamiliar world.

12 Reading "No Speak English" helped me to see that the courage to emigrate involves not only leaving the old behind but also accepting the new. *13* Sandra Cisneros's character, Mamacita, shows what happens when a person leaves home physically but never really accepts the change. *14* My grandmother endured many painful adjustments to life in New York City during the Depression. *15* She claims that one of her biggest challenges was finding work, but she faced that and all the other challenges for the sake of the better future she believed in. *16* According to her, she merely did what she had to do to survive, but to me it is clear that she made bold decisions and courageous adjustments to new situations. *17* For me she represents the true immigrant—the one who wanted to arrive in a new world and who wanted to stay and succeed.

THE PERSUASIVE ESSAY

The purpose of a **persuasive essay** is to convince readers that your point of view or opinion about a topic is reasonable. Persuasion may involve influencing your audience to change its mind or to take a certain action. To achieve your purpose, be sure to present logical arguments and sound evidence to support your opinion. If you know your readers well, you might also appeal to their emotions, interests, or values. When choosing a topic for a persuasive essay, select an issue your really care about so that you will be motivated to present the strongest case possible. The model essay that follows is in response to the Unit 3 writing assignment on page 369.

WHOSE DREAM IS IT?

1 The selections in Unit 3, "Struggle and Recognition," made me reconsider what the United States is and what it can be. 2 Is it a melting pot in which groups blend or a "cultural bouillabaisse," as Ishmael Reed proposes in "America: The Multinational Society"? 3 To me, the United States is a land of promises not yet realized, but still being shaped by the lives and imaginations of millions of people from many cultures.

4 The long struggle of African Americans to win their full rights as U.S. citizens reflects the incomplete realization of that dream. 5 In his sermon in Memphis in April 1968, Dr. Martin Luther King, Jr., said, "And I've seen the promised land. I may not get there with you. But I want you to know that we as a people will get to the promised land." 6 Dr. King's words affirm the dream but also the reality that not all African Americans have achieved equal rights in U.S. society.

7 Nearly 25 years have passed since Dr. King spoke these words. 8 Although the civil rights struggles of the 1960s helped shatter many forms of racism, prejudice is still widespread in the United States. 9 Many African Americans still have not reached "the promised land" of equality nor have they merged into the "melting pot" of a standard national identity.

1-2. The first two sentences pose an issue and raise a question.

3. The third sentence states the writer's point of view, or thesis, about the issue.

4. An example from history is used to support the first part of the thesis.
5-6. The historical example is illustrated by a direct quotation.

7-9. Facts of contemporary life and an appeal to emotion are used to support the thesis.

10-11. A quotation from a poem is used to support the second part of the thesis.

12-13. Analysis of poetic technique clarifies how the theme of the poem supports the thesis.

14. The issue is restated in the first sentence of the final paragraph.

15-16. Facts and a rhetorical question build up to a conclusion.

17. The final sentence expands the thesis with a reference to an author in the unit.

10 Today's U.S. citizens, like those who came before, are children "of many diaspora, born into this continent at a crossroads." 11 These words from "Ending Poem," by Aurora Levins Morales and Rosario Morales, express the complex identity many Americans feel. 12 "Ending Poem" captures that complex identity by a very effective use of repeated lines, beginning with "I": "I am Puerto Rican. I am U.S. American. . . . / I am an immigrant . . . / I am caribeña, island grown. . . . / I am a child of many mothers." 13 The poem ends, however, by moving from "I" to "we," suggesting that diverse traditions within an individual and a society can come together to form a unity: "And we are whole."

14 How can we "make America again," in the words of Langston Hughes? 15 First, we must realize that "we" includes millions of newcomers from places such as Asia, South America, Mexico, and the Caribbean who are reshaping the reality of the United States. 16 All Americans—both former and recent newcomers—share a dream of what this country can be. 17 Ishmael Reed's vision of a rich cultural stew, in which individual ingredients affect the flavor of the whole without losing their own identity, seems to me the right recipe for the future of our nation.

LISTING OF LITERARY TERMS

ALLITERATION *Alliteration* is the repetition of similar sounds, usually initial consonants, in a group of words. Note the repeated *d* sound in this phrase from "The Slave Auction" by Frances E. W. Harper: "sobs of *deep despair*." Poets and other writers use alliteration to connect and emphasize ideas and to create rhythmic and musical effects.

ALLUSION An *allusion* is a spoken or written reference to a well-known person, place, event, literary work, or work of art. Classical mythology, the Bible, Shakespeare, and world history are frequent sources of allusions in literature. Martin Luther King, Jr., makes several biblical allusions in his speech "I See the Promised Land." Contemporary writers sometimes make allusions to current events and to the particular history or experience of the audience they are addressing.

AUTOBIOGRAPHY An *autobiography* is an account of a person's life written by that person. Since autobiographies are written from the first-person point of view, using the pronouns *I* and *me*, they may not present the most objective account of events. However, they often offer vivid descriptions of events and people that only an eyewitness can provide. A good example is "The Slave Ship," written by an enslaved African who became a powerful spokesperson for freedom.

CHARACTER A *character* is a person or animal that plays a role in a literary work. Characters are called *flat* or *round* depending on how they are developed by an author. Flat characters are one-dimensional, having one or two qualities that define and limit them. The characters in myths and fables are often flat, such as the cunning Tortoise in *Things Fall Apart* by Chinua Achebe. Round characters are more complex, with a mixture of qualities that make them seem more like real people. Rosie in "Seventeen Syllables," by Hisaye Yamamoto, is an example of a round character.

CHARACTERIZATION *Characterization* is the method by which a writer develops a character. Characterization can be *direct* or *indirect*. In direct characterization, the writer simply tells the reader what a character is like, as Pablita Velarde does in "The Stars": "he [Long Sash] was a great warrior who had won many battles." In indirect characterization, the writer may reveal the character by means of the words, thoughts, and actions of the character. Indirect characterization requires the reader to draw conclusions from the information the writer provides.

CONFLICT A *conflict* in a literary work is a struggle between opposing forces. Sometimes the struggle is *internal*, meaning it takes place in the mind of a character. Hana's struggle with her own fear and anxiety in *Picture Bride*, by Yoshiko Uchida, is an internal conflict. Other conflicts are external. An *external* conflict may be a struggle between characters (as with the mother and daughter in *The Joy Luck Club*, by Amy Tan), between a character and society (as in "In the American Storm," by Constantine Panunzio), or between a character and a force of nature (as in "The Circuit," by Francisco Jiménez).

DIALECT A *dialect* is a unique form of a language spoken by the people of a particular region or cultural group. Writers often use dialect in a literary work to convey a realistic sense of character and setting, as in *Their Eyes Were Watching God*, by Zora Neale Hurston. Dialectical differences appear in vocabulary, pronunciation, and grammar.

DRAMA A *drama*, or play, is a literary work written to be performed by actors on a stage, for example, *Fences*, by August Wilson. The playwright develops the story through *dialogue*, or the conversations of the characters. *Stage directions* give instructions about props, lighting, costumes, scenery, and the movement and gestures of the actors. Plays can be read and enjoyed as literature, but true drama exists only in performance.

ESSAY An *essay* is a short piece of nonfiction, usually focused on a single topic. Essays can be written for a variety of purposes and with different tones. The tone is usually determined by the purpose. An essay meant to inform or persuade usually has a more *formal* tone and structure than one meant to amuse or entertain. An example of a formal essay is "They Are Taking the Holy Elements from Mother Earth," by Asa Bazhonoodah. Personal essays usually focus on the personal experience of the authors. These essays are often *informal* and conversational in tone. An example of the personal style of essay is "America: The Multinational Society," by Ishmael Reed.

FANTASY *Fantasy elements* in literature stress imaginative possibilities not found in real life. These include nonhuman characters, magical powers, and the suspension of the laws of nature, time, and space. *Realistic details*, on the other hand, are used to make the characters, action, and setting seem true to life. *Bless Me, Ultima*, by Rudolfo A. Anaya is an example of a novel with both fantasy elements and realistic details.

FICTION *Fiction* is prose writing that deals with invented or imaginary events. Short stories such as "To Da-duh, In Memoriam," by Paule Marshall, and novels such as *Roots*, by Alex Haley, are examples of fiction.

FIGURATIVE LANGUAGE *Figurative language* is language that is not meant to be taken literally, or at face value. Figurative language paints a picture in the reader's mind that is different from that conveyed by the dictionary meaning of individual words. For example, in the poem "Black Hair," Gary Soto uses figurative language in the phrase "my black torch of hair." Metaphors, similes, and personification are examples of figurative language.

FLASHBACK A *flashback* is a device used in a literary work to introduce a scene that occurred before the current action. Flashbacks sometimes take the form of dreams or daydreams, allowing the author to contrast two different scenes or ideas. In "Lali" by Nicholasa Mohr, for instance, the main character, Lali, lies in bed in New York in February thinking about the cold, dirty snow outside her window. She then vividly recalls how beautiful and warm the summers were in Puerto Rico when she was a child.

FOLKTALE A *folktale* is a story about common people that usually teaches a lesson about living in the world. Often folktales involve a clear struggle between good and evil that may be resolved by magic or other supernatural means. Many folktales are composed orally and are passed down from generation to generation by word of mouth. "The Sheep of San Cristóbal" is an example of a folktale.

FREE VERSE *Free Verse* is poetry without regular rhythm or rhyme. In free verse, poets try to invent a rhythm uniquely suited to their subject. Repetition of words and sentences as well as creative placement of words on the page are common in free verse poems, such as "i yearn" by Richard Sánchez.

IMAGERY *Imagery* is the use of descriptive words to re-create a sensory experience for readers, including sights, sounds, tastes, smells, and textures. Imagery contributes to the feeling or tone of a poem and can range from violent to gentle. The imagery in "Napa, California," by Ana Castillo, for example, expresses weariness and pain.

IRONY *Irony* refers to a contradiction between what appears to be true and what actually is true. In *verbal irony*, what is said is the opposite of what is really meant, for example, calling a deceptive person "noble." In *dramatic irony*, there is a contrast between what a character knows or expects and what the audience or reader knows. In *situational irony*, an event takes place that contradicts the expectations of the characters and the audience. The surprise ending is an example of situational irony.

METAPHOR A *metaphor* is a figure of speech in which one thing is spoken of as though it were something else. In a metaphor, a comparison is suggested through identification. For example, in *I Am Joaquín* by Rodolfo Gonzales, the speaker compares physical places with states of mind when he speaks of "suburbs of bigotry," "mines of social snobbery," and "prisons of dejection."

MOOD *Mood* is the feeling, or atmosphere, created by a literary work or passage. Writers create mood by their choice of words, images, characters, and setting. For example, the mood of joyous celebration in "AmeRícan," by Tato Laviera, is created by phrases such as "strutting beautifully alert, alive/many turning eyes wondering,/admiring!"

NONFICTION *Nonfiction* is prose writing that presents and explains ideas or that tells about real people, places, events, or objects. Autobiographies, biographies, journalism, reports, diaries, and letters are examples of nonfiction writing.

NOVEL A *novel* is a long work of fiction. Novels often have a complicated plot, many major and minor characters, several settings, and more than one theme. Popular types of novels include historical novels, mysteries, science fiction novels, romances, and thrillers. Excerpts from the novels *Roots*, by Alex Haley, *In Nueva York*, by Nicholasa Mohr, and *Picture Bride*, by Yoshiko Uchida, appear in this book.

PERSONIFICATION *Personification* is a type of figurative language in which a nonhuman subject is given human qualities. Animals and forces of nature are frequently personified in poetry, folktales, and myths. In the song "The Drinking Gourd," personification is applied to trees in the line "The dead trees show you the way."

PLOT The *plot* is the sequence of events in a literary work. In most dramas, novels, and short stories, the plot involves characters in a *central conflict*. The conflict is usually developed by means of a series of complications until it reaches a climax. The *climax* is the point of highest tension when *suspense*, or the reader's curiosity about the outcome, reaches its maximum intensity. The climax is usually followed by the *resolution*, or end, of the conflict.

POETRY *Poetry* is one of the three major types, or *genres*, of literature, along with prose (fiction and nonfiction) and drama. Language in poetry is usually more condensed and musical than in prose. Poems are made up of single units called *lines*, which are often grouped together in larger units called *stanzas*. All poems have rhythm, and some have regular rhythm and rhyme patterns. Most poems also contain vivid imagery and figurative language.

POINT OF VIEW The *point of view* is the perspective from which a story is told. The person who tells the story is called the *narrator*. In stories using the *first-person point of view*, the narrator is a character in the story and refers to himself or herself as "I," as in the short story "To Da-duh, In Memoriam," by Paule Marshall. In stories told from the *third-person point of view*, the narrator is outside the story and refers to the characters by name or as "he" or "she." The *limited* third-person narrator of "Seventeen Syllables," by Hisaye Yamamoto, sees everything through the eyes of one character, Rosie. An *omniscient* third-person narrator knows and tells what *all* the characters think and feel. The narrator in "Lali," by Nicholasa Mohr, is omniscient because the reader is told the thoughts of Lali, Rudi, and Chiquitín.

REPETITION *Repetition* is the use of a sound, word, or group of words more than once to achieve a specific effect. Writers use repetition to emphasize meaning, link ideas, and create rhythm. A *refrain* is a phrase, line, or group of lines that is repeated at regular intervals in a poem or song. Refrains often convey the main idea or theme of the work. The phrase "Runagate Runagate," from the poem "Runagate Runagate," is repeated several times both to link the poem's sections and to create the feeling of people running.

RHYTHM *Rhythm* is the pattern of beats, or stresses, in spoken or written language. Traditional poetry usually has *meter*, a regular rhythmic pattern of stressed and unstressed syllables. Much modern poetry is *free verse*, which has its own irregular rhythms that suit its meaning.

SETTING The *setting* of a literary work is the time and place of the action. Setting provides a background for the action and is sometimes a crucial element in the plot or conflict. Often the setting creates a mood or atmosphere that helps convey the theme of the work, as in "Those Who Don't," "No Speak English," and "The Three Sisters" from *The House on Mango Street* by Sandra Cisneros.

SHORT STORY A *short story* is a brief work of fiction. Short stories usually have a single setting and only a few characters who are involved in a central conflict. For example, "To Da-duh, In Memoriam," by Paule Marshall, focuses on one setting, the island of Barbados. The simple plot centers on an encounter between two characters—the narrator and her grandmother.

SIMILE A *simile* is a figure of speech in which two things are compared using the words *like* or *as*. In the poem "Refugee Ship," Lorna Dee Cervantes uses a simile in the following lines: "like wet cornstarch/ i slide past *mi abuelita's* eyes.

SPEAKER The *speaker* is the imaginary voice talking in a poem. As with the narrator of a story, the speaker in a poem does not necessarily represent the writer. Poets often create a fictional character to be the voice in a poem. For example, in *I Am Joaquín*, by Rodolfo Gonzales, the speaker assumes various identities, as in the lines: "I am the masses of my people" and "I am Aztec Prince and Christian Christ."

SPEECH A *speech* is an oral presentation of ideas. Formal speeches are planned ahead of time and are more organized than are informal or impromptu talks. An effective speech has a clear purpose and is tailored to its audience. Speeches are frequently delivered for the purpose of persuading an audience to think in a certain way or take a course of action. In the speech "I See the Promised Land," Martin Luther King, Jr., urges his audience to continue the nonviolent struggle for civil rights.

SYMBOL A *symbol* is a person, place, or object that stands for something beyond itself. For example, the mountain that N. Scott Momaday describes in *The Way to Rainy Mountain* is not just a physical feature of the landscape where the Kiowa people live. The mountain is also a symbol of their identity and their origins.

THEME The *theme* is the central idea or message about life that a writer conveys in a literary work. A theme may be stated directly, as in Chinua Achebe's *Things Fall Apart*: "I have learned that a man who makes trouble for others is also making it for himself." More often, however, writers communicate the theme indirectly, through characterization, plot, and setting. For example, in *Black Boy*, Richard Wright uses indirect methods to develop the theme that race is a dangerous and painful topic in the United States for all cultures.

TONE The *tone* of a literary work is the writer's attitude toward the subject, the characters, or the reader. The tone might be lighthearted, amusing, reflective, impatient, or angry. Tone is conveyed by the choice of characters and situations and by the choice of language, or *diction*. Many words have *connotations*, emotional associations for the reader, in addition to their *denotations*, or literal meanings. The connotations of the words a writer chooses affect the tone of a work. For example, Margaret Walker uses words with strong emotional connotations to create the inspiring, celebratory tone of her poem "For My People."

INDEX OF SKILLS

Artists Unknown

INDEX OF AUTHORS AND TITLES

ACKNOWLEDGMENTS

Grateful acknowledgment is made to the following publishers, authors, and other copyright holders:

Margaret Walker Alexander, author, for "For My People" from *This Is My Century, New and Collected Poems* by Margaret Walker. Copyright ©1942, 1989 by Margaret Walker Alexander. Published by University of Georgia Press. Reprinted by permission of the author.

Alurista, author, for "address" from *Floricanto en Aztlan* by Alurista, ©copyright 1971 by the Regents of the University of California. Published by the Chicano Studies Center, UCLA. Reprinted by permission of the author.

Arno Press, Inc., for Constantine M. Panunzio, excerpt of "In the American Storm" from *The Soul of an Immigrant*. Available from Ayer Company Publishers, Box 958, Salem, NH 03079. Copyright ©1969 by Arno Press, Inc. All rights reserved.

Arte Publico Press for "Refugee Ship" from *Revista* (now *The American Review*) by Lorna Dee Cervantes, copyright ©1981, Lorna Dee Cervantes, reprinted by permission of Arte Publico Press, University of Houston; for "Lali" from *In Nueva York* by Nicholasa Mohr, copyright ©1977 by Nicholasa Mohr, reprinted by permission of Arte Publico Press, University of Houston; and for "AmeRícan" from *AmeRícan* by Tato Laviera, copyright 1985 by Tato Laviera, all rights reserved, reprinted by permission of Arte Publico Press, University of Houston.

Atheneum Publishers for "America: The Multinational Society" from *Writin' is Fightin'* by Ishmael Reed. Copyright ©1988 by Ishmael Reed. Reprinted by permission of Atheneum Publishers.

Susan Bergholz Literary Service for "Those Who Don't," "No Speak English," and "The Three Sisters" from *The House on Mango Street* by Sandra Cisneros, copyright ©1989 by Sandra Cisneros, published in the United States by Vintage Books, a division of Random House, Inc., New York, and distributed in Canada by Random House of Canada Limited, Toronto, originally published in somewhat different form by Arte Publico Press in 1984 and revised in 1989, reprinted by permission of Susan Bergholz Literary Service, New York; and for "Napa, California" from *Women Are Not Roses*, by Ana Castillo, copyright ©by Ana Castillo 1984.

Originally published by Arte Publico Press, reprinted by permission of Susan Bergholz Literary Service, New York.

Terri Bueno for "The Sheep of San Cristóbal." Every effort has been made to contact Terri Bueno. The publishers would be very interested to hear from the copyright owner.

Virginia Cerenio, author, for "We Who Carry the Endless Seasons" by Virginia Cerenio from *Breaking Silence*. Copyright by V.R. Cerenio. Reprinted by permission of the author.

Diana Chang, author, for "Saying Yes." Copyright ©1985 by Diana Chang. Reprinted by permission of the author.

Chronicle Books for "Letter to America" from *Body in Flames* by Francisco X. Alarcón. Copyright ©1990 by Francisco X. Alarcón. All rights reserved. Reprinted by permission of Chronicle Books.

Clear Light Publishers for "The Stars" from *Old Father Story Teller* by Pablita Velarde. Copyright ©1989 Pablita Velarde. Reprinted by permission of Clear Light Publishers, Sante Fe, New Mexico.

Doubleday, a division of Bantam Doubleday Dell Publishing Group, Inc., for excerpt from *Roots* by Alex Haley. Copyright ©1976 by Alex Haley. Used by permission of Doubleday, a division of Bantam Doubleday Dell Publishing Group, Inc.

Paul Edwards for "The Slave Ship" from *Equiano's Travels* by Olaudah Equiano. Edited by Paul Edwards. ©Paul Edwards, 1967. Reprinted by permission.

Farrar, Straus & Giroux for "Instructions for joining a new society" from *A Fountain, A House of Stone* by Heberto Padilla. Translated by Alastair Reid and Alexander Coleman. English translation copyright ©1991 by Alastair Reid and Alexander Coleman. All rights reserved. Reprinted by permission of Farrar, Straus & Giroux.

The Feminist Press for "To Da-duh, In Memoriam" from *Reena and Other Stories* by Paule Marshall, copyright ©1967, 1983 by Paule Marshall, published by The Feminist Press at the City University of New York, all rights reserved; and for "The Slave Auction" from *A Brighter Day Coming, A Frances Ellen Watkins*

Harold Ober Associates, Inc.

Oxford University Press, Inc., for excerpt of "The Slave who Dared to Feel like a Man." from *Incidents in the Life of a Slave Girl: Written by Herself* by Harriet A. Jacobs, copyright ©1988 by Oxford University Press, Inc., reprinted by permission; and for "Speech of Sojourner Truth" from *Narrative of Sojourner Truth: A Bondswoman of Olden Time, With a History of Her Labors and Correspondence Drawn from Her "Book of Life"* by Sojourner Truth, copyright ©1991 by Oxford University Press, Inc., reprinted by permission.

Partisan Review for Hisaye Yamamoto, excerpt of "Seventeen Syllables" from *Seventeen Syllables: 5 Stories of Japanese American Life*. First published in *Partisan Review*, November 1949. Copyright ©1985 by Hisaye Yamamoto.

Pathfinder Press for excerpt of "See for yourself, listen for yourself, think for yourself" from *Malcolm X Talks to Young People: Speeches in the U.S., Britain, and Africa* by Malcolm X. Edited by Steve Clark. Copyright ©1965, 1970, 1991 by Betty Shabazz and Pathfinder Press. All rights reserved. Reprinted by permission of Pathfinder Press.

The Putnam Publishing Group for excerpt from "Four Directions" from *The Joy Luck Club* by Amy Tan. Copyright ©1989 by Amy Tan. Reprinted by permission of The Putnam Publishing Group.

Random House, Inc., for "ALONE/december/night" from *Snaps* by Victor Hernandez Cruz. Copyright ©1968, 1969 by Victor Hernandez Cruz. Reprinted by permission of Random House, Inc.

Red Earth Press for "Ellis Island" from *The Remembered Earth* by Joseph Bruchac, edited by Geary Hobson. Albuquerque: Red Earth Press, 1979. Reprinted by permission of Joseph Bruchac.

The Regents of the University of California for "Immigration Blues" from *Songs of Gold Mountain: Cantonese Rhymes from San Francisco Chinatown* by Marlon Hom, copyright ©1987, The Regents of the University of California, reprinted by permission.

Roslyn Targ Literary Agency, Inc., for "Petey and Yotsee and Mario" by Henry Roth. Copyright ©1956 by Henry Roth; copyright © renewed by Henry Roth.

Originally published in *The New Yorker* magazine. Reprinted by permission of Roslyn Targ Literary Agency, Inc., New York.

Ricardo Sánchez, author, for "i yearn" by Ricardo Sánchez from *American Literature*. Copyright ©1975 by Ricardo Sánchez, Ph.D., Associate Professor/English, Dept. of Comparative American Cultures, CUSU. Reprinted by permission of the author.

Jay Schulman for "They Are Taking the Holy Elements from Mother Earth" by Asa Bazhonoodah, from *Pride and Protest: Ethnic Roots in America*, ed. Jay Schulman, Aubrey Shatter, and Rosalie Ehrlich. Copyright Jay Schulman. Laurel Edition published by Dell Publishing, a division of Bantam Doubleday Dell Publishing Group, 1977. Reprinted by permission of Jay Schulman.

Charles Scribner's Sons, an imprint of Macmillan Publishing Company, for excerpts of "I Leave South Africa" from *Kaffir Boy in America* by Mark Mathabane. Copyright ©1989 Mark Mathabane. Reprinted by permission of Charles Scribner's Sons, an imprint of Macmillan Publishing Company.

Leslie Marmon Silko, author, for "Humaweepi, The Warrior Priest" by Leslie Silko. Copyright ©Leslie Marmon Silko, 1974. Reprinted by permission of the author.

Syracuse University Press for excerpt from "The Constitution of the Five Nations" in *Parker on the Iroquois* by Arthur C. Parker, edited with an introduction by William N. Fenton. Published by Syracuse University Press, Syracuse, New York, 1968. Reprinted by permission.

TQS Publications for excerpt from *Bless Me, Ultima* by Rudolfo A. Anaya. ©by Rudolfo A. Anaya 1972. The novel is available through TQS Publications, P.O. Box 9275, Berkeley, CA 94709.

University of Nebraska Press for excerpt from "Wasichus in the Hills," an excerpt from *Black Elk Speaks: Being the Life Story of a Holy Man of the Ogalala Sioux*, as told to John G. Neihardt. Copyright 1932, 1959, 1972 by John G. Neihardt. Copyright ©1961 by The John G. Neihardt Trust. Reprinted by permission of University of Nebraska Press.

The University of New Mexico Press for excerpt from *The Way to Rainy Mountain* by N. Scott Momaday. Copyright ©1969, The University of New Mexico Press. Introduction first published in *The Reporter*, 26 January, 1967. Reprinted by permission of The University of New Mexico Press.

The University of Oklahoma Press for "The Indians' Night Promises to be Dark" by Chief Seattle from *Indian Oratory: Famous Speeches by Noted Indian Chieftains*. Compiled by W. C. Vanderwerth. Copyright ©1971 by the University of Oklahoma Press. Reprinted by permission.

The University of Pittsburgh Press for "Black Hair" from *A Fire in My Hands* by Gary Soto. First published in *Black Hair* by Gary Soto. ©1985 by Gary Soto. Reprinted by permission of the University of Pittsburgh Press.

Viking Penguin for *In the Land of Small Dragon: A Vietnamese Folktale* by Dang Manh Kha. As told to Ann Nolan Clark. Copyright ©1979 Ann Nolan Clark. Reprinted by permission of Viking Penguin, a division of Penguin Books USA Inc.

Yoshiko Uchida, author, for Chapter One from *Picture Bride* by Yoshiko Uchida. ©1987 by Yoshiko Uchida. Reprinted by permission.

The following piece is in the public domain:

"Steal Away"

Grateful acknowledgment is made to the following for illustrations, photographs, and reproductions on the pages indicated:

Unit 1: Origins and Ceremonies.
p. 2: (top) *North Mountain*, Haskay Yah Ne Yah (Harrison Begay), ©659, Museum of Northern Arizona, photo by Kevin Orlerich; (bottom left) Bronze mask from the Kingdom of Benin, Giraudon/Art Resource; (bottom right) *The Tree of Life*, Heron Martinez, Girard Foundation Collection in the Museum of International Folk Art, a unit of the Museum of New Mexico, photograph by Michael Monteaux.

Theme 1: A Heritage of Traditional Stories.
p. 6: *Tatei Urianaka, Goddess of the Earth Ready for Planting*, Cresencio Peréz Robles, The Fine Arts Museums of San Francisco, gift of Peter F. Young; **p.13:** Male storyteller with 17 children, Helen Cordero, ©Jerry Jacka Photography; **p. 17:** Shepherd and sheep, Nelson Rockefeller Collection of Mexican Folk Art, Mexican Museum of San Francisco; **p. 26:** Gaming chips or counters from the Beti culture of Cameroon, West Africa, artist unknown, Staatliches Museum fur Volkerkunde; **p. 34:** T'âm arrives at the Emperor's palace, illustrated by Tony Chen, published by Viking; **p. 36:** The Temple of Literature in Hanoi, ©John Spragens, Jr./Photo Researchers; **p. 37:** (top) Vietnamese ceramic jar and platter, Asian Art Museum of San Francisco, The Avery Brundage Collection; (bottom) Vietnamese scholar teaching calligraphy, ©Lawrence Migdale; **p. 42:** *The Fiddler of Glenbirnie*, I. Kay, Culver Pictures, Inc.

Theme 2: Exploring Ancestral Roots.
p. 44: Bronze horn player from the kingdom of Benin, ©Lee Boltin; **p. 47:** Market scene, Girard Foundation Collection in The Museum of International Folk Art, a division of a unit of The Museum of New Mexico, photographs by Michael Monteaux; **p. 54:** *November in New Mexico*, Andrew Michael Dasburg, Albert M. Bender Collection, gift of Albert M. Bender; **p. 58:** 19th-century bronze staff of office from the Abeokuta culture, Collection of High Museum of Art, Atlanta, The Fred and Rita Richman Collection, 1980.500.74; **p. 66:** Photograph of woman of Barbados, ©Bernard Wolff/Photo Researchers, Inc.; **p. 69:** Photograph of deserted beach with palm trees on the Atlantic coast of Barbados, ©Elyse Reider/Photo Researchers, Inc.; **p. 78:** Devil's Tower, Al Momaday, illustration from *The Way to Rainy Mountain* by N. Scott Momaday, University of New Mexico Press.

Theme 3: Celebrating Growth and Change.
p. 87: Photograph of a Japanese bride dressed in traditional wedding garments, E. Heiniger/Rapho, Division of Photo Researchers, Inc.; **p. 90**: *The Poetess Ono-No-Komaki*, Scala/Art Resource; **p. 103**: Native American standing on a cliff, Edward Curtis, The Rare Book Room, New York Public Library; **p. 111**: (top) Dakota Sun Dance, Short Bull, Neg. #326848, Courtesy Department Library Services, American Museum of Natural History; (bottom) Painted buffalo skull used in the Sun Dance ceremony by the Arapaho people, National Museum of the American Indian, Smithsonian Institution, photo by Carmelo Guadagno; **p. 117**: *My Brother*, Oswaldo Guayasamin, Collection, The Museum of Modern Art, New York, Inter-American Fund.

Unit 2: Arrival and Settlement.
p. 120: (top) Photograph of a Chinatown street in San Francisco about 1900, Brown Brothers; (middle) Photograph of an immigrant family looking at the Statue of Liberty from Ellis Island in 1930, The Granger Collection; (bottom) Photograph of Cuban Americans at Miami Airport welcoming newcomers from Havana in May 1961, UPI/Bettmann Newsphotos.

Theme 4: Voices of the First Nations.
p. 124: Navajo wall painting depicting a Spanish cavalry expedition against the Navajo in 1804-1805, ©Jerry Jacka Photography; **p. 128**: Black Elk of the Oglala Lakota nation, Joseph Epes, South Dakota Historical Society; **p. 134**: *The Washington Covenant Belt*, New York State Museum catalogue #37310; **p. 140**: Photograph of Chief Seattle of the Suquamish and Duwamish nations of the present-day northwestern United States, Brown Brothers; **p. 144**: A Navajo weaver, ©David Barnes/Photo Researchers, Inc.; **p. 145**: (top) Pueblo pottery, Photograph courtesy of National Museum of the American Indian, Smithsonian Institution; (bottom) Navajo squashblossom necklaces, ©Jerry Jacka Photography; **p. 148**: Photograph of Navajos and their hogans, or dwellings, taken in 1895, Seaver Center for Western History Research, Natural History Museum of Los Angeles County.

Theme 5: The Long Road from Slavery.
p. 152: *Underground Railroad*, Jerry Pinkney, National Geographic Society; **p. 155**: Engraving of a fugitive enslaved African American, Culver Pictures, Inc.; **p. 158**: Photograph of the auction block in Fredericksburg, Virginia, The Bettmann Archive; **p. 162**: *Portrait of Olaudah Equiano*, Royal Albert Memorial Museum, Exeter, England; **p. 166**: Panel painting depicting the living quarters of enslaved African

Americans, Jacob Lawrence, Hampton University Museum; **p. 176**: *Swing Low, Sweet Chariot*, William H. Johnson, National Museum of American Art.

Theme 6: Stories of Newcomers.
p. 181: *The Immigrants*, Allen Lewis, Special Collections, The New York Public Library; **p. 184**: *Casa con Arboles (House with Trees)*, Jose A. Torres Martino, Collection of Institute of Puerto Rican Culture; **p. 192**: Photograph of Japanese picture brides taken in 1931, Bettmann Archive Newsphotos; **p. 201**: Photograph of Mark Mathabane, ©1986, Nicole Bengiveno/People Weekly; **p. 208**: Photograph of missionaries at work with European immigrants on Ellis Island, Brown Brothers; **p. 210**: Photograph of Ellis Island in New York Harbor, Culver Pictures, Inc.; **p. 211**: (top) *Hester Street*, George Benjamin Luks, 1905, The Brooklyn Museum, #40.339, Dick S. Ramsay Fund; (bottom) Asian immigrants at Angel Island, State of California Department of Parks and Recreation; **p. 216**: *Portrait of Nina Ibarra*, Rosa Ibarra, Courtesy of Rosa Ibarra.

Unit 3: Struggle and Recognition.
p. 220: (top) Photograph of James Meredith in graduation procession at the University of Mississippi in 1963, Charles Moore, ©Charles Moore/Black Star; (middle) Photograph of Manzanar War Relocation Center, Ansel Adams, ©Owen Franken/Sygma; (bottom) Photograph of Native Americans protesting unfair treatment by the U.S. government in front of the White House in 1978, ©Arthur Grace/Sygma.

Theme 7: The Quest for Equality.
p. 224: "Remember I *Had* a Dream . . .," Franco, Franken/Sygma; **p. 230**: Photograph of the Reverend Martin Luther King, Jr., speaking in 1960, ©Henriques/Magnum Photos, Inc.; **p. 235**: Photograph of a mural of Malcolm X, ©Andrew Holbrooke/Black Star; **p. 241**: Engraving of Chinese laborers at work on the Central Pacific Railroad in 1867, Culver Pictures, Inc.; **p. 250**: Photograph of César Chávez, ©Burton Berinsky; **p. 254**: *Chicano Farm Workers*, Jesse Treviño, Dagenbela Graphics; **p. 258**: *Cakewalk*, Carmen Lomas Garza, ©Carmen Lomas Garza; **p. 259**: (top) *Tribute to the Chicano Working Class*, Emigdio Vasquez, Courtesy of the Artist, Photo by Shifra M. Goldman; (bottom) Zia Mission, ©Courtesy Museum of New Mexico; **p. 262**: *Sojourner Truth and Booker T. Washington*, Charles White, The Granger Collection; **p. 265**: *El Pantalon Rosa*, Cesar Martinez, ©Tony Ortega; **p. 271**: Photograph of the Mochida family, The Bettmann Archive; **p. 281**: Photograph of Italian im-

migrants arriving in the United States around 1900, The Granger Collection.

Theme 8: Recognizing Differences.

p. 284: Photograph of Chinese New Year celebration in Chinatown, New York City, ©Eugene Gordon/Photo Researchers, Inc.; **p. 287**: *Jennie*, Lois M. Jones, Collection Gallery of Art, Howard University; **p. 290**: *Portrait of Klavia*, Rosa Ibarra, Courtesy of Rosa Ibarra; **p. 298**: *Farm Boy*, Charles Alston, Atlanta University Collection of Afro-American Art, Atlanta, Georgia; **p. 305**: *Self-Portrait*, Heeyoung S. Kimm, Dagenbela Graphics; **p. 311**: Photograph of Chinese American boy holding a flag, Photograph collection Chinese Children (Stellman Collection) California Section, California State Library; **p. 319**: Illustration of a fruit and vegetable market on a city street, Beth Peck, from *Matthew and Tilly* by Rebecca C. Jones, illustrated by Beth Peck, copyright ©1991 by Beth Peck for illustrations, used by permission of Dutton Children's Books, a division of Penguin Books USA Inc.; **p. 325**: Photograph of 1985 Yale Repertory production of *Fences*, Ron Scherl Photography/Opera Stock; **p. 329**: Photograph of 1985 Yale Repertory production of *Fences*, Ron Scherl Photography/Opera Stock.

Theme 9: Breaking Down Barriers and Building Communities.

p. 332: Photograph of children from different cultural backgrounds, ©Shelley Rotner/Omni-Photo Communications, Inc.; **p. 335**: *Main Street*, Mick Wooten, ©Mick Wooten; **p. 342**: *Yesterday, Today and Tomorrow*, Charles White, ©Charles White Heritage; **p. 348**: Jelly Roll Morton and band, The Granger Collection; **p. 349**: (top) *Rise, Shine for Thy Light Has Come*, Aaron Douglas, Howard University, Washington, DC, The Gallery of Art; (bottom) Portrait of Richmond Barthe, Betsy Graves Reyneau, National Portrait Gallery, Smithsonian Institution, Gift of the Harmon Foundation; **p. 354**: Photograph of adolescent boys on a city street, ©Erika Stone/Peter Arnold; **p. 367**: Photograph of a medicine wheel in Boynton Canyon near Sedona, Arizona, ©Christina Thomson/Woodfin Camp.

Arts of the Tapestry.

p. A1: Old Father Story Teller, Pablita Velarde, Clear Light Publishers, Santa Fe, NM; **p. A2**: (top) Taino vessel, Gift of Brian & Florence Mahony, Collection of El Museo del Barrio, photograph by Ken Showell; (bottom) *Rice Eaters*, Tomie Arai, Asian American Society; **p. A3**: *The Holy Family*, José Benito Ortega, Museum of International Folk Art; **p. A4**: (top) *La Cama (The Bed)*, Pepón Osorio, Collection El Museo del Barrio, New York, photograph by Ken Showell; (bottom) Man sprouting leaves, Bill Traylor, Ricco/Maresca Gallery; **p. A5**: *Apache Crown Dance*, Allan Houser, Denver Art Museum; **p. A6**: (top) Kwakiutl dance apron, Philbrook Art Center; (bottom) Seneca (Iroquois) leather headdress, National Museum of the American Indian, Smithsonian Institution; **p. A7**: (left) *Jumper*, Jaune Quick-to-See Smith, Bernice Steinbaum Gallery; (right) Tlingit speaker's staff, Philbrook Art Center, #82.1-63; **p. A8**: *Forward, 1967*, Jacob Lawrence, North Carolina Museum of Art, Raleigh, NC, purchased with funds from the State of North Carolina, #70.8.1; **p. A9**: (top) *Sunday Morning*, Jonathan Green, June Kelly Gallery; (bottom) *Into Bondage*, Aaron Douglas, Evans-Tibbs Collection, Washington, DC; **p. A10**: (top) *Dinner*, J. Mejias, Courtesy Bernice Steinbaum Gallery; **p. A10-11**: (bottom) *The Block*, Romare Bearden, Metropolitan Museum of Art, Gift of Mr. & Mrs. Samuel Shore, 1978; **p. A11**: (top) *Young Bride*, Bo Jia, Courtesy of Bo Jia; **p. A12**: *If You Believe in Woman*, Jane Evershed, oil on canvas painting by Jane Evershed, Jane Evershed Card Collection, from the *Power of Woman* series notecards; **p. A13**: Photograph of a wall painting in Harrisburg, Pennsylvania, ©Leonard Freed/Magnum Photos; **p. A14**: Hunchback Yei, Joe Ben, Jr., ©Jerry Jacka Photography; **p. A15**: (top) *Sepia 1900*, Hung Liu; (bottom) *Under the Portal #1*, Elias Rivera, Munson Gallery; **p. A16**: *Subway Graffiti #3*, Faith Ringgold.

ACHEBE, CHINUA. *Things Fall Apart.* New York: Bantam, 1959.

ALARCÓN, FRANCISCO X. "Letter to America." In *Body in Flames.* San Francisco, CA: Chronicle Books, 1990.

ALURISTA. "address." In *Floricanto en Aztlan.* Berkeley, CA: The Regents of the University of California, 1971.

ANAYA, RUDOLFO A. *Bless Me, Ultima.* Berkeley, CA: TQS Publications, 1972.

BAZHONOODAH, ASA. "They Are Taking the Holy Elements from Mother Earth." In *Pride and Protest: Ethnic Roots in America*, edited by Jay Schulman, Aubrey Shatter, and Rosalie Ehrlich. New York: Dell Publishing, 1977.

BLACK ELK. "Wasichus in the Hills." In *Black Elk Speaks.* New York: William Morrow & Co., 1932, 1959, 1972.

BRUCHAC, JOSEPH. "Ellis Island." In *The Remembered Earth*, edited by Geary Hobson. Albuquerque, NM: Red Earth Press, 1979.

CAMPBELL, PAUL. "Follow the Drinkin' Gourd." New York: Folkways Music Publishers, 1951 (renewed).

CASTILLO, ANA. "Napa, California." In *Women Are Not Roses.* Houston, TX: Arte Publico Press, 1984.

CERVANTES, LORNA DEE. "Refugee Ship." In *Revista.* Houston, TX: Arte Publico Press, 1981.

CHIEF SEATTLE. "The Indians' Night Promises to be Dark." In *Indian Oratory: Famous Speeches by Noted Indian Chieftains*, compiled by W.C. Vanderwerth. Norman, OK: University of Oklahoma Press, 1971.

CISNEROS, SANDRA. "Those Who Don't," "No Speak English," and "The Three Sisters." In *The House on Mango Street.* New York: Vintage Books, 1989.

CROW DOG, MARY AND RICHARD ERDOES. "Cante Ishta—The Eye of the Heart." In *Lakota Woman.* Grove Press, 1990.

CRUZ, VICTOR HERNANDEZ. "ALONE/december/night." In *Snaps.* New York: Random House, 1968.

EQUIANO, OLAUDAH. "The Slave Ship." In *Equiano's Travels.* New York: Frederick A. Praeger, 1967.

GONZALES, RODOLFO. *I Am Joaquín.* New York: Bantam Books, 1967.

HALEY, ALEX. *Roots.* Boston, MA: G.K. Hall & Co., 1976.

HAMILTON, VIRGINIA. "The People Could Fly." In *The People Could Fly.* Alfred A. Knopf, 1985.

HARPER, FRANCES E.W. "The Slave Auction." In *A Brighter Day Coming, A Frances Ellen Watkins Harper Reader*, edited by Frances Smith Foster. New York: The Feminist Press at the City University of New York, 1990.

HAYDEN, ROBERT. "Runagate Runagate." In *Angle of Ascent: New and Selected Poems.* New York: Liveright Publishing Corp, 1975, 1972, 1970, 1966.

HOM, MARLON. "Immigration Blues." In *Songs of Gold Mountain: Cantonese Rhymes from San Francisco Chinatown.* Berkeley, CA: The Regents of the University of California, 1987.

HOUSTON, JEANNE WAKATSUKI AND JAMES D. HOUSTON. "Free to Go." In *Farewell to Manzanar.* Boston, MA: Houghton Mifflin Co., 1973.

HUGHES, LANGSTON. "Let America Be America Again." In *Poetry of the Negro*, edited by Langston Hughes and Arne Bontemps, 1970.

HURSTON, ZORA NEALE. *Their Eyes Were Watching God.* New York: Harper & Row, 1937, 1965.

JACOBS, HARRIET A. "The Slave who Dared to Feel like a Man." In *Incidents in the Life of a Slave Girl: Written by Herself.* New York: Oxford University Press, 1988.

JIMÉNEZ, FRANCISCO. "The Circuit." In *Cuentos Chicanos*, edited by Rudolfo A. Anaya and Antonio Marquez. Albuquerque, NM: University of New Mexico Press, 1984.

KHA, DANG MANH. *In the Land of Small Dragon: A Vietnamese Folktale*, as told to Ann Nolan Clark. New York: Viking Press, 1979.

KING, MARTIN LUTHER, JR. "I See the Promised

Land." In *A Testament of Hope: The Essential Writings of Martin Luther King, Jr.*, edited by James Melvin Washington. New York: Harper Collins, 1986.

KINGSTON, MAXINE HONG. *China Men*. New York: Alfred A. Knopf, 1980.

LAVIERA, TATO. *AmeRícan*. Houston, TX: Arte Publico Press, 1985.

MALCOLM X. "See for yourself, listen for yourself, think for yourself." In *Malcolm X Talks to Young People: Speeches in the U.S., Britain, and Africa*, edited by Steve Clark. New York: Pathfinder Press, 1965, 1970, 1991.

MARSHALL, PAULE. "To Da-duh, In Memoriam." In *Reena and Other Stories*. New York: The Feminist Press, 1983.

MATHABANE, MARK. "I Leave South Africa." In *Kaffir Boy in America*. New York: Charles Scribner's Sons, 1989.

MOHR, NICHOLASA. "Lali." In *In Nueva York*. Houston, TX: Arte Publico Press, 1977.

MOMADAY, N. SCOTT. *The Way to Rainy Mountain*. Albuquerque, NM: University of New Mexico Press, 1969.

MORALES, AURORA LEVINS AND ROSARIO MORALES "Ending Poem." In *Getting Home Alive*. Ithaca, NY: Firebrand Books, 1986.

PADILLA, HEBERTO "Instructions for joining a new society." In *A Fountain, a House of Stone*. English translation by Alastair Reid and Alexander Coleman. New York: Farrar, Straus & Giroux, 1991.

PANUNZIO, CONSTANTINE M "In the American Storm." In *The Soul of an Immigrant*. Salem, NH: Ayer Company Publishers, 1969.

PARKER, ARTHUR C "The Constitution of the Five Nations." In *Parker on the Iroquois*, edited with an introduction by William N. Fenton. Syracuse, NY: Syracuse University Press, 1968.

PETRAKIS, HARRY MARK. *Stelmark: A Family Recollection*. New York: David McKay Co., 1970.

REED, ISHMAEL. "America: The Multinational So-ciety." In *Writin' is Fightin.'* New York: Atheneum Publishers, 1988.

ROTH, HENRY. "Petey and Yotsee and Mario." In *Shifting Landscape*. Philadelphia, PA: The Jewish Publication Society, 1987.

SILKO, LESLIE MARMON. "Humaweepi, the Warrior Priest." In *The Man to Send Rain Clouds*. New York: Random House, 1975.

SOTO, GARY. "Black Hair." In *A Fire in My Hands*. New York: Scholastic, 1990.

STORM, HYEMEYOHSTS *Seven Arrows*. New York: Ballantine Books, 1972.

TAN, AMY "Four Directions." In *The Joy Luck Club*. New York: G. P. Putnam's Sons, 1989.

TIMONEY, MICHAEL JAMES AND SÉAMAS Ó CATHAIN "The Man Who Had No Story." In *Irish Folktales*, edited by Henry Glassie. New York: Pantheon Books, 1985.

TRUTH, SOJOURNER "Speech of Sojourner Truth." In *Narrative of Sojourner Truth: A Bondswoman of Olden Time, With a History of Her Labors and Correspondence Drawn from Her "Book of Life."* New York: Oxford University Press, 1991.

UCHIDA, YOSHIKO. *Picture Bride*. New York: Fireside Books, 1987.

VELARDE, PABLITA. "The Stars." In *Old Father Story Teller*. Santa Fe, NM: Clear Light Publishers, 1989.

WALKER, MARGARET. "For My People." In *This Is My Century, New and Collected Poems*. Athens, GA: University of Georgia Press, 1942, 1989.

WILSON, AUGUST. *Fences*. New York: New American Library, 1986.

WRIGHT, RICHARD *Black Boy: A Record of Childhood*. New York: Harper & Row, 1937, 1942, 1944, 1945.

YAMAMOTO, HISAYE. "Seventeen Syllables." In *Seventeen Syllables: 5 Stories of Japanese American Life*. Latham, NY: Kitchen Table: Women of Color Press, Inc., 1988.